STRATEGY FOR
CONQUEST

STRATEGY FOR CONQUEST

Communist Documents On Guerrilla Warfare

Edited and with an Indroduction by
JAY MALLIN

Foreword by
S. L. A. MARSHALL

UNIVERSITY OF MIAMI PRESS
Coral Gables, Florida

To
the 27 Americans killed
in the Dominican uprising
and to all Americans
who have died in Cuba, Viet Nam,
and elsewhere in the
so-called "Cold War"

"... *With firmness in the right, as God gives us to see the right, let us strive on to finish the work we are in; to bind up the nation's wounds; to care for him who shall have borne the battle, and for his widow, and his orphan—to do all which may achieve and cherish a just, and a lasting peace, among ourselves and with all nations.*"

CONTENTS

FOREWORD

The Mind of the Enemy

We have in this book the profiles of a small number of lead characters whose enterprises have made irregular warfare a fearsome specter, spoiling the sleep of free societies in our time while not yet wholly shattering the American dream of peace everlasting.

Accompanying the character sketches are briefs or abstracts of what these men, some living, others dead, have contributed to the theory and practice of how war is best to be waged by inferior forces against an organized society, or more specifically, the established order wherever it is non-Communist. For the common denominator of the cast under study is that they are Communist and so being are implacably set against the values and ideals cherished by peoples of the free world. They have set their course and they will never yield. Where there is an appearance of compromise or accomodation, it is at best and worst a short-term maneuver aimed to achieve ultimately a long-term advantage.

This above all is the one thing best worth remembering. It is the oldest of adages that the prime requirement, if one is to conduct war successfully, is to know the mind of the enemy. In our past trials at arms we have occasionally failed of that aim, though the blighting effects were always temporarily discomfiting and never finally fatal.

Today it is a good question whether the American people, and more particularly the men at the top who shape policy and make the pivotal decisions, have even begun to understand the minds of such men as General Giap and Ho Chi Minh. More disturbing, it is no more possible to give a positive answer to the question now than it was a decade ago, though in ten years of ever-broadening contact one should make some advance through hard-won experience.

Most of what is to be read of these men's ideas, from this source and others, is of a doctrinal nature, with the laying down of broad principles. It is hence generalized and tending toward vagueness, quite unsatisfactory to the technician in that it exposes few, if any, secrets. There is practically nothing that would be of value to the platoon or company leader of Americans in Vietnam or that would have helped me when afield I was collecting the data on our operations so that our forces might avoid repetitiously falling for the same traps and snares.

That vacuum had to be expected. Such men are not limitlessly clever, but, on the other hand, they are never altogether fools. They write of our vulnerability, our gullibility, our weaknesses, the confusions and uncertainties in our politics that thwart unity over the long haul under great national stress, and of the superior will and durability of a people's army. It is party-lining all the way, an untiring reiteration of the theme, "We will always be able to outlast you," and this should be enough for them. We have not yet proved the opposite in Korea after almost twenty years.

Now I turn to ourselves and to our way of mobilizing and mustering, once the decision is tentatively made to come to grips with such a diehard antagonist. So doing, and looking backward, I am reminded of something heard in my youth to the effect that a thousand monkeys strumming on typewriters for one hundred years would by the laws of chance reproduce all of the books in the British Museum.

The reflection is appropriate to the early Kennedy years after the decision was taken to intervene, if somewhat delicately and without undue risk, in the going war in Vietnam. Today it reads like something from Broadway, a burlesque of a great nation, under guidance, preparing itself for such terrible adventure, the end of which may never be certain.

Platoons of scientists, scholars, and consultants from the defense agencies were assembled in Washington at government expense, there to ponder the problem of how to defeat communism in Vietnam, this during a two- to five-day seminar. Each man was permitted to speak his piece, though not one in five knew anything about irregular warfare or war of any kind. There were more such seminars to be counted than the number of assistant secretaries and special assistants to the assistants in the Pentagon.

The same whirligig exercise was being conducted at various military bases and numerous college campuses, this well before anti-Vietnam war sit-ins became a faculty vogue. Folks got together. There was great pow-wow, and after less than mountainous labor, out came mice.

But if one arose, as I did, at any of these conferences, to suggest that the prime requirement was organization of a data basis afield so that we might know how this enemy moved, lived, and thought, the response was an outright negative. We have never had one in the Vietnam war. The only attempt to set up such a system was killed by Defense Secretary Robert S. McNamara.

While the seminars were spinning, the printing presses were whirling. Like Lucky Strike Green, the publishers had gone to war, reacting to political pressure. Scores of texts on guerrillas and how to fight them hit the market. In the preceding twenty years there was but one that I recall, a book by Yank Levy.

It was as if government and all who respond to it had fallen for the illusion that the fundamental ideas that make for success in military operations may be produced massively along an assembly line at wholesale cost by turning the right switch. Where today are the seminars, the freshets of books, the hustle and bustle of little groups of serious thinkers? The fad began to die when the signs of frightful mismanagement at the highest levels became no less self-apparent than the proof that a determining number of the public was wearying of the war at a rate far exceeding that of the gains made in the field. Hanoi had counted on exactly this happening when its councils made the decision to risk a full-length commitment in South Vietnam.

Almost from the start of the American buildup under the late President John F. Kennedy, the chief executive and his immediate circle of civilian advisers took over responsibility not only for the higher strategic direction of the war, which is the rightful province of political leadership, but for major tactical decisions, which with rare exceptions have always been the military prerogative. That covers target selection in enemy country and in fact any movement of forces over its borders or against contiguous neutral territory. While it may be argued that the situation has ever been so sensitive and the risk of an expanded war has been so great that the alternative would have been unacceptable, it must be answered in truth that the White House—meaning the president and his chief counselors—cannot possibly find the time to give undivided attention to the direction of the war, and its intermittent effort has undeniably put the national interests in the gravest jeopardy. To contend that something else might have been worse refutes logic when we know that what we've got is dilemma beyond solution.

The record says that for nine years the White House went wrong on its estimates of situation, of which came main decision. Whether the measurings of the other side's military capabilities were letter-perfect or grossly in error may be of interest, but is no more relevant to the point under discussion than is the question of how much bad guessing was done by the Joint Chiefs of Staff about our own requirements. The military do not run the government and they have not been the top managers of the war. The pivotal blunders were made in calculating the enemy's intentions, and though the JCS and others may have given bad advice, the crucial decisions had to be made by one president or another acting on the assumption that he knew the mind of the enemy when he obviously did not.

Be they military or civilian, it is easy for men in power in a state as affluent, industrially strong, and heretofore successful at arms as is the United States to become persuaded that final truths and solutions must always be at their beck and call. The Washington atmosphere is conducive to such a delusion. It is no less easy to fall for the new and untried formula, the panacea, the slicker and less costly way of doing things, the conviction that a new day requires the rejection of truths which look shopworn because they have been so repeatedly tested.

Some of the Pentagon's brains went this way after the atom bomb came along. They decided there was a new science which they called the study of limited war, its first requirement being a new approach to operations, dubbed escalation though the dictionary of the time gave the word only a maritime application. So began the age of hocus-pocus and the rejection of the reality that there is only one way to wage war successfully —to get in swiftly with enough power to win it quickly, which is the best insurance against its spreading. Several of the false prophets of limited war became the Fair-Haired Favorites of the White House as South Vietnam began to heat up. Of that came trouble compounded.

To speculate on whether the ultimate consequences of this bit of folly will be more or less painful than what comes of the White House arrogation of war power that it cannot properly exercise would be like comparing Tweedledee and Tweedledum. The unveiling of the cockeyed hypothesis is as obnoxious as the launching of the over-wishful expectation. The latter we have had in surfeit over the past decade. Let's call the roll.

. . . . The Kennedy decision to beef up a small advisory force in Vietnam by expanding same, strengthening the Special Force contingent, and fielding a few helicopter companies to the scene. Victory over the Viet Cong was the object, proclaimed by a blast of trumpets. McNamara made a speech: "We now know how to defeat Communist guerrillas and will stay in Indochina until we do." The tactical prescription was akin to fighting organic disease with a poultice, and Hanoi was served warning of the national intent.

. . . . The Johnson decision to bomb the North following the raid on Holloway Barracks. It illuminated, far better than the Tonkin Gulf incident, how far short was the White House view of the enemy, as of the problem. Nothing in human experience suggested that a tightly restricted bombing could bring about the defeat or pull back of a people under full control by a revolutionary dictatorship. NVA units were then crossing into South Vietnam. We neither planned nor projected a force buildup of any real significance. Instead, we waited.

. . . . The Johnson statement, on posting the 1st Cavalry Division to Vietnam, that it might well take seven or eight years to win the war. There was in 1965 no likelihood that the flux in our domestic politics would permit of such a prolongation. That, the Communists knew.

. . . . The Johnson decision to reach for the first Communist truce bid, however entangling, as a trout goes for a fly. He was virtually on his knees pleading for some response. An attitude of aloof contempt might better have served the American people, though possibly not his person or party.

. . . . The Johnson decision to suspend bombing of the North just prior to the national election when the NVA in South Vietnam was at nadir, bleeding from every pore and incapable of mounting any large-scale action. Johnson and his councilors actually believed that the magnanimous gesture would bring forth immediate reciprocal concessions from the Communist side. Senators Mansfield, McGovern, Kennedy, and Church, to name a few, hold that to get peace we need but stack arms. Naïveté knows no limits.

. . . . The Nixon decision to play along with Paris instead of declaring an ultimatum on Communist stalling at the table under the threat that full-scale operations would be resumed on a given date, implying the resumption of bombing the North. It was his main chance and he missed the bus, possibly after accepting the advice that Hanoi would change its tune once it felt the firm grip of the new man.

A more dismal showing by presidents of the United States in coping with the problems of the nation at war is not to be found in our history. That is not because the enemy has a genius beyond the comprehension of other mortals or because the combatting of Communist-directed insurgency is complicated by ruses, strategems, and feints beyond the contending power of the leaders and willing followers in a free society. The back of my hand to those who so say. The thing happens because men in highest place either will not listen or they have the wrong advisers who would rather be loved than be right at the expense of hitting the skids. Not one of the blunders here described was imperceivable in the hour when the decision was taken. That's the pity of it.

As I write, the appearance is that nothing good can come out of Vietnam for our side. All auguries point that way. There is also a redundance of official talk to the effect that there will be no more Vietnams in our future, though what is intended by that ambiguity must baffle any informed person with a respect for the language as for history. Enough to say then that there should be no more Vietnams, if the meaning is that we stumble forward blindly into a deep thicket because someone who dreams he knows the way, though he has never truly studied it, cries: "March on!" The purpose of any book should be to make men wiser, though most books in our day make one wonder about that. My only reservation about the book at hand is a regret that it was not possible to launch it on the sea of knowledge ten years earlier.

S. L. A. MARSHALL

Dherran Dhoun
Birmingham, Michigan

PREFACE

In the course of my journalistic career, I have covered four wars and many revolutions, riots, and other manifestations of political violence. Traveling through Asia and Latin America, I have collected a considerable quantity of books and other documents dealing with Communist subversion and guerrilla warfare, the theoretical as well as the practical aspects of these. From these documents, I have culled the seven contained in this book, which I believe present a fundamental view of Communist thinking on guerrilla warfare as a method for conquest.

Before each selection, I have included a biographical sketch of the author. The varying lengths of these sketches are not meant to be indicative of relative importance. A great deal has been written about Mao, Giap, and Lin; very little about Raúl Castro. Having at hand material I had gathered as a correspondent in Cuba, I therefore utilized this to provide a somewhat longer introduction to Raúl, whose importance has been overshadowed by the theatrics of his brother Fidel.

For reading this manuscript and making comments and corrections, my warm appreciation goes to Dr. Ernst Halperin, Center for International Studies, Massachusetts Institute of Technology; Dr. Nikolai Khokhlov, San Bernardino State College; and Mr. Bernard Yoh, who not only knows guerrilla warfare but has himself been a guerrilla.

My thanks also to Dr. Mose Harvey, director of the Center for Advanced International Studies, University of Miami, for his encouragement.

Finally, my thanks to Dr. Mario Llerena, for his fine assistance, and to Mrs. Georgina Palomares and Miss Rhoda Stanford for helping to prepare the manuscript for publication.

J. M.

STRATEGY FOR
CONQUEST

INTRODUCTION

The town of Simacota, in Colombia, has a population of 5,000 and lies along the Suárez River in cattle-raising country. The area is ruggedly mountainous, and Simacota is located at a height of about 2,600 feet on the western side of a mountain range. The town is 225 miles from Bogotá, the capital of the country.

Shortly after dawn one morning, a group of about one hundred guerrillas invaded and rapidly took over Simacota. The guerrillas, including at least one young woman, placed guards on all roads and at key points inside the town. Wearing khaki uniforms, olive green berets, and armbands bearing the initials "EL," the guerrillas were equipped with revolvers, rifles, and submachine guns. They were members of the Communist *Ejército de Liberación Nacional* (Army of National Liberation).

One detachment went directly to the small police station and quickly captured it, killing three of four policemen who were there. A young girl was also killed, evidently by a stray bullet.

Other guerrillas were busy elsewhere in the town. They had split up into small groups and set about carrying out various tasks. One group charged into the telephone office and severed the phone lines. Another group entered the municipal offices, destroyed a two-way radio and a public address system, and scattered office files and furniture. Other guerrillas went into stores and looted them of food, medicines, and merchandise. The guerrillas also helped themselves to cash at a brewery and at the home of a well-to-do local citizen. At the government's Agrarian Bank they forced the manager and cashier at gunpoint to open the safe, and from this the guerrillas removed $5,300 in Colombian currency. They then counted the money on adding machines and meticulously checked it against the bank's books. Upon completing their looting, the guerrillas rounded up the citizens of Simacota in the town's main plaza, and there subjected them to a political harangue urging them to overthrow the government of Colombia.

The rebels held Simacota for about two hours, and then, their mission accomplished, they faded back into the hills. When an army detachment set out in pursuit, it fell into an ambush and three soldiers were killed. One guerrilla also died.

The taking of Simacota, in January of 1965, was a classic guerrilla maneuver. By boldly seizing a town, the guerrillas meant to demonstrate their own strength and the government's weakness. More important than the local situation, however, was the fact that Communist forces were seizing a populated location, not in Asia, but in the heart of South America, supposedly a bulwark of Western inviolability under the protection of the United States shield.

World War I did not end all wars, and neither did World War II. Since the latter conflagration ended, there have been more than forty wars. Twenty years after World War II, a list published by a newsmagazine included the following conflicts ("40 wars since '45"):[1]

PLACE AND DATE	OPPONENTS (Winner in Italics)
Indonesia 1945-47	Netherlands v. *rebels*
China 1945-49	Nationalists v. *Reds*
Kashmir 1947-49	India v. Pakistan
Greece 1946-49	*Govt.* v. ELAS rebels
Israel 1948-49	*Israel* v. Arabs
Philippines 1948-52	*Government* v. Huks
Indo-China 1945-54	France v. *Viet Minh*
Malaya 1945-54	*Britain* v. Red rebels
Korea 1950-53	*U.N. & South Korea* v. Red China & N. Korea
Formosa 1950-current	U.S. v. Red China
Kenya 1952-53	*Britain* v. Mau Mau
Sinai 1956	*Israel* v. Egypt
Suez 1956	G.B. & France v. *Egypt*
Hungary 1956	*Russia* v. rebels
Quemoy-Matsu 1954-58	Chinese Nationalists v. Chinese Communists
Lebanon 1958	*U.S. & Lebanese* v. rebels
Tibet 1950-59	*Chinese Communists* v. Tibetans
Cyprus 1955-59	Britain v. *EOKA rebels*
Algeria 1956-62	France v. *rebels*
Cuba 1958-59	Govt. v. *Castro rebels*
Laos 1959-current	Government v. Pathet Lao
Kuwait 1961	*Britain* v. Iraq
Goa 1961	*India* v. Portugal
Yemen 1962-current	Royalists v. government & Egypt

Congo 1960-62	*Govt. & U.N. v.* mutineers & secessionists
Cuba 1961 (Bay of Pigs)	Cuban refugees & U.S. *v. government*
South Viet Nam 1959-current	U.S. & S. Vietnam *v.* Viet Cong & N. Vietnam
Himalayas 1959-62	India *v. Red China*
Angola 1960-current	Portugal *v.* rebels
West New Guinea 1962	Netherlands *v. Indonesia*
Colombia 1960-current	Government *v.* rebels
Cuba 1962	Russia & Cuba *v. U.S.*
Algeria-Morocco 1963	Algeria *v.* Morocco
Venezuela 1963	*Government v.* rebels
Malaysia 1963-current	Britain & Malaysia *v.* Indonesia
Congo 1964-current	Govt. *v.* Simba rebels
Thailand 1964-current	Govt. *v.* Red terrorists
Dominican Rep. 1965	Govt. & U.S. *v.* rebels
Peru 1965	Government *v.* rebels
Pakistan-India 1965	Pakistan *v.* India

Commenting on these conflicts, *Time* noted that "23 of the 40 wars . . . involved Communists." It also may be noted that although in a number of cases the Communists engaged in, or attempted, outright land grabs, as in Korea and Tibet, the more frequent Communist method was the utilization of guerrilla warfare, as in Greece, the Philippines, Colombia, and Venezuela. Outright seizures of territory, particularly when engaged in by major powers, run the risk of triggering nuclear warfare. Preferable is limited warfare, which hopefully will bring only limited response. Using the term "wars of liberation," Soviet Premier Nikita Khrushchev set the policy line for Communist participation in this type of conflict in a famous speech delivered in January of 1961. He stated:

> There will be wars of liberation as long as imperialism exists, as long as colonialism exists. There are revolutionary wars. Such wars are not only possible but inevitable, since the colonialists will not voluntarily grant the peoples independence. Therefore, the peoples can win their freedom and independence only through struggle, including armed struggle. . . . Can such wars occur in the future? They can. Can there be such uprisings? There can. These are precisely wars of popular rebellion. Can conditions in other countries come to where the people exhaust their patience and rise up with arms in hand? They can. What attitude do Marxists have toward such uprisings? The most favorable. These uprisings must not be identified with wars among states, with local wars, because in these uprisings the people are fighting to exercise their right to self-determination and for the social and

independent national development; these are uprisings against rotten reactionary regimes and against colonialists. Communists fully and unreservedly support such just wars and march in the van of the peoples fighting wars of liberation.[2]

Clearly, not every internal struggle since World War II has been sparked by the Communists. There have been legitimate anticolonial conflicts, as the Indonesians against the Dutch and the Algerians against the French. In other cases, however, the Communists have launched guerrilla campaigns, thinly veiled as "wars of liberation" but actually nothing more than Communist attempts to seize power. The latter has generally been the pattern in Latin America and Southeast Asia. Three of the more significant Communist guerrilla movements—each on a different continent— were as follows:

Greece (1946–1949): Today the initials VC, for *Viet Cong,* immediately bring to mind Communist guerrillas. A few years ago, however, other initials were in men's minds when thinking of a Communist threat: EAM, for *Ethnikon Apeleftherotikon Metopon* (National Liberation Front), and ELAS, for *Ethnikos Laikos Apeleftherotikon Stratos* (National Popular Liberation Army). The EAM was a Communist-dominated political movement, and the ELAS was its fighting arm. Ostensibly organized to fight Greece's German and Italian invaders in World War II, the ELAS actually only fought the foreigners to the extent that it was necessary to maintain its popular role in Greece. Much of its efforts were directed toward eliminating rival guerrilla groups that might pose a threat once Greece was liberated, for the Communists were primarily interested in preparing the ground for seizing control of Greece after peace had come. At the end of September 1944, the Germans retreated from Greece, and British and Greek units returned to assume control. On December 3 the Communists staged a demonstration in Athens that turned into a bloody affair when panic-stricken police opened fire. The occurrence sparked an all-out attack by the ELAS on Athens, an attack that was not defeated until the arrival of two British divisions. A peace agreement signed by the Communists brought only temporary peace to Greece. The Communists surrendered a portion of their weapons but kept their better equipment. Some 8,000 ELAS guerrillas hid in the mountains, and over 4,000 sought sanctuary in neighboring Communist countries. Early in 1946 the Communists began to mount a guerrilla campaign. They struck at lonely villages, isolated army and police posts, and lines of communication. They followed the usual guerrilla tactics: swift strikes followed by swift retreats, sometimes across the borders into Albania, Yugoslavia, and Bulgaria. The Greek army was ill-prepared to cope with the problem: its men were poorly trained, it lacked good leaders, and it was troubled by Communist penetration and beset by politicians who demanded that their areas be protected. The guerrillas grew in numbers and boldness; previously operating along the borders, they now moved through the Pindus Mountains deep into Greece. Early in 1949, however, a dramatic change began to take place. General Alexandros Papagos, retired hero of the 1940–1941 war against Italy, was named supreme commander of land forces, given the rank of field marshal, and provided with broad powers over the organization of the army, formulation of military policy, and carrying out of operations. Other factors were also at play: American and British economic and advisory assistance was helping to strengthen Greece and its army. And Yugoslavia's Tito had broken with the Comintern, depriving the guerrillas of one of their key support areas. Papagos, developing armed peasant units into a National Defense Corps, utilized this corps to guard towns and villages, thus freeing regular army units for offensive operations. The Communist bastion was emplaced in the Grammos-Vitsi area near the Albanian border. Papagos' strategy called for sweeping through southern and central Greece first, a task which the army accomplished by arresting known and suspected Communist informers (depriving the guerrillas of their intelligence networks), followed by the determined, day and night pursuit of guerrilla units. Once the Peloponnesus and the central portion of the country had been cleared, Papagos was ready to tackle the Communist redoubt in northern Greece. Operation Torch, as the offensive was known, began on 10 August 1949 with a heavy air attack, followed by additional raids that prepared the way for a ground assault. So effective were the air strikes that the army was able to overrun the Communist positions with comparatively few casualties. By the end of the month, the Greek Communists were beaten and the war had been won.

Indochina (1946–1954): Following the termination of World War II, Indochina, which had been occupied by the Vichy French and the Japanese, became a bone of contention among the victorious Chinese, British, and French allies. After considerable military and diplomatic maneuvering, French control was reestablished in this land that had been a French colony for over eighty years. The French position, however, was far from secure: in Saigon, they and the British—assisted by their recent Japanese foe—had to put down a Vietnamese uprising. In the northern portion of the country, the *Viet Nam Doc Lap Dong Minh* (League for the Independence of Viet Nam) had set up a provisional government for what it called the "Democratic Republic of Viet Nam." The league, best known simply as the *Viet Minh*, was a Communist-dominated organization established on 19 May 1941 by an old-time Communist revolutionary, Ho Chi Minh. During the war years, the Viet Minh had set up jungle bases, organized and trained guerrilla forces, and extended its control through rural areas where neither the French nor the Japanese ventured. With the collapse of the Japanese forces, Ho announced the formation of the "Democratic Republic," with himself at the head of it. Chinese forces occupying northern Indochina had cooperated with Ho's government, but the Chinese pulled out upon reaching an agreement with the French. Ho then negotiated an accord with the French under which the "Democratic Republic" was recognized as an "independent state" within the Indochinese Federation. The agreement, however, was at best superficial and temporary. Fundamentally, the French wanted to retain control of Indochina; the Communists and nationalists wanted an independent state. In November 1946 shooting broke out in the port city of Haiphong, and the subsequent French bombardment of the city reportedly killed more than 6,000 Vietnamese. The Viet Minh attacked the French in Hanoi, Hue, and other cities, and a full-scale conflict was under way. It was a war that would last eight years, cause heavy casualties, and be a severe financial drain not only on the immediate combatants but also on the Western and Communist powers supporting each side—and it was a war that would eventually lead to an even greater conflict involving the United States. In the early months of 1947, the French forces established control over the principal towns in central and north Viet Nam, the regions where the Viet Minh had been strongest. Ho and his military commander, Vo Nguyen Giap, adopted the guerrilla tactics that became the chief characteristic of the conflict. The guerrillas used the jungle to neutralize French firepower and mobility. Striking at opportune moments, withdrawing when faced with superior strength, the Communists kept the French on the defensive as often as they were on the offensive. In an effort to encourage Vietnamese nationalists to join in the fight against the Communists, the French set up a government under former Emperor Bao Dai and provided it with certain rights, including the establishment of a Vietnamese army. The struggle, nevertheless, remained one essentially between the French and Viet Minh. After three years of war, the French still held the major cities, but the Viet Minh had won large areas of the countryside. One of France's foremost military figures, General Jean de Lattre de Tassigny, built a strong line of bunkers in the Red River Delta and regrouped his forces there. The guerrillas struck from the rear. Upon De

Tassigny's death (due to cancer), the French command was assumed by General Henri-Eugène Navarre. Navarre regrouped and reorganized his forces into strong mobile units, capable of breaking up Communist offensives and striking into guerrilla-held regions. To counter this strategy and get the French off base once more—the French were using the Red River Delta as a concentration zone—the Viet Minh moved into Laos to support Communist fighters there, thus forcing the French to disperse their own units again. The war was stalemated: where tanks could go, the French could control; in the mountains, jungles, and rice paddies, the Communists were in control. In April 1954 an international conference was convened in Geneva to seek an end to the war. Even as the conference got under way, one last, great battle was being fought at the heavily fortified town of Dien Bien Phu.[3] The French gambled that if they could draw the Communists into a stand-up battle, the French might score a major, perhaps decisive, victory. But, after fifty-five days and fifty-five nights of bloody battle, the French garrison was all but annihilated. On May 1954 one of the most gallant defenses of modern times ended. Bernard B. Fall, perhaps the leading historian of Viet Nam's two wars, has stated that the 8,000 Viet Minh and 2,000 French Union troops who died at Dien Bien Phu "may have done more to shape the fate of the world than the soldiers at Agincourt, Waterloo, or Stalingrad."[4] In Geneva, a peace agreement was reached: Laos, Cambodia, and Viet Nam became independent nations; Viet Nam was split along the seventeenth parallel, with the Communists in control of the northern portion of the country.

Bolivia: The most bizarre of guerrilla operations (1967) occurred in the heartland of Latin America. It revolved around the figure of Ernesto "Che" Guevara, the colorful Argentine who helped Castro come to power in Cuba. Guevara held high military and economic positions in the Castro regime, but his primary concern was with subversion: he wrote theoretical works on guerrilla warfare and developed and directed a vast campaign of subversion aimed at the other Latin American countries.[5] Much of Guevara's attention centered on setting up guerrilla operations in target countries. Despite Guevara's prolonged and determined effort, however, not a single guerrilla movement developed successfully to the point where a Castroite regime was able to come to power. Faced with repeated failures and probably affected by the wanderlust that had marked so much of his life, Guevara, apparently dressed in clerical garb, secretly slipped out of Cuba in order to lead personally a guerrilla operation in Africa, where he felt that the United States could not as easily exercise its power as in Latin America. In Africa, however, Guevara again failed. Returning eventually to Cuba, he laid the groundwork, including special training given to a group of Cuban army officers, for a guerrilla operation that was to be launched in Bolivia. In November 1966, again traveling secretly, Guevara entered Bolivia and went to a hinterland farm that had previously been purchased to serve as the guerrillas' base. There Guevara put together a guerrilla unit composed of Cubans and Bolivians. On 23 March 1967 the guerrillas staged their first ambush of a Bolivian army patrol. The attack was a success—the Bolivian troops killed, captured, or in flight—and the guerrillas followed this attack with others that were equally successful. The guerrilla movement, nevertheless, failed to gain significant momentum. Guevara found the Bolivian peasantry apathetic, and he failed to gain support from the local Bolivian Communist parties. He might be a Communist, but he was a foreigner, and even Latin American Communists have strong streaks of nationalism. Guevara's long-range plan was aimed not so much at the Bolivian government as at the entire South American continent. He hoped to use his Bolivian movement as a spawning ground for additional guerrilla operations in adjoining countries, and he expected that this would then draw the United States into a new Viet Nam-like morass. The United States, however, did not bite the bait. Instead of sending troops into Bolivia, it dispatched supplies for the Bolivian army and advisers to train Bolivian troops. The tide turned against Guevara and his men. They were running short of food; the army had encircled their area with large numbers of troops; a clandestine apparatus that had been providing support from the cities was uncovered and destroyed. The guerrillas were on the run; fragmented into small groups, they were hunted down. The Bolivian Second Ranger Battalion, trained by American personnel, patrolled aggressively and engaged in a relentless pursuit of Guevara and sixteen other men, all that remained of a group that at its peak had numbered some fifty members. At mid-morning, October 8, the government troops caught up with the last of the guerrillas. There was a fire fight, and Guevara and one of his men attempted to break away and escape. Guevara was wounded, however, and when the other guerrilla sought to drag him to safety, both were captured. With the destruction of this rebel group, Guevara's dream of continental conquest was smashed. Others might try again, but never he. Placed on a blanket, Guevara was carried by four soldiers to a schoolhouse in the town of La Higuera. He was interrogated by Bolivian and American officials, and then the order came from La Paz that he was to be executed. The Bolivian government feared that an imprisoned Guevara would be troublesome, the focus of international attention and agitation. The execution order was carried out by a Bolivian sergeant, who first fortified himself with beer. Guevara was the first high-ranking Communist captured on the field of battle and the first executed at Western hands.

Three men in particular, plus a number of lesser figures, have provided the basic thoughts and practical tactics that have played fundamental roles in the guerrilla campaigns of the past twenty-five years—the time of the Cold War. The three men were Mao, Giap, and Guevara. This volume includes a selection of their writings, plus the writings of four other individuals who have also contributed to the Communist strategies of guerrilla conflict. All of the men whose works are herein included have one thing in common: all were warriors. Beyond that, however, their works vary considerably, ranging from the theoretical pieces by Mao and Giap to the instructional questions and answers of Bayo. Despite the variance, all of these men have had a hand in the Communist quest for conquest. The men whose works are included are the following:

Mao Tse-tung: Mao is the father of Communist guerrilla warfare. He did not invent it; he was the first Communist leader to utilize it on a large scale. Mao's career spans a long period that has carried him from a cave headquarters in Chinese mountains to the nuclear summit as leader of one of the world's great powers. Today Mao is known as the man who wrote the Little Red Book, supposedly carried out a swift nine-mile swim, and launched the Cultural Revolution that has convulsed China. Once, however, Mao was a revolutionary who wrote thoughtfully on guerrilla warfare. It is to Mao that the concept of three stages of guerrilla conflict is credited, a concept that has been adopted by other Communist theoreticians. It was also Mao who emphasized the need for popular support if a guerrilla movement is to succeed. He stated, "Especially in guerrilla combat, we must rely on the force of the popular masses, for it is only thus that we can have a guarantee of success."[6]

Mao learned of warfare by reading the works of Chinese and Western theoreticians and combining this with his own experiences as the warrior leader of China's Communists. He wrote a number of essays on guerrilla combat. Although these essays were written within the context of the Chinese war against the Japanese invaders, much of what Mao had to say remains highly relevant today. He counseled the importance of base areas:

> It is a characteristic of guerrilla warfare behind the enemy lines that it is fought without a rear, for the guerrilla forces are severed from the country's general rear. But guerrilla warfare could not last long or grow without base areas. The base areas, indeed, are its rear.[7]

Mao advised the concentration of "a superior force to destroy the en-

emy forces one by one"—a tactic particularly important for guerrillas
who are usually in the numerical minority. Mao set forth the tactic thus:

> ... When the enemy employs many brigades (or regiments) and ad-
> vances against our army in several columns from several directions,
> our army must concentrate an absolutely superior force—six, five,
> four, or at least three times the enemy strength—and pick an oppor-
> tune moment to encircle and wipe out one enemy brigade (or regi-
> ment) first. It should be one of the enemy's weaker brigades (or
> regiments), or one that has less support, or one stationed where the
> terrain and the people are most favorable to us and unfavorable to
> the enemy. We should tie down the other enemy brigades (or regi-
> ments) with small forces in order to prevent them from rushing re-
> inforcements to the brigade (or regiment) we are encircling and at-
> tacking, so that we can destroy it first. When this has been achieved,
> we should, according to the circumstances, either wipe out one or
> several more enemy brigades or retire to rest and consolidate for fur-
> ther fighting ...[8]

One of Mao's most important writings was "On Protracted War," an
essay based on a series of lectures he delivered in 1938. It is here that he
set forth his theory of "three stages" of guerrilla warfare, and it is here
that he emphasized the need for "universal and thoroughgoing political
mobilization" to support a "revolutionary war." Mao also expressed his
belief that guerrilla warfare was secondary to regular warfare (". . . Guerrilla warfare cannot shoulder the main responsibility in deciding the outcome")—a view that was modified by later Communist guerrilla theoreticians. But Mao also set forth the necessity of a protracted war, because
in a drawn-out conflict, "the enemy's advantages can be reduced and
his shortcomings aggravated by our efforts," whereas, at the same time,
". . . our advantages can be enhanced and our shortcomings remedied by
our efforts." Mao recognized Chinese military inferiority in the face of
the Japanese attack, but he pointed out that "the enemy's strength and
our weakness have been relative and not absolute." He could add, therefore, that:

> ... Circumstances are continually changing. In the course of the war,
> provided we employ correct military and political tactics, make no
> mistakes of principle, and exert our best efforts, the enemy's disad-
> vantages and China's advantages will both grow as the war is drawn
> out, with the inevitable result that there will be continual change in
> the difference in comparative strength and hence in the relative posi-
> tion of the two sides. . . .

The view that time is a crucial factor in the conduct of a guerrilla

operation has been an essential element of all modern Communist guerrilla theory. It has been of vital importance in the Communist conduct of
the war in Viet Nam.

Vo Nguyen Giap: General Giap, commander in chief of North Vietnamese forces, has been at war longer—with only brief intervals of peace
—than any other military chief in the world today. First he fought the
Vichy French and the Japanese, then the post-World War II French
troops, and now he is engaged in combatting the American-South Vietnamese allied forces. In all of these conflicts he has had to fight armies
that enjoyed superiority in numbers and equipment. To be able to do this,
Giap has relied primarily on guerrilla warfare, utilizing and elaborating
on the tactics set forth by Mao. Giap has stated:

> Armed struggle in the south has another characteristic: In guerrilla
> warfare or in limited regular warfare, the revolutionary armed strug-
> gle is fully capable of solving the question of outdoing an enemy
> equipped with modern weapons, like the U.S. armed forces. In the
> south, not only the regular army but also the regional army and the
> militia and guerrillas can wipe out American and puppet troops and
> foil their most modern tactics. This is a new development of the
> revolutionary military art, the main content of which is to rely
> mostly on man, on his patriotism and revolutionary spirit, to bring
> into full play all weapons and techniques available to defeat an enemy
> with very modern weapons and equipment.[9]

Giap has emphasized the totality of war, the necessity of "combining
military operations with political and economic action."[10] Giap has also
pointed out the importance of propaganda, saying that *"political activities
were more important than military activities, and fighting less important
than propaganda."*[11] (Italics Giap's.) Giap called this "armed propaganda," a term particularly apt since various uses of force, including kidnapping and killing, have been adapted by the Communists—notably
Giap himself—for use primarily to achieve propaganda goals. Raúl Castro's abduction of a group of Americans in Cuba, related in "Operation
Antiaircraft," which is included in this volume, was a typical case of
armed propaganda: the kidnapping demonstrated the strength of the
rebels, and concurrently, the weakness of the established government.
Giap has elevated the use of terrorism to a theoretical level. He has stated
bluntly, *". . . the most correct path to be followed by the peoples to liberate themselves is revolutionary violence and revolutionary war."*[12] (Italics
Giap's.) Giap believes that "only by revolutionary violence can the masses
defeat aggressive imperialism and its lackeys and overthrow the reactionary administration to take power."[13]

Giap places his greatest reliance for victory on the element of time. In time, he feels, he will wear down the Allies in South Viet Nam, and achieve victory there, too. In his "The Big Victory; the Great Task," the full text of which is included in this volume, he states, "Protracted resistance is an essential strategy of a people of a country which is not large and crowded and which has restricted economic and military potentials, but who are determined to defeat an enemy and aggressor having large and well-armed forces."

This article is of considerable significance because in it Giap clearly sets forth his thinking on how the better-equipped allied army can be defeated. Giap refers to the necessity of utilizing "flexible and creative tactics," of maintaining "high fighting spirit" and "troop quality," of waging war "on all fronts—military, political, cultural, diplomatic." But continually Giap harkens back to the essential factor: the struggle must be a drawn-out one if it is to succeed. He says: ". . . national liberation wars must allow some time, and a long time, to be able to crush the aggressive desire of the colonialist imperialists and to win final victory." In Giap's view, the Allies in South Viet Nam are fighting not only his forces, but time, as well. Eventually, he hopes, their will to fight will collapse, particularly on the home fronts.

Ernesto "Che" Guevara: Giap built on Mao, and Guevara built on both of these men, adopting much of their theory on the conduct of guerrilla warfare. Guevara, too, spoke of the "three stages" and of the need for "bases of support." Guevara, however, carried guerrilla theory beyond the confines set by Mao and Giap. They had seen this type of combat as a phase of struggle that would evolve eventually into regular warfare. Guevara believed that guerrilla warfare would itself develop quantitatively until victory was achieved by the guerrilla forces.

Guevara also believed that a nucleus of well-trained men could be introduced into a country, and this nucleus would grow into a revolutionary movement capable of sweeping into power. Guevara argued that it was "not always necessary to await the existence of all the conditions for revolution; the insurrectional focus can create them."[14] This belief laid the basis for the adventurism of Fidel Castro and his regime, which has affected much of Latin America.

Of the various Communist countries, Cuba has most doggedly pursued a policy of utilizing guerrilla warfare as a means of attempted conquest. Castro and Guevara built a mystique of invincibility around this method of combat—and they themselves came to believe the mystique completely. Guevara believed in it so firmly that he staked his life on it. Castro and Guevara became convinced that Cuba's 1956–1958 revolution had been won because of guerrilla warfare, thus conveniently overlooking the ground swell of popular unrest that overwhelmed Batista, a ground swell that the guerrillas rode but never controlled.

Castro and Guevara believed they could develop guerrilla warfare in other Latin American countries, and thus eventually take over the continent. Latin America of the sixties was not Cuba 1958, however. Latin American armies, remembering the disintegration and destruction of the Cuban army, moved with dispatch and determination to stamp out guerrillas wherever they poked up their heads. The military were not about to sit around and let the guerrillas run rampant, steadily growing in strength. Each day that a guerrilla movement survives, the harder it is to eliminate it. Conversely, the quicker an army moves against a guerrilla movement, the easier it is to destroy. Guerrillas win if they don't lose; a regular army loses if it doesn't win. The military of Haiti, the Dominican Republic, Nicaragua, Peru, Argentina, Panama, and Bolivia did not dally when confronted with Castroite guerrilla threats.

A note regarding Guevara and extremists within the United States proper: In writing his "Guerrilla Warfare: A Method," Guevara was thinking primarily of the applicability of his ideas in Latin America. The fundamental theories expressed therein, however, do not necessarily have geographical boundaries. Guevara expressed the belief that military dictatorships were easier targets for Communism than democratic regimes. He said:

> . . . Forcing the dictatorship to appear undisguised—that is, in its true aspect of violent dictatorship of the reactionary classes—will contribute to its unmasking, which will intensify the struggle to such extremes that then there is no turning back. The manner in which the people's forces, dedicated to the task of making the dictatorship define itself—holding back or unleashing the battle—carry out their function depends on the firm beginning of a long-range armed action.

Transferred and applied to the United States and given a broader meaning, Guevara's viewpoint would be that a Fascistic society would be preferable to the present democratic regime (although Guevara would never have admitted the democratic nature of the American republic). How does one go about opening the way for fascism? In simple terms, by causing a reaction against a genuinely enlightened cause, such as civil rights. Extremist militants, in making demands and doing deeds that are outrageous, would appear to be working against their own causes, converting possible public sympathy into outright antagonism. This is precisely what Guevara would have counseled: make the populace angry, create a reaction that will lead to a Fascistic state. The militants who follow the Communist line do not seek understanding, but enmity. If they can create a deep cleavage between the blacks and whites, polarizing the nation into two opposing forces, then the United States will have truly been crippled. Guerrilla warfare need not be limited to the lowlands of Bolivia nor the jungles of Viet Nam; in the Communist view, the cities of America are also potential battlegrounds.[15] One of the leading extremist groups in the United States is the SDS (Students for a Democratic Society). It must not be ignored that members of the SDS have been traveling to Communist Cuba for years, there to receive training and indoctrination. The danger to the United States lies in confusing militant extremism with legitimate human causes; only the extremists can benefit from a blurring of goals.

Lin Piao: Lin, Mao's heir designate and commander of Red China's military forces, wrote his "Long Live the Victory of People's War!" to mark the twentieth anniversary of China's (and the Allies') victory over Japan. Much of this article is a reflection of Mao's writings on "people's war," but its importance lies in Lin's extension of guerrilla theory from an intranational plane to the international sphere. Lin projects the rural-urban concept to the world stage, relating the developed countries, such as the United States and Russia, to the cities, and the underdeveloped areas—Asia, Africa, and Latin America—to the rural areas. Lin states:

> . . . In a sense, the contemporary world revolution . . . presents a picture of the encirclement of cities by the rural areas. In the final analysis, the whole cause of world revolution hinges on the revolutionary struggles of the Asian, African, and Latin American peoples who make up the overwhelming majority of the world's population. The socialist countries should regard it as their internationalist duty to support the people's revolutionary struggles in Asia, Africa, and Latin America.

With this definition of the world's power structures serving as a theoretical basis, Mao and Communist China have sought the leadership of underdeveloped areas. Red Chinese have openly participated in African and Southeast Asian affairs, and only geographical considerations have minimized their efforts in Latin America.[16]

Alberto Bayo: Bayo, a former officer in the Spanish Republican army, gave Castro and his men their basic training in Mexico before they launched their 1956 expedition to Cuba. Bayo's *One Hundred and Fifty Questions to a Guerrilla* was written as a handbook providing fundamental information for guerrillas, and as such it has been utilized by the

Castro government in its program of subversion directed against other Latin American countries. Bayo's instructions cover a wide span of facts and advice useful to prospective guerrilla fighters: basic equipment, physical training, how to assault a police barracks, how to make grenades and time bombs, what to do if unexpectedly attacked, even such matters as how to dig a tunnel and tasks to be assigned to female volunteers. Bayo's instructions were printed in the form of small paperback books which could be carried easily in pockets. (Early editions bore the pseudonym "Alejandro Gener B.," but later ones carried Bayo's name.) It is not known how many editions have been printed—one edition known to the editor bears the notation that it was the twenty-eighth. Bayo added more material to the later editions, but this was only illustrative matter that did not alter the basic tenets he originally set forth.

Raúl Castro: Neither Fidel Castro nor his younger brother Raúl have written much. Castro prefers to deliver frequent and lengthy speeches in order to set forth the policies and ideology of the Cuban Revolution. Raúl, however, wrote a little-known but significant article that was published in the Cuban Communist daily *Hoy* and in two successive issues of the Cuban military magazine *Verde Olivo.* Titled "Operation Antiaircraft," the article detailed the 1958 kidnapping by guerrillas led by Raúl of forty-eight Americans and two Canadians. The reason for the kidnapping was the supposed delivery of weapons by the United States to Cuban dictator Fulgencio Batista. The kidnapping, however, served a much wider purpose: it demonstrated the strength of the Cuban rebels, at the same time showing the weakness of the Batista regime, unable to provide protection for foreigners. This mass abduction was to have considerable importance in future years. Earlier in the year, Cuban rebels had kidnapped auto racing champion Juan Manuel Fangio in Havana. Such acts were to serve as a model for other similar ones by Communist guerrilla and clandestine organizations elsewhere in the hemisphere. In Venezuela, for example, a Communist group went so far as to hijack a freighter on the high seas, thus attracting worldwide attention. In Brazil, the American ambassador was abducted and held until the Brazilian government released fifteen political prisoners. Today, kidnappings and hijackings for publicity purposes are an accepted tactic of Communist activists, particularly in this hemisphere.

Hoang Van Thai: Thai has long been one of the military leaders of North Viet Nam. Thai's pamphlet, *Some Aspects of Guerrilla Warfare in Vietnam,* is a basic handbook on the conduct of a guerrilla campaign. Much of Thai's thinking is a reflection of the ideas of his chief, Vo Nguyen Giap, but Thai does set down five "main lessons" that the Vietnamese Communists have learned, lessons that encompass basic concepts of guerrilla conflict. Humor is a human condition ordinarily lacking in the deadly affair of war. Thai, however, has included a section on "guerrilla stratagems," anecdotal accounts written with earthy humor. Thai explains how even such things as toads, shaddocks, bananas, hens, and wasps can be utilized by guerrillas and their supporters.

Since the termination of World War II, the two areas of greatest conflict have been the Middle East and Viet Nam. The four mid-east wars have been basically conventional in nature, although guerrilla actions have flared along the peripheries of the conflicts.

The wars in Viet Nam—the French against the Viet Minh, the Americans and South Vietnamese and their allies against the Viet Cong and North Vietnamese—have fundamentally been guerrilla conflicts. United States participation in the Vietnamese war has been a source of considerable controversy, not only in the United States itself but in foreign lands as well. This editor, having witnessed at firsthand Communist moves in Cuba, the Dominican Republic, and other countries, feels that American intervention is justified when a strategically vital area is threatened by a Communist take-over, the local population and defense forces are unable to cope with the problem on their own, and the national government requests American assistance.[17]

Serious questions can be raised, however, regarding the military conduct of the war in Viet Nam. And one must then wonder whether, had the Vietnamese campaign been better handled militarily, there might not have been less opposition to the American involvement.

Despite some attention given to meeting the distinctive problems of guerrilla threats—such as the teaching of courses in counterinsurgency and the establishment of such units as the army's special forces and the air force's air commandos—too much of the American military still appears overly dominated by "conventional" thinking, planning, and execution of plans. Yet the war in Viet Nam has not been a conventional conflict. It has, in fact, had to be fought on three different—although interrelated—levels:

1. Guerrilla warfare. The Viet Cong have employed hit-and-run tactics in the countryside. This has been complemented by terror attacks in the cities (urban guerrilla warfare). American and South Vietnamese units have also engaged in "special operations" to harass the enemy.

2. The battle for the minds and loyalties of the citizenry. Vietnamese peasants, like peasants all over the world, are content with the status quo as long as it is not oppressive to them (exorbitant taxation, forced con-

scription, tyrannical local rulers). Both sides in the war have hurt the peasantry; both sides have tried to win them over; neither side has fully succeeded in its efforts.

3. Conventional warfare. There have been a number of stand-up, knock-out battles between United States and North Vietnamese units.

With three separate levels—or spheres—of conflict, the Vietnamese struggle has been virtually unique in the annals of warfare. On occasion, of course, the three levels have overlapped—for example, American warplanes hitting a village held by the Viet Cong are not likely to win the hearts of non-Viet Cong householders in the area.[18] Clearly, in the fluid situations characteristic of the fighting in Viet Nam, no field or staff commander can be expected to follow rigid rules applicable to each type of conflict in which his troops are involved.

American commanders, however, particularly at the very top level, have not always shown full perception of the complicated human-military problems with which they have been faced. At least part of this failure appears to stem from not understanding well the thinking and tactics of the Communists. Conventional commanders will fight for a piece of real estate. When they have won it, or defended it, as the case may be, they consider that they have won a victory. General Giap, however, thinks in a different dimension: the loss of territory means little, the loss of men means little. In an interview, Giap admitted, with apparent unconcern, that his forces had lost 500,000 men in fighting the Americans[19]—a considerable number in view of the fact that the total population of North Viet Nam is around 20,000,000. To Giap, the important dimension is time: if men and land must be lost in order to prolong the conflict, so be it. After eight years of conflict, the French no longer had the will for fighting in Indochina. Giap feels that the Americans, too, will tire of the war and accept a peace favorable to the Communists. As he said in the aforementioned interview: ". . . This isn't a war that can be won in a few years. War against the United States takes time, time. . . . They'll be beaten with time, worn out. And to wear them out we have to go on, to endure . . ."[20]

General William C. Westmoreland, commander of United States forces in Viet Nam, thinking in conventional terms of tactics and territory, believed in 1967 that the Communist forces would stage attacks in the northern portion of South Viet Nam. In an official report, Westmoreland stated, "Based on our intelligence, I foresaw an even higher level of enemy effort in the far northern provinces in the future."[21] Instead, during *Tet* (celebration of the lunar new year) the Communists struck at cities and towns throughout South Viet Nam, even in the very heart of Saigon where the American embassy itself came under attack. Westmoreland admitted in his report:

> Frankly, those of us who had been in Vietnam for a long period of time found it hard to believe that the enemy would expose his forces to almost certain decimation by engaging us frontally at great distances from his base areas and border sanctuaries. He would have to expose his forces to attack the population because we had, by 1967, destroyed or neutralized most of his large close-in bases. However, in 1968 this is exactly what he did—and in doing it he lost the cream of his army.[22]

This is precisely the point. Westmoreland should not have been surprised. He should not have to admit that even after his command became "certain that a major offensive action was planned by the enemy at *Tet*, we did not surmise the true nature or scope of the countryside attack."[23] If the *Tet* offensive had brought Giap a comparative victory—the conquest of significant towns and cities—then the human price would have been worth the gains. But even if no geographical victories were obtained, Giap would still be ahead, in his view. He would be prolonging the war, he would be setting back the pacification program, he would be striking psychologically at the American-South Vietnamese allied forces by hitting them in their inner areas, he would be fueling the dissension on the United States home front. Americans would be confronted with vivid news dispatches, photographs, and television films of GIs fighting and suffering casualties. Giap would be buying this with human lives, but Communist leaders have historically not been hesitant in spending human lives as coin for the purchase of strategic aims.

There have been other instances where poor judgment has been displayed by the American forces in Viet Nam. A tendency to overuse artillery has been criticized by Brigadier General S. L. A. Marshall (Ret.), one of today's foremost military writers. Marshall reported:

> . . . Hundreds of probes go forth every month seeking to fix the enemy and then call on the bombers and artillery to finish him . . .
>
> Not more than 20 per cent of them move to a worthwhile contact. Of those that succeed in finding the Viet Cong, in nine cases out of 10, the circumstances of the fight that ensues are such that the use of infantry weapons by both sides mainly determines the outcome. The effect of intervention by the big guns to rearward and by tactical air and gunships is more often unproductive than decisive, and most of the time is strictly marginal.[24]

Again here there appears to be a question of levels of warfare. In a pitched battle, no combat group will doubt the value of the assistance provided by supporting air and artillery units. Planes and artillery have helped break up Viet Cong assaults, and have softened enemy resistance at strongpoints being attacked by Allied units. In other cases, however, such as the bombing or shelling of towns where VC are possibly holed up, or jungle areas in which they are fleeing in a dispersed fashion, air and artillery attacks are of questionable worth. This is somewhat akin to hunting fleas with elephant guns. Nevertheless, air power does have a vital role in guerrilla fighting; this will be discussed at length further on in this Introduction.

Military actions against guerrillas must be carried out concurrently with activities aimed at winning and holding the loyalty of the peasantry in zones where the guerrillas are operating. In an effort to win the friendship of local citizenry in troubled areas, the U.S. military have evolved the concept of "nation building" (carried out by the U.S. military in foreign lands) and "civic action" (carried out by the local military). This concept, in its simplest terms, calls for the military to be of assistance to the citizenry in realistic ways: digging wells, providing medical care, building roads that enable farmers to reach markets, and so on. Some successes in this sphere have been scored in Viet Nam. But here again the sometime failure to see different levels of struggle has been detrimental. Lieutenant Colonel William R. Corson (Ret.), a marine veteran of Viet Nam, has pointed out what happens when military techniques disregard broader nation-building goals. Corson has written:

> . . . We had chosen a battering-ram to get through the door to the enemy and in so doing had made a shambles of the entire house. By mid-1965 the ARVN [Army of the Republic of Viet Nam] had chosen to sit on the sidelines and watch us incur the enmity of the people while we flailed about like a dog with a sack over its head. The more we "succeeded" in our search-and-destroy efforts the more the enemy gained by the concomitant destruction of the Vietnamese social structure. *The cause* of thousands of refugees filled with despair, children turned into delinquents, abandoned rice fields, and mountains of American trash was never attributed to our actions. Each of our actions was rationalized in terms of response to the Communist threat. Each action provided the excuse for the next. We could, as we have, fight the same battles over and over without ever achieving a victory. . . .[25]

For four years, on and off, the United States bombed targets in North Viet Nam in an effort to dishearten the North Vietnamese and thus stem the flow of men and supplies southward. Yet, once the bombing of that country was halted in 1968, intelligence reports indicated that whereas the bombings had had a unifying effect on the North Vietnamese, there were now signs of lowered morale, antagonism toward the continuing war, and increased trading on the black market. The bombing, carried out in an escalated manner, had not been sufficient to deter the North Vietnamese; it had only been enough to harden morale and provide the Communists with a propaganda weapon that could be utilized worldwide. Far too often, when political considerations become uppermost—precisely as occurred at the Bay of Pigs, where the invaders were not supported once they landed—then military effectiveness is blunted. Perhaps all-out bombing would not have ended the war; no nation has yet been brought to its knees by nonnuclear bombing. On the other hand, limited bombing is, from the military point of view, largely ineffective. In fact, it works adversely against the very political considerations that limited it in the first place. It serves to stiffen the morale of the target country and makes the bombing nation into an international villain—and for a prolonged period, at that.

Admiral U. S. Grant Sharp (Ret.), who was commander in chief of United States forces in the Pacific from mid-1964 to mid-1968, a command which included Viet Nam, has been highly critical of the use of escalated air warfare. He has said:

> We had tremendous air power within easy striking range of North Vietnam—on aircraft carriers in the Gulf of Tonkin and at bases in Thailand and South Vietnam. Yet never in the entire course of the war have we used our air power to its full advantage. This tragic failure to do so is, in my opinion, perhaps the most serious error we have made in all of American military history. It has resulted in needless casualties. It has added billions of dollars to the cost of the war, and each month that passes causes our worldwide prestige to sink lower and lower.[26]

Sharp states that former Defense Secretary Robert S. McNamara "must take a large share of the responsibility" for the American failure. "His insistence that we pursue the campaign of a gradualistic basis gave the enemy," Sharp asserts, "plenty of time to cope with our every move. He was, I submit, dead wrong."[27]

General Maxwell D. Taylor (Ret.), one of the most distinguished American military figures, whose career has taken him from combat commander in World War II to chairman of the Joint Chiefs of Staff and the ambassadorship to South Viet Nam, has also been critical of escalation. Taylor has pointed out:

Because of the tendency to move cautiously to avoid the risk of World War III, as a matter of deliberate policy we have exercised extreme prudence in applying military pressures in Vietnam. But however praiseworthy this restraint may be from some aspects, this slow application of military force is antithetical to the American disposition. It requires too much time and patience to obtain results. And we are finding in Vietnam, as in former episodes of our history, that these are national virtues in short supply.[28]

Perhaps history will view Westmoreland as President Johnson's McClellan. Both generals wanted their armies to be in perfect shape, and did not get the most out of the forces they already had. Westmoreland, instead of relying on more flexible tactics, kept calling for more men. Manpower is important, but successful antiguerrilla campaigns have demonstrated that tactics are even more important. For one thing, the use of the helicopter has been a great boon to the American forces. This editor once asked a French officer who had been in Indochina why the French had lost. "We didn't have the helicopter," he replied succinctly. Helicopters provide antiguerrilla forces with a mobility and flexibility that the guerrilla confined to the ground cannot hope to match. Westmoreland liked to engage in grand sweeps of Viet Cong territory, but the Viet Cong, forewarned by the massive preparation and movement of troops, usually managed to elude the American forces.

Westmoreland's successor in Viet Nam, General Creighton W. Abrams, was able to increase pressure on the Communists, not by launching bigger sweeps but rather by undertaking more numerous small-scale actions. *Time* magazine carried this report:

> . . . Abrams has found that forays by sub-battalion-size units—companies, platoons, even squads—can be mounted more quickly, more often and in more places. Such surprise sweeps also achieve better results. Thus the general's stingray tactics, designed to interdict the movement of North Vietnamese units and supplies, involve the same number of men but hundreds, and sometimes thousands more of what Abrams prefers to call "initiatives" rather than "offensives."[29]

A major American omission appears to have been the failure to encourage and assist the Vietnamese forces to build up their own fighting capabilities to the fullest. Rather than preparing the South Vietnamese—by training and equipping them—to take over the major portion of the fighting, the United States instead continually poured more and more of its own men into the conflict. This in itself, a vast flow of foreign fighting men, is sufficient to dishearten local combatants and make them shrug and feel that this is a foreigners' war, not worthwhile risking one's neck for. Some feeling of South Vietnamese fighting inadequacy seems to have permeated the American command. It is illogical, however, to think that there is a real difference in the fighting abilities of the North and South Vietnamese, simply because of an artificial boundary between their two countries. A parallel situation existed in Korea during that nation's conflict, when the South Korean fighting ability was denigrated. Later, however, once the South Koreans had been adequately organized and trained for war, they were able to shoulder a major share of the fighting burden— and years later to participate on a significant scale in the Vietnamese conflict. In a letter to the editor from Viet Nam, an American special forces captain expressed the following bitter opinion:

> The Vietnamese Special Forces are about as worthless a group of human beings as I've ever seen. Cowardly, lazy, inept, with a don't give a damn attitude. The policy of placing them in command and utilizing the U.S. Special Forces as advisors was a gross error of the greatest magnitude.

Perhaps General Westmoreland held similar feelings. An article published in *Life* magazine on General Abrams carried this revealing paragraph:

> Abrams had not been in Vietnam long before it became apparent that he and Westmoreland were quite different men. As Westmoreland's deputy, Abrams would come home from field trips bubbling with stories about the Vietnamese, slapping his thigh and roaring with laughter. Westmoreland, says a colleague, would listen politely enough but always a bit uncertainly, bewildered by this unknown quantity who for some unfathomable reason genuinely relished things Vietnamese.[30]

A report issued by the American command in Viet Nam on the pacification program in a northern district carried this description of the South Vietnamese soldiers who make up the regional and popular forces (militia-type units whose primary task is to maintain security in their zones):

> The individual RF/PF is a product of the villages and hamlets of rural Vietnam. Although he has conformed to the mores and social restrictions of his village, disciplined conformation to rules, regulations, or precise group behavior is foreign to his background. To accomplish a task by 1200 hours rather than 1800 hours, or even to do it today rather than tomorrow, has never been important—so long

as necessary tasks were accomplished within the broad framework imposed by the season or custom. His three months of military training have not fundamentally altered this attitude. Consequently, individual and unit discipline is not as highly developed as in a U.S. unit. Fire discipline is generally poor—the RF/PF reconnoiters by fire when and where the mood strikes him, his rucksack becomes a home for stray chickens, small pigs, rice, or other items that he passes. He is not by nature and training a "hard charger" who tenaciously presses to overcome all obstacles to the accomplishment of his mission. When tired he would rather rest and push toward his objective later. Especially on initial combined operations, the size, firepower, and boisterousness of the average trooper inhibit RF/PF aggressiveness and incline him to let his U.S. partners lead the way.[31]

The report goes on to point out, however, that his local background provides the Vietnamese with "certain inherent skills and acquired knowledge which the U.S. trooper cannot duplicate." The report states:

> ... Operating in the vicinity of their native village, the RF/PF know the area like the back of their hands and, in this respect, are the equal of the VC. They know in detail all trails, streams, hedges, canals, and other features of the countryside. They are intimately acquainted with the people and their patterns of activity. They know who lives in what house and how much rice is required by the occupants, who works each paddy, which families have relatives fighting with the VC. They know which villagers to question and what type of information each could reasonably be expected to know. What would pass unnoticed by an American may immediately telegraph a message to the RF/PF. . . .[32]

The report further points out that the local forces—and, clearly, soldiers of the regular army, too—"have much to offer as fighting allies." When treated with respect, "they are reliable and effective." When properly trained, "they are quite capable of carrying out any reasonable assignment." In this particular province, the American forces showed "sympathetic recognition and understanding of RF/PF characteristics and capabilities," and with this attitude were able to foster "increasingly responsible missions" by these local forces. Under American tutelage, the Vietnamese displayed increasing "aggressiveness, proficiency, and esprit." As a result of American-South Vietnamese cooperation and coordination, Communist influence was virtually eliminated in the district. "This success was achieved not by contacts by major forces or large-scale cordon operations, but rather by the less dynamic day-to-day execution of a harmonious and well-integrated U.S./Vietnamese campaign."[33] Another goal, in addition to that of clearing out the VC, was achieved when the regional and popular forces became responsible for providing security in the area. The local inhabitants knew that these forces were there to stay and, unlike in the possible case of the Americans, would not at some future date be deployed to some other area.

General Westmoreland and the American command may have preferred to build up their own forces, rather than those of a nation—allied though it might be—that they did not fully understand nor perhaps respect. But what the American command should have known is that the difference in the fighting qualities of the North and South Vietnamese was not the seventeenth parallel but rather the motivation, training, leadership, and equipment provided to the warring forces. If the South Vietnamese did not enjoy these elements, then it was there that the search must begin as well as the effort to set right the situation—and not simply by pouring more American troops into what could be an inexhaustible predicament. Not until the American government began to pressure the South Vietnamese into building a sounder, more widespread political base, not until the U.S. forces under General Abrams began to pay more attention to preparing the South Vietnamese to take over a greater share of the fighting responsibility, not until then did a glimmer of a "solution" to the conflict begin to appear on the horizon.

This has been a critical look at the military conduct of the war. Viet Nam has been one of the two great problems (the other is civil rights) with which the United States has been confronted in this decade. The war in Viet Nam has been a direct outgrowth of the concepts of conflict developed by Mao, Giap, Lin, and their brethren. There have been times when the policy makers and tacticians of the United States have seemed not to understand fully the Communist methods and challenges, and therefore our answers have not been adequate. Reference has been made to specific instances. This is not to say, obviously, that the United States and its allies have failed completely to comprehend Communist unconventional warfare. Quite the contrary, considerable progress has indeed been made in developing answers. The point is that more might have been accomplished if more were understood. Certainly on the plus side have been the development of civic-action programs and the use of national troops to fight Communist guerrillas (a tactic successfully utilized in Bolivia against Guevara, and now belatedly moving toward fuller accomplishment in Viet Nam).

Perhaps the most significant counterguerrilla development has been the use of air power. A few years ago it seemed inconceivable that air power could have much bearing on guerrilla warfare—the foot soldier prowling through the jungle, invisible from the air; the aircraft flashing through the sky, out of range and soon out of sight of the land-bound guerrilla.

Despite the apparently unbridgeable apartness of the two modes of combat, the last few years have seen the development of techniques and equipment which have indeed enabled the twain to meet, with aerial forces playing important, often decisive, roles in the unfolding or destruction of guerrilla operations.

When the growing guerrilla problem in Southeast Asia led to increased American intervention, it was far from clear what role the U.S. Air Force would play. In fact, there was little enthusiasm with the problem on the part of airmen. Thinking in those days held to the belief that you tramped around in the jungle, found a guerrilla and shot him or stuck a knife in his ribs. How could you possibly fight a shadow in the night with an airplane?

But an answer—a number of answers—developed in the following years. In the initial stages of the Vietnamese conflict, political policy dictated that only propeller planes be used for air strikes. This worked out well because prop planes could be flown from small fields, they were slower and thus better for low-level activity (reconnaissance, strafing), and it would be easier to give Vietnamese on-the-job training in these craft.

Utilizing T-28s, C-47s, and B-26s, the Air Force discovered that the airplane had several characteristics similar to those of the guerrillas themselves. It had the characteristic of surprise. It could arrive on the scene with no warning, strike hard, and disappear. It could be "hidden"—on an airbase hundreds of miles away.

Guerrillas operated at night, and therefore aircraft must do so, also. The flare was rediscovered. There was no need to fly in darkness: flares converted night into day at any action scene. Later, sophisticated new equipment—such as heat-detecting devices—provided aircraft with additional "eyes" in the night.

The mammoth B-52 bombers had been developed for intercontinental warfare. There appeared to be no function for them in—or over—the jungles of Viet Nam. Good intelligence work and speedy communications, however, did provide the big bombers with an important role to play. An air force officer who served in Viet Nam described this role:

> The B-52 can turn a safe haven into a green hell of instant swimming pools. A delayed action bomb, falling from 40,000 feet, shakes loose enough earth to make even the best VC tunnel a crypt. You don't get a body count, but the VC know what's going on, and they have a few morale problems. The B-52, big as it is, is completely silent. It arrives over target so high the VC can't hear it. The strike comes without warning. Destruction is terrific, leaving the survivors stunned and wondering when it might happen again.[34]

Even the lowly spotter plane has a job to do in guerrilla hunting. One effective technique that has been developed is as follows: A pilot in a small L-19 observation craft flies a regular "beat," each day covering a set area and becoming thoroughly familiar with it. One day he spots something out of the ordinary (an unusual number of bicyclists on a road, a lack of activity in an otherwise bustling village). The pilot circles low. VC, hiding below, become apprehensive and fire at the plane. The pilot radios his base, and within minutes swift jets arrive to attack the VC concentration.

Planes are a useful defensive weapon, as well. Consider the plight of the VC commander. A few years ago he could scout a special-forces camp, wait until he thought the time was ripe, and attack. He still can. But previously it was several days before help arrived, and the guerrillas had time to fade back into the jungle. Today he has only a matter of minutes from the time he fires his first shot until a flare is dropped (if it is night) from an AC-47 or AC-130 gun ship on patrol in various sectors of Viet Nam. A few seconds later a solid stream of machine gun and cannon fire rips through the forest. Then, in five to fifteen minutes, fighter planes arrive with napalm and rockets.

Aircraft fill other functions, too. They drop leaflets over enemy-held territory. They broadcast, via loudspeakers, to enemy soldiers, urging them to surrender. Aircraft participate in civic action programs, winning over local natives by bringing them medical assistance, food supplies, building materials.

The helicopter is perhaps the greatest boon ever given to the guerrilla hunter. Previously, a guerrilla group could strike and then rapidly disappear into a jungle. The pursuer had to march or run faster than the guerrilla if he was to catch him. Now, however, the helicopter provides the pursuer with a method of transportation that is considerably swifter than the guerrilla. The guerrilla faces the danger not only of land pursuit but of vertical envelopment from the air as well. The helicopter is a versatile vehicle. It not only transports troops, it also serves as an airborne gun platform, as a reconnaissance craft, as an aerial ambulance, as a rescue craft for downed airmen, and as a means for infiltrating and exfiltrating scouts and agents in and out of enemy-controlled territory.

The employment of air power against guerrillas has been a notable military step in the Cold War. The American defense establishment must continue to develop concepts, methods, and techniques with which to meet the problem of warfare waged "unconventionally." It is preferable, of course, to prevent a conflict, but once the struggle begins in any area of the world, it must be contested effectively by the free forces. In June of 1962, addressing the graduating class at West Point, President Kennedy spoke of the wars that have followed World War II and said:

> . . . No nuclear weapons have been fired. No massive nuclear retaliation has been considered appropriate. This is another type of war, new in its intensity, ancient in its origin—war by guerrillas, subversives, insurgents, assassins, war by ambush instead of by combat; by infiltration, instead of aggression, seeking victory by eroding and exhausting the enemy instead of engaging him. It is a form of warfare uniquely adapted to what has been strangely called "wars of liberation," to undermine the efforts of new and poor countries to maintain the freedom that they have finally achieved. It preys on economic unrest and ethnic conflicts. It requires in those situations where we must counter it, and these are the kinds of challenges that will be before us in the next decade if freedom is to be saved, a whole new kind of strategy, a wholly different kind of force, and therefore a new and wholly different kind of military training.[35]

Now, as we enter a new decade, the same challenges remain before us. We can best meet these if we fully comprehend their nature. To assist in this task is the purpose of this book, by setting forth the thoughts of the Communist guerrilla captains in their own words.

What follows in this volume are some of the most dangerous writings of our time. Distilled here are the ideologies, theories, and tactics that have assaulted the Free World for many years. If we understand, however, what the foe thinks, we are in a far better position to forestall and counter his moves.

ON PROTRACTED WAR 1

by Mao Tse-tung

Mao Tse-tung led Communists guerrilla forces in China during more than a decade and a half of continuous fighting, first against the Nationalists, then against the Japanese, and then once more against the Nationalists. The long struggle finally culminated in the conquest in 1949 of all of China (except Taiwan) by the Communists.

Mao was born in 1893 in Hunan Province, the son of a land-holding family. This enabled him to receive a thorough education through primary, secondary, and normal schools. After graduating from normal school in 1917, he took a position in the library of Peking University. Here he began learning about Marxism and, when the Chinese Communist Party (CCP) was organized in 1921, he became a member.

China was in ferment in the twenties, and Mao returned to Hunan to agitate among the peasants. Nationalist forces under Chiang Kai-shek were taking over the country, and Chiang made an alliance with the Communists. The alliance, however, did not last long. The Communists established a zone of their own in a mountainous section of the Fukien-Kiangsi area. There they built their own army and by the early thirties were at war with the Nationalists. The Nationalists launched four military campaigns against the Communists in southern China. Each one was successfully executed, but as soon as the Nationalists were pulled out, the Communists were back. A fifth campaign, called "encirclement and suppression," was similar to the "clear and hold" tactics used by the British in Malaya. Civic action programs were also undertaken—such as a farmers' bank to extend low-interest loans—in order to win the support of the peasants. The Communists, led by Mao, were forced to abandon their zone and begin their legendary "Long March" of about 6,800 miles across China. A year later—in October 1935—the Communist advance group arrived at its goal, Yenan, in mountainous Shensi Province. Only about 20,000 Communists survived the march, of the 90,000 who set out, but the Communists firmly established themselves in their new area. From then on this would be their base in their campaigns against the Nationalists.

Since 1935 Mao has been the leader of the Chinese Communist Party. He is believed to have put down in a bloody purge in 1930 revolutionaries who opposed his orders. His claim to the party leadership was henceforth only a question of time. Later purges insured his continuing control. He launched a first "Rectification Campaign" to purify the party of the followers of a local leader, Chang Kuo-tao, who defected in 1938. In 1955 it became known that he had ousted a leftwing deviation group when Kao Kang from Manchuria and Jao Shu-shih from the east were accused of having formed an anti-party group. In September 1959 Mao dismissed a group of high-ranking army officers who were thought to oppose policies within the army. In 1957–58 Mao conducted another Rectification Campaign. In the sixties, Mao's "Cultural Revolution" has convulsed the nation and purged the hierarchy from top to bottom.

On the establishment of the Central People's Government in 1949, after the defeat of the Nationalist forces, Mao became chairman of the Government Council, of the Chinese People's Political Consultative Conference (CPPCC), and of the People's Revolutionary Military Council. In January 1953 Mao was chairman of the Constitution Drafting Committee and, upon the consequent reorganization of the government structure in 1954, he was elected chairman of the republic and ex officio became chairman of the National Defense Council. The CPPCC remained in function as the organizational side of a united front of ostensibly independent political parties. It put the Central People's Government into power with an agreed "Common Program," but power lay with the Communists and the Common Program was replaced by a new Communist-style constitution that based power on the principle of "democratic centralism."

Mao was seriously ill during 1953 and 1954, and little was heard of him until July 1955 when he came back to call for the rapid, full-scale socialization of agriculture. After this he generally has remained in the public eye, and all major policies have been ascribed personally to him.

In 1956 he launched the "Hundred Flowers Campaign" with the order, "Let one hundred flowers bloom, one hundred schools of thought contend." This was to be China's answer to de-Stalinization. The campaign had to be terminated the following year because there was more criticism of the party than Mao had anticipated. The Flowers Campaign coincided with Mao's "Great Leap Forward" policies that culminated in the ill-conceived communes. The communes not only failed to overcome poor harvests and natural disasters but also seriously dislocated the nation's economic structure.

In December 1958 it was announced that Mao was about to retire from the chairmanship of the republic "in order to devote himself more to ideological study." His retirement came in April 1959. Mao, however, retains the post of chairman of the Central Committee of the CCP. In an effort to revitalize the revolution, Mao launched the Cultural Revolution, the full effects of which are still not clear. A considerable purge was carried out, but the bitterness that resulted carried the nation close to civil war. Today Mao still appears to be on top. He continues to be treated, at least officially, as the leader and father of the Chinese people.

ON PROTRACTED WAR*

May 1938

Statement of the Problem

1. IT WILL SOON be July 7, the first anniversary of the great War of Resistance Against Japan. For almost a year the forces of the whole nation, rallying in unity, persevering in resistance and persevering in the united front, have been valiantly fighting the enemy. The people of the whole world are attentively following this war, which has no precedent in the history of the East, and which will go down as a great war in world history too. Every Chinese suffering from the disasters of the war and fighting for the survival of his nation daily yearns for victory. But what actually will be the course of the war? Can we win? Can we win quickly? Many people are talking about a protracted war, but why is it a protracted war? How to carry on a protracted war? Many people are talking about final victory, but why will final victory be ours? How shall we strive for final victory? Not everyone has found answers to these questions; in fact, to this day most people have not done so. Therefore the defeatist exponents of the theory of national subjugation have come forward to tell people that China will be subjugated, that final victory will not be China's. On the other hand, some impetuous friends have come forward to tell people that China will win very quickly without having to exert any great effort. But are these views correct? We have said all along they are not. However, most people have not yet grasped what we have been saying. This is partly because we did not do enough propaganda and explanatory work, and partly because the development of objective events had not yet fully and clearly revealed their inherent nature and their features to the people, who were thus not in a position to foresee the overall trend and the outcome and hence to decide on a complete set of policies and tactics. Now things are better; the experience of ten months of war has been quite sufficient to explode the utterly baseless theory of national subjugation and to dissuade our impetuous friends from their theory of quick victory. In these circumstances many people are asking for an explanation in the nature of a summing-up. All the more so with regard to protracted war, not only because of the opposing theories of national subjugation and quick vic-

---

* This series of lectures was delivered by Comrade Mao Tse-tung from May 26 to June 3, 1938, at the Yenan Association for the Study of the War of Resistance Against Japan.

tory but also because of the shallow understanding of its nature. "Our four hundred million people have been making a concerted effort since the Lukouchiao Incident, and the final victory will belong to China." This formula has a wide currency. It is a correct formula but needs to be given more content. Our perseverance in the War of Resistance and in the united front has been possible because of many factors. Internally, they comprise all the political parties in the country from the Communist Party to the Kuomintang, all the people from the workers and peasants to the bourgeoisie, and all the armed forces from the main forces to the guerrillas; internationally, they range from the land of socialism to justice-loving people in all countries; in the camp of the enemy, they range from those people in Japan who are against the war to those Japanese soldiers at the front who are against the war. In short, all these forces have contributed in varying degrees to our War of Resistance. Every man with a conscience should salute them. We Communists, together with all the other anti-Japanese political parties and the whole people, have no other course than to strive to unite all forces for the defeat of the diabolical Japanese invaders. July 1 this year will be the 17th anniversary of the founding of the Communist party of China. A serious study of the protracted war is necessary in order to enable every Communist to play a better and greater part in the War of Resistance. Therefore my lectures will be devoted to such a study. I shall try to speak on all the problems relevant to the protracted war, but I cannot possibly go into everything in one series of lectures.

2. All the experience of the ten months of war proves the error both of the theory of China's inevitable subjugation and of the theory of China's quick victory. The former gives rise to the tendency to compromise and the latter to the tendency to underestimate the enemy. Both approaches to the problem are subjective and one-sided, or, in a word, unscientific.

3. Before the War of Resistance, there was a great deal of talk about national subjugation. Some said, "China is inferior in arms and is bound to lose in a war." Others said, "If China offers armed resistance, she is sure to become another Abyssinia." Since the beginning of the war, open talk of national subjugation has disappeared, but secret talk, and quite a lot of it too, still continues. For instance, from time to time an atmosphere of compromise arises and the advocates of compromise argue that "the continuance of the war spells subjugation."[1] In a letter from Hunan a student has written:

In the countryside everything seems difficult. Doing propaganda work on my own, I have to talk to people when and where I find them. The people I have talked to are by no means ignoramuses; they all have some understanding of what is going on and are very interested in what I have to say. But when I run into my own relatives, they always say: "China cannot win; she is doomed." They make one sick! Fortunately, they do not go around spreading their views, otherwise things would really be bad. The peasants would naturally put more stock in what they say.

Such exponents of the theory of China's inevitable subjugation form the social basis of the tendency to compromise. They are to be found everywhere in China, and therefore the problem of compromise is liable to crop up within the anti-Japanese front at any time and will probably remain with us right until the end of the war. Now that Hsuchow has fallen and Wuhan is in danger, it will not be unprofitable, I think, to knock the bottom out of the theory of national subjugation.

4. During these ten months of war all kinds of views which are indicative of impetuosity have also appeared. For instance, at the outset of the war many people were groundlessly optimistic, underestimating Japan and even believing that the Japanese could not get as far as to Shansi. Some belittled the strategic role of guerrilla warfare in the War of Resistance and doubted the proposition, "With regard to the whole, mobile warfare is primary and guerrilla warfare supplementary; with regard to each part, guerrilla warfare is primary and mobile warfare supplementary." They disagreed with the Eighth Route Army's strategy, "Guerrilla warfare is basic, but lose no chance for mobile warfare under favorable conditions," which they regarded as a "mechanical" approach.[2] During the battle of Shanghai some people said: "If we can fight for just three months, the international situation is bound to change, the Soviet Union is bound to send troops, and the war will be over." They pinned their hopes for the future of the War of Resistance chiefly on foreign aid.[3] After the Taierhchuang victory,[4] some people advocated that the Hsuchow campaign should be fought as a "virtually decisive campaign" and that the policy of protracted war should be changed. They said such things as, "This campaign marks the last desperate struggle of the enemy," or, "If we win, the Japanese warlords will be demoralized and able only to await their Day of Judgement."[5] The victory at Pinghsingkuan turned some people's heads, and further victory at Taierhchuang has turned more people's heads. Doubts have arisen as to whether the enemy will attack Wuhan. Many people think "probably not," and many others "definitely not." Such doubts may affect all major issues. For instance, is our anti-Japanese strength already sufficient? Some people may answer affirmatively that our present strength is already sufficient to check the enemy's

advance, so why increase it? Or, for instance, is the slogan "Consolidate and expand the Anti-Japanese National United Front" still correct? Some people may answer negatively that the united front in its present state is already strong enough to repulse the enemy, so why consolidate and expand it? Or, for instance, should our efforts in diplomacy and international propaganda be intensified? Here again the answer may be in the negative. Or, for instance, should we proceed in earnest to reform the military and political systems, develop the mass movement, enforce education for national defence, suppress traitors and Trotskyites, develop war industries and improve the people's livelihood? Or, for instance, are the slogans calling for the defence of Wuhan, of Canton and of the Northwest and for the vigorous development of guerrilla warfare in the enemy's rear still correct? The answers might all be in the negative. There are even some people who, the moment a slightly favorable turn occurs in the war situation, are prepared to intensify the friction between the Kuomintang and the Communist party, diverting attention from external to internal matters. This almost invariably occurs whenever a comparatively big battle is won or the enemy's advance comes to a temporary halt. All the above can be termed political and military short-sightedness. Such talk, however plausible, is actually specious and groundless. To sweep away such verbiage should help the victorious prosecution of the War of Resistance.

5. The question now is: Will China be subjugated? The answer is, No, she will not be subjugated, but will win final victory. Can China win quickly? The answer is, No, she cannot win quickly, and the War of Resistance will be a protracted war.

6. As early as two years ago, we broadly indicated the main arguments on these questions. On July 16, 1936, five months before the Sian Incident and twelve months before the Lukouchiao Incident, in a talk with the American correspondent, Mr. Edgar Snow, I made a general estimate of the situation with regard to war between China and Japan and advanced various principles for winning victory. The following excerpts may serve as a reminder: [6]

> *Question:* Under what conditions do you think the Chinese people can defeat and exhaust the forces of Japan?
> *Answer:* Three conditions will guarantee our success: first, the achievement of the National United Front against Japanese imperialism in China; second, the formation of a World Anti-Japanese United Front; third, the rise of the revolutionary movement among the people in Japan and the Japanese colonies. Of these, the central necessity is the union of the Chinese people themselves.

Question: How long do you think such a war would last?

Answer: That depends on the strength of the Chinese People's Front, many conditioning factors in China and Japan, and the degree of international help given to China, as well as the rate of revolutionary development in Japan. If the Chinese People's Front is powerfully developed, if it is effectively organized horizontally and vertically, if the international aid to China is considerable from those governments and peoples which recognize the menace of Japanese imperialism to their own interests, if revolution comes quickly in Japan, the war will be short and victory speedily won. If these conditions are not realized, however, the war will be very long, but in the end, just the same, Japan will be defeated, China will certainly win, only the sacrifices will be extensive and it will be a painful period for the whole world.

Question: What is your opinion of the probable course of development of such a war, politically and militarily?

Answer: Now, the Japanese continental policy is already fixed and it is well known. Those who imagine that by further sacrifices of Chinese sovereignty, by making economic, political or territorial compromises and concessions, they can halt the advance of Japan, are only indulging in Utopian fancy. But we know well enough that the Lower Yangtse Valley and our southern seaports are already included in the Japanese continental program. Moreover, it is just as clear that the Japanese aspire to seize the Philippines, Siam, Indo-China, Malaya, and the Dutch East Indies. In the event of war, Japan will try to make them her strategic bases, cutting off Great Britain, France and America from China, and monopolizing the seas of the southern Pacific. These moves are included in Japan's maritime strategy. In such a period, it is beyond doubt that China will be in an extremely difficult position. But the majority of the Chinese people believe that such difficulties can be overcome; only the rich in the big port cities are defeatists because they are afraid of losing their property. Many people think it would be impossible for China to continue her fight against Japan, once the latter enforced a blockade. This is nonsense. To refute it we have only to refer to the history of the Red Army. In the anti-Japanese war the Chinese people would have on their side greater advantages than those the Red Army has utilized in its struggle with the Kuomintang. China is a very big nation; if Japan should succeed in occupying even a large section of China, getting possession of an area with as many as one hundred or even two hundred million people, we would still be far from defeated. We would still have left a great force to fight against Japan's warlords, who would have to fight defensive battles in their own rear throughout the war. Economically, of course, China is not unified. But the uneven development of China's economy also presents advantages in a war. For example, to sever Shanghai from the rest of China is not as disastrous to the country as would be, for instance, the severance of New York from the rest of America. Moreover, it is impossible for Japan to isolate all of China: China's Northwest, Southwest and West cannot be blockaded by Japan. Thus, once more the central point of the problem becomes the mobilization and unification of the entire Chinese people and the building up of a United Front, such as has been advocated by the Communist party.

Question: If the war drags on for a long time and Japan is not completely defeated, would the Communist party agree to the negotiation of a peace with Japan and recognize her rule in northeastern China?

Answer: No. Like the people of the whole country, the Chinese Communist party will not allow Japan to retain an inch of Chinese territory.

Question: What, in your opinion, should be the main strategy and tactics to be followed in this "war of liberation"?

Answer: Our strategy should be to employ our main forces in mobile warfare, over an extended, shifting and indefinite front, a strategy depending for success on a high degree of mobility in difficult terrain and featured by swift attack and withdrawal, swift concentration and dispersal. It will be a large-scale war of movement rather than a positional war depending exclusively on defensive works with deep trenches, high fortresses and successive defensive positions. This does not mean the abandonment of vital strategic points, which can be defended by positional warfare as long as profitable. But the pivotal strategy must be a war of movement. Positional warfare must be utilized, but it will be of auxiliary and secondary strategic importance. Geographically the theatre of the war is so vast that it is possible for us to conduct mobile warfare most efficiently. In the face of our vigorous actions the Japanese forces will have to be cautious. Theirs is a ponderous slow-moving war-machine, with limited efficiency. Deep concentration and the exhausting defence of a vital position or two on a narrow front would be to throw away all the tactical advantages of our geography and economic organization, and to repeat the mistake of the Abyssinians. We must avoid great decisive battles in the early stages of the war, and must first employ mobile warfare gradually to break the morale, the fighting spirit and the military efficiency of the living forces of the enemy.

Besides employing trained armies to carry on mobile warfare, we must organize and equip great numbers of guerrilla detachments among the peasantry. What has been accomplished by the anti-Japanese volunteer units of this type in Manchuria is only a very minor demonstration of the latent power of resistance that can be mobilized from the revolutionary peasantry of all China. China's peasants have very great latent power. Properly led and organized, such units can keep the Japanese busy twenty-four hours a day and worry them to death. It must be remembered that the war will be fought in China. This means that the Japanese will be entirely surrounded by a hostile Chinese people. The Japanese will be forced to move in all their provisions and guard them, maintaining large numbers of troops along all lines of communications to be on constant guard against attacks, and heavily garrisoning their bases in Manchuria and Japan as well.

The process of the war will present to China the possibility of capturing many Japanese prisoners, arms, ammunition, war-machines, and so forth. A point will be reached where it will become more and more possible to engage Japan's armies on a basis of positional warfare, using fortifications and deep entrenchment, for, as the war progresses, the technical equipment of the anti-Japanese forces will greatly improve, and will be reinforced by foreign help. Japan's economy will crack under the strain of a long, expensive occupation of China and the morale of her forces will break under the trial of a war of innumerable but indecisive battles. The great reservoirs of human material in the revolutionary Chinese people will still be pouring forth men ready to fight for their freedom into our front lines. All these and other factors will condition the war and will enable us to make the final and decisive attacks on Japan's fortifications and strategic bases and to drive Japan's army of occupation from China.

The above views have been proved correct in the light of the experience of the ten months of war and will be borne out in the future.

7. As far back as August 25, 1937, less than two months after the Lukouchiao Incident, the Central Committee of the Chinese Communist Party clearly pointed out in its "Decision on the Current Situation and the Tasks of the Party":

> The Japanese invaders' provocation at Lukouchiao and their occupation of Peiping and Tientsin are only the beginning of their large-scale invasion of China south of the Great Wall. They have already begun total mobilization in Japan. Their propaganda that they have "no desire to aggravate the situation" is only a smoke-screen for their invasion.
>
> The resistance of July 7 at Lukouchiao marked the starting point of China's nation-wide War of Resistance.
>
> A new stage in China's political situation has begun, the stage of actual resistance. The stage of preparation for resistance is over. The crucial task of the present stage is to mobilize all forces for victory in the War of Resistance.
>
> The key to victory is to develop the War of Resistance already begun into a total nation-wide anti-Japanese war. Only such a total nation-wide war can bring final victory.
>
> As there are still serious weaknesses in the War of Resistance, many difficulties may arise in its future course—setbacks and retreats, internal divisions and betrayals, temporary and partial compromises. We must therefore realize that this will be a hard-fought, protracted war. But we believe that, through the efforts of our Party and the whole people, the War of Resistance which has already begun is sure to overcome all obstacles and continue to progress and develop.

The above thesis, too, has been proved correct in the light of the experience of the ten months of war and will be borne out in the future.

8. Epistemologically speaking, the source of all erroneous views on war lies in idealist and mechanistic tendencies on the question of war. People with such tendencies have a subjective and one-sided approach to problems. They either indulge in groundless and purely subjective talk, or, basing themselves upon a single aspect or a temporary manifestation, magnify it with similar subjectivity into the whole of the problem. But there are two categories of erroneous views, one comprising fundamental and therefore consistent errors which are hard to correct, and the other comprising accidental and therefore temporary errors which are easy to correct. Since both are wrong, both need to be corrected. Therefore, only by opposing idealist and mechanistic tendencies and taking an objective and all-sided view in making a study of war can we draw correct conclusions on the question of war.

The Basis of the Problem

9. Why is the War of Resistance Against Japan a protracted war? Why will the final victory be China's? What is the basis for these statements?

The Sino-Japanese War is not just any war, it is specifically a war of life and death between semicolonial and semifeudal China and imperialist Japan, fought in the nineteen thirties. Herein lies the basis of the whole problem of the war. The two sides in the war have many contrasting features, which will be considered in turn below.

10. *The Japanese side.* First, Japan is a powerful imperialist country, which ranks first in the East in military, economic, and political-organizational power, and is one of the five or six foremost imperialist countries of the world. These are the basic factors in Japan's war of aggression. The inevitability of the war and the impossibility of quick victory for China are due to Japan's imperialist system and her great military, economic and political-organizational power. Secondly, however, the imperialist character of Japan's social economy determines the imperialist character of her war, a war that is retrogressive and barbarous. In the nineteen thirties, the internal and external contradictions of Japanese imperialism have driven it not only to embark on an adventurist war unparalleled in scale but also to approach its final collapse. In terms of social development, Japan is no longer a thriving country; the war will not lead to the prosperity sought by her ruling classes but to the very reverse, the doom of

Japanese imperialism. This is what we mean by the retrogressive nature of Japan's war. It is this reactionary quality, coupled with the military-feudal character of Japanese imperialism, that gives rise to the peculiar barbarity of Japan's war. All of which will arouse to the utmost the class antagonisms within Japan, the antagonism between the Japanese and the Chinese nations, and the antagonism between Japan and most other countries of the world. The reactionary and barbarous character of Japan's war constitutes the primary reason for her inevitable defeat. Thirdly, Japan's war is conducted on the basis of her great military, economic, and political-organizational power, but at the same time it rests on an inadequate natural endowment. Japan's military, economic, and political-organizational power is great but quantitatively inadequate. Japan is a comparatively small country, deficient in manpower and in military, financial, and material resources, and she cannot stand a prolonged war. Japan's rulers are endeavouring to resolve this difficulty through war, but again they will get the very reverse of what they desire; that is to say, the war they have launched to resolve this difficulty will end in adding to it and even in exhausting Japan's original resources. Fourthly and lastly, while Japan can get international support from the Fascist countries, the international opposition she is bound to encounter will be greater than her international support. This opposition will gradually grow and eventually not only cancel out the support but even bear down upon Japan herself. Such is the law that an unjust cause finds meagre support, and such is the consequence of the very nature of Japan's war. To sum up, Japan's advantage lies in her great capacity to wage war, and her disadvantages lie in the reactionary and barbarous nature of her war, in the inadequacy of her manpower and material resources, and in her meagre international support. These are the characteristics on the Japanese side.

11. *The Chinese side.* First, we are a semicolonial and semifeudal country. The Opium War, the Taiping Revolution, the Reform Movement of 1898,[7] the Revolution of 1911 and the Northern Expedition—the revolutionary or reform movements which aimed at extricating China from her semicolonial and semifeudal state—all met with serious setbacks, and China remains a semicolonial and semifeudal country. We are still a weak country and manifestly inferior to the enemy in military, economic, and political-organizational power. Here again one can find the basis for the inevitability of the war and the impossibility of quick victory for China. Secondly, however, China's liberation movement, with its cumulative development over the last hundred years, is now different from that of any previous period. Although the domestic and foreign forces opposing it have caused it serious setbacks, at the same time they

have tempered the Chinese people. Although China today is not so strong as Japan militarily, economically, politically, and culturally, yet there are factors in China more progressive than in any other period of her history. The Communist party of China and the army under its leadership represent these progressive factors. It is on the basis of this progress that China's present war of liberation can be protracted and can achieve final victory. By contrast with Japanese imperialism, which is declining, China is a country rising like the morning sun. China's war is progressive, hence its just character. Because it is a just war, it is capable of arousing the nation to unity, of evoking the sympathy of the people in Japan, and of winning the support of most countries in the world. Thirdly, and again by contrast with Japan, China is a very big country with vast territory, rich resources, a large population and plenty of soldiers, and is capable of sustaining a long war. Fourthly and lastly, there is broad international support for China stemming from the progressive and just character of her war, which is again exactly the reverse of the meagre support for Japan's unjust cause. To sum up, China's disadvantage lies in her military weakness, and her advantages lie in the progressive and just character of her war, her great size and her abundant international support. These are China's characteristics.

12. Thus it can be seen that Japan has great military, economic, and political-organizational power, but that her war is reactionary and barbarous, her manpower and material resources are inadequate, and she is in an unfavorable position internationally. China, on the contrary, has less military, economic, and political-organizational power, but she is in her era of progress, her war is progressive and just, she is moreover a big country, a factor which enables her to sustain a protracted war, and she will be supported by most countries. The above are the basic, mutually contradictory characteristics of the Sino-Japanese War. They have determined and are determining all the political policies and military strategies and tactics of the two sides; they have determined and are determining the protracted character of the war and the fact that the final victory will go to China and not to Japan. The war is a contest between these characteristics. They will change in the course of the war, each according to its own nature; and from this everything else will follow. These characteristics exist objectively and are not invented to deceive people; they constitute all the basic elements of the war, and are not incomplete fragments; they permeate all big and small problems on both sides and all stages of the war, and they are not matters of no consequence. If anyone forgets these characteristics in studying the Sino-Japanese War, he will surely go wrong; and even though some of his ideas win credence

for a time and may seem right, they will inevitably be proved wrong by the course of the war. On the basis of these characteristics we shall now proceed to explain the problems to be dealt with.

Refutation of the Theory of National Subjugation

13. The theorists of national subjugation, who see nothing but the contrast between the enemy's strength and our weakness, used to say, "Resistance will mean subjugation," and now they are saying, "The continuance of the war spells subjugation." We shall not be able to convince them merely by stating that Japan, though strong, is small, while China, though weak, is large. They can adduce historical instances, such as the destruction of the Sung Dynasty by the Yuan and the destruction of the Ming Dynasty by the Ching, to prove that a small but strong country can vanquish a large but weak one and, moreover, that a backward country can vanquish an advanced one. If we say these events occurred long ago and do not prove the point, they can cite the British subjugation of India to prove that a small but strong capitalist country can vanquish a large but weak and backward country. Therefore, we have to produce other grounds before we can silence and convince all the subjugationists, and supply everyone engaged in propaganda with adequate arguments to persuade those who are still confused or irresolute and so strengthen their faith in the War of Resistance.

14. What then are the grounds we should advance? The characteristics of the epoch. These characteristics are concretely reflected in Japan's retrogression and paucity of support and in China's progress and abundance of support.

15. Our war is not just any war, it is specifically a war between China and Japan fought in the nineteen thirties. Our enemy, Japan, is first of all a moribund imperialist power; she is already in her era of decline and is not only different from Britain at the time of the subjugation of India, when British capitalism was still in the era of its ascendency, but also different from what she herself was at the time of World War I twenty years ago. The present war was launched on the eve of the general collapse of world imperialism and, above all, of the Fascist countries; that is the very reason the enemy has launched this adventurist war, which is in the nature of a last desperate struggle. Therefore, it is an inescapable certainty that it will not be China but the ruling circles of Japanese imperialism which will be destroyed as a result of the war. Moreover, Japan has

undertaken this war at a time when other countries have been or are about to be embroiled in war, when we are all fighting or preparing to fight against barbarous aggression, and China's fortunes are linked with those of most of the countries and peoples of the world. This is the root cause of the opposition Japan has aroused and will increasingly arouse among those countries and peoples.

16. What about China? The China of today cannot be compared with the China of any other historical period. She is a semi-colony and a semi-feudal society in character and she is consequently considered a weak country. At the same time, she is historically in her era of progress; this is the primary reason for her ability to defeat Japan. When we say that the War of Resistance Against Japan is progressive, we do not mean progressive in the ordinary or general sense, nor do we mean progressive in the sense that the Abyssinian war against Italy, or the Taiping Revolution or the 1911 Revolution were progressive, we mean progressive in the sense that China is progressive today. In what way is the China of today progressive? She is progressive because she is no longer a completely feudal country and because we already have some capitalism in China, we have a bourgeoisie and a proletariat, we have vast numbers of people who have awakened or are awakening, we have a Communist party, we have a politically progressive army—the Chinese Red Army led by the Communist party—and we have the tradition and the experience of many decades of revolution, and especially the experience of the seventeen years since the founding of the Chinese Communist Party. This experience has schooled the people and the political parties of China and forms the very basis for the present unity against Japan. If it is said that without the experience of 1905 the victory of 1917 would have been impossible in Russia, then we can also say that without the experience of the last seventeen years it would be impossible to win our War of Resistance. Such is the internal situation.

In the existing international situation, China is not isolated in the war, and this fact too is without precedent in history. In past history, China's wars, and India's too, were wars fought in isolation. It is only today that we meet with world-wide popular movements, extraordinary in breadth and depth, which have arisen or are arising and which are supporting China. The Russian Revolution of 1917 also received international support, and thus the Russian workers and peasants won; but that support was not so broad in scale and deep in nature as ours today. The popular movements in the world today are developing on a scale and with a depth that are unprecedented. The existence of the Soviet Union is a particularly vital factor in present-day international politics, and the Soviet

Union will certainly support China with the greatest enthusiasm; and there was no such thing twenty years ago. All these factors have created and are creating important conditions indispensable to China's final victory. Large-scale direct assistance is as yet lacking and will come only in the future, but China is progressive and is a big country, and these are the factors enabling her to protract the war and to promote as well as await international help.

17. There is the additional factor that while Japan is a little country with a small territory, few resources, a small population and a limited number of soldiers, China is a big country with vast territory, rich resources, a large population, and plenty of soldiers, so that, besides the contrast between strength and weakness, there is the contrast between a small country, retrogression, and meagre support and a big country, progress, and abundant support. This is the reason why China will never be subjugated. It follows from the contrast between strength and weakness that Japan can ride roughshod over China for a certain time and to a certain extent, that China must unavoidably travel a hard stretch of road, and that the War of Resistance will be a protracted war and not a war of quick decision; nevertheless, it follows from the other contrast—a small country, retrogression and meagre support versus a big country, progress and abundant support—that Japan cannot ride roughshod over China indefinitely but is sure to meet final defeat, while China can never be subjugated but is sure to win final victory.

18. Why was Abyssinia vanquished? First, she was not only weak but also small. Second, she was not as progressive as China; she was an old country passing from the slave to the serf system, a country without any capitalism or bourgeois political parties, let alone a Communist party, and with no army such as the Chinese army, let alone one like the Eighth Route Army. Third, she was unable to hold out and wait for international assistance and had to fight her war in isolation. Fourth, and most important of all, there were mistakes in the direction of her war against Italy. Therefore Abyssinia was subjugated. But there is still quite extensive guerrilla warfare in Abyssinia, which, if persisted in, will enable the Abyssinians to recover their country when the world situation changes.

19. If the subjugationists quote the history of the failure of liberation movements in modern China to prove their assertions first that "resistance will mean subjugation," and then that "the continuance of the war spells subjugation," here again our answer is, "Times are different." China herself, the internal situation in Japan and the international environment are all different now. It is a serious matter that Japan is stronger than before while China in her unchanged semicolonial and semifeudal position is

still fairly weak. It is also a fact that for the time being Japan can still control her people at home and exploit international contradictions in order to invade China. But during a long war, these things are bound to change in the opposite direction. Such changes are not yet accomplished facts, but they will be so in the future. The subjugationists dismiss this point. As for China, we already have new people, a new political party, a new army and a new policy of resistance to Japan, a situation very different from that of over a decade ago, and what is more, all these will inevitably make further progress. It is true that historically the liberation movements met with repeated setbacks with the result that China could not accumulate greater strength for the present War of Resistance—this is a very painful historical lesson, and never again should we destroy any of our revolutionary forces. Yet even on the present basis, by exerting great efforts we can certainly forge gradually ahead and increase the strength of our resistance. All such efforts should converge on the great Anti-Japanese National United Front. As for international support, though direct and large-scale assistance is not yet in sight, it is in the making, the international situation being fundamentally different from what it was. The countless failures in the liberation movement of modern China had their subjective and objective causes, but the situation today is entirely different. Today, although there are many difficulties which make the War of Resistance arduous— such as the enemy's strength and our weakness, and the fact that his difficulties are just starting, while our own progress is far from sufficient— nevertheless many favorable conditions exist for defeating the enemy; we need only add our subjective efforts, and we shall be able to overcome the difficulties and win through to victory. These are favorable conditions such as never existed before in any period of our history, and that is why the War of Resistance Against Japan, unlike the liberation movements of the past, will not end in failure.

Compromise or Resistance?
Corruption or Progress?

20. It has been fully explained above that the theory of national subjugation is groundless. But there are many people who do not subscribe to this theory; they are good, honest patriots, who are nevertheless deeply worried about the present situation. Two things are worrying them, fear of a compromise with Japan and doubts about the possibility of political progress. These two vexing questions are being widely discussed and no key has been found to their solution. Let us now examine them.

21. As previously explained, the question of compromise has social roots, and as long as the roots exist the question is bound to arise. But compromise will not work. To prove the point, again we need only look for substantiation to Japan, China, and the international situation. Take first Japan. At the very beginning of the War of Resistance, we estimated that the time would come when an atmosphere conducive to compromise would arise, in other words, that after occupying northern China, Kiangsu, and Chekiang, Japan would probably resort to the scheme of inducing China to capitulate. True enough, she did resort to the scheme, but the crisis soon passed, one reason being that the enemy everywhere pursued a barbarous policy and practised naked plunder. Had China capitulated, every Chinese would have become a slave without a country. The enemy's predatory policy, the policy of subjugating China, has two aspects, the material and the spiritual, both of which are being applied universally to all Chinese, not only to the people of the lower strata but also to members of the upper strata; of course the latter are treated a little more politely, but the difference is only one of degree, not of principle. In the main the enemy is transplanting into the interior of China the same old measures he adopted in the three northeastern provinces. Materially, he is robbing the common people even of their food and clothing, making them cry out in hunger and cold; he is plundering the means of production, thus ruining and enslaving China's national industries. Spiritually, he is working to destroy the national consciousness of the Chinese people. Under "the flag of the Rising Sun" no Chinese could avoid being a docile subject, a beast of burden forbidden to show the slightest trace of Chinese national spirit. This barbarous enemy policy will be carried deeper into the interior of China. Japan with her voracious appetite is unwilling to stop the war. As was inevitable, the policy set forth in the Japanese cabinet's statement of January 16, 1938,[8] is still being obstinately carried out, which has enraged all strata of the Chinese people. This rage is engendered by the reactionary and barbarous character of Japan's war—"there is no escape from fate," and hence an absolute hostility has crystallized. It is to be expected that on some future occasion the enemy will once again resort to the scheme of inducing China to capitulate and that certain subjugationists will again crawl out and most probably collude with certain foreign elements (to be found in Britain, the United States, and France, especially among the upper strata in Britain) as partners in crime. But the general trend of events will not permit capitulation; the obstinate and peculiarly barbarous character of Japan's war has decided this aspect of the question.

22. Second, let us take China. There are three factors contributing to

China's perseverance in the War of Resistance. In the first place, the Communist party, which is the reliable force leading the people to resist Japan. Next, the Kuomintang, which depends on Britain and the United States and hence will not capitulate to Japan unless they tell it to. Finally, the other political parties and groups, most of which oppose compromise and support the War of Resistance. With unity among these three, whoever compromises will be standing with the traitors, and anybody will have the right to punish him. All those unwilling to be traitors have no choice but to unite and carry on the War of Resistance to the end; therefore compromise is scarcely possible.

23. Third, take the international aspect. Except for Japan's allies and certain elements in the upper strata of other capitalist countries, the whole world is in favor of China's resistance, not of compromise by China. This factor reinforces China's hopes. Today the people throughout the country cherish the hope that international forces will gradually give China increasing help. It is not a vain hope; the existence of the Soviet Union in particular encourages China in her War of Resistance. The socialist Soviet Union, now strong as never before, has always shared China's joys and sorrows. In direct contrast to all the upper class elements in all the capitalist countries who seek nothing but profits, the Soviet Union considers it her duty to help all weak nations and all revolutionary wars. That China is not fighting her war in isolation has its basis not only in international assistance in general but in Soviet assistance in particular. China and the Soviet Union are in close geographical proximity, which aggravates Japan's crisis and facilitates China's War of Resistance. Geographical proximity to Japan increases the difficulties of China's resistance. Proximity to the Soviet Union, on the other hand, is a favorable condition for the War of Resistance.

24. Hence we may conclude that the danger of compromise exists but can be overcome. Even if the enemy can modify his policy to some extent, he cannot alter it fundamentally. In China the social roots of compromise are present, but the opponents of compromise are in the majority. Internationally, also, some forces favor compromise but the main forces favor resistance. The combination of these three factors makes it possible to overcome the danger of compromise and persist to the end in the War of Resistance.

25. Let us now answer the second question. Political progress at home and perseverance in the War of Resistance are inseparable. The greater the political progress, the more we can persevere in the war, and the more we persevere in the war, the greater the political progress. But, fundamentally, everything depends on our perseverance in the War of Resist-

ance. The unhealthy phenomena in various fields under the Kuomintang regime are very serious, and the accumulation of these undesirable factors over the years has caused great anxiety and vexation among the broad ranks of our patriots. But there is no ground for pessimism, since experience in the War of Resistance has already proved that the Chinese people have made as much progress in the last ten months as in many years in the past. Although the cumulative effects of long years of corruption are seriously retarding the growth of the people's strength to resist Japan, thus reducing the extent of our victories and causing us losses in the war, yet the overall situation in China, in Japan and in the world is such that the Chinese people cannot but make progress. This progress will be slow because of the factor of corruption, which impedes progress. Progress and the slow pace of progress are two characteristics of the present situation, and the second ill accords with the urgent needs of the war, which is a source of great concern to patriots. But we are in the midst of a revolutionary war, and revolutionary war is an antitoxin which not only eliminates the enemy's poison but also purges us of our own filth. Every just, revolutionary war is endowed with tremendous power, which can transform many things or clear the way for their transformation. The Sino-Japanese War will transform both China and Japan; provided China perseveres in the War of Resistance and in the united front, the old Japan will surely be transformed into a new Japan and the old China into a new China, and people and everything else in both China and Japan will be transformed during and after the war. It is proper for us to regard the anti-Japanese war and our national reconstruction as interconnected. To say that Japan can also be transformed is to say that the war of aggression by her rulers will end in defeat and may lead to a revolution by the Japanese people. The day of triumph of the Japanese people's revolution will be the day Japan is transformed. All this is closely linked with China's War of Resistance and is a prospect we should take into account.

The Theory of National Subjugation is Wrong and the Theory of Quick Victory is Likewise Wrong

26. In our comparative study of the enemy and ourselves with respect to the basic contradictory characteristics, such as relative strength, relative size, progress or reaction, and the relative extent of support, we have already refuted the theory of national subjugation, and we have explained why compromise is unlikely and why political progress is possible. The subjugationists stress the contradiction between strength and weakness

and puff it up until it becomes the basis of their whole argument on the question, neglecting all the other contradictions. Their preoccupation with the contrast in strength shows their one-sidedness, and their exaggeration of this one side of the matter into the whole shows their subjectivism. Thus, if one looks at the matter as a whole, it will be seen that they have no ground to stand on and are wrong. As for those who are neither subjugationists nor confirmed pessimists, but who are in a pessimistic frame of mind for the moment simply because they are confused by the disparity between our strength and that of the enemy at a given time and in certain respects or by the corruption in the country, we should point out to them that their approach also tends to be one-sided and subjective. But in their case correction is relatively easy; once they are alerted, they will understand, for they are patriots and their error is only momentary.

27. The exponents of quick victory are likewise wrong. Either they completely forget the contradiction between strength and weakness, remembering only the other contradictions, or they exaggerate China's advantages beyond all semblance of reality and beyond recognition, or they presumptuously take the balance of forces at one time and place for the whole situation, as in the old saying, "A leaf before the eye shuts out Mount Tai." In a word, they lack the courage to admit that the enemy is strong while we are weak. They often deny this point and consequently deny one aspect of the truth. Nor do they have the courage to admit the limitations of our advantages, and thus they deny another aspect of the truth. The result is that they make mistakes, big and small, and here again it is subjectivism and one-sidedness that are doing the mischief. These friends have their hearts in the right place, and they, too, are patriots. But while "the gentlemen's aspirations are indeed lofty," their views are wrong, and to act according to them would certainly be to run into a brick wall. For if appraisal does not conform to reality, action cannot attain its objective; and to act notwithstanding would mean the army's defeat and the nation's subjugation, so that the result would be the same as with the defeatists. Hence this theory of quick victory will not do either.

28. Do we deny the danger of national subjugation? No, we do not. We recognize that China faces two possible prospects, liberation or subjugation, and that the two are in violent conflict. Our task is to achieve liberation and to avert subjugation. The conditions for liberation are China's progress, which is basic, the enemy's difficulties, and international support. We differ from the subjugationists. Taking an objective and many-sided view, we recognize the two possibilities of national subjugation and liberation, stress that liberation is the dominant possibility, point out the

conditions for its achievement, and strive to secure them. The subjuga-tionists, on the other hand, taking a subjective and one-sided view, recog-nize only one possibility, that of subjugation; they do not admit the possi-bility of liberation, and still less point out the conditions necessary for liberation or strive to secure them. Moreover, while acknowledging the tendency to compromise and the corruption, we see other tendencies and phenomena which, we indicate, will gradually prevail and which are al-ready in violent conflict with the former; in addition, we point out the conditions necessary for the healthy tendencies and phenomena to pre-vail, and we strive to overcome the tendency to compromise and to change the state of corruption. Therefore, contrary to the subjugationists, we are not at all pessimistic.

29. Not that we would not like a quick victory; everybody would be in favor of driving the "devils" out overnight. But we point out that in the absence of certain definite conditions quick victory is something that exists only in our minds and not in objective reality, and that it is a mere illusion, a false theory. Accordingly, having made an objective and com-prehensive appraisal of all the circumstances concerning both the enemy and ourselves, we point out that the only way to final victory is the strat-egy of protracted war, and we reject the completely groundless theory of quick victory. We maintain that we must strive to secure all the condi-tions indispensable to final victory, and the more fully and the earlier these conditions are secured, the surer we shall be of victory and the earlier we shall win it. We believe that only in this way can the course of the war be shortened, and we reject the theory of quick victory, which is just idle talk and an effort to get things on the cheap.

Why a Protracted War?

30. Let us now examine the problem of protracted war. A correct an-swer to the question "Why a protracted war?" can be arrived at only on the basis of all the fundamental contrasts between China and Japan. For instance, if we say merely that the enemy is a strong imperialist power while we are a weak semicolonial and semifeudal country, we are in dan-ger of falling into the theory of national subjugation. For neither in theory nor in practice can a struggle be protracted by simply pitting the weak against the strong. Nor can it be protracted by simply pitting the big against the small, the progressive against the reactionary, or abundant sup-port against meagre support. The annexation of a small country by a big one or of a big country by a small one is a common occurrence. It often

happens that a progressive country which is not strong is destroyed by a big, reactionary country, and the same holds for everything that is progressive but not strong. Abundant or scanty support is an important but a subsidiary factor, and the degree of its effect depends upon the fundamental factors on both sides. Therefore when we say that the War of Resistance Against Japan is a protracted war, it is a conclusion derived from the interrelations of all the factors at work on both sides. The enemy is strong and we are weak, and the danger of subjugation is there. But in other respects the enemy has shortcomings and we have advantages. The enemy's advantages can be reduced and his shortcomings aggravated by our efforts. On the other hand, our advantages can be enhanced and our shortcomings remedied by our efforts. Hence, we can win final victory and avert subjugation, while the enemy will ultimately be defeated and cannot avert the collapse of his whole imperialist system.

31. Since the enemy has only one advantage but shortcomings in all other respects and we have shortcomings in only one respect but advantages in all others, why has this produced not a balance, but, on the contrary, a superior position for him and an inferior position for us at the present time? Quite clearly, we cannot consider the question in such a formal way. The fact is that the disparity between the enemy's strength and our own is now so great that the enemy's shortcomings have not developed and, for the time being, cannot develop to a degree sufficient to offset his strength, while our advantages have not developed and, for the time being, cannot develop to a degree sufficient to compensate for our weakness. Therefore there can as yet be no balance, only imbalance.

32. Although our efforts in persevering in the War of Resistance and the united front have somewhat changed the enemy's strength and superiority as against our weakness and inferiority, there has as yet been no basic change. Hence during a certain stage of the war, to a certain degree the enemy will be victorious and we shall suffer defeat. But why is it that in this stage the enemy's victories and our defeats are definitely restricted in degree and cannot be transcended by complete victory or complete defeat? The reason is that, first, the enemy's strength and our weakness have been relative and not absolute from the very beginning, and that, second, our efforts in persevering in the War of Resistance and in the united front have further emphasized this relativeness. In comparison with the original situation, the enemy is still strong, but unfavorable factors have reduced his strength, although not yet to a degree sufficient to destroy his superiority, and similarly we are still weak, but favorable factors have compensated for our weakness, although not yet to a degree sufficient to transform our inferiority. Thus it turns out that the enemy is

relatively strong and we are relatively weak, that the enemy is in a relatively superior and we are in a relatively inferior position. On both sides, strength and weakness, superiority and inferiority, have never been absolute, and besides, our efforts in persevering in resistance to Japan and in the united front during the war have brought about further changes in the original balance of forces between us and the enemy. Therefore, in this stage the enemy's victory and our defeat are definitely restricted in degree, and hence the war becomes protracted.

33. But circumstances are continually changing. In the course of the war, provided we employ correct military and political tactics, make no mistakes of principle and exert our best efforts, the enemy's disadvantages and China's advantages will both grow as the war is drawn out, with the inevitable result that there will be continual change in the difference in comparative strength and hence in the relative position of the two sides. When a new stage is reached, a great change will take place in the balance of forces, resulting in the enemy's defeat and our victory.

34. At present the enemy can still manage to exploit his strength, and our War of Resistance has not yet fundamentally weakened him. His insufficiency in manpower and material resources is not yet such as to prevent his offensive; on the contrary, they can still sustain his offensive to a certain extent. The reactionary and barbarous nature of his war, a factor which intensifies both class antagonisms within Japan and the resistance of the Chinese nation, has not yet brought about a situation which radically impedes his advance. The enemy's international isolation is increasing but is not yet complete. In many countries which have indicated they will help us, the capitalists dealing in munitions and war materials and bent solely on profit are still furnishing Japan with large quantities of war supplies,[9] and their governments[10] are still reluctant to join the Soviet Union in practical sanctions against Japan. From all this it follows that our War of Resistance cannot be won quickly and can only be a protracted war. As for China, although there has been some improvement with regard to her weakness in the military, economic, political, and cultural spheres in the ten months of resistance, it is still a long way from what is required to prevent the enemy's offensive and prepare our counteroffensive. Moreover, quantitatively speaking, we have had to sustain certain losses. Although all the factors favorable to us are having a positive effect, it will not be sufficient to halt the enemy's offensive and to prepare for our counteroffensive unless we make an immense effort. Neither the abolition of corruption and the acceleration of progress at home, nor the curbing of the pro-Japanese forces and the expansion of the anti-Japanese forces

abroad, is yet a fact. From all this it follows that our war cannot be won quickly but can only be a protracted war.

The Three Stages of the Protracted War

35. Since the Sino-Japanese War is a protracted one and final victory will belong to China, it can reasonably be assumed that this protracted war will pass through three stages. The first stage covers the period of the enemy's strategic offensive and our strategic defensive. The second stage will be the period of the enemy's strategic consolidation and our preparation for the counteroffensive. The third stage will be the period of our strategic counteroffensive and the enemy's strategic retreat. It is impossible to predict the concrete situation in the three stages, but certain main trends in the war may be pointed out in the light of present conditions. The course of objective events will be exceedingly rich and varied, with many twists and turns, and nobody can cast a "horoscope" for the Sino-Japanese War; nevertheless it is necessary for the strategic direction of the war to make an outline sketch of its trends. Although our sketch may not be in full accord with the subsequent facts and will be amended by them, it is still necessary to make such a sketch in order to give firm and purposeful strategic direction to the protracted war.

36. The first stage has not yet ended. The enemy's design is to occupy Canton, Wuhan, and Lanchow and link up these three points. To accomplish this aim the enemy will have to use at least fifty divisions, or about one and a half million men, spend from one and a half to two years, and expend more than ten thousand million yen. In penetrating so deeply, the enemy will encounter immense difficulties, with consequences disastrous beyond imagination. As for attempting to occupy the entire length of the Canton-Hankow Railway and the Sian-Lanchow Highway, he will have to fight perilous battles and even so may not fully accomplish his design. But in drawing up our operational plan we should base ourselves on the assumption that the enemy may occupy the three points and even certain additional areas, as well as link them up, and we should make dispositions for a protracted war, so that even if he does so, we shall be able to cope with him. In this stage the form of fighting we should adopt is primarily mobile warfare, to be supplemented by guerrilla and positional warfare. Through the subjective errors of the Kuomintang military authorities, positional warfare was assigned the primary role in the first phase of this stage, but, nevertheless, it is supplementary from the point of view of the

stage as a whole. In this stage, China has already built up a broad united front and achieved unprecedented unity. Although the enemy has used and will continue to use base and shameless means to induce capitulation in the attempt to realize his plan for a quick decision and to conquer the whole of China without much effort, he has failed so far, nor is he likely to succeed in the future. In this stage, in spite of considerable losses, China has made considerable progress, which will become the main basis for her continued resistance in the second stage. In the present stage the Soviet Union has already given substantial aid to China. On the enemy side, there are already signs of flagging morale, and the momentum of attack of his army is less in the middle phase of this stage than in the initial phase and will diminish still further in the concluding phase. His finances and economy are beginning to show signs of exhaustion; war-weariness is beginning to set in among his people and troops; and within the clique that is running the war, "war frustrations" are beginning to manifest themselves and pessimism about the prospects of the war is growing.

37. The second stage may be termed one of strategic stalemate. At the tail end of the first stage, the enemy will be forced to fix certain terminal points to his strategic offensive owing to his shortage of troops and our firm resistance, and upon reaching them he will stop his strategic offensive and enter the stage of safeguarding his occupied areas. In the second stage, the enemy will attempt to safeguard the occupied areas and to make them his own by the fraudulent method of setting up puppet governments, while plundering the Chinese people to the limit; but again he will be confronted with stubborn guerrilla warfare. Taking advantage of the fact that the enemy's rear is unguarded, our guerrilla warfare will develop extensively in the first stage, and many base areas will be established, seriously threatening the enemy's consolidation of the occupied areas, and so in the second stage there will still be widespread fighting. In this stage, our form of fighting will be primarily guerrilla warfare, supplemented by mobile warfare. China will still retain a large regular army, but she will find it difficult to launch the strategic counteroffensive immediately because, on the one hand, the enemy will adopt a strategically defensive position in the big cities and along the main lines of communication under his occupation and, on the other hand, China will not yet be adequately equipped technically. Except for the troops engaged in frontal defence against the enemy, our forces will be switched in large numbers to the enemy's rear in comparatively dispersed dispositions, and, basing themselves on all the areas not actually occupied by the enemy and coordinating with the people's local armed forces, they will launch extensive, fierce guerrilla warfare against enemy-occupied places, keeping the enemy on

the move as far as possible in order to destroy him in mobile warfare, as is now being done in Shansi Province. The fighting in the second stage will be ruthless, and the country will suffer serious devastation. But the guerrilla warfare will be successful, and if it is well conducted the enemy may be able to retain only about one-third of his occupied territory, with the remaining two-thirds back in our hands, which will constitute a great defeat for the enemy and a great victory for China. By then the enemy-occupied territory as a whole will fall into three categories: first, the enemy base areas; second, our base areas for guerrilla warfare; and, third, the guerrilla areas contested by both sides. The duration of this stage will depend on the degree of change in the balance of forces between us and the enemy and on the changes in the international situation; generally speaking, we should be prepared to see this stage last a comparatively long time and to weather its hardships. It will be a very painful period for China; the two big problems will be economic difficulties and the disruptive activities of the traitors. The enemy will go all out to wreck China's united front, and the traitor organizations in all the occupied areas will merge into a so-called "unified government." Owing to the loss of big cities and the hardships of war, vacillating elements within our ranks will clamor for compromise, and pessimism will grow to a serious extent. Our tasks will then be to mobilize the whole people to unite as one man and carry on the war with unflinching perseverance, to broaden and consolidate the united front, sweep away all pessimism and ideas of compromise, promote the will to hard struggle and apply new war-time policies, and so to weather the hardships. In the second stage, we will have to call upon the whole country resolutely to maintain a united government, oppose splits, and systematically improve our fighting technique, reform the armed forces, mobilize the entire people, and prepare for the counteroffensive. The international situation will become still more unfavorable to Japan and the main international forces will incline towards giving more help to China, even though there may be talk of "realism" of the Chamberlain type which accommodates itself to *faits accomplis*. Japan's threat to Southeast Asia and Siberia will become greater, and there may even be another war. As regards Japan, scores of her divisions will be inextricably bogged down in China. Widespread guerrilla warfare and the people's anti-Japanese movement will wear down this big Japanese force, greatly reducing it and also disintegrating its morale by stimulating the growth of homesickness, war-weariness, and even anti-war sentiment. Though it would be wrong to say that Japan will achieve no results at all in her plunder of China, yet, being short of capital and harassed by guerrilla warfare, she cannot possibly achieve rapid or substantial results. This second stage will be the transitional stage of the entire war; it will be the most trying period but also the pivotal one. Whether China becomes an independent country or is reduced to a colony will be determined not by the retention or loss of the big cities in the first stage but by the extent to which the whole nation exerts itself in the second. If we can persevere in the War of Resistance, in the united front and in the protracted war, China will in that stage gain the power to change from weak to strong. It will be the second act in the three-act drama of China's War of Resistance. And through the efforts of the entire cast it will be possible to perform a most brilliant last act.

38. The third stage will be the stage of the counteroffensive to recover our lost territories. Their recovery will depend mainly upon the strength which China has built up in the preceding stage and which will continue to grow in the third stage. But China's strength alone will not be sufficient, and we shall also have to rely on the support of international forces and on the changes that will take place inside Japan, or otherwise we shall not be able to win; this adds to China's tasks in international propaganda and diplomacy. In the third stage, our war will no longer be one of strategic defensive, but will turn into a strategic counteroffensive manifesting itself in strategic offensives; and it will no longer be fought on strategically interior lines, but will shift gradually to strategically exterior lines. Not until we fight our way to the Yalu River can this war be considered over. The third stage will be the last in the protracted war, and when we talk of persevering in the war to the end, we mean going all the way through this stage. Our primary form of fighting will still be mobile warfare, but positional warfare will rise to importance. While positional defence cannot be regarded as important in the first stage because of the prevailing circumstances, positional attack will become quite important in the third stage because of the changed conditions and the requirements of the task. In the third stage guerrilla warfare will still provide strategic support by supplementing mobile and positional warfare, but it will not be the primary form as in the second stage.

39. It is thus obvious that the war is protracted and consequently ruthless in nature. The enemy will not be able to gobble up the whole of China but will be able to occupy many places for a considerable time. China will not be able to oust the Japanese quickly, but the greater part of her territory will remain in her hands. Ultimately the enemy will lose and we will win, but we shall have a hard stretch of road to travel.

40. The Chinese people will become tempered in the course of this long and ruthless war. The political parties taking part in the war will also be steeled and tested. The united front must be persevered in; only by

persevering in the united front can we persevere in the war; and only by presevering in the united front and in the war can we win final victory. Only thus can all difficulties be overcome. After traveling the hard stretch of road we shall reach the highway to victory. This is the natural logic of the war.

41. In the three stages the changes in relative strength will proceed along the following lines. In the first stage, the enemy is superior and we are inferior in strength. With regard to our inferiority we must reckon on changes of two different kinds from the eve of the War of Resistance to the end of this stage. The first kind is a change for the worse. China's original inferiority will be aggravated by war losses, namely, decreases in territory, population, economic strength, military strength and cultural institutions. Towards the end of the first stage, the decrease will probably be considerable, especially on the economic side. This point will be exploited by some people as a basis for their theories of national subjugation and of compromise. But the second kind of change, the change for the better, must also be noted. It includes the experience gained in the war, the progress made by the armed forces, the political progress, the mobilization of the people, the development of culture in a new direction, the emergence of guerrilla warfare, the increase in international support, etc. In the first stage, what is on the downgrade is the old quantity and the old quality, the manifestations being mainly quantitative. What is on the upgrade is the new quantity and the new quality, the manifestations being mainly qualitative. It is the second kind of change that provides a basis for our ability to fight a protracted war and win final victory.

42. In the first stage, changes of two kinds also occur on the enemy's side. The first kind is a change for the worse and manifests itself in hundreds of thousands of casualties, the drain on arms and ammunition, deterioration of troop morale, popular discontent at home, shrinkage of trade, the expenditure of over ten thousand million yen, condemnation by world opinion, etc. This trend also provides a basis for our ability to fight a protracted war and win final victory. But we must likewise reckon with the second kind of change on the enemy's side, a change for the better, that is, his expansion in territory, population, and resources. This too is a basis for the protracted nature of our War of Resistance and the impossibility of quick victory, but at the same time certain people will use it as a basis for their theories of national subjugation and of compromise. However, we must take into account the transitory and partial character of this change for the better on the enemy's side. Japan is an imperialist power heading for collapse, and her occupation of China's territory is temporary. The vigorous growth of guerrilla warfare in China will re-

strict her actual occupation to narrow zones. Moreover, her occupation of Chinese territory is creating and intensifying contradictions between Japan and other foreign countries. Besides, generally speaking, such occupation involves a considerable period in which Japan will make capital outlay without drawing any profits, as is shown by the experience in the three northeastern provinces. All of which again gives us a basis for demolishing the theories of national subjugation and of compromise and for establishing the theories of protracted war and of final victory.

43. In the second stage, the above changes on both sides will continue to develop. While the situation cannot be predicted in detail, on the whole Japan will continue on the downgrade and China on the upgrade.[11] For example, Japan's military and financial resources will be seriously drained by China's guerrilla warfare, popular discontent will grow in Japan, the morale of her troops will deteriorate further, and she will become more isolated internationally. As for China, she will make further progress in the political, military and cultural spheres and in the mobilization of the people; guerrilla warfare will develop further; there will be some new economic growth on the basis of the small industries and the widespread agriculture in the interior; international support will gradually increase; and the whole picture will be quite different from what it is now. This second stage may last quite a long time, during which there will be a great reversal in the balance of forces, with China gradually rising and Japan gradually declining. China will emerge from her inferior position, and Japan will lose her superior position; first the two countries will become evenly matched, and then their relative positions will be reversed. Thereupon, China will in general have completed her preparations for the strategic counteroffensive and will enter the stage of the counteroffensive and the expulsion of the enemy. It should be reiterated that the change from inferiority to superiority and the completion of preparations for the counteroffensive will involve three things, namely, an increase in China's own strength, an increase in Japan's difficulties, and an increase in international support; it is the combination of all these forces that will bring about China's superiority and the completion of her preparations for the counteroffensive.

44. Because of the unevenness in China's political and economic development, the strategic counteroffensive of the third stage will not present a uniform and even picture throughout the country in its initial phase but will be regional in character, rising here and subsiding there. During this stage, the enemy will not relax his divisive tricks to break China's united front, hence the task of maintaining internal unity in China will become all the more important, and we shall have to ensure that the stra-

tegic counteroffensive does not collapse halfway through internal dissension. In this period the international situation will become very favorable to China. China's task will be to take advantage of it in order to attain complete liberation and establish an independent democratic state, which at the same time will mean helping the world anti-Fascist movement.

45. China moving from inferiority to parity and then to superiority, Japan moving from superiority to parity and then to inferiority; China moving from the defensive to stalemate and then to the counteroffensive, Japan moving from the offensive to the safeguarding of her gains and then to retreat—such will be the course of the Sino-Japanese War and its inevitable trend.

46. Hence the questions and the conclusions are as follows: Will China be subjugated? The answer is, No, she will not be subjugated, but will win final victory. Can China win quickly? The answer is, No, she cannot win quickly, and the war must be a protracted one. Are these conclusions correct? I think they are.

47. At this point, the exponents of national subjugation and of compromise will again rush in and say, "To move from inferiority to parity China needs a military and economic power equal to Japan's, and to move from parity to superiority she will need a military and economic power greater than Japan's. But this is impossible, hence the above conclusions are not correct."

48. This is the so-called theory that "weapons decide everything,"[12] which constitutes a mechanical approach to the question of war and a subjective and one-sided view. Our view is opposed to this; we see not only weapons but also people. Weapons are an important factor in war, but not the decisive factor; it is people, not things, that are decisive. The contest of strength is not only a contest of military and economic power, but also a contest of human power and morale. Military and economic power is necessarily wielded by people. If the great majority of the Chinese, of the Japanese and of the people of other countries are on the side of our War of Resistance Against Japan, how can Japan's military and economic power, wielded as it is by a small minority through coercion, count as superiority? And if not, then does not China, though wielding relatively inferior military and economic power, become the superior? There is no doubt that China will gradually grow in military and economic power, provided she perseveres in the War of Resistance and in the united front. As for our enemy, weakened as he will be by the long war and by internal and external contradictions, his military and economic power is bound to change in the reverse direction. In these circumstances, is there any reason why China cannot become the superior? Nor

is that all. Although we cannot as yet count the military and economic power of other countries as being openly and to any great extent on our side, is there any reason why we will not be able to do so in the future? If Japan's enemy is not just China, if in future one or more other countries make open use of their considerable military and economic power defensively or offensively against Japan and openly help us, then will not our superiority be still greater? Japan is a small country, her war is reactionary and barbarous, and she will become more and more isolated internationally; China is a big country, her war is progressive and just, and she will enjoy more and more support internationally. Is there any reason why the long-period development of these factors should not definitely change the relative position between the enemy and ourselves?

49. The exponents of quick victory, however, do not realize that war is a contest of strength, and that before a certain change has taken place in the relative strength of the belligerents, there is no basis for trying to fight strategically decisive battles and shorten the road to liberation. Were their ideas to be put into practice, we should inevitably run our heads into a brick wall. Or perhaps they are just talking for their own pleasure without really intending to put their ideas into practice. In the end Mr. Reality will come and pour a bucket of cold water over these chatterers, showing them up as mere windbags who want to get things on the cheap, to have gains without pains. We have had this kind of idle chatter before and we have it now, though not very much so far; but there may be more as the war develops into the stage of stalemate and then of counteroffensive. But in the meantime, if China's losses in the first stage are fairly heavy and the second stage drags on very long, the theories of national subjugation and of compromise will gain great currency. Therefore, our fire should be directed mainly against them and only secondarily against the idle chatter about quick victory.

50. That the war will be protracted is certain, but nobody can predict exactly how many months or years it will last, as this depends entirely upon the degree of the change in the balance of forces. All those who wish to shorten the war have no alternative but to work hard to increase our own strength and reduce that of the enemy. Specifically, the only way is to strive to win more battles and wear down the enemy's forces, develop guerrilla warfare to reduce enemy-occupied territory to a minimum, consolidate and expand the united front to rally the forces of the whole nation, build up new armies and develop new war industries, promote political, economic, and cultural progress, mobilize the workers, peasants, businessmen, intellectuals, and other sections of the people, disintegrate the enemy forces and win over their soldiers, carry on interna-

tional propaganda to secure foreign support, and win the support of the Japanese people and other oppressed peoples. Only by doing all this can we reduce the duration of the war. There is no magic shortcut.

A War of Jig-saw Pattern

51. We can say with certainty that the protracted War of Resistance Against Japan will write a splendid page unique in the war history of mankind. One of the special features of this war is the interlocking "jig-saw" pattern which arises from such contradictory factors as the barbarity of Japan and the shortage of her troops on the one hand, and the progressiveness of China and the extensiveness of her territory on the other. There have been other wars of jig-saw pattern in history, the three years' civil war in Russia after the October Revolution being a case in point. But what distinguishes this war in China is its especially protracted and extensive character, which will set a record in history. Its jig-saw pattern manifests itself as follows.

52. *Interior and exterior lines.* The anti-Japanese war as a whole is being fought on interior lines; but as far as the relation between the main forces and the guerrilla units is concerned, the former are on the interior lines while the latter are on the exterior lines, presenting a remarkable spectacle of pincers around the enemy. The same can be said of the relationship between the various guerrilla areas. From its own viewpoint each guerrilla area is on interior lines and the other areas are on exterior lines; together they form many battle fronts, which hold the enemy in pincers. In the first stage of the war, the regular army operating strategically on interior lines is withdrawing, but the guerrilla units operating strategically on exterior lines will advance with great strides over wide areas to the rear of the enemy—they will advance even more fiercely in the second stage—thereby presenting a remarkable picture of both withdrawal and advance.

53. *Possession and nonpossession of a rear area.* The main forces, which extend the front lines to the outer limits of the enemy's occupied areas, are operating from the rear area of the country as a whole. The guerrilla units, which extend the battle lines into the enemy rear, are separated from the rear area of the country as a whole. But each guerrilla area has a small rear of its own, upon which it relies to establish its fluid battle lines. The case is different with the guerrilla detachments which are dispatched by a guerrilla area for short-term operations in the rear of the enemy in the same area; such detachments have no rear, nor do they have

a battle line. "Operating without a rear" is a special feature of revolutionary war in the new era, wherever a vast territory, a progressive people, and an advanced political party and army are to be found; there is nothing to fear but much to gain from it, and far from having doubts about it we should promote it.

54. *Encirclement and counterencirclement.* Taking the war as a whole, there is no doubt that we are strategically encircled by the enemy, because he is on the strategic offensive and operating on exterior lines, while we are on the strategic defensive and operating on interior lines. This is the first form of enemy encirclement. We on our part can encircle one or more of the enemy columns advancing on us along separate routes, because we apply the policy of fighting campaigns and battles from tactically exterior lines by using numerically preponderant forces against these enemy columns advancing on us from strategically exterior lines. This is the first form of our counterencirclement of the enemy. Next, if we consider the guerrilla base areas in the enemy's rear, each area taken singly is surrounded by the enemy on all sides, like the Wutai mountain area, or on three sides, like the northwestern Shansi area. This is the second form of enemy encirclement. However, if one considers all the guerrilla base areas together and in their relation to the positions of the regular forces, one can see that we in turn surround a great many enemy forces. In Shansi Province, for instance, we have surrounded the Tatung-Puchow Railway on three sides (the east and west flanks and the southern end) and the city of Taiyuan on all sides; and there are many similar instances in Hopei and Shantung Provinces. This is the second form of our counterencirclement of the enemy. Thus there are two forms of encirclement by the enemy forces and two forms of encirclement by our own—rather like a game of *weichi*.[13] Campaigns and battles fought by the two sides resemble the capturing of each other's pieces, and the establishment of enemy strongholds (such as Taiyuan) and our guerrilla base areas (such as the Wutai Mountains) resembles moves to dominate spaces on the board. If the game of *weichi* is extended to include the world, there is yet a third form of encirclement as between us and the enemy, namely, the interrelation between the front of aggression and the front of peace. The enemy encircles China, the Soviet Union, France, and Czechoslovakia with his front of aggression, while we counterencircle Germany, Japan, and Italy with our front of peace. But our encirclement, like the hand of Buddha, will turn into the Mountain of Five Elements lying athwart the Universe, and the modern Sun Wu-kungs—the Fascist aggressors—will finally be buried underneath it, never to rise again.[14] Therefore, if on the international plane we can create an anti-Japanese front in the Pacific region, with

China as one strategic unit, with the Soviet Union and other countries which may join it as other strategic units, and with the Japanese people's movement as still another strategic unit, and thus form a gigantic net from which the Fascist Sun Wu-kungs can find no escape, that will be our enemy's day of doom. Indeed, the day when this gigantic net is formed will undoubtedly be the day of the complete overthrow of Japanese imperialism. We are not jesting; this is the inevitable trend of the war.

55. *Big areas and little areas.* There is a possibility that the enemy will occupy the greater part of Chinese territory south of the Great Wall, and only the smaller part will be kept intact. That is one aspect of the situation. But within this greater part, which does not include the three northeastern provinces, the enemy can actually hold only the big cities, the main lines of communication and some of the plains—which may rank first in importance, but will probably constitute only the smaller part of the occupied territory in size and population, while the greater part will be taken up by the guerrilla areas that will grow up everywhere. That is another aspect of the situation. If we go beyond the provinces south of the Great Wall and include Mongolia, Sinkiang, Chinghai, and Tibet, then the unoccupied area will constitute the greater part of China's territory, and the enemy-occupied area will become the smaller part, even with the three northeastern provinces. That is yet another aspect of the situation. The area kept intact is undoubtedly important, and we should devote great efforts to developing it, not only politically, militarily, and economically but, what is also important, culturally. The enemy has transformed our former cultural centres into culturally backward areas, and we on our part must transform the former culturally backward areas into cultural centres. At the same time, the work of developing extensive guerrilla areas behind the enemy lines is also extremely important, and we should attend to every aspect of this work, including the cultural. All in all, big pieces of China's territory, namely, the rural areas, will be transformed into regions of progress and light, while the small pieces, namely, the enemy-occupied areas and especially the big cities, will temporarily become regions of backwardness and darkness.

56. Thus it can be seen that the protracted and far-flung War of Resistance Against Japan is a war of a jig-saw pattern militarily, politically, economically, and culturally. It is a marvellous spectacle in the history of war, a heroic undertaking by the Chinese nation, a magnificent and earth-shaking feat. This war will not only affect China and Japan, strongly impelling both to advance, but will also affect the whole world, impelling all nations, especially the oppressed nations such as India, to march forward. Every Chinese should consciously throw himself into this war of a jig-saw

pattern, for this is the form of war by which the Chinese nation is liberating itself, the special form of war of liberation waged by a big semicolonial country in the nineteen thirties and the nineteen forties.

Fighting for Perpetual Peace

57. The protracted nature of China's anti-Japanese war is inseparably connected with the fight for perpetual peace in China and the whole world. Never has there been a historical period such as the present in which war is so close to perpetual peace. For several thousands of years since the emergence of classes, the life of mankind has been full of wars; each nation has fought countless wars, either internally or with other nations. In the imperialist epoch of capitalist society, wars are waged on a particularly extensive scale and with a peculiar ruthlessness. The first great imperialist war of twenty years ago was the first of its kind in history, but not the last. Only the war which has now begun comes close to being the final war, that is, comes close to the perpetual peace of mankind. By now one-third of the world's population has entered the war. Look! Italy, then Japan; Abyssinia, then Spain, then China. The population of the countries at war now amounts to almost 600 million, or nearly a third of the total population of the world. The characteristics of the present war are its uninterruptedness and its proximity to perpetual peace. Why is it uninterrupted? After attacking Abyssinia, Italy attacked Spain, and Germany joined in; then Japan attacked China. What will come next? Undoubtedly Hitler will fight the great powers. "Fascism is war"[15]—this is perfectly true. There will be no interruption in the development of the present war into a world war; and mankind will not be able to avoid the calamity of war. Why then do we say the present war is near to perpetual peace? The present war is the result of the development of the general crisis of world capitalism which began with World War I; this general crisis is driving the capitalist countries into a new war and, above all, driving the Fascist countries into new war adventures. This war, we can foresee, will not save capitalism, but will hasten its collapse. It will be greater in scale and more ruthless than the war of twenty years ago, all nations will inevitably be drawn in, it will drag on for a very long time, and mankind will suffer greatly. But, owing to the existence of the Soviet Union and the growing political consciousness of the people of the world, great revolutionary wars will undoubtedly emerge from this war to oppose all counterrevolutionary wars, thus giving this war the character of a struggle for perpetual peace. Even if later there should be another period of

war, perpetual world peace will not be far off. Once man has eliminated capitalism, he will attain the era of perpetual peace, and there will be no more need for war. Neither armies, nor warships, nor military aircraft, nor poison gas will then be needed. Thereafter and for all time, mankind will never again know war. The revolutionary wars which have already begun are part of the war for perpetual peace. The war between China and Japan, which have a combined population of over 500 million, will take an important place in this war for perpetual peace, and out of it will come the liberation of the Chinese nation. The liberated new China of the future will be inseparable from the liberated new world of the future. Hence our War of Resistance Against Japan takes on the character of a struggle for perpetual peace.

58. History shows that wars are divided into two kinds, just and unjust. All wars that are progressive are just, and all wars that impede progress are unjust. We Communists oppose all unjust wars that impede progress, but we do not oppose progressive, just wars. We Communists not only do not oppose just wars, but we actively participate in them. As for unjust wars, World War I is an instance in which both sides fought for imperialist interests; therefore the Communists of the whole world firmly opposed that war. The way to oppose a war of this kind is to do everything possible to prevent it before it breaks out and, once it breaks out, to oppose war with war, to oppose unjust war with just war, whenever possible. Japan's war is an unjust war that impedes progress, and the peoples of the world, including the Japanese people, should oppose it and are opposing it. In our country the people and the government, the Communist party and the Kuomintang, have all raised the banner of righteousness in the national revolutionary war against aggression. Our war is sacred and just, it is progressive, and its aim is peace. The aim is peace not just in one country but throughout the world, not just temporary but perpetual peace. To achieve this aim we must wage a life-and-death struggle, be prepared for any sacrifice, persevere to the end, and never stop short of the goal. However great the sacrifice and however long the time needed to attain it, a new world of perpetual peace and brightness already lies clearly before us. Our faith in waging this war is based upon the new China and the new world of perpetual peace and brightness for which we are striving. Fascism and imperialism wish to perpetuate war, but we wish to put an end to it in the not too distant future. The great majority of mankind should exert their utmost efforts for this purpose. The 450 million people of China constitute one quarter of the world's population, and if by their concerted efforts they overthrow Japanese imperialism and create a new China of freedom and equality, they will most certainly be

making a tremendous contribution to the struggle for perpetual world peace. This is no vain hope, for the whole world is approaching this point in the course of its social and economic development, and provided that the majority of mankind work together, our goal will surely be attained in several decades.

The Role of Conscious Activity in War

59. We have so far explained why the war is a protracted war and why the final victory will be China's, and in the main dealt with what protracted war really is. Now we shall turn to the question of what to do and what not to do. How to conduct protracted war? How to win the final victory? These are the questions answered below. We shall therefore successively discuss the following problems: the role of conscious activity in war, war and politics, political mobilization for the War of Resistance, the object of war, offence within defence, quick decisions within a protracted war, exterior lines within interior lines, initiative, flexibility, planning, mobile warfare, guerrilla warfare, positional warfare, war of annihilation, war of attrition, the possibilities of exploiting the enemy's mistakes, the question of decisive engagements in the anti-Japanese war, and the army and the people as the foundation of victory. Let us start with the problem of conscious activity.

60. When we say we are opposed to a subjective approach to problems, we mean that we must oppose ideas which are not based upon or do not correspond to objective facts because such ideas are fanciful and fallacious and will lead to failure if acted on. But whatever is done has to be done by human beings; protracted war and final victory will not come about without human action. For such action to be effective there must be people who derive ideas, principles or views from the objective facts, and put forward plans, directives, policies, strategies, and tactics. Ideas, etc. are subjective, while deeds or actions are the subjective translated into the objective, but both represent the conscious activity peculiar to human beings. We term this kind of conscious activity "self-conscious activity," and it is a characteristic that distinguishes man from all other beings. All ideas based upon and corresponding to objective facts are correct ideas, and all deeds or actions based upon correct ideas are correct actions. We must give full scope to such ideas and actions, such conscious activity. The anti-Japanese war is being waged to drive out imperialism and transform the old China into a new China; this can be achieved only when the whole Chinese people are mobilized and full scope is given to their con-

scious activity in resisting Japan. If we just sit by and take no action, only subjugation awaits us and there will be neither protracted war nor final victory.

61. Conscious activity is a human characteristic. Man strongly displays this characteristic in war. True, victory or defeat in war is decided by the military, political, economic, and geographical conditions on both sides, the nature of the war each side is waging and the international support each enjoys, but it is not decided by these alone; in themselves, all these provide only the possibility of victory or defeat but do not decide the issue. To decide the issue, subjective effort must be added, namely, the directing and waging of war, man's conscious activity in war.

62. In seeking victory, those who direct a war cannot overstep the limitations imposed by the objective conditions; within these limitations, however, they can and must exercise conscious activity in striving for victory. The stage of action for commanders in a war must be built upon objective possibilities, but on that stage they can direct the performance of many a drama, full of sound and color, power and grandeur. Given the objective material foundations, the commanders in the anti-Japanese war should display their prowess and marshal all their forces to crush the national enemy, transform the present situation in which our country and society are suffering from aggression and oppression, and create a new China of freedom and equality; here is where our subjective faculties for directing war can and must be exercised. We do not want any of our commanders in the war to detach himself from the objective conditions and become a blundering hothead, but we decidedly want every commander to become a general who is both bold and sagacious. Our commanders should have not only the boldness to overwhelm the enemy but also the ability to remain masters of the situation throughout the changes and vicissitudes of the entire war. Swimming in the ocean of war, they must not flounder but make sure of reaching the opposite shore with measured strokes. Strategy and tactics, as the laws for directing war, constitute the art of swimming in the ocean of war.

War and Politics

63. "War is the continuation of politics." In this sense war is politics and war itself is a political action; since ancient times there has never been a war that did not have a political character. The anti-Japanese war is a revolutionary war waged by the whole nation, and victory is inseparable from the political aim of the war—to drive out Japanese imperialism and

build a new China of freedom and equality—inseparable from the general policy of persevering in the War of Resistance and in the united front, from the mobilization of the entire people, and from such political principles as the unity between officers and men, the unity between army and people and the disintegration of the enemy forces, and inseparable from the effective application of united front policy, from mobilization on the cultural front, and from the efforts to win international support and the support of the people inside Japan. In a word, war cannot for a single moment be separated from politics. Any tendency among the anti-Japanese armed forces to belittle politics by isolating war from it and advocating the idea that "war is absolute" is wrong and should be corrected.

64. But war has its own particular characteristics and in this sense it cannot be equated with politics in general. "War is simply the continuation of politics by other . . . means."[16] When politics develops to a certain stage beyond which it cannot proceed by the usual means, war breaks out to sweep away the obstacles in the way. For instance, the semi-independent status of China is an obstacle to the political growth of Japanese imperialism, hence Japan has unleashed a war of aggression to sweep away that obstacle. What about China? Imperialist oppression has long been an obstacle to China's bourgeois-democratic revolution, hence many wars of liberation have been waged in the effort to sweep it away. Japan is now using war for the purpose of oppressing China and completely blocking the advance of the Chinese revolution, and therefore China is compelled to wage the War of Resistance in her determination to sweep away this obstacle. When the obstacle is removed, our political aim will be attained and the war concluded. But if the obstacle is not completely swept away, the war will have to continue till the aim is fully accomplished. Thus anyone who seeks a compromise before the task of the anti-Japanese war is fulfilled is bound to fail, because even if a compromise were to occur for one reason or another, the war would break out again, since the broad masses of the people would certainly not submit but would continue the war until its political objective was achieved. It can therefore be said that politics is war without bloodshed while war is politics with bloodshed.

65. From the particular characteristics of war there arise a particular set of organizations, a particular series of methods and a process of a particular kind. The organizations are the armed forces and everything that goes with them. The methods are the strategy and tactics for directing war. The process is the particular form of social activity in which the opposing armed forces attack each other or defend themselves against one another, employing strategy and tactics favorable to themselves and un-

favorable to the enemy. Hence war experience is a particular kind of experience. All who take part in war must rid themselves of their customary ways and accustom themselves to war before they can win victory.

Political Mobilization for the War of Resistance

66. A national revolutionary war as great as ours cannot be won without universal and thoroughgoing political mobilization. Before the anti-Japanese war there was no political mobilization for resistance to Japan, and this was a great drawback, as a result of which China has already lost a move to the enemy. After the war began, political mobilization was very far from extensive, let alone thoroughgoing. It was the enemy's gunfire and the bombs dropped by enemy aeroplanes that brought news of the war to the great majority of the people. That was also a kind of mobilization, but it was done for us by the enemy, we did not do it ourselves. Even now the people in the remoter regions beyond the noise of the guns are carrying on quietly as usual. This situation must change, or otherwise we cannot win in our life-and-death struggle. We must never lose another move to the enemy; on the contrary, we must make full use of this move, political mobilization, to get the better of him. This move is crucial; it is indeed of primary importance, while our inferiority in weapons and other things is only secondary. The mobilization of the common people throughout the country will create a vast sea in which to drown the enemy, create the conditions that will make up for our inferiority in arms and other things, and create the prerequisites for overcoming every difficulty in the war. To win victory, we must persevere in the War of Resistance, in the united front, and in the protracted war. But all these are inseparable from the mobilization of the common people. To wish for victory and yet neglect political mobilization is like wishing to "go north by driving a chariot south," and the result would inevitably be to forfeit victory.

67. What is political mobilization? First, it means telling the army and the people about the political aim of the war. It is necessary for every soldier and civilian to understand why the war must be fought and how it concerns him. The political aim of the war is "to drive out Japanese imperialism and build a new China of freedom and equality"; we must proclaim this aim to everybody, to all the soldiers and civilians, before we can create an anti-Japanese upsurge and unite hundreds of millions as one man to contribute their all to the war. Secondly, it is not enough merely to

explain the aim to them; the steps and policies for its attainment must also be given, that is, there must be a political programme. We already have the Ten-Point Programme for Resisting Japan and Saving the Nation and also the Programme of Armed Resistance and National Reconstruction; we should popularize both of them in the army and among the people and mobilize everyone to carry them out. Without a clear-cut, concrete political programme it is impossible to mobilize all the armed forces and the whole people to carry the fight against Japan through to the end. Thirdly, how should we mobilize them? By word of mouth, by leaflets and bulletins, by newspapers, books and pamphlets, through plays and films, through schools, through the mass organizations and through our cadres. What has been done so far in the Kuomintang areas is only a drop in the ocean, and moreover it has been done in a manner ill-suited to the people's tastes and in a spirit uncongenial to them; this must be drastically changed. Fourthly, to mobilize once is not enough, and political mobilization for the War of Resistance must be continuous. Our job is not to recite our political programme mechanically to the people, for nobody will listen to such recitations; we must link the political mobilization for the war with developments in the war and with the life of the soldiers and the people, and make it a continuous movement. This is a matter of immense importance on which our victory in the war primarily depends.

The Object of War

68. Here we are not dealing with the political aim of war; the political aim of the War of Resistance Against Japan has been defined above as "to drive out Japanese imperialism and build a new China of freedom and equality." Here we are dealing with the elementary object of war, war as "man's politics with bloodshed," as mutual slaughter by opposing armies. The object of war is specifically "to preserve oneself and to destroy the enemy." (To destroy the enemy is to disarm him or "deprive him of the power to resist," and not to destroy every member of his forces physically.) In ancient warfare, the spear and the shield were used, the spear to attack and destroy the enemy, and the shield to defend and preserve oneself. To the present day, all weapons are still an extension of the spear and the shield. The bomber, the machine gun, the long-range gun and poison gas are developments of the spear, while the air-raid shelter, the steel helmet, the concrete fortification and the gas mask are developments of the shield. The tank is a new weapon combining the functions of both spear and shield. Attack is the chief means of destroying the enemy, but de-

fence cannot be dispensed with. In attack the immediate object is to destroy the enemy, but at the same time it is self-preservation, because if the enemy is not destroyed, you will be destroyed. In defence the immediate object is to preserve yourself, but at the same time defence is a means of supplementing attack or preparing to go over to the attack. Retreat is in the category of defence and is a continuation of defence, while pursuit is a continuation of attack. It should be pointed out that destruction of the enemy is the primary object of war and self-preservation the secondary, because only by destroying the enemy in large numbers can one effectively preserve oneself. Therefore attack, the chief means of destroying the enemy, is primary, while defence, a supplementary means of destroying the enemy and one means of self-preservation, is secondary. In actual warfare the chief role is played now by defence and now by attack, but if war is taken as a whole, attack remains primary.

69. How do we justify the encouragement of heroic sacrifice in war? Does it not contradict "self-preservation"? No, it does not; sacrifice and self-preservation are both opposite and complementary to each other. War is politics with bloodshed and exacts a price, sometimes an extremely high price. Partial and temporary sacrific (nonpreservation) is incurred for the sake of general and permanent preservation. This is precisely why we say that attack, which is basically a means of destroying the enemy, also has the function of self-preservation. It is also the reason why defence must be accompanied by attack and should not be defence pure and simple.

70. The object of war, namely, the preservation of oneself and the destruction of the enemy, is the essence of war and the basis of all war activities, an essence which pervades all war activities, from the technical to the strategic. The object of war is the underlying principle of war, and no technical, tactical, or strategic concepts or principles can in any way depart from it. What for instance is meant by the principle of "taking cover and making full use of fire-power" in shooting? The purpose of the former is self-preservation, of the latter to destroy the enemy. The former gives rise to such techniques as making use of the terrain and its features, advancing in spurts, and spreading out in dispersed formation. The latter gives rise to other techniques, such as clearing the field of fire and organizing a fire net. As for the assault force, the containing force and the reserve force in a tactical operation, the first is for annihilating the enemy, the second for preserving oneself, and the third is for either purpose according to circumstances—either for annihilating the enemy (in which case it reinforces the assault force or serves as a pursuit force), or for self-preservation (in which case it reinforces the containing force or serves as

a covering force). Thus, no technical, tactical, or strategical principles or operations can in any way depart from the object of war, and this object pervades the whole of a war and runs through it from beginning to end.

71. In directing the anti-Japanese war, leaders at the various levels must not lose sight of the contrast between the fundamental factors on each side and of the object of this war. In the course of military operations these contrasting fundamental factors unfold themselves in the struggle by each side to preserve itself and to destroy the other. In our war we strive in every engagement to win a victory, big or small, and to disarm a part of the enemy and to destroy a part of his men and *matériel*. We must accumulate the results of these partial destructions of the enemy into major strategic victories and so achieve the final political aim of expelling the enemy, protecting the motherland and building a new China.

Offence Within Defence, Quick Decisions Within A Protracted War, Exterior Lines Within Interior Lines

72. Now let us examine the specific strategy of the War of Resistance Against Japan. We have already said that our strategy for resisting Japan is that of protracted war, and indeed this is perfectly right. But this strategy is general, not specific. Specifically, how should the protracted war be conducted? We shall now discuss this question. Our answer is as follows. In the first and second stages of the war, i.e., in the stages of the enemy's offensive and preservation of his gains, we should wage offensive campaigns and battles within the strategic defence, campaigns and battles of quick decision within the strategically protracted war, and campaigns and battles on exterior lines within strategic interior lines. In the third stage, we should launch the strategic counteroffensive.

73. Since Japan is a strong imperialist power and we are a weak semi-colonial and semifeudal country, she has adopted the policy of the strategic offensive while we are on the strategic defensive. Japan is trying to execute the strategy of a war of quick decision; we should consciously execute the strategy of protracted war. Japan is using dozens of army divisions of fairly high combat effectiveness (now numbering thirty) and part of her navy to encircle and blockade China from both land and sea, and is using her air force to bomb China. Her army has already established a long front stretching from Paotow to Hangchow and her navy has reached Fukien and Kwangtung; thus exterior-line operations have taken shape on a vast scale. On the other hand, we are in the position of operat-

ing on interior lines. All this is due to the fact that the enemy is strong while we are weak. This is one aspect of the situation.

74. But there is another and exactly opposite aspect. Japan, though strong, does not have enough soldiers. China, though weak, has a vast territory, a large population and plenty of soldiers. Two important consequences follow. First, the enemy, employing his small forces against a vast country, can only occupy some big cities, and main lines of communication and part of the plains. Thus there are extensive areas in the territory under his occupation which he has had to leave ungarrisoned and which provide a vast arena for our guerrilla warfare. Taking China as a whole, even if the enemy manages to occupy the line connecting Canton, Wuhan, and Lanchow and its adjacent areas, he can hardly seize the regions beyond, and this gives China a general rear and vital bases from which to carry on the protracted war to final victory. Secondly, in pitting his small forces against large forces, the enemy is encircled by our large forces. The enemy is attacking us along several routes, strategically he is on exterior lines while we are on interior lines, strategically he is on the offensive while we are on the defensive; all this looks very much to our disadvantage. However, we can make use of our two advantages, namely, our vast territory and large forces, and instead of stubborn positional warfare, carry on flexible mobile warfare, employing several divisions against one enemy division, several tens of thousands of our men against ten thousand of his, several columns against one of his columns, and suddenly encircling and attacking a single column from the exterior lines of the battlefield. In this way, while the enemy is on exterior lines and on the offensive in strategic operations, he will be forced to fight on interior lines and on the defensive in campaigns and battles. And for us, interior lines and the defensive in strategic operations will be transformed into exterior lines and the offensive in campaigns and battles. This is the way to deal with one or indeed with any advancing enemy column. Both the consequences discussed above follow from the fact that the enemy forces are small while ours are large. Again, the enemy forces, though small, are strong (in weapons and training) while our forces, though large, are weak (in weapons and training but not in morale), and in campaigns and battles, therefore, we should not only employ large forces against small and operate from exterior against interior lines, but also follow the policy of seeking quick decisions. In general, to achieve quick decision, we should attack a moving and not a stationary enemy. We should concentrate a big force under cover beforehand alongside the route which the enemy is sure to take, and while he is on the move, advance suddenly to encircle and attack

him before he knows what is happening, and thus quickly conclude the battle. If we fight well, we may destroy the entire enemy force or the greater part or some part of it, and even if we do not fight so well, we may still inflict heavy casualties. This applies to any and every one of our battles. If each month we could win one sizable victory like that at Pinghsingkuan or Taierhchuang, not to speak of more, it would greatly demoralize the enemy, stimulate the morale of our own forces and evoke international support. Thus our strategically protracted war is translated in the field into battles of quick decision. The enemy's war of strategic quick decision is bound to change into protracted war after he is defeated in many campaigns and battles.

75. In a word, the above operational principle for fighting campaigns and battles is one of "quick-decision offensive warfare on exterior lines." It is the opposite of our strategic principle of "protracted defensive warfare on interior lines," and yet it is the principle that is indispensable for carrying out this strategy. If we should use "protracted defensive warfare on interior lines" as the principle for campaigns and battles too, as we did at the beginning of the War of Resistance, it would be totally unsuited to the circumstances in which the enemy is small while we are big and the enemy is strong while we are weak; in that case we could never achieve our strategic objective of a protracted war and we would be defeated by the enemy. That is why we have always advocated the organization of the forces of the entire country into a number of large field armies, each counterposed to one of the enemy's field armies but having two, three, or four times its strength, and so keeping the enemy engaged in extensive theatres of war in accordance with the principle outlined above. This principle of "quick-decision offensive warfare on exterior lines" can and must be applied in guerrilla as well as in regular warfare. It is applicable not only to any one stage of the war but to its entire course. In the stage of strategic counteroffensive, when we are better equipped technically and are no longer in the position of the weak fighting the strong, we shall be able to capture prisoners and booty on a large scale all the more effectively if we continue to employ superior numbers in quick-decision offensive battles from exterior lines. For instance, if we employ two, three, or four mechanized divisions against one mechanized enemy division, we can be all the more certain of destroying it. It is common sense that several hefty fellows can easily beat one.

76. If we resolutely apply "exterior-line quick-decision offensive warfare" on a battlefield, we shall not only change the balance of forces on that battlefield, but also gradually change the general situation. On the battlefield we shall be on the offensive and the enemy on the defensive, we

shall be employing superior numbers on exterior lines and the enemy inferior numbers on interior lines, and we shall seek quick decisions, while the enemy, try as he may, will not be able to protract the fighting in expectation of reinforcements; for all these reasons, the enemy's position will change from strong to weak, from superior to inferior, while that of our forces will change from weak to strong, from inferior to superior. After many such battles have been victoriously fought, the general situation between us and the enemy will change. That is to say, through the accumulation of victories on many battlefields by quick-decision offensive warfare on exterior lines, we shall gradually strengthen ourselves and weaken the enemy, which will necessarily affect the general balance of forces and bring about changes in it. When that happens, these changes, together with other factors on our side and together with the changes inside the enemy camp and a favorable international situation, will turn the overall situation between us and the enemy first into one of parity and then into one of superiority for us. That will be the time for us to launch the counteroffensive and drive the enemy out of the country.

77. War is a contest of strength, but the original pattern of strength changes in the course of war. Here the decisive factor is subjective effort —winning more victories and committing fewer errors. The objective factors provide the possibility for such change, but in order to turn this possibility into actuality both correct policy and subjective effort are essential. It is then that the subjective plays the decisive role.

Initiative, Flexibility, and Planning

78. In quick-decision offensive campaigns and battles on exterior lines, as discussed above, the crucial point is the "offensive"; "exterior lines" refers to the sphere of the offensive and "quick-decision" to its duration. Hence the name "exterior-line quick-decision offensive warfare." It is the best principle for waging a protracted war and it is also the principle for what is known as mobile warfare. But it cannot be put into effect without initiative, flexibility, and planning. Let us now study these three questions.

79. We have already discussed conscious activity, so why do we talk about the initiative again? By conscious activity we mean conscious action and effort, a characteristic unique to man, and this human characteristic manifests itself most strongly in war; all this has been discussed already. The initiative here means an army's freedom of action as distinguished from an enforced loss of freedom. Freedom of action is the very life of an army and, once it is lost, the army is close to defeat or destruction. The

disarming of a soldier is the result of his losing freedom of action and of his being forced into a passive position. The same is true of the defeat of an army. For this reason both sides in war do all they can to gain the initiative and avoid passivity. It may be said that the quick-decision offensive warfare on exterior lines which we advocate and the flexibility and planning necessary for its execution are designed to gain the initiative and thus force the enemy into a passive position and achieve the object of preserving ourselves and destroying the enemy. But initiative or passivity is inseparable from superiority or inferiority in the capacity to wage war. Consequently it is also inseparable from the correctness or incorrectness of the subjective direction of war. In addition, there is the question of exploiting the enemy's misconceptions and unpreparedness to gain the initiative and force the enemy into passivity. These points are analysed below.

80. Initiative is inseparable from superiority in capacity to wage war, while passivity is inseparable from inferiority in capacity to wage war. Such superiority or inferiority is the objective basis of initiative or passivity. It is natural that the strategic initiative can be better maintained and developed through a strategic offensive, but to maintain the initiative always and everywhere, that is, to have the absolute initiative, is possible only when there is absolute superiority matched against absolute inferiority. When a strong, healthy man wrestles with an invalid, he has the absolute initiative. If Japan were not riddled with insoluble contradictions, if, for instance, she could throw in a huge force of several million or ten million men all at once, if her financial resources were several times what they are, if she had no opposition from her own people or from other countries, and if she did not pursue the barbarous policies which arouse the desperate resistance of the Chinese people, then she would be able to maintain absolute superiority and have the absolute initiative always and everywhere. In history, such absolute superiority rarely appears in the early stages of a war or a campaign but is to be found towards its end. For instance, on the eve of Germany's capitulation in World War I, the Allied Powers became absolutely superior and Germany absolutely inferior, so that Germany was defeated and the Allied Powers were victorious; this is an example of absolute superiority and inferiority towards the end of a war. Again, on the eve of the Chinese victory at Taierhchuang, the isolated Japanese forces there were reduced after bitter fighting to absolute inferiority while our forces achieved absolute superiority, so that the enemy was defeated and we were victorious; this is an example of absolute superiority and inferiority towards the end of a campaign. A war or campaign may also end in a situation of relative superiority or of

parity, in which case there is compromise in the war or stalemate in the campaign. But in general it is absolute superiority and inferiority that decide victory and defeat. All this holds for the end of a war or a campaign, and not for the beginning. The outcome of the Sino-Japanese War, it can be predicted, will be that Japan will become absolutely inferior and be defeated and that China will become absolutely superior and gain victory. But at present superiority or inferiority is not absolute on either side, but is relative. With the advantages of her military, economic, and political-organizational power, Japan enjoys superiority over us with our military, economic, and political-organizational weakness, which creates the basis for her initiative. But since quantitatively her military and other power is not great and she has many other disadvantages, her superiority is reduced by her own contradictions. Within China, her superiority has been reduced still further because she has come up against our vast territory, large population, great numbers of troops, and resolute nation-wide resistance. Hence, Japan's general position has become one of only relative superiority, and her ability to exercise and maintain the initiative, which is thereby restricted, has likewise become relative. As for China, though placed in a somewhat passive position strategically because of her inferior strength, she is nevertheless quantitatively superior in territory, population, and troops, and also superior in the morale of her people and army and their patriotic hatred of the enemy; this superiority, together with other advantages, reduces the extent of her inferiority in military, economic, and other power, and changes it into a relative strategic inferiority. This also reduces the degree of China's passivity so that her strategic position is one of only relative passivity. Any passivity, however, is a disadvantage, and one must strive hard to shake it off. Militarily, the way to do so is resolutely to wage quick-decision offensive warfare on exterior lines, to launch guerrilla warfare in the rear of the enemy, and so secure overwhelming local superiority and initiative in many campaigns of mobile and guerrilla warfare. Through such local superiority and local initiative in many campaigns, we can gradually create strategic superiority and strategic initiative and extricate ourselves from strategic inferiority and passivity. Such is the interrelation between initiative and passivity, between superiority and inferiority.

81. From this we can also understand the relationship between initiative or passivity and the subjective directing of war. As already explained, it is possible to escape from our position of relative strategic inferiority and passivity, and the method is to create local superiority and initiative in many places, so depriving the enemy of local superiority and initiative and plunging him into inferiority and passivity. These local successes will

add up to strategic superiority and initiative for us and strategic inferiority and passivity for the enemy. Such a change depends upon correct subjective direction. Why? Because while we seek superiority and the initiative, so does the enemy; viewed from this angle, war is a contest in subjective ability between the commanders of the opposing armies in their struggle for superiority and for the initiative on the basis of material conditions such as military forces and financial resources. Out of the contest there emerge a victor and a vanquished; leaving aside the balance of objective material conditions, the victor will necessarily owe his success to correct subjective direction and the vanquished his defeat to wrong subjective direction. We admit that the phenomenon of war is more elusive and is characterized by greater uncertainty than any other social phenomenon, in other words, that it is more a matter of "probability." Yet war is in no way supernatural, but a mundane process governed by necessity. That is why Sun Wu Tzu's axiom, "Know the enemy and know yourself, and you can fight a hundred battles with no danger of defeat,"[17] remains a scientific truth. Mistakes arise from ignorance about the enemy and about ourselves, and moreover the peculiar nature of war makes it impossible in many cases to have full knowledge about both sides; hence the uncertainty about military conditions and operations, and hence mistakes and defeats. But whatever the situation and the moves in a war, one can know their general aspects and essential points. It is possible for a commander to reduce errors and give generally correct direction, first through all sorts of reconnaissance and then through intelligent inference and judgement. Armed with the weapon of "generally correct direction," we can win more battles and transform our inferiority into superiority and our passivity into initiative. This is how initiative or passivity is related to the correct or incorrect subjective direction of a war.

82. The thesis that incorrect subjective direction can change superiority and initiative into inferiority and passivity and that correct subjective direction can effect a reverse change becomes all the more convincing when we look at the record of defeats suffered by big and powerful armies and of victories won by small and weak armies. There are many such instances in Chinese and foreign history. Examples in China are the Battle of Chengpu between the states of Tsin and Chu,[18] the Battle of Chengkao between the states of Chu and Han,[19] the Battle in which Han Hsin defeated the Chao armies,[20] the Battle of Kunyang between the states of Hsin and Han,[21] the Battle of Kuantu between Yuan Shao and Tsao Tsao,[22] the Battle of Chihpi between the states of Wu and Wei,[23] the Battle of Yiling between the states of Wu and Shu,[24] the Battle of Feishui between the states of Chin and Tsin,[25] etc. Among examples to be found

abroad are most of Napoleon's campaigns and the civil war in the Soviet Union after the October Revolution. In all these instances, victory was won by small forces over big and by inferior over superior forces. In every case, the weaker force, pitting local superiority and initiative against the enemy's local inferiority and passivity, first inflicted one sharp defeat on the enemy and then turned on the rest of his forces and smashed them one by one, thus transforming the overall situation into one of superiority and initiative. The reverse was the case with the enemy who originally had superiority and held the initiative; owing to subjective errors and internal contradictions, it sometimes happened that he completely lost an excellent or fairly good position in which he enjoyed superiority and initiative, and became a general without an army or a king without a kingdom. Thus it can be seen that although superiority or inferiority in the capacity to wage war is the objective basis determining initiative or passivity, it is not in itself actual initiative or passivity; it is only through a struggle, a contest of ability, that actual initiative or passivity can emerge. In the struggle, correct subjective direction can transform inferiority into superiority and passivity into initiative, and incorrect subjective direction can do the opposite. The fact that every ruling dynasty was defeated by revolutionary armies shows that mere superiority in certain respects does not guarantee the initiative, much less the final victory. The inferior side can wrest the initiative and victory from the superior side by securing certain conditions through active subjective endeavor in accordance with the actual circumstances.

83. To have misconceptions and to be caught unawares may mean to lose superiority and initiative. Hence, deliberately creating misconceptions for the enemy and then springing surprise attacks upon him is one means—indeed an important means—of achieving superiority and seizing the initiative. What are misconceptions? "To see every bush and tree on Mount Pakung as an enemy soldier"[26] is an example of misconception. And "making a feint to the east but attacking in the west" is a way of creating misconceptions among the enemy. When the mass support is sufficiently good to block the leakage of news, it is often possible by various ruses to succeed in leading the enemy into a morass of wrong judgements and actions so that he loses his superiority and the initiative. The saying, "There can never be too much deception in war," means precisely this. What does "being caught unawares" mean? It means being unprepared. Without preparedness superiority is not real superiority and there can be no initiative either. Having grasped this point, a force which is inferior but prepared can often defeat a superior enemy by surprise attack. We say an enemy on the move is easy to attack precisely because he is

then off guard, that is, unprepared. These two points—creating misconceptions among the enemy and springing surprise attacks on him—mean transferring the uncertainties of war to the enemy while securing the greatest possible certainty for ourselves and thereby gaining superiority, the initiative, and victory. Excellent organization of the masses is the prerequisite for attaining all this. Therefore it is extremely important to arouse all the people who are opposed to the enemy, in order that they may arm themselves to the last man, make widespread raids on the enemy, and also prevent the leakage of news and provide a screen for our own forces; thus the enemy is kept in the dark about where and when our forces will attack, and an objective basis is created for misconceptions and unpreparedness on his part. It was largely owing to the organized, armed masses of the people that the weak and small force of the Chinese Red Army was able to win many battles in the period of the Agrarian Revolutionary War. Logically, a national war should win broader mass support than an agrarian revolutionary war; however, as a result of past mistakes[27] the people are in an unorganized state, cannot be promptly drawn in to serve the cause, and are sometimes even made use of by the enemy. The resolute rallying of the people on a broad scale is the only way to secure inexhaustible resources to meet all the requirements of the war. Moreover, it will definitely play a big part in carrying out our tactics of defeating the enemy by misleading him and catching him unawares. We are not Duke Hsiang of Sung and have no use for his asinine ethics.[28] In order to achieve victory we must as far as possible make the enemy blind and deaf by sealing his eyes and ears and drive his commanders to distraction by creating confusion in their minds. The above concerns the way in which the initiative or passivity is related to the subjective direction of the war. Such subjective direction is indispensable for defeating Japan.

84. By and large, Japan has held the initiative, in the stage of her offensive, by reason of her military power and her exploitation of our subjective errors, past and present. But her initiative is beginning to wane to some extent because of her many inherent disadvantages and of the subjective errors she too has committed in the course of the war (of which more later) and also because of our many advantages. The enemy's defeat at Taierhchuang and his predicament in Shansi prove this clearly. The widespread development of guerrilla warfare in the enemy's rear has placed his garrisons in the occupied areas in a completely passive position. Although he is still on the offensive strategically and still holds the initiative, his initiative will end when his strategic offensive ends. The first reason why the enemy will not be able to maintain the initiative is that his shortage of troops renders it impossible for him to carry on the offensive

indefinitely. Our offensive warfare in campaigns and our guerrilla warfare behind the enemy lines, together with other factors, constitute the second reason why he will have to cease his offensive at a certain limit and will not be able to keep his initiative. The existence of the Soviet Union and changes in the international situation constitute the third reason. Thus it can be seen that the enemy's initiative is limited and can be shattered. If, in military operations, China can keep up offensive warfare by her main forces in campaigns and battles, vigorously develop guerrilla warfare in the enemy's rear, and mobilize the people on a broad scale politically, we can gradually build up a position of strategic initiative.

85. Let us now discuss flexibility. What is flexibility? It is the concrete realization of the initiative in military operations; it is the flexible employment of armed forces. The flexible employment of armed forces is the central task in directing a war, a task most difficult to perform well. In addition to organizing and educating the army and the people, the business of war consists in the employment of troops in combat, and all these things are done to win the fight. Of course it is difficult to organize an army, etc., but it is even more difficult to employ it, particularly when the weak are fighting the strong. To do so requires subjective ability of a very high order and requires the overcoming of the confusion, obscurity and uncertainty peculiar to war and the discovery of order, clarity, and certainty in it; only thus can flexibility in command be realized.

86. The basic principle of field operations for the War of Resistance Against Japan is quick-decision offensive warfare on exterior lines. There are various tactics or methods for giving effect to this principle, such as dispersion and concentration of forces, diverging advance and converging attack, the offensive and the defensive, assault and containment, encirclement and outflanking, advance and retreat. It is easy to understand these tactics, but not at all easy to employ and vary them flexibly. Here the three crucial links are the time, the place, and the troops. No victory can be won unless the time, the place, and the troops are well chosen. For example, in attacking an enemy force on the move, if we strike too early, we expose ourselves and give the enemy a chance to prepare, and if we strike too late, the enemy may have encamped and concentrated his forces, presenting us a hard nut to crack. This is the question of the time. If we select a point of assault on the left flank and it actually turns out to be the enemy's weak point, victory will be easy; but if we select the right flank and hit a snag, nothing will be achieved. This is the question of the place. If a particular unit of our forces is employed for a particular task, victory may be easy; but if another unit is employed for the same task, it may be hard to achieve results. This is the question of the troops. We

should know not only how to employ tactics but how to vary them. For flexibility of command the important task is to make changes such as from the offensive to the defensive or from the defensive to the offensive, from advance to retreat or from retreat to advance, from containment to assault or from assault to containment, from encirclement to outflanking or from outflanking to encirclement, and to make such changes properly and in good time according to the circumstances of the troops and terrain on both sides. This is true of command in battles, command in campaigns, and strategic command.

87. The ancients said: "Ingenuity in varying tactics depends on mother wit"; this "ingenuity," which is what we mean by flexibility, is the contribution of the intelligent commander. Flexibility does not mean recklessness; recklessness must be rejected. Flexibility consists in an intelligent commander's ability to take timely and appropriate measures on the basis of objective conditions after "judging the hour and sizing up the situation" (the "situation" includes the enemy's situation, our situation, and the terrain), and this flexibility is "ingenuity in varying tactics." On the basis of this ingenuity, we can win more victories in quick-decision offensive warfare on exterior lines, change the balance of forces in our favor, gain the initiative over the enemy, and overwhelm and crush him so that the final victory will be ours.

88. Let us now discuss the question of planning. Because of the uncertainty peculiar to war, it is much more difficult to prosecute war according to plan than is the case with other activities. Yet, since "affairs succeed when prepared and fail when unprepared," there can be no victory in war without advance planning and preparations. There is no absolute certainty in war, and yet it is not without some degree of relative certainty. We are comparatively certain about our own situation. We are very uncertain about the enemy's, but here too there are signs for us to read, clues to follow, and sequences of phenomena to ponder. These form what we call a degree of relative certainty, which provides an objective basis for planning in war. Modern technical developments (telegraphy, radio, aeroplanes, automobiles, railways, steamships, etc.) have added to the possibilities of planning in war. However, because there is only very limited and transient certainty in war, complete or stable planning is difficult; the plan must change with the movement (flow or change) of the war and vary in scope according to the scale of the war. Tactical plans, such as plans for attack or defence by small formations or units, often have to be changed several times a day. A plan of campaign, that is, of action by large formations, can generally stand till the conclusion of the campaign, in the course of which, however, it is often changed partially or

sometimes even wholly. A strategic plan based on the overall situation of both belligerents is still more stable, but it too is applicable only in a given strategic stage and has to be changed when the war moves toward a new stage. The making and changing of tactical, campaign, and strategic plans in accordance with scope and circumstance is a key factor in directing a war; it is the concrete expression of flexibility in war, in other words, it is also ingenuity in varying one's tactics. Commanders at all levels in the anti-Japanese war should take note.

89. Because of the fluidity of war, some people categorically deny that war plans or policies can be relatively stable, describing such plans or policies as "mechanical." This view is wrong. In the preceding section we fully recognized that, because the circumstances of war are only relatively certain and the flow (movement or change) of war is rapid, war plans or policies can be only relatively stable and have to be changed or revised in good time in accordance with changing circumstances and the flow of the war; otherwise we would become mechanists. But one must not deny the need for war plans or policies that are relatively stable over given periods; to negate this is to negate everything, including the war itself as well as the negator himself. As both military conditions and operations are relatively stable, we must grant the relative stability of the war plans and policies resulting from them. For example, since both the circumstances of the war in northern China and the dispersed operational actions of the Eighth Route Army are relatively stable for a particular stage, it is absolutely necessary during this stage to acknowledge the relative stability of the Eighth Route Army's strategic principle of operation, namely, "guerrilla warfare is basic, but lose no chance for mobile warfare under favorable conditions." The period of validity of a plan for a campaign is shorter than that of a strategic plan, and for a tactical plan it is shorter still, but each is stable over a given period. Anyone denying this point would have no way of handling warfare and would become a relativist in war with no settled views, for whom one course is just as wrong or just as right as another. No one denies that even a plan valid for a given period is fluid; otherwise, one plan would never be abandoned in favor of another. But it is fluid within limits, fluid within the bounds of the various war operations undertaken for carrying it out, but not fluid as to its essence; in other words, it is quantitatively but not qualitatively fluid. Within such a given period of time, this essence is definitely not fluid, which is what we mean by relative stability within a given period. In the great river of the war as a whole, in which fluidity is absolute, there are various stretches, each of which is relatively stable; this is our view regarding the essence of war plans or policies.

90. Having dealt with protracted defensive warfare on interior lines in strategy and quick-decision offensive warfare on exterior lines in campaigns and battles, and also with the initiative, flexibility, and planning, we can now sum up briefly. The anti-Japanese war must have a plan. War plans, which are the concrete application of strategy and tactics, must be flexible so that they can be adapted to the circumstances of the war. We should always seek to transform our inferiority into superiority and our passivity into the initiative so as to change the situation as between the enemy and ourselves. The expression of all this is quick-decision offensive warfare on exterior lines in campaigns and battles and protracted defensive warfare on interior lines in strategy.

Mobile Warfare, Guerrilla Warfare, and Positional Warfare

91. In content, our war is quick-decision offensive warfare on exterior lines in campaigns and battles within the framework of the strategy of interior lines, protracted war, and defence, and in form, it is mobile warfare. Mobile warfare is the form in which regular armies wage quick-decision offensive campaigns and battles on exterior lines along extensive fronts and over big areas of operation. At the same time, it includes "mobile defence," which is conducted when necessary to facilitate such offensive battles; it also includes positional attack and positional defence in a supplementary role. Its characteristics are regular armies, superiority of forces in campaigns and battles, the offensive, and fluidity.

92. China has a vast territory and an immense number of soldiers, but her troops are inadequately equipped and trained; the enemy's forces, on the other hand, are inadequate in number, but better equipped and trained. In this situation, there is no doubt that we must adopt offensive mobile warfare as our primary mode of operations, supplementing it by others and integrating them all into mobile warfare. We must oppose "only retreat, never advance," which is flight-ism, and at the same time oppose "only advance, never retreat," which is desperate recklessness.

93. One of the characteristics of mobile warfare is fluidity, which not only permits but requires a field army to advance and to withdraw in great strides. However, it has nothing in common with flight-ism of the Han Fu-chu brand.[29] The primary requirement of war is to destroy the enemy, and the other requirement is self-preservation. The object of self-preservation is to destroy the enemy, and to destroy the enemy is in turn the most effective means of self-preservation. Hence mobile warfare is in no

way an excuse for people like Han Fu-chu and can never mean moving only backward, and never forward; that kind of "moving" which negates the basically offensive character of mobile warfare would, in practice, "move" China out of existence despite her vastness.

94. However, the other view, which we call the desperate recklessness of "only advance, never retreat," is also wrong. We advocate mobile warfare, the substance of which is quick-decision offensive warfare on exterior lines in campaigns and battles; it also includes positional warfare in a supplementary role, "mobile defence," and retreat, without which mobile warfare cannot be fully carried out. Desperate recklessness is military short-sightedness, originating often from fear of losing territory. A man who acts with desperate recklessness does not know that one characteristic of mobile warfare is fluidity, which not only permits but requires a field army to advance and to withdraw in great strides. In a positive situation, in order to draw the enemy into a fight unfavorable to him but favorable to us, it is usually necessary that he should be on the move and that we should have a number of advantages, such as favorable terrain, a vulnerable enemy, a local population that can prevent the leakage of information, and the enemy's fatigue and unpreparedness. This requires that the enemy should advance, and we should not grudge a temporary loss of part of our territory. For the temporary loss of part of our territory is the price we pay for the permanent preservation of all our territory and for the recovery of lost territory. In a negative situation, whenever we are forced into a disadvantageous position which fundamentally endangers the preservation of our forces, we should have the courage to retreat so as to preserve our forces and hit the enemy when new opportunities arise. In their ignorance of this principle, the advocates of desperate action will contest a city or a piece of ground even when the position is obviously and definitely unfavorable; as a result, they not only lose the city or ground but fail to preserve their forces. We have always advocated the policy of "luring the enemy in deep," precisely because it is the most effective military policy for a weak army strategically on the defensive to employ against a strong.

95. Among the forms of warfare in the anti-Japanese war mobile warfare comes first and guerrilla warfare second. When we say that in the entire war mobile warfare is primary and guerrilla warfare supplementary, we mean that the outcome of the war depends mainly on regular warfare, especially in its mobile form, and that guerrilla warfare cannot shoulder the main responsibility in deciding the outcome. It does not follow, however, that the role of guerrilla warfare is unimportant in the strategy of the war. Its role in the strategy of the war as a whole is sec-

ond only to that of mobile warfare, for without its support we cannot defeat the enemy. In saying this we also have in mind the strategic task of developing guerrilla warfare into mobile warfare. Guerrilla warfare will not remain the same throughout this long and cruel war, but will rise to a higher level and develop into mobile warfare. Thus the strategic role of guerrilla warfare is twofold: to support regular warfare and to transform itself into regular warfare. Considering the unprecedented extent and duration of guerrilla warfare in China's War of Resistance, it is all the more important not to underestimate its strategic role. Guerrilla warfare in China, therefore, has not only its tactical but also its peculiar strategic problems. I have already discussed this in "Problems of Strategy in Guerrilla War Against Japan." As indicated above, the forms of warfare in the three strategic stages of the War of Resistance are as follows. In the first stage mobile warfare is primary, while guerrilla and positional warfare are supplementary. In the second stage guerrilla warfare will advance to the first place and will be supplemented by mobile and positional warfare. In the third stage mobile warfare will again become the primary form and will be supplemented by positional and guerrilla warfare. But the mobile warfare of the third stage will no longer be undertaken solely by the original regular forces; part, possibly quite an important part, will be undertaken by forces which were originally guerrillas but which will have progressed from guerrilla to mobile warfare. From the viewpoint of all three stages in China's War of Resistance Against Japan, guerrilla warfare is definitely indispensable. Our guerrilla war will present a great drama unparalleled in the annals of war. For this reason, out of the millions of China's regular troops, it is absolutely necessary to assign at least several hundred thousand to disperse through all enemy-occupied areas, arouse the masses to arm themselves, and wage guerrilla warfare in coordination with the masses. The regular forces so assigned should shoulder this sacred task conscientiously, and they should not think their status lowered because they fight fewer big battles and for the time being do not appear as national heroes. Any such thinking is wrong. Guerrilla warfare does not bring as quick results or as great renown as regular warfare, but "a long road tests a horse's strength and a long task proves a man's heart," and in the course of this long and cruel war guerrilla warfare will demonstrate its immense power; it is indeed no ordinary undertaking. Moreover, such regular forces can conduct guerrilla warfare when dispersed and mobile warfare when concentrated, as the Eighth Route Army has been doing. The principle of the Eighth Route Army is, "Guerrilla warfare is basic, but lose no chance for mobile warfare under favorable conditions." This principle is perfectly correct; the views of its opponents are wrong.

96. At China's present technical level, positional warfare, defensive or offensive, is generally impracticable, and this is where our weakness manifests itself. Moreover, the enemy is also exploiting the vastness of our territory to bypass our fortified positions. Hence positional warfare cannot be an important, still less the principal, means for us. But in the first and second stages of the war, it is possible and essential, within the scope of mobile warfare, to employ localized positional warfare in a supplementary role in campaigns. Semipositional "mobile defence" is a still more essential part of mobile warfare undertaken for the purpose of resisting the enemy at every step, thereby depleting his forces and gaining extra time. China must strive to increase her supplies of modern weapons so that she can fully carry out the tasks of positional attack in the stage of the strategic counteroffensive. In this third stage positional warfare will undoubtedly play a greater role, for then the enemy will be holding fast to his positions and we shall not be able to recover our lost territory unless we launch powerful positional attacks in support of mobile warfare. Nevertheless, in the third stage too, we must exert our every effort to make mobile warfare the primary form of warfare. For the art of directing war and the active role of man are largely nullified in positional warfare such as that fought in Western Europe in the second half of World War I. It is only natural that the war should be taken "out of the trenches," since the war is being fought in the vast expanses of China and since our side will remain poorly equipped technically for quite a long time. Even during the third stage, when China's technical position will be better, she will hardly surpass her enemy in that respect and so will have to concentrate on highly mobile warfare without which she cannot achieve final victory. Hence, throughout the War of Resistance China will not adopt positional warfare as primary; the primary or important forms are mobile warfare and guerrilla warfare. These two forms of warfare will afford full play to the art of directing war and to the active role of man—what a piece of good fortune out of our misfortune!

War of Attrition and War of Annihilation

97. As we have said before, the essence, or the object, of war is to preserve oneself and to destroy the enemy. There are three forms of warfare, mobile, positional, and guerrilla, for achieving this object, and since they differ in degrees of effectiveness, there arises the broad distinction between war of attrition and war of annihilation.

98. To begin with, we may say that the anti-Japanese war is at once a

war of attrition and a war of annihilation. Why? Because the enemy is still exploiting his strength and retains strategic superiority and strategic initiative, and, therefore, unless we fight campaigns and battles of annihilation, we cannot effectively and speedily reduce his strength and break his superiority and initiative. We still have our weakness and have not yet rid ourselves of strategic inferiority and passivity, and, therefore, unless we fight campaigns and battles of annihilation, we cannot win time to improve our internal and international situation and alter our unfavorable position. Hence campaigns of annihilation are the means of attaining the objective of strategic attrition. In this sense war of annihilation *is* war of attrition. It is chiefly by using the method of attrition through annihilation that China can wage protracted war.

99. But the objective of strategic attrition may also be achieved by campaigns of attrition. Generally speaking, mobile warfare performs the task of annihilation, positional warfare performs the task of attrition, and guerrilla warfare performs both simultaneously; the three forms of warfare are thus distinguished from one another. In this sense war of annihilation is different from war of attrition. Campaigns of attrition are supplementary but necessary in protracted war.

100. Speaking theoretically and in terms of China's needs, in order to achieve the strategic objective of greatly depleting the enemy's forces, China in her defensive stage should not only exploit the function of annihilation, which is fulfilled primarily by mobile warfare and partially by guerrilla warfare, but also exploit the function of attrition, which is fulfilled primarily by positional warfare (which itself is supplementary) and partially by guerrilla warfare. In the stage of stalemate we should continue to exploit the functions of annihilation and attrition fulfilled by guerrilla and mobile warfare for further large-scale depletion of the enemy's forces. All this is aimed at protracting the war, gradually changing the general balance of forces and preparing the conditions for our counteroffensive. During the strategic counteroffensive, we should continue to employ the method of attrition through annihilation so as finally to expel the enemy.

101. But as a matter of fact, it was our experience in the last ten months that many or even most of the mobile warfare campaigns became campaigns of attrition, and guerrilla warfare did not adequately fulfill its proper function of annihilation in certain areas. The positive aspect is that at least we depleted the enemy's forces, which is important both for the protracted warfare and for our final victory, and did not shed our blood in vain. But the drawbacks are, first, that we did not sufficiently deplete the enemy, and second, that we were unable to avoid rather heavy

losses and captured little war booty. Although we should recognize the objective cause of this situation, namely, the disparity between us and the enemy in technical equipment and in the training of troops, in any case it is necessary, both theoretically and practically, to urge that our main forces should fight vigorous battles of annihilation whenever circumstances are favorable. And although our guerrilla units have to wage battles of pure attrition in performing specific tasks such as sabotage and harassment, it is necessary to advocate and vigorously carry out campaigns and battles of annihilation whenever circumstances are favorable, so as greatly to deplete the enemy's forces and greatly replenish our own.

102. The "exterior lines," the "quick-decision" and the "offensive" in quick-decision offensive warfare on exterior lines and the "mobility" in mobile warfare find their main operational expression in the use of encirclement and outflanking tactics; hence the necessity for concentrating superior forces. Therefore concentration of forces and the use of encirclement and outflanking tactics are the prerequisites for mobile warfare, that is, for quick-decision offensive warfare on exterior lines. All this is aimed at annihilating the enemy forces.

103. The strength of the Japanese army lies not only in its weapons but also in the training of its officers and men—its degree of organization, its self-confidence arising from never having been defeated, its superstitious belief in the Mikado and in supernatural beings, its arrogance, its contempt for the Chinese people, and other such characteristics, all of which stem from long years of indoctrination by the Japanese warlords and from the Japanese national tradition. This is the chief reason why we have taken very few prisoners, although we have killed and wounded a great many enemy troops. It is a point that has been underestimated by many people in the past. To break down these enemy characteristics will be a long process. The first thing to do is to give the matter serious attention, and then patiently and systematically to work at it in the political field and in the fields of international propaganda and the Japanese people's movement; in the military sphere war of annihilation is of course one of the means. In these enemy characteristics pessimists may find a basis for the theory of national subjugation, and passively-minded military men a basis for opposition to war of annihilation. We, on the contrary, maintain that these strong points of the Japanese army can be broken down and that their destruction has already begun. The chief method of destroying them is to win over the Japanese soldiers politically. We should understand, rather than hurt, their pride and channel it in the proper direction and, by treating prisoners of war leniently, lead the Japanese soldiers to see the Japanese rulers' aggressiveness which is directed against the people.

On the other hand, we should demonstrate to the Japanese soldiers the indomitable spirit and the heroic, stubborn fighting capacity of the Chinese army and the Chinese people, that is, we should deal them blows in battles of annihilation. Our experience in the last ten months of military operations shows that it is possible to annihilate enemy forces—witness the Pinghsingkuan and Taierhchuang campaigns. The Japanese army's morale is beginning to sag, its soldiers do not understand the aim of the war, they are engulfed by the Chinese armies and by the Chinese people, in assault they show far less courage than the Chinese soldiers, and so on; all these are objective factors favorable to waging battles of annihilation, and they will, moreover, steadily develop as the war becomes protracted. From the viewpoint of destroying the enemy's overweening arrogance through battles of annihilation, such battles are one of the prerequisites for shortening the war and accelerating the emancipation of the Japanese soldiers and the Japanese people. Cats make friends with cats, and nowhere in the world do cats make friends with mice.

104. On the other hand, it must be admitted that for the present we are inferior to the enemy in technical equipment and in troop training. Therefore, it is often difficult to achieve the maximum in annihilation, such as capturing the whole or the greater part of an enemy force, especially when fighting on the plains. In this connection the excessive demands of the theorists of quick victory are wrong. What should be demanded of our forces in the anti-Japanese war is that they should fight battles of annihilation as far as possible. In favorable circumstances, we should concentrate superior forces in every battle and employ encircling and outflanking tactics—encircle part if not all of the enemy forces, capture part if not all of the encircled forces, and inflict heavy casualties on part of the encircled forces if we cannot capture them. In circumstances which are unfavorable for battles of annihilation, we should fight battles of attrition. In favorable circumstances, we should employ the principle of concentration of forces, and in unfavorable circumstances that of their dispersion. As for the relationship of command in campaigns, we should apply the principle of centralized command in the former and that of decentralized command in the latter. These are the basic principles of field operations for the War of Resistance Against Japan.

The Possibilities of Exploiting
The Enemy's Mistakes

105. The enemy command itself provides a basis for the possibility of

defeating Japan. History has never known an infallible general, and the enemy makes mistakes just as we ourselves can hardly avoid doing so; in fact, the possibility exists of exploiting the enemy's errors. In the ten months of his war of aggression the enemy has already made many mistakes in strategy and tactics. There are five major ones.

First, piecemeal reinforcement. This is due to the enemy's underestimation of China and also to his shortage of troops. The enemy has always looked down on us. After grabbing the four northeastern provinces at small cost, he occupied eastern Hopei and northern Chahar, all by way of strategic reconnaissance. The conclusion the enemy came to was that the Chinese nation is a heap of loose sand. Thus, thinking that China would crumble at a single blow, he mapped out a plan of "quick decision," attempting with very small forces to send us scampering in panic. He did not expect to find such great unity and such immense powers of resistance as China has shown during the past ten months, forgetting as he did that China is already in an era of progress and already has an advanced political party, an advanced army and an advanced people. Meeting with setbacks, the enemy then increased his forces piecemeal from about a dozen to thirty divisions. If he wants to advance, he will have to augment his forces still further. But because of Japan's antagonism with the Soviet Union and her inherent shortage of manpower and finances, there are inevitable limits to the maximum number of men she can throw in and to the furthest extent of her advance.

Second, absence of a main direction of attack. Before the Taierhchuang campaign, the enemy had divided his forces more or less evenly between northern and central China and had again divided them evenly inside each of these areas. In northern China, for instance, he divided his forces evenly among the Tientsin-Pukow, the Peiping-Hankow, and the Tatung-Puchow railways, and along each of these lines he suffered some casualties and left some garrisons in the places occupied, after which he lacked the forces for further advances. After the Taierhchuang defeat from which he learned a lesson, the enemy concentrated his main forces in the direction of Hsuchow, and so temporarily corrected this mistake.

Third, lack of strategic coordination. On the whole coordination exists within the groups of enemy forces in northern China and in central China, but there is glaring lack of coordination between the two. When his forces on the southern section of the Tientsin-Pukow railway attacked Hsiaopengpu, those on the northern section made no move, and when his forces on the northern section attacked Taierhchuang, those on the southern section made no move. After the enemy came to grief at both places, the Japanese minister of war arrived on an inspection tour and the chief of General Staff turned up to take charge, and for the moment, it seemed, there was coordination. The landlord class, the bourgeoisie and the war-lords of Japan have very serious internal contradictions, which are grow-ing, and the lack of military coordination is one of the concrete mani-festations of this fact.

Fourth, failure to grasp strategic opportunities. This failure was con-spicuously shown in the enemy's halt after the occupation of Nanking and Taiyuan, chiefly because of his shortage of troops and his lack of a stra-tegic pursuit force.

Fifth, encirclement of large but annihilation of small numbers. Before the Taierhchuang campaign, in the campaigns of Shanghai, Nanking, Tsangchow, Paoting, Nankow, Hsinkou, and Linfen, many Chinese troops were routed but few were taken prisoner, which shows the stu-pidity of the enemy command.

These five errors—piecemeal reinforcement, absence of a main direc-tion of attack, lack of strategic coordination, failure to grasp opportuni-ties, and encirclement of large but annihilation of small numbers—were all points of incompetence in the Japanese command before the Taierh-chuang campaign. Although the enemy has since made some improve-ments, he cannot possibly avoid repeating his errors because of his short-age of troops, his internal contradictions and other such factors. Moreover, what he gains at one point he loses at another. For instance, when he concentrated his forces in northern China on Hsuchow, he left a great vacuum in the occupied areas in northern China, which gave us full scope for developing guerrilla warfare. These mistakes were of the enemy's own making and not induced by us. On our part, we can deliberately make the enemy commit errors, that is, we can mislead him and maneuver him into the desired position by clever and effective actions behind the screen of a well-organized local population, for example, by "making a feint to the east but attacking in the west." This possibility has already been discussed. All the above shows that in the enemy's command, too, we can find some basis for victory. Of course, we should not take it as an important basis for our strategic planning; on the contrary, the only reliable course is to base our planning on the assumption that the enemy will make few mis-takes. Besides, the enemy can exploit our mistakes just as we can exploit his. It is the duty of our command to allow him the minimum of oppor-tunities for doing so. Actually, the enemy command has committed errors, will again commit errors in the future, and can be made to do so through our endeavors. All these errors we can exploit, and it is the business of our generals in the War of Resistance to do their utmost to seize upon them. However, although much of the enemy's strategic and campaign command is incompetent, there are quite a few excellent points in his battle command, that is, in his unit and small formation tactics, and here we should learn from him.

The Question of Decisive Engagements in the Anti-Japanese War

106. The question of decisive engagements in the anti-Japanese war should be approached from three aspects: we should resolutely fight a decisive engagement in every campaign or battle in which we are sure of victory; we should avoid a decisive engagement in every campaign or battle in which we are not sure of victory; and we should absolutely avoid a strategically decisive engagement on which the fate of the whole nation is staked. The characteristics differentiating our anti-Japanese war from many other wars are also revealed in this question of decisive engagements. In the first and second stages of the war, which are marked by the enemy's strength and our weakness, the enemy's objective is to have us concentrate our main forces for a decisive engagement. Our objective is exactly the opposite. We want to choose conditions favorable to us, concentrate superior forces, and fight decisive campaigns or battles only when sure of victory, as in the battles at Pinghsingkuan, Taierhchuang, and other places; we want to avoid decisive engagements under unfavorable conditions when we are not sure of victory, this being the policy we adopted in the Changteh and other campaigns. As for fighting a strategically decisive engagement on which the fate of the whole nation is staked, we simply must not do so, as witness the recent withdrawal from Hsuchow. The enemy's plan for a "quick decision" was thus foiled, and now he cannot help fighting a protracted war with us. These principles are impracticable in a country with a small territory, and hardly practicable in a country that is very backward politically. They are practicable in China because she is a big country and is in an era of progress. If strategically decisive engagements are avoided, then "as long as the green mountains are there, we need not worry about firewood," for even though some of our territory may be lost, we shall still have plenty of room for maneuver and thus be able to promote and await domestic progress, international support, and the internal disintegration of the enemy; that is the best policy for us in the anti-Japanese war. Unable to endure the arduous trials of a protracted war and eager for an early triumph, the impetuous theorists of quick victory clamor for a strategically decisive engagement the moment the situation takes a slightly favorable turn. To do what they

want would be to inflict incalculable damage on the entire war, spell finis to the protracted war, and would land us in the enemy's deadly trap; actually, it would be the worst policy. Undoubtedly, if we are to avoid decisive engagements, we shall have to abandon territory, and we must have the courage to do so when (and only when) it becomes completely unavoidable. At such times we should not feel the slightest regret, for this policy of trading space for time is correct. History tells us how Russia made a courageous retreat to avoid a decisive engagement and then defeated Napoleon, the terror of his age. Today China should do likewise.

107. Are we not afraid of being denounced as "nonresisters"? No, we are not. Not to fight at all but to compromise with the enemy—that is nonresistance, which should not only be denounced but must never be tolerated. We must resolutely fight the War of Resistance, but in order to avoid the enemy's deadly trap, it is absolutely necessary that we should not allow our main forces to be finished off at one blow, which would make it difficult to continue the War of Resistance—in brief, it is absolutely necessary to avoid national subjugation. To have doubts on this point is to be short-sighted on the question of the war and is sure to lead one into the ranks of the subjugationists. We have criticized the desperate recklessness of "only advance, never retreat" precisely because, if it became the fashion, this doctrine would make it impossible to continue the War of Resistance and would lead to the danger of ultimate national subjugation.

108. We are for decisive engagements whenever circumstances are favorable, whether in battles or in major or minor campaigns, and in this respect we should never tolerate passivity. Only through such decisive engagements can we achieve the objective of annihilating or depleting the enemy forces, and every soldier in the anti-Japanese war should resolutely play his part. For this purpose considerable partial sacrifices are necessary; to avoid any sacrifice whatsoever is the attitude of cowards and of those afflicted by the fear of Japan and must be firmly opposed. The execution of Li Fu-ying, Han Fu-chu, and other flightists was justified. Within the scope of correct war planning, encouraging the spirit and practice of heroic self-sacrifice and dauntless advance in battle is absolutely necessary and inseparable from the waging of protracted war and the achievement of final victory. We have strongly condemned the flight-ism of "only retreat, never advance" and have supported the strict enforcement of discipline, because it is only through heroic decisive engagements, fought under a correct plan, that we can vanquish the powerful enemy; flight-ism, on the contrary, gives direct support to the theory of national subjugation.

109. Is it not self-contradictory to fight heroically first and then abandon territory? Will not our heroic fighters have shed their blood in vain? That is not at all the way questions should be posed. To eat and then to empty your bowels—is this not to eat in vain? To sleep and then to get up—is this not to sleep in vain? Can questions be posed in such a way? I would suppose not. To keep on eating, to keep on sleeping, to keep on fighting heroically all the way to the Yalu River without a stop—these are subjectivist and formalist illusions, not realities of life. As everybody knows, although in fighting and shedding our blood in order to gain time and prepare the counteroffensive we have had to abandon some territory, in fact we have gained time, we have achieved the objective of annihilating and depleting the enemy, we have acquired experience in fighting, we have aroused hitherto inactive people and improved our international standing. Has our blood been shed in vain? Certainly not. Territory has been given up in order to preserve our military forces and indeed to preserve territory, because if we do not abandon part of our territory when conditions are unfavorable but blindly fight decisive engagements without the least assurance of winning, we shall lose our military forces and then be unable to avoid the loss of all our territory, to say nothing of recovering territory already lost. A capitalist must have capital to run his business, and if he loses it all he is no longer a capitalist. Even a gambler must have money to stake, and if he risks it all on a single throw and his luck fails, he cannot gamble any more. Events have their twists and turns and do not follow a straight line, and war is no exception; only formalists are unable to comprehend this truth.

110. I think the same will also hold true for the decisive engagements in the stage of strategic counteroffensive. Although by then the enemy will be in the inferior and we in the superior position, the principle of "fighting profitable decisive engagements and avoiding unprofitable ones" will still apply and will continue to apply until we have fought our way to the Yalu River. This is how we will be able to maintain our initiative from beginning to end, and as for the enemy's "challenges" and other people's "taunts" we should imperturbably brush them aside and ignore them. In the War of Resistance only those generals who show this kind of firmness can be deemed courageous and wise. This is beyond the ken of those who "jump whenever touched." Even though we are in a more or less passive position strategically in the first stage of the war, we should have the initiative in every campaign; and of course we should have the initiative throughout the later stages. We are for protracted war and final victory, we are not gamblers who risk everything on a single throw.

The Army and the People Are
the Foundation of Victory

111. Japanese imperialism will never relax in its aggression against and repression of revolutionary China; this is determined by its imperialist nature. If China did not resist, Japan would easily seize all China without firing a single shot, as she did the four provinces in the northeast. Since China is resisting, it is an inexorable law that Japan will try to repress this resistance until the force of her repression is exceeded by the force of China's resistance. The Japanese landlord class and bourgeoisie are very ambitious, and in order to drive south to Southeast Asia and north to Siberia, they have adopted the policy of breaking through in the centre by first attacking China. Those who think that Japan will know where to stop and be content with the occupation of northern China and of Kiangsu and Chekiang Provinces completely fail to perceive that imperialist Japan, which has developed to a new stage and is approaching extinction, differs from the Japan of the past. When we say that there is a definite limit both to the number of men Japan can throw in and to the extent of her advance, we mean that with her available strength, Japan can only commit part of her forces against China and penetrate China as far as their capacity allows, for she wants to attack in other directions and has to defend herself against other enemies; at the same time China has given proof of progress and power of stubborn resistance, and it is inconceivable that there should be fierce attacks by Japan without inevitable resistance by China. Japan cannot occupy the whole of China, but she will spare no effort to suppress China's resistance in all the areas she can reach, and will not stop until internal and external developments push Japanese imperialism to the brink of the grave. There are only two possible outcomes to the political situation in Japan. Either the downfall of her entire ruling class occurs rapidly, political power passes to the people, and war thus comes to an end, which is impossible at the moment, or her landlord class and bourgeoisie become more and more Fascist and maintain the war until the day of their downfall, which is the very road Japan is now traveling. There can be no other outcome. Those who hope that the moderates among the Japanese bourgeoisie will come forward and stop the war are only harboring illusions. The reality of Japanese politics for many years has been that the bourgeois moderates of Japan have fallen captive to the landlords and the financial magnates. Now that Japan has launched war against China, so long as she does not suffer a fatal blow from Chinese resistance and still retains sufficient strength, she is bound to attack Southeast Asia or Siberia, or even both. She will do so once war breaks out in

Europe; in their wishful calculations, the rulers of Japan have it worked out on a grandiose scale. Of course, it is possible that Japan will have to drop her original plan of invading Siberia and adopt a mainly defensive attitude towards the Soviet Union on account of Soviet strength and of the serious extent to which Japan herself has been weakened by her war against China. But in that case, so far from relaxing her aggression against China she will intensify it, because then the only way left to her will be to gobble up the weak. China's task of persevering in the War of Resistance, the united front, and the protracted war will then become all the more weighty, and it will be all the more necessary not to slacken our efforts in the slightest.

112. Under the circumstances the main prerequisites for China's victory over Japan are nationwide unity and all-round progress on a scale ten or even a hundred times greater than in the past. China is already in an era of progress and has achieved a splendid unity, but her progress and unity are still far from adequate. That Japan has occupied such an extensive area is due partly to her strength but also partly to China's weakness; this weakness is entirely the cumulative effect of the various historical errors of the last hundred years, and especially of the last ten years, which have confined progress to its present bounds. It is impossible to vanquish so strong an enemy without making an extensive and long-term effort. There are many things we have to exert ourselves to do; here I will deal only with two fundamental aspects, the progress of the army and the progress of the people.

113. The reform of our military system requires its modernization and improved technical equipment, without which we cannot drive the enemy back across the Yalu River. In our employment of troops we need progressive, flexible strategy and tactics, without which we likewise cannot win victory. Nevertheless, soldiers are the foundation of an army; unless they are imbued with a progressive political spirit, and unless such a spirit is instilled through progressive political work, it will be impossible to achieve genuine unity between officers and men, impossible to arouse their enthusiasm for the War of Resistance to the full, and impossible to provide a sound basis for the most effective use of all our technical equipment and tactics. When we say that Japan will finally be defeated despite her technical superiority, we mean that the blows we deliver through annihilation and attrition, apart from inflicting losses, will eventually shake the enemy army's morale which is not on a level with its weapons. With us, on the contrary, officers and men are at one on the political aim of the War of Resistance. This gives us the foundation for political work among all the anti-Japanese forces. A proper measure of democracy should be

put into effect in the army, chiefly by abolishing the feudal practice of bullying and beating and by having officers and men share weal and woe. Once this is done, unity will be achieved between officers and men, the combat effectiveness of the army will be greatly increased, and there will be no doubt of our ability to sustain the long, cruel war.

114. The richest source of power to wage war lies in the masses of the people. It is mainly because of the unorganized state of the Chinese masses that Japan dares to bully us. When this defect is remedied, then the Japanese aggressor, like a wild bull crashing into a ring of flames, will be surrounded by hundreds of millions of our people standing upright, the mere sound of their voices will strike terror into him, and he will be burned to death. China's armies must have an uninterrupted flow of reinforcements, and the abuses of press-ganging and of buying substitutes,[30] which now exist at the lower levels, must immediately be banned and replaced by widespread and enthusiastic political mobilization, which will make it easy to enlist millions of men. We now have great difficulties in raising money for the war, but once the people are mobilized, finances too will cease to be a problem. Why should a country as large and populous as China suffer from lack of funds? The army must become one with the people so that they see it as their own army. Such an army will be invincible, and an imperialist power like Japan will be no match for it.

115. Many people think that it is wrong methods that make for strained relations between officers and men and between the army and the people, but I always tell them that it is a question of basic attitude (or basic principle) of having respect for the soldiers and the people. It is from this attitude that the various policies, methods, and forms ensue. If we depart from this attitude, then the policies, methods, and forms will certainly be wrong, and the relations between officers and men and between the army and the people are bound to be unsatisfactory. Our three major principles for the army's political work are, first, unity between officers and men; second, unity between the army and the people; and third, the disintegration of the enemy forces. To apply these principles effectively, we must start with this basic attitude of respect for the soldiers and the people, and of respect for the human dignity of prisoners of war once they have laid down their arms. Those who take all this as a technical matter and not one of basic attitude are indeed wrong, and they should correct their view.

116. At this moment, when the defence of Wuhan and other places has become urgent, it is a task of the utmost importance to arouse the active enthusiasm of the whole army and the whole people to the full in support of the war. There is no doubt that the task of defending Wuhan

and other places must be seriously posed and seriously performed. But whether we can be certain of holding them depends not on our subjective desires but on concrete conditions. Among the most important of these conditions is the political mobilization of the whole army and people for the struggle. If a strenuous effort is not made to secure all the necessary conditions, or even one of these conditions is missing, disasters like the loss of Nanking and other places are bound to be repeated. China will have her Madrids in places where the conditions are present. So far China has not had a Madrid, and from now on we should work hard to create several, but it all depends on the conditions. The most fundamental of these is extensive political mobilization of the whole army and people.

117. In all our work we must persevere in the Anti-Japanese National United Front as the general policy. For only with this policy can we persevere in the War of Resistance and in protracted warfare, bring about a widespread and profound improvement in the relations between officers and men and between the army and the people, arouse to the full the active enthusiasm of the entire army and the entire people in the fight for the defence of all the territory still in our hands and for the recovery of what we have lost, and so win final victory.

118. This question of the political mobilization of the army and the people is indeed of the greatest importance. We have dwelt on it at the risk of repetition precisely because victory is impossible without it. There are, of course, many other conditions indispensable to victory, but political mobilization is the most fundamental. The Anti-Japanese National United Front is a united front of the whole army and the whole people, it is certainly not a united front merely of the headquarters and members of a few political parties; our basic objective in initiating the Anti-Japanese National United Front is to mobilize the whole army and the whole people to participate in it.

Conclusions

119. What are our conclusions? They are:

"Under what conditions do you think the Chinese people can defeat and exhaust the forces of Japan?" "Three conditions will guarantee our success: first, the acnievement of the National United Front against Japanese imperialism in China; second, the formation of a World Anti-Japanese United Front; third, the rise of the revolutionary movement among the people in Japan and the Japanese colonies. Of these, the central necessity is the union of the Chinese people themselves."

"How long would such a war last?" "That depends on the strength of the Chinese People's Front, many conditioning factors in China and Japan...."

"If these conditions are not realized, however, the war will be very long, but in the end, just the same, Japan will be defeated, China will certainly win, only the sacrifices will be extensive and it will be a painful period for the whole world."

"Our strategy should be to employ our main forces in mobile warfare, over an extended, shifting, and indefinite front, a strategy depending for success on a high degree of mobility in difficult terrain."

"Besides employing trained armies to carry on mobile warfare, we must organize and equip great numbers of guerrilla detachments among the peasantry."

"A point will be reached where it will become more and more possible to engage Japan's armies on a basis of positional warfare, using fortifications and deep entrenchment, for, as the war progresses, the technical equipment of the anti-Japanese forces will greatly improve. . . . Japan's economy will crack under the strain of a long, expensive occupation of China and the morale of her forces will break under the trial of a war of innumerable but indecisive battles. The great reservoirs of human material in the revolutionary Chinese people will still be pouring forth men ready to fight for their freedom into our front lines. All these and other factors will condition the war and will enable us to make the final and decisive attacks on Japan's fortifications and strategic bases and to drive Japan's army of occupation from China." (From an interview with Edgar Snow in July 1936.)

"A new stage in China's political situation has begun. . . . The crucial task of the present stage is to mobilize all forces for victory in the War of Resistance."

"The key to victory is to develop the War of Resistance already begun into a total nation-wide anti-Japanese war. Only such a total nation-wide war can bring final victory."

"As there are still serious weaknesses in the War of Resistance, many difficulties may arise in its future course—setbacks and retreats, internal divisions and betrayals, temporary and partial compromises. We must therefore realize that this will be a hard-fought, protracted war. But we believe that, through the efforts of our Party and the whole people, the War of Resistance which has already begun is sure to overcome all obstacles and continue to progress and develop." ("Decision on the Current Situation and the Tasks of the Party," adopted by the Central Committee of the Communist party of China, August 1937.)

These are our conclusions. In the eyes of the subjugationists the enemy are supermen and we Chinese are worthless, while in the eyes of the theorists of quick victory we Chinese are supermen and the enemy are worthless. Both are wrong. We take a different view; the War of Resistance Against Japan is a protracted war, and the final victory will be China's. These are our conclusions.

120. My lectures end here. The great War of Resistance Against Japan is unfolding, and many people are hoping for a summary of experience to facilitate the winning of complete victory. What I have discussed is simply the general experience of the past ten months, and it may perhaps serve as a kind of summary. The problem of protracted war deserves wide attention and discussion; what I have given is only an outline, which I hope you will examine and discuss, amend and amplify.

LONG LIVE THE VICTORY OF PEOPLE'S WAR! 2

by Lin Piao

Lin Piao is a veteran Communist and military leader. An outstanding strategist in the Sino-Japanese War, Lin was the author of the "short attack" with which he defeated on 25 September 1937 the crack Japanese Itagaki Division. In May 1958 he was elected vice-chairman of the Chinese Communist Party (CCP) Central Committee and Politburo, at the time when the communes were started as the basic form of China's society. In 1959 he replaced the minister of defense who was said to have opposed the communes policy as adversely affecting the army.

Lin Piao was born in Hupeh in 1908, the son of a factory owner. He went from a middle school in Wuchang to the Whampao Military Academy, from which he graduated in 1925. A year earlier, Lin had joined the Kuomintang (KMT—or Nationalist party) and in 1925 became a member of the Communist party—the two then being in alliance. At the age of 20, in 1927, Lin was a colonel in the KMT's Fourth Army, and when the split in the alliance came, he led his troops over to the Communists in the abortive Nanchang uprisings. After the further unsuccessful uprisings at Swatow and Canton, he took his troops to join Chu Teh in Hunan; they both made their way to join Mao Tse-tung in the Kiangsi Soviet area.

There, in 1932, Lin became commander of the First Red Army and made the "Long March" (1934–35) with Mao to the north. In Yenan, Lin was appointed in 1936 president of the Red Academy. A year later, he became director of the Anti-Japanese Military and Political University. Lin commanded the 115th Division of the Eighth Route Army in Shansi and Hopei when hostilities with Japan broke out; he was severely wounded. In 1938 he went to the Soviet Union for medical treatment, staying there until 1942, when he returned to resume his university post.

After the Allied defeat of Japan, Lin briefly took part in the abortive 1945 negotiations in Chungking between Nationalists and Communists. He went to Manchuria and there recruited the Manchurian army, which became the Communist Fourth Field Army. In the civil war between the Nationalists and Communists, Lin captured Tientsin in January 1949, then moved south to capture Hankow in the late spring and Kwantung and Kwangsi in the autumn. Later, when Communist China intervened in Korea, Lin led the Fourth Field Army against the United Nations forces.

A Central Committee member since 1945, Lin served on the 1949 preparatory Chinese People's Political Consultative Conference (CPP CC), which put the Central People's Government into power that October. He was appointed a member of the Government Administrative Council, vice-chairman of the Revolutionary Military Council, and a Standing Committee member of the CPPCC, which remained as the organizational form of the united front of ostensibly independent political parties.

On its foundation in 1950, Lin was appointed director of the Central South Military and Political Commission and continued as first secretary of the Central South Party Bureau. In August 1950 he was appointed director of the Commission's Committee of Finance, then actively engaged in securing control of assets and bending business, businessmen, and the economy to Communist control. Lin was appointed a member of the National Planning Committee when it was set up in 1952 to give more centralized direction to the economy.

After centralization was completed in September 1954 under a new Communist-style constitution and new electoral laws, Lin became a vice-premier of the new government, a member of the National People's Congress, and vice-chairman of the National Defense Council. In December of the same year he was elected a vice-president of the Sino-Soviet Friendship Association—it was a period of great Soviet economic aid. In April 1955 Lin became the youngest member of the party Politburo, and in September he was made marshal of the Chinese People's Republic. In May 1958 Lin was brought into the highest party conclaves, being made a vice-chairman of the Central Committee and a member of the Standing Committee of the Politburo.

As China veered away from the Soviet model into its "Great Leap Forward" and independent foreign policies, Mao had perceived that the professionals in the army did not approve of his new course. If nothing more, the professionals could no longer accept responsibility for China's defense against atomic attack; in June 1959 Russian opposition to "Great Leap Forward" policies had led the Soviet Union to tear up the two-year-old agreement for Sino-Soviet sharing of nuclear weapons. As head of the Communist party's Military Affairs Committee, Mao purged as well as reorganized the army. Lin was appointed minister of defense. He was considered to be unswervingly loyal and personally close to Mao, having lived and fought by his side for years.

Lin has carried out programs aimed at raising the revolutionary spirit of the troops and establishing closer ties between them and the populace. In June 1965 Lin abolished ranks within the army, thereby restoring the "internal army democracy" of the guerrilla days. At the present time, army men are supposed to refer to each other by job title—e.g., Squad Leader Chang, Combatant Li, or Minister of Defense Lin—or, even more democratically, simply by the title of "comrade." There are no more marshals or privates.

Possibly the most important of Lin's reforms was that he greatly strengthened the army's General Political Department and made it the command center for all internal army political activities and civil-military campaigns. One of Lin's objectives was to reassert the party's control over the army, which had slipped badly under his predecessor.

In order to ensure effective civilian party control over party organizations within the army, the General Political Department directed on 26 April 1961 that army party committees be placed under the joint control and supervision of local *hsien* (county) or urban civilian party committees and of the party committee of the army's military region branch. In matters pertaining to the organization and training of militia cadres, party and Young Communist League activities within the militia, and the use of the militia to maintain public order, army party organs were placed under the exclusive jurisdiction of local civilian party committees. This control of army party organs by nonmilitary party units is perpetuated all the way up the military hierarchy. At the apex of the army's hierarchy, the party-army distinction disappears as all senior officers of the army are also members of the Communist party.

Lin's tight control of the military paid off when Mao launched his "Cultural Revolution" in 1966. The greater portion of the army remained loyal to Lin and Mao. Lin was given additional power when he was placed in command of the Red Guards, the youthful hordes who rampaged through China in the name of revolution. For his loyalty in supporting Mao, Lin was rewarded by being made heir designate—the probable future ruler of vast and powerful China.

LONG LIVE THE VICTORY
OF PEOPLE'S WAR!

FULL TWENTY years have elapsed since our victory in the great War of Resistance Against Japan.

After a long period of heroic struggle, the Chinese people, under the leadership of the Communist party of China and Comrade Mao Tse-tung, won final victory two decades ago in their war against the Japanese imperialists who had attempted to subjugate China and swallow up the whole of Asia.

The Chinese people's War of Resistance was an important part of the world war against German, Japanese, and Italian fascism. The Chinese people received support from the people and the anti-Fascist forces all over the world. And in their turn, the Chinese people made an important contribution to victory in the anti-Fascist war as a whole.

Of the innumerable anti-imperialist wars waged by the Chinese people in the past hundred years, the War of Resistance Against Japan was the first to end in complete victory. It occupies an extremely important place in the annals of war, in the annals of both the revolutionary wars of the Chinese people and the wars of the oppressed nations of the world against imperialist aggression.

It was a war in which a weak semicolonial and semifeudal country triumphed over a strong imperialist country. For a long period after the invasion of China's northeastern provinces by the Japanese imperialists, the Kuomintang followed a policy of nonresistance. In the early stage of the War of Resistance, the Japanese imperialists exploited their military superiority to drive deep into China and occupy half her territory. In the face of the massive attacks of the aggressors and the anti-Japanese upsurge of the people throughout the country, the Kuomintang was compelled to take part in the War of Resistance, but soon afterwards it adopted the policy of passive resistance to Japan and active opposition to the Communist party. The heavy responsibility of combating Japanese imperialism thus fell on the shoulders of the Eighth Route Army, the New Fourth Army, and the people of the liberated areas, all led by the Communist party. At the outbreak of the war, the Eighth Route and New Fourth armies had only a few tens of thousands of men and suffered from extreme inferiority in both arms and equipment, and for a long time they were under the crossfire of the Japanese imperialists on the one hand and the Kuomintang troops on the other. But they grew stronger and stronger in the course of the war and became the main force in defeating Japanese imperialism.

How was it possible for a weak country finally to defeat a strong country? How was it possible for a seemingly weak army to become the main force in the war?

The basic reasons were that the War of Resistance Against Japan was a genuine people's war led by the Communist party of China and Comrade Mao Tse-tung, a war in which the correct Marxist-Leninist political and military lines were put into effect, and that the Eighth Route and New Fourth armies were genuine people's armies which applied the whole range of strategy and tactics of people's war as formulated by Comrade Mao Tse-tung.

Comrade Mao Tse-tung's theory of and policies for people's war have creatively enriched and developed Marxism-Leninism. The Chinese people's victory in the anti-Japanese war was a victory for people's war, for Marxism-Leninism and the thought of Mao Tse-tung.

Prior to the war against Japan, the Communist party of China had gone through the First Revolutionary Civil War of 1924-27 and the Second Revolutionary Civil War of 1927-36 and summed up the experience and lessons of the successes and failures in those wars, and the leading role of Mao Tse-tung's thought had become established within the party. This was the fundamental guarantee of the party's ability to lead the Chinese people to victory in the War of Resistance.

The Chinese people's victory in the War of Resistance paved the way for their seizure of state power throughout the country. When the Kuomintang reactionaries, backed by the U.S. imperialists, launched a nationwide civil war in 1946, the Communist party of China and Comrade Mao Tse-tung further developed the theory of people's war, led the Chinese people in waging a people's war on a still larger scale, and in the space of a little over three years the great victory of the People's Liberation War was won, the rule of imperialism, feudalism and bureaucrat-capitalism in our country ended and the People's Republic of China founded.

The victory of the Chinese people's revolutionary war breached the imperialist front in the East, wrought a great change in the world balance of forces, and accelerated the revolutionary movement among the people of all countries. From then on, the national liberation movement in Asia, Africa, and Latin America entered a new historical period.

Today, the U.S. imperialists are repeating on a worldwide scale the past actions of the Japanese imperialists in China and other parts of Asia. It has become an urgent necessity for the people in many countries to master and use people's war as a weapon against U.S. imperialism and its lackeys. In every conceivable way U.S. imperialism and its lackeys are trying to extinguish the revolutionary flames of people's war. The

Khrushchev revisionists, fearing people's war like the plague, are heaping abuse on it. The two are colluding to prevent and sabotage people's war. In these circumstances, it is of vital practical importance to review the historical experience of the great victory of the people's war in China and to recapitulate Comrade Mao Tse-tung's theory of people's war.

The Principal Contradiction in the Period of the War of Resistance Against Japan and the Line of the Communist Party of China

The Communist party of China and Comrade Mao Tse-tung were able to lead the Chinese people to victory in the War of Resistance Against Japan primarily because they formulated and applied a Marxist-Leninist line.

Basing himself on the fundamental tenets of Marxism-Leninism and applying the method of class analysis, Comrade Mao Tse-tung analysed, first, the mutual transformation of China's principal and non-principal contradictions following the invasion of China by Japanese imperialism, second, the consequent changes in class relations within China and in international relations, and, third, the balance of forces as between China and Japan. This analysis provided the scientific basis upon which the political and military lines of the War of Resistance were formulated.

There had long been two basic contradictions in China—the contradiction between imperialism and the Chinese nation, and the contradiction between feudalism and the masses of the people. For ten years before the outbreak of the War of Resistance, the Kuomintang reactionary clique, which represented the interests of imperialism, the big landlords and the big bourgeoisie, had waged civil war against the Communist party of China and the Communist-led Workers' and Peasants' Red Army, which represented the interests of the Chinese people. In 1931, Japanese imperialism invaded and occupied northeastern China. Subsequently, and especially after 1935, it stepped up and expanded its aggression against China, penetrating deeper and deeper into our territory. As a result of its invasion, Japanese imperialism sharpened its contradiction with the Chinese nation to an extreme degree and brought about changes in class relations within China. To end the civil war and to unite against Japanese aggression became the pressing nationwide demand of the people. Changes of varying degrees also occurred in the political attitudes of the national bourgeoisie and the various factions within the Kuomintang. And the Sian Incident[1] of 1936 was the best case in point.

How was one to assess the changes in China's political situation, and what conclusion was to be drawn? This question had a direct bearing on the very survival of the Chinese nation.

For a period prior to the outbreak of the War of Resistance, the "Left" opportunists represented by Wang Ming within the Chinese Communist Party were blind to the important changes in China's political situation caused by Japanese aggression since 1931 and denied the sharpening of the Sino-Japanese national contradiction and the demands of various social strata for a war of resistance; instead, they stressed that all the counterrevolutionary factions and intermediate forces in China and all the imperialist countries were a monolithic bloc. They persisted in their line of "closed-doorism" and continued to advocate, "Down with the whole lot."

Comrade Mao Tse-tung resolutely fought the "Left" opportunist errors and penetratingly analysed the new situation in the Chinese revolution.

He pointed out that the Japanese imperialist attempt to reduce China to a Japanese colony heightened the contradiction between China and Japan and made it the principal contradiction; that China's internal class contradictions—such as those between the masses of the people and feudalism, between the peasantry and the landlord class, between the proletariat and the bourgeoisie, and between the peasantry and urban petty bourgeoisie on the one hand and the bourgeoisie on the other—still remained, but that they had all been relegated to a secondary or subordinate position as a result of the war of aggression unleashed by Japan; and that throughout China opposition to Japanese imperialism had become the common demand of the people of all classes and strata, except for a handful of pro-Japanese traitors among the big landlords and the big bourgeoisie.

As the contradiction between China and Japan ascended and became the principal one, the contradiction between China and imperialist countries such as Britain and the United States descended to a secondary or subordinate position. The rift between Japan and the other imperialist countries had widened as a result of Japanese imperialism's attempt to turn China into its own exclusive colony. This rendered it possible for China to make use of these contradictions to isolate and oppose Japanese imperialism.

In the face of Japanese imperialist aggression, was the party to continue with the civil war and the Agrarian Revolution? Or was it to hold aloft the banner of national liberation, unite with all the forces that could be united to form a broad national united front and concentrate on fighting the Japanese aggressors? This was the problem sharply confronting our party.

The Communist party of China and Comrade Mao Tse-tung formu-

lated the line of the Anti-Japanese National United Front on the basis of
their analysis of the new situation. Holding aloft the banner of national
liberation, our party issued the call for national unity and united resistance to Japanese imperialism, a call which won fervent support from the
people of the whole country. Thanks to the common efforts of our party
and of China's patriotic armies and people, the Kuomintang ruling clique
was eventually compelled to stop the civil war, and a new situation with
Kuomintang-Communist cooperation for joint resistance to Japan was
brought about.

In the summer of 1937 Japanese imperialism unleashed its all-out war
of aggression against China. The nationwide War of Resistance thus
broke out.

Could the War of Resistance be victorious? And how was victory to
be won? These were the questions to which all the Chinese people demanded immediate answers.

The defeatists came forward with the assertion that China was no
match for Japan and that the nation was bound to be subjugated. The
blind optimists came forward with the assertion that China could win
very quickly, without much effort.

Basing himself on a concrete analysis of the Chinese nation and of
Japanese imperialism—the two aspects of the principal contradiction—
Comrade Mao Tse-tung showed that while the "theory of national subju-
gation" was wrong, the "theory of quick victory" was untenable, and he
concluded that the War of Resistance would be a protracted one in which
China would finally be victorious.

In his celebrated work *On Protracted War*, Comrade Mao Tse-tung
pointed out the contrasting features of China and Japan, the two sides in
the war. Japan was a powerful imperialist country. But Japanese imperialism was in its era of decline and doom. The war it had unleashed was a
war of aggression, a war that was retrogressive and barbarous; it was deficient in manpower and material resources and could not stand a protracted war; it was engaged in an unjust cause and therefore had meagre
support internationally. China, on the other hand, was a weak semicolonial and semifeudal country. But she was in her era of progress. She was
fighting a war against aggression, a war that was progressive and just; she
had sufficient manpower and material resources to sustain a protracted
war; internationally, China enjoyed extensive sympathy and support.
These comprised all the basic factors in the Sino-Japanese war.

He went on to show how these factors would influence the course of
the war. Japan's advantage was temporary and would gradually diminish
as a result of our efforts. Her disadvantages were fundamental; they could

not be overcome and would gradually grow in the course of the war. China's disadvantage was temporary and could be gradually overcome. China's advantages were fundamental and would play an increasingly positive role in the course of the war. Japan's advantage and China's disadvantage determined the impossibility of quick victory for China. China's advantages and Japan's disadvantages determined the inevitability of Japan's defeat and China's ultimate victory.

On the basis of this analysis Comrade Mao Tse-tung formulated the strategy for a protracted war. China's War of Resistance would be protracted, and prolonged efforts would be needed gradually to weaken the enemy's forces and expand our own, so that the enemy would change from being strong to being weak and we would change from being weak to being strong and accumulate sufficient strength finally to defeat him. Comrade Mao Tse-tung pointed out that with the change in the balance of forces between the enemy and ourselves the War of Resistance would pass through three stages, namely, the strategic defensive, the strategic stalemate, and the strategic offensive. The protracted war was also a process of mobilizing, organizing, and arming the people. It was only by mobilizing the entire people to fight a people's war that the War of Resistance could be persevered in and the Japanese aggressors defeated.

In order to turn the anti-Japanese war into a genuine people's war, our party firmly relied on the broadest masses of the people, united with all the anti-Japanese forces that could be united, and consolidated and expanded the Anti-Japanese National United Front. The basic line of our party was: boldly to arouse the masses of the people and expand the people's forces so that, under the leadership of the party, they could defeat the aggressors and build a new China.

The War of Resistance Against Japan constituted a historical stage in China's new-democratic revolution. The line of our party during the War of Resistance aimed not only at winning victory in the war but also at laying the foundations for the nation-wide victory of the new-democratic revolution. Only the accomplishment of the new-democratic revolution makes it possible to carry out a socialist revolution. With respect to the relations between the democratic and the socialist revolutions, Comrade Mao Tse-tung said: "In the writing of an article the second half can be written only after the first half is finished. Resolute leadership of the democratic revolution is the prerequisite for the victory of socialism."[2]

The concrete analysis of concrete conditions and the concrete resolution of concrete contradictions are the living soul of Marxism-Leninism. Comrade Mao Tse-tung has invariably been able to single out the principal contradiction from among a complexity of contradictions, analyse the two aspects of this principal contradiction concretely and, "pressing on irresistibly from this commanding height," successfully solve the problem of understanding and handling the various contradictions.

It was precisely on the basis of such scientific analysis that Comrade Mao Tse-tung correctly formulated the political and military lines for the people's war during the War of Resistance Against Japan, developed his thought on the establishment of rural base areas and the use of the countryside to encircle the cities and finally capture them, and formulated a whole range of principles and policies, strategy and tactics in the political, military, economic, and cultural fields for the carrying out of the people's war. It was this that ensured victory in the War of Resistance and created the conditions for the nationwide victory of the new-democratic revolution.

Correctly Apply the Line and Policy of the United Front

In order to win a people's war, it is imperative to build the broadest possible united front and formulate a series of policies which will ensure the fullest mobilization of the basic masses as well as the unity of all the forces that can be united.

The Anti-Japanese National United Front embraced all the anti-Japanese classes and strata. These classes and strata shared a common interest in fighting Japan, an interest which formed the basis of their unity. But they differed in the degree of their firmness in resisting Japan, and there were class contradictions and conflicts of interest among them. Hence the inevitable class struggle within the united front.

In formulating the party's line of the Anti-Japanese National United Front, Comrade Mao Tse-tung made the following class analysis of Chinese society.

The workers, the peasants, and the urban petty bourgeoisie firmly demanded that the War of Resistance should be carried through to the end; they were the main force in the fight against Japanese aggression and constituted the basic masses who demanded unity and progress.

The bourgeoisie was divided into the national and the comprador bourgeoisie. The national bourgeoisie formed the majority of the bourgeoisie; it was rather flabby, often vacillated, and had contradictions with the workers, but it also had a certain degree of readiness to oppose imperialism and was one of our allies in the War of Resistance. The comprador bourgeoisie was the bureaucrat-capitalist class, which was very small in number but occupied the ruling position in China. Its members attached themselves to different imperialist powers, some of them being pro-Japanese and others pro-British and pro-American. The pro-Japanese section of the comprador bourgeoisie were the capitulators, the overt and covert traitors. The pro-British and pro-American section of this class favored resistance to Japan to a certain extent, but they were not firm in their resistance and very much wished to compromise with Japan, and by their nature they were opposed to the Communist party and the people.

The landlords fell into different categories; there were the big, the middle, and the small landlords. Some of the big landlords became traitors, while others favored resistance but vacillated a great deal. Many of the middle and small landlords had the desire to resist, but there were contradictions between them and the peasants.

In the face of these complicated class relationships, our party's policy regarding work within the united front was one of both alliance and struggle. That is to say, its policy was to unite with all the anti-Japanese classes and strata, try to win over even those who could be only vacillating and temporary allies, and adopt appropriate policies to adjust the relations among these classes and strata so that they all served the general cause of resisting Japan. At the same time, we had to maintain our party's principle of independence and initiative, make the bold arousing of the masses and expansion of the people's forces the centre of gravity in our work, and wage the necessary struggles against all activities harmful to resistance, unity, and progress.

Our party's Anti-Japanese National United Front policy was different both from Chen Tu-hsiu's Right opportunist policy of all alliance and no struggle, and from Wang Ming's "Left" opportunist policy of all struggle and no alliance. Our party summed up the lessons of the Right and "Left" opportunist errors and formulated the policy of both alliance and struggle.

Our party made a series of adjustments in its policies in order to unite all the anti-Japanese parties and groups, including the Kuomintang, and all the anti-Japanese strata in a joint fight against the foe. We pledged ourselves to fight for the complete realization of Dr. Sun Yat-sen's revolutionary Three People's Principles. The government of the Shensi-Kansu-Ningsia revolutionary base area was renamed the Government of the Shensi-Kansu-Ningsia Special Region of the Republic of China. Our Workers' and Peasants' Red Army was redesignated the Eighth Route Army and the New Fourth Army of the National Revolutionary Army. Our land policy, the policy of confiscating the land of the landlords, was changed to one of reducing rent and interest. In our own base areas we carried out the "three thirds system"[3] in our organs of political power, drawing in those representatives of the petty bourgeoisie, the national bourgeoisie, and the enlightened gentry and those members of the Kuomintang who stood for resistance to Japan and did not oppose the Communist party. In accordance with the principles of the Anti-Japanese National United Front, we also made necessary and appropriate changes in our policies relating to the economy, taxation, labor and wages, anti-espionage, people's rights, culture and education, etc.

While making these policy adjustments, we maintained the independence of the Communist party, the people's army, and the base areas. We also insisted that the Kuomintang should institute a general mobilization, reform the government apparatus, introduce democracy, improve the people's livelihood, arm the people, and carry out a total war of resistance. We waged a resolute struggle against the Kuomintang's passive resistance to Japan and active opposition to the Communist party, against its suppression of the people's resistance movement and its treacherous activities for compromise and capitulation.

Past experience had taught us that "Left" errors were liable to crop up after our party had corrected Right errors, and that Right errors were liable to crop up after it had corrected "Left" errors. "Left" errors were liable to occur when we broke with the Kuomintang ruling clique, and Right errors were liable to occur when we united with it.

After the overcoming of "Left" opportunism and the formation of the Anti-Japanese National United Front, the main danger in our party was Right opportunism or capitulationism.

Wang Ming, the exponent of "Left" opportunism during the Second Revolutionary Civil War, went to the other extreme in the early days of the War of Resistance Against Japan and became the exponent of Right opportunism, i.e., capitulationism. He countered Comrade Mao Tsetung's correct line and policies with an out-and-out capitulationist line of his own and a series of ultra-Right policies. He voluntarily abandoned proletarian leadership in the Anti-Japanese National United Front and willingly handed leadership to the Kuomintang. By his advocacy of "everything through the united front" or "everything to be submitted to the united front," he was in effect advocating that everything should go through or be submitted to Chiang Kai-shek and the Kuomintang. He opposed the bold mobilization of the masses, the carrying out of democratic reforms and the improvement of the livelihood of the workers and peasants, and wanted to undermine the worker-peasant alliance which was the foundation of the united front. He did not want the Communist-led base areas of the people's revolutionary forces but wanted to cut off the people's revolutionary forces from their roots. He rejected a people's army led by the Communist party and wanted to hand over the people's armed forces to Chiang Kai-shek, which would have meant handing over everything the people had. He did not want the leadership of the party and advocated an alliance between the youth of the Kuomintang and that of the Communist party to suit Chiang Kai-shek's design of corroding the Communist party. He decked himself out and presented himself to Chiang Kai-shek, hoping to be given some official appointment. All this was revisionism, pure and simple. If we had acted on Wang Ming's revisionist line and his set of policies, the Chinese people would have been unable to win the War of Resistance Against Japan, still less the subsequent nationwide victory.

For a time during the War of Resistance, Wang Ming's revisionist line caused harm to the Chinese people's revolutionary cause. But the leading role of Comrade Mao Tse-tung had already been established in the Central Committee of our party. Under his leadership, all the Marxist-Leninists in the party carried out a resolute struggle against Wang Ming's errors and rectified them in time. It was this struggle that prevented Wang Ming's erroneous line from doing greater and more lasting damage to the cause of the party.

Chiang Kai-shek, our teacher by negative example, helped us to correct Wang Ming's mistakes. He repeatedly lectured us with cannons and machine guns. The gravest lesson was the Southern Anhwei Incident, which took place in January 1941. Because some leaders of the New Fourth Army disobeyed the directives of the Central Committee of the party and followed Wang Ming's revisionist line, its units in southern Anhwei suffered disastrous losses in the surprise attack launched by Chiang Kai-shek and many heroic revolutionary fighters were slaughtered by the Kuomintang reactionaries. The lessons learned at the cost of blood helped to sober many of our comrades and increase their ability to distinguish the correct from the erroneous line.

Comrade Mao Tse-tung constantly summed up the experience gained by the whole party in implementing the line of the Anti-Japanese National United Front and worked out a whole set of policies in good time. They were mainly as follows:

1. All people favoring resistance (that is, all the anti-Japanese workers, peasants, soldiers, students and intellectuals, and businessmen) were to unite and form the Anti-Japanese National United Front.

2. Within the united front, our policy was to be one of independence and initiative, i.e., both unity and independence were necessary.

3. As far as military strategy was concerned, our policy was to be

guerrilla warfare waged independently and with the initiative in our own hands, within the framework of a unified strategy; guerrilla warfare was to be basic, but no chance of waging mobile warfare was to be lost when the conditions were favorable.

4. In the struggle against the anti-Communist die-hards headed by Chiang Kai-shek, our policy was to make use of contradictions, win over the many, oppose the few; and destroy our enemies one by one; and to wage struggles on just grounds, to our advantage, and with restraint.

5. In the Japanese-occupied and Kuomintang areas our policy was, on the one hand, to develop the united front to the greatest possible extent and, on the other, to have selected cadres working underground. With regard to the forms of organization and struggle, our policy was to assign selected cadres to work under cover for a long period, so as to accumulate strength and bide our time.

6. As regards the alignment of the various classes within the country, our basic policy was to develop the progressive forces, win over the middle forces and isolate the anti-Communist die-hard forces.

7. As for the anti-Communist die-hards, we followed a revolutionary dual policy of uniting with them, insofar as they were still capable of bringing themselves to resist Japan, and of struggling against and isolating them, insofar as they were determined to oppose the Communist party.

8. With respect to the landlords and the bourgeoisie—even the big landlords and big bourgeoisie—it was necessary to analyse each case and draw distinctions. On the basis of these distinctions we were to formulate different policies so as to achieve our aim of uniting with all the forces that could be united.

The line and the various policies of the Anti-Japanese National United Front formulated by Comrade Mao Tse-tung stood the test of the War of Resistance and proved to be entirely correct.

History shows that when confronted by ruthless imperialist aggression, a Communist party must hold aloft the national banner and, using the weapon of the united front, rally around itself the masses and the patriotic and anti-imperialist people who form more than ninety percent of a country's population, so as to mobilize all positive factors, unite with all the forces that can be united and isolate to the maximum the common enemy of the whole nation. If we abandon the national banner, adopt a line of "closed-doorism," and thus isolate ourselves, it is out of the question to exercise leadership and develop the people's revolutionary cause, and this in reality amounts to helping the enemy and bringing defeat on ourselves.

History shows that within the united front the Communist party must maintain its ideological, political, and organizational independence, adhere to the principle of independence and initiative, and insist on its leading role. Since there are class differences among the various classes in the united front, the party must have a correct policy in order to develop the progressive forces, win over the middle forces, and oppose the die-hard forces. The party's work must centre on developing the progressive forces and expanding the people's revolutionary forces. This is the only way to maintain and strengthen the united front. "If unity is sought through struggle, it will live; if unity is sought through yielding, it will perish."[4] This is the chief experience gained in our struggle against the die-hard forces.

History shows that during the national-democratic revolution there must be two kinds of alliance within this united front, first, the worker-peasant alliance and, second, the alliance of the working people with the bourgeoisie and other nonworking people. The worker-peasant alliance is an alliance of the working class with the peasants and all other working people in town and country. It is the foundation of the united front. Whether the working class can gain leadership of the national-democratic revolution depends on whether it can lead the broad masses of the peasants in struggle and rally them around itself. Only when the working class gains leadership of the peasants, and only on the basis of the worker-peasant alliance, is it possible to establish the second alliance, form a broad united front, and wage a people's war victoriously. Otherwise, everything that is done is unreliable, like castles in the air or so much empty talk.

Rely on the Peasants and Establish
Rural Base Areas

The peasantry constituted more than eighty percent of the entire population of semicolonial and semifeudal China. They were subjected to the threefold oppression and exploitation of imperialism, feudalism, and bureaucrat-capitalism, and they were eager for resistance against Japan and for revolution. It was essential to rely mainly on the peasants if the people's war was to be won.

But at the outset not all comrades in our party saw this point. The history of our party shows that in the period of the First Revolutionary Civil War, one of the major errors of the Right opportunists, represented by Chen Tu-hsiu, was their failure to recognize the importance of the peasant question and their opposition to arousing and arming the peasants. In the period of the Second Revolutionary Civil War, one of the major errors of the "Left" opportunists, represented by Wang Ming, was likewise their failure to recognize the importance of the peasant question. They did not realize that it was essential to undertake long-term and painstaking work among the peasants and establish revolutionary base areas in the countryside; they were under the illusion that they could rapidly seize the big cities and quickly win nationwide victory in the revolution. The errors of both the Right and the "Left" opportunists brought serious setbacks and defeats to the Chinese revolution.

As far back as the period of the First Revolutionary Civil War, Comrade Mao Tse-tung had pointed out that the peasant question occupied an extremely important position in the Chinese revolution, that the bourgeois-democratic revolution against imperialism and feudalism was in essence a peasant revolution and that the basic task of the Chinese proletariat in the bourgeois-democratic revolution was to give leadership to the peasants' struggle.

In the period of the War of Resistance Against Japan, Comrade Mao Tse-tung again stressed that the peasants were the most reliable and the most numerous ally of the proletariat and constituted the main force in the War of Resistance. The peasants were the main source of manpower for China's armies. The funds and the supplies needed for a protracted war came chiefly from the peasants. In the anti-Japanese war it was imperative to rely mainly on the peasants and to arouse them to participate in the war on the broadest scale.

The war of Resistance Against Japan was in essence a peasant revolutionary war led by our party. By arousing and organizing the peasant masses and integrating them with the proletariat, our party created a powerful force capable of defeating the strongest enemy.

To rely on the peasants, build rural base areas, and use the countryside to encircle and finally capture the cities—such was the way to victory in the Chinese revolution.

Basing himself on the characteristics of the Chinese revolution, Comrade Mao Tse-tung pointed out the importance of building rural revolutionary base areas:

> Since China's key cities have long been occupied by the powerful imperialists and their reactionary Chinese allies, it is imperative for the revolutionary ranks to turn the backward villages into advanced, consolidated base areas, into great military, political, economic, and cultural bastions of the revolution from which to fight their vicious enemies who are using the cities for attacks on the rural districts, and in this way gradually to achieve the complete victory of the revolution through protracted fighting; it is imperative for them to do so if they do not wish to compromise with imperialism and its lackeys but

are determined to fight on, and if they intend to build up and temper their forces, and avoid decisive battles with a powerful enemy while their own strength is inadequate.[5]

Experience in the period of the Second Revolutionary Civil War showed that, when this strategic concept of Comrade Mao Tse-tung's was applied, there was an immense growth in the revolutionary forces and one Red base area after another was built. Conversely, when it was violated and the nonsense of the "Left" opportunists was applied, the revolutionary forces suffered severe damage, with losses of nearly 100 percent in the cities and ninety percent in the rural areas.

During the War of Resistance Against Japan, the Japanese imperialist forces occupied many of China's big cities and the main lines of communication, but owing to the shortage of troops they were unable to occupy the vast countryside, which remained the vulnerable sector of the enemy's rule. Consequently, the possibility of building rural base areas became even greater. Shortly after the beginning of the War of Resistance, when the Japanese forces surged into China's hinterland and the Kuomintang forces crumbled and fled in one defeat after another, the Eighth Route and New Fourth armies, led by our party, followed the wise policy laid down by Comrade Mao Tse-tung and boldly drove into the areas behind the enemy lines in small contingents and established base areas throughout the countryside. During the eight years of the war, we established nineteen anti-Japanese base areas in northern, central, and southern China. With the exception of the big cities and the main lines of communication, the vast territory in the enemy's rear was in the hands of the people.

In the anti-Japanese base areas, we carried out democratic reforms, improved the livelihood of the people, and mobilized and organized the peasant masses. Organs of anti-Japanese democratic political power were established on an extensive scale and the masses of the people enjoyed the democratic right to run their own affairs; at the same time we carried out the policies of "a reasonable burden" and "the reduction of rent and interest," which weakened the feudal system of exploitation and improved the people's livelihood. As a result, the enthusiasm of the peasant masses was deeply aroused, while the various anti-Japanese strata were given due consideration and were thus united. In formulating our policies for the base areas, we also took care that these policies should facilitate our work in the enemy-occupied areas.

In the enemy-occupied cities and villages, we combined legal with illegal struggle, united the basic masses and all patriots, and divided and disintegrated the political power of the enemy and his puppets so as to prepare ourselves to attack the enemy from within in coordination with operations from without when conditions were ripe.

The base areas established by our party became the centre of gravity in the Chinese people's struggle to resist Japan and save the country. Relying on these bases, our party expanded and strengthened the people's revolutionary forces, persevered in the protracted war, and eventually won the War of Resistance Against Japan.

Naturally, it was impossible for the development of the revolutionary base areas to be plain sailing all the time. They constituted a tremendous threat to the enemy and were bound to be attacked. Therefore, their development was a tortuous process of expansion, contraction, and then renewed expansion. Between 1937 and 1940 the population in the anti-Japanese base areas grew to 100,000,000. But in 1941–42 the Japanese imperialists used the major part of their invading forces to launch frantic attacks on our base areas and wrought havoc. Meanwhile, the Kuomintang, too, encircled these base areas, blockaded them, and went so far as to attack them. So by 1942, the anti-Japanese base areas had contracted and their population was down to less than 50,000,000. Placing complete reliance on the masses, our party resolutely adopted a series of correct policies and measures, with the result that the base areas were able to hold out under extremely difficult circumstances. After this setback, the army and the people in the base areas were tempered and grew stronger. From 1943 onwards, our base areas were gradually restored and expanded, and by 1945 the population had grown to 160,000,000. Taking the entire course of the Chinese revolution into account, our revolutionary base areas went through even more ups and downs and they weathered a great many tests before the small, separate base areas, expanding in a series of waves, gradually developed into extensive and contiguous base areas.

At the same time, the work of building the revolutionary base areas was a grand rehearsal in preparation for nationwide victory. In these base areas, we built the party, ran the organs of state power, built the people's armed forces and set up mass organizations; we engaged in industry and agriculture and operated cultural, educational, and all other undertakings necessary for the independent existence of a separate region. Our base areas were in fact a state in miniature. And with the steady expansion of our work in the base areas, our party established a powerful people's army, trained cadres for various kinds of work, accumulated experience in many fields, and built up both the material and the moral strength that provided favorable conditions for nationwide victory.

The revolutionary base areas established in the War of Resistance later became the springboards for the People's War of Liberation, in which the Chinese people defeated the Kuomintang reactionaries. In the War of Liberation we continued the policy of first encircling the cities from the countryside and then capturing the cities, and thus won nationwide victory.

Build a People's Army of a New Type

"Without a people's army the people have nothing."[6] This is the conclusion drawn by Comrade Mao Tse-tung from the Chinese people's experience in their long years of revolutionary struggle, experience that was bought in blood. This is a universal truth of Marxism-Leninism.

The special feature of the Chinese revolution was armed revolution against armed counterrevolution. The main form of struggle was war and the main form of organization was the army which was under the absolute leadership of the Chinese Communist Party, while all the other forms of organization and struggle led by our party were coordinated, directly or indirectly, with the war.

During the First Revolutionary Civil War, many fine party comrades took an active part in the armed revolutionary struggle. But our party was then still in its infancy and did not have a clear understanding of this special feature of the Chinese revolution. It was only after the First Revolutionary Civil War, only after the Kuomintang had betrayed the revolution, massacred large numbers of Communists and destroyed all the revolutionary mass organizations, that our party reached a clearer understanding of the supreme importance of organizing revolutionary armed forces and of studying the strategy and tactics of revolutionary war, and created the Workers' and Peasants' Red Army, the first people's army under the leadership of the Communist party of China.

During the Second Revolutionary Civil War, the Workers' and Peasants' Red Army created by Comrade Mao Tse-tung grew considerably and at one time reached a total of 300,000 men. But it later lost nine-tenths of its forces as a result of the wrong political and military lines followed by the "Left" opportunist leadership.

At the start of the War of Resistance Against Japan, the people's army led by the Chinese Communist Party had only a little over 40,000 men. The Kuomintang reactionaries attempted to restrict, weaken, and destroy this people's army in every conceivable way. Comrade Mao Tse-tung pointed out that, in these circumstances, in order to sustain the War of Resistance and defeat the Japanese aggressors, it was imperative greatly to expand and consolidate the Eighth Route and New Fourth armies and all the guerrilla units led by our party. The whole party should give close attention to war and study military affairs. Every party member should be ready at all times to take up arms and go to the front.

Comrade Mao Tse-tung also incisively stated that Communists do not fight for personal military power but must fight for military power for the party and for the people.

Guided by the party's correct line of expanding the revolutionary armed forces, the Communist-led Eighth Route and New Fourth armies and anti-Japanese guerrilla units promptly went to the forefront at the very beginning of the war. We spread the seeds of the people's armed forces in the vast areas behind the enemy lines and kindled the flames of guerrilla warfare everywhere. Our people's army steadily expanded in the struggle, so that by the end of the war it was already a million strong, and there was also a militia of over two million. That was why we were able to engage nearly two-thirds of the Japanese forces of aggression and ninety-five percent of the puppet troops and to become the main force in the War of Resistance Against Japan. While resisting the Japanese invading forces, we repulsed three large-scale anti-Communist onslaughts launched by the Kuomintang reactionaries in 1939, 1941, and 1943, and smashed their countless "friction-mongering" activities.

Why were the Eighth Route and New Fourth armies able to grow big and strong from being small and weak and to score such great victories in the War of Resistance Against Japan?

The fundamental reason was that the Eighth Route and New Fourth armies were founded on Comrade Mao Tse-tung's theory of army building. They were armies of a new type, a people's army which wholeheartedly serves the interests of the people.

Guided by Comrade Mao Tse-tung's theory on building a people's army, our army was under the absolute leadership of the Chinese Communist Party and most loyally carried out the party's Marxist-Leninist line and policies. It had a high degree of conscious discipline and was heroically inspired to destroy all enemies and conquer all difficulties. Internally there was full unity between cadres and fighters, between those in higher and those in lower positions of responsibility, between the different departments and between the various fraternal army units. Externally, there was similarly full unity between the army and the people and between the army and the local government.

During the anti-Japanese war our army staunchly performed the three tasks set by Comrade Mao Tse-tung, namely, fighting, mass work, and production, and it was at the same time a fighting force, a political work force, and a production corps. Everywhere it went, it did propaganda work among the masses, organized and armed them and helped them set up revolutionary political power. Our armymen strictly observed the Three Main Rules of Discipline and the Eight Points for Attention,[7] carried out campaigns to "support the government and cherish the people," and did good deeds for the people everywhere. They also made use of every possibility to engage in production themselves so as to overcome economic difficulties, better their own livelihood and lighten the people's burden. By their exemplary conduct they won the whole-hearted support of the masses, who affectionately called them "our own boys."

Our army consisted of local forces as well as of regular forces; moreover, it energetically built and developed the militia, thus practising the system of combining the three military formations, i.e., the regular forces, the local forces, and the militia.

Our army also pursued correct policies in winning over enemy officers and men and in giving lenient treatment to prisoners of war. During the anti-Japanese war we not only brought about the revolt and surrender of large numbers of puppet troops, but succeeded in converting not a few Japanese prisoners, who had been badly poisoned by fascist ideology. After they were politically awakened, they organized themselves into anti-war organizations such as the League for the Liberation of the Japanese People, the Anti-War League of the Japanese in China and the League of Awakened Japanese, helped us to disintegrate the Japanese army and cooperated with us in opposing Japanese militarism. Comrade Sanzo Nosaka, the leader of the Japanese Communist Party, who was then in Yenan, gave us great help in this work.

The essence of Comrade Mao Tse-tung's theory of army building is that in building a people's army prominence must be given to politics, i.e., the army must first and foremost be built on a political basis. Politics is the commander, politics is the soul of everything. Political work is the lifeline of our army. True, a people's army must pay attention to the constant improvement of its weapons and equipment and its military technique, but in its fighting it does not rely purely on weapons and technique, it relies mainly on politics, on the proletarian revolutionary consciousness and courage of the commanders and fighters, on the support and backing of the masses.

Owing to the application of Comrade Mao Tse-tung's line on army building, there has prevailed in our army at all times a high level of proletarian political consciousness, an atmosphere of keenness to study the thought of Mao Tse-tung, an excellent morale, a solid unity and a deep hatred for the enemy, and thus a gigantic moral force has been brought into being. In battle it has feared neither hardships nor death, it has been able to charge or hold its ground as the conditions require. One man can play the role of several, dozens, or even hundreds, and miracles can be performed.

All this makes the people's army led by the Chinese Communist Party fundamentally different from any bourgeois army, and from all the armies of the old type which served the exploiting classes and were driven and utilized by a handful of people. The experience of the people's war in China shows that a people's army created in accordance with Comrade Mao Tse-tung's theory of army building is incomparably strong and invincible.

Carry Out the Strategy and Tactics of People's War

Engels said, "The emancipation of the proletariat, in its turn, will have its specific expression in military affairs and create its specific, new military method."[8] Engels' profound prediction has been fulfilled in the revolutionary wars waged by the Chinese people under the leadership of the Chinese Communist Party. In the course of protracted armed struggle, we have created a whole range of strategy and tactics of people's war by which we have been able to utilize our strong points to attack the enemy at his weak points.

During the War of Resistance Against Japan, on the basis of his comprehensive analysis of the enemy and ourselves, Comrade Mao Tse-tung laid down the following strategic principle for the Communist-led Eighth Route and New Fourth armies: "Guerrilla warfare is basic, but lose no chance for mobile warfare under favorable conditions."[9] He raised guerrilla warfare to the level of strategy, because, if they are to defeat a formidable enemy, revolutionary armed forces should not fight with a reckless disregard for the consequences when there is a great disparity between their own strength and the enemy's. If they do, they will suffer serious losses and bring heavy setbacks to the revolution. Guerrilla warfare is the only way to mobilize and apply the whole strength of the people against the enemy, the only way to expand our forces in the course of the war, deplete and weaken the enemy, gradually change the balance of forces between the enemy and ourselves, switch from guerrilla to mobile warfare, and finally defeat the enemy.

In the initial period of the Second Revolutionary Civil War, Comrade Mao Tse-tung enumerated the basic tactics of guerrilla warfare as follows:

The enemy advances, we retreat; the enemy camps, we harass; the enemy tires, we attack; the enemy retreats, we pursue.[10]

Guerrilla war tactics were further developed during the War of Resistance Against Japan. In the base areas behind the enemy lines, everybody joined in the fighting—the troops and the civilian population, men and women, old and young; every single village fought. Various ingenious methods of fighting were devised, including "sparrow warfare,"[11] landmine warfare, tunnel warfare, sabotage warfare, and guerrilla warfare on lakes and rivers.

In the later period of the War of Resistance Against Japan and during the Third Revolutionary Civil War, we switched our strategy from that of guerrilla warfare as the primary form of fighting to that of mobile warfare in the light of the changes in the balance of forces between the enemy and ourselves. By the middle, and especially the later, period of the Third Revolutionary Civil War, our operations had developed into large-scale mobile warfare, including the storming of big cities.

War of annihilation is the fundamental guiding principle of our military operations. This guiding principle should be put into effect regardless of whether mobile or guerrilla warfare is the primary form of fighting. It is true that in guerrilla warfare much should be done to disrupt and harass the enemy, but it is still necessary actively to advocate and fight battles of annihilation whenever conditions are favorable. In mobile warfare superior forces must be concentrated in every battle so that the enemy forces can be wiped out one by one. Comrade Mao Tse-tung has pointed out:

> A battle in which the enemy is routed is not basically decisive in a contest with a foe of great strength. A battle of annihilation, on the other hand, produces a great and immediate impact on any enemy. Injuring all of a man's ten fingers is not as effective as chopping off one, and routing ten enemy divisions is not as effective as annihilating one of them.[12]

Battles of annihilation are the most effective way of hitting the enemy; each time one of his brigades or regiments is wiped out, he will have one brigade or one regiment less, and the enemy forces will be demoralized and will disintegrate. By fighting battles of annihilation, our army is able to take prisoners of war or capture weapons from the enemy in every battle, and the morale of our army rises, our army units get bigger, our weapons become better, and our combat effectiveness continually increases.

In his celebrated ten cardinal military principles Comrade Mao Tse-tung pointed out:

> In every battle, concentrate an absolutely superior force (two, three, four, and sometimes even five or six times the enemy's strength), encircle the enemy forces completely, strive to wipe them out thoroughly and do not let any escape from the net. In special circumstances, use the method of dealing crushing blows to the enemy, that is, concentrate all our strength to make a frontal attack and also to attack one or both of his flanks, with the aim of wiping out one part and routing another so that our army can swiftly move its troops to smash other enemy forces. Strive to avoid battles of attrition in which we lose more than we gain or only break even. In this way, although we are inferior as a whole (in terms of numbers), we are absolutely superior in every part and every specific campaign, and this ensures victory in the campaign. As time goes on, we shall become superior as a whole and eventually wipe out all the enemy.[13]

At the same time, he said that we should first attack dispersed or isolated enemy forces and only attack concentrated and strong enemy forces later; that we should strive to wipe out the enemy through mobile warfare; that we should fight no battle unprepared and fight no battle we are not sure of winning; and that in any battle we fight we should develop our army's strong points and its excellent style of fighting. These are the major principles of fighting a war of annihilation.

In order to annihilate the enemy, we must adopt the policy of luring him in deep and abandon some cities and districts of our own accord in a planned way, so as to let him in. It is only after letting the enemy in that the people can take part in the war in various ways and that the power of a people's war can be fully exerted. It is only after letting the enemy in that he can be compelled to divide up his forces, take on heavy burdens, and commit mistakes. In other words, we must let the enemy become elated, stretch out all his ten fingers, and become hopelessly bogged down. Thus, we can concentrate superior forces to destroy the enemy forces one by one, to eat them up mouthful by mouthful. Only by wiping out the enemy's effective strength can cities and localities be finally held or seized. We are firmly against dividing up our forces to defend all positions and putting up resistance at every place for fear that our territory might be lost and our pots and pans smashed; this can neither wipe out the enemy forces nor hold cities or localities.

Comrade Mao Tse-tung has provided a masterly summary of the strategy and tactics of people's war: You fight in your way and we fight in ours; we fight when we can win and move away when we can't.

In other words, you rely on modern weapons and we rely on highly conscious revolutionary people; you give full play to your superiority and we give full play to ours; you have your way of fighting and we have ours. When you want to fight us, we don't let you and you can't even find us. But when we want to fight you, we make sure that you can't get away and we hit you squarely on the chin and wipe you out. When we are able to wipe you out, we do so with a vengeance; when we can't, we see to it that you don't wipe us out. It is opportunism if one won't fight when one can win. It is adventurism if one insists on fighting when one can't win. Fighting is the pivot of all our strategy and tactics. It is because of the necessity of fighting that we admit the necessity of moving away. The sole purpose of moving away is to fight and bring about the final and complete destruction of the enemy. This strategy and these tactics can be applied only when one relies on the broad masses of the people, and such application brings the superiority of people's war into full play. However superior he may be in technical equipment and whatever tricks he may resort to, the enemy will find himself in the passive position of having to receive blows, and the initiative will always be in our hands.

We grew from a small and weak to a large and strong force and finally defeated formidable enemies at home and abroad because we carried out the strategy and tactics of people's war. During the eight years of War of Resistance Against Japan, the people's army led by the Chinese Communist Party fought more than 125,000 engagements with the enemy and put out of action more than 1,700,000 Japanese and puppet troops. In the three years of the War of Liberation, we put eight million of the Kuomintang's reactionary troops out of action and won the great victory of the people's revolution.

Adhere to the Policy of Self-Reliance

The Chinese people's War of Resistance Against Japan was an important part of the Anti-Fascist World War. The victory of the Anti-Fascist War as a whole was the result of the common struggle of the people of the world. By its participation in the war against Japan at the final stage, the Soviet army under the leadership of the Communist party of the Soviet Union headed by Stalin played a significant part in bringing about the defeat of Japanese imperialism. Great contributions were made by the peoples of Korea, Viet Nam, Mongolia, Laos, Cambodia, Indonesia, Burma, India, Pakistan, Malaya, the Philippines, Thailand, and certain other Asian countries. The people of the Americas, Oceania, Europe, and Africa also made their contribution.

Under extremely difficult circumstances, the Communist Party of Japan and the revolutionary forces of the Japanese people kept up their valiant and staunch struggle, and played their part in the defeat of Japanese fascism.

The common victory was won by all the peoples, who gave one another support and encouragement. Yet each country was, above all, liberated as a result of its own people's efforts.

The Chinese people enjoyed the support of other peoples in winning both the War of Resistance Against Japan and the People's Liberation War, and yet victory was mainly the result of the Chinese people's own efforts. Certain people assert that China's victory in the War of Resistance was due entirely to foreign assistance. This absurd assertion is in tune with that of the Japanese militarists.

The liberation of the masses is accomplished by the masses themselves— this is a basic principle of Marxism-Leninism. Revolution or people's war in any country is the business of the masses in that country and should be carried out primarily by their own efforts; there is no other way.

During the War of Resistance Against Japan, our party maintained that China should rely mainly on her own strength while at the same time trying to get as much foreign assistance as possible. We firmly opposed the Kuomintang ruling clique's policy of exclusive reliance on foreign aid. In the eyes of the Kuomintang and Chiang Kai-shek, China's industry and agriculture were no good, her weapons and equipment were no good, nothing in China was any good, so that if she wanted to defeat Japan, she had to depend on other countries, and particularly on the U.S.-British imperialists. This was completely slavish thinking. Our policy was diametrically opposed to that of the Kuomintang. Our party held that it was possible to exploit the contradictions between U.S.-British imperialism and Japanese imperialism, but that no reliance could be placed on the former. In fact, the U.S.-British imperialists repeatedly plotted to bring about a "Far Eastern Munich" in order to arrive at a compromise with Japanese imperialism at China's expense, and for a considerable period of time they provided the Japanese aggressors with war *matériel*. In helping China during that period, the U.S. imperialists harbored the sinister design of turning China into a colony of their own.

Comrade Mao Tse-tung said: "China has to rely mainly on her own efforts in the War of Resistance."[14] He added, "We hope for foreign aid but cannot be dependent on it; we depend on our own efforts, on the creative power of the whole army and the entire people."[15]

Self-reliance was especially important for the people's armed forces and the Liberated Areas led by our party.

The Kuomintang government gave the Eighth Route and New Fourth armies some small allowances in the initial stage of the anti-Japanese war but gave them not a single penny later. The Liberated Areas faced great difficulties as a result of the Japanese imperialists' savage attacks and brutal "mopping-up" campaigns, of the Kuomintang's military encirclement and economic blockade, and of natural calamities. The difficulties were particularly great in the years 1941 and 1942, when we were very short of food and clothing.

What were we to do? Comrade Mao Tse-tung asked: How has mankind managed to keep alive from time immemorial? Has it not been by men using their hands to provide for themselves? Why should we, their latter-day descendants, be devoid of this tiny bit of wisdom? Why can't we use our own hands?

The Central Committee of the party and Comrade Mao Tse-tung put forward the policies of "ample food and clothing through self-reliance" and "develop the economy and ensure supplies," and the army and the people of the Liberated Areas accordingly launched an extensive production campaign, with the main emphasis on agriculture.

Difficulties are not invincible monsters. If everyone cooperates and fights them, they will be overcome. The Kuomintang reactionaries thought that it could starve us to death by cutting off allowances and imposing an economic blockade, but in fact it helped us by stimulating us to rely on our own efforts to surmount our difficulties. While launching the great campaign for production, we applied the policy of "better troops and simpler administration" and economized in the use of manpower and material resources; thus we not only surmounted the severe material difficulties and successfully met the crisis, but lightened the people's burden, improved their livelihood and laid the material foundations for victory in the anti-Japanese war.

The problem of military equipment was solved mainly by relying on the capture of arms from the enemy, though we did turn out some weapons too. Chiang Kai-shek, the Japanese imperialists, and the U.S. imperialists have all been our "chiefs of transportation corps." The arsenals of the imperialists always provide the oppressed peoples and nations with arms.

The people's armed forces led by our party independently waged people's war on a large scale and won great victories without any material aid from outside, both during the more than eight years of the anti-Japanese war and during the more than three years of the People's War of Liberation.

Comrade Mao Tse-tung has said that our fundamental policy should rest on the foundation of our own strength. Only by relying on our own efforts can we in all circumstances remain invincible.

The peoples of the world invariably support each other in their struggles against imperialism and its lackeys. Those countries which have won victory are duty bound to support and aid the peoples who have not yet done so. Nevertheless, foreign aid can only play a supplementary role.

In order to make a revolution and to fight a people's war and be victorious, it is imperative to adhere to the policy of self-defence, rely on the strength of the masses in one's own country, and prepare to carry on the fight independently even when all material aid from outside is cut off. If one does not operate by one's own efforts, does not independently ponder and solve the problems of the revolution in one's own country, and does not rely on the strength of the masses but leans wholly on foreign aid—even though this be aid from socialist countries which persist in revolution—no victory can be won or be consolidated even if it is won.

The International Significance of Comrade Mao Tse-tung's Theory of People's War

The Chinese revolution is a continuation of the great October Revolution. The road of the October Revolution is the common road for all people's revolutions. The Chinese revolution and the October Revolution have in common the following basic characteristics: (1) Both were led by the working class with a Marxist-Leninist party as its nucleus. (2) Both were based on the worker-peasant alliance. (3) In both cases state power was seized through violent revolution and the dictatorship of the proletariat was established. (4) In both cases the socialist system was built after victory in the revolution. (5) Both were component parts of the proletarian world revolution.

Naturally, the Chinese revolution had its own peculiar characteristics. The October Revolution took place in imperialist Russia, but the Chinese revolution broke out in a semicolonial and semifeudal country. The former was a proletarian socialist revolution, while the latter developed into a socialist revolution after the complete victory of the new-democratic revolution. The October Revolution began with armed uprisings in the cities and then spread to the countryside, while the Chinese revolution won nationwide victory through the encirclement of the cities from the rural areas and the final capture of the cities.

Comrade Mao Tse-tung's great merit lies in the fact that he has succeeded in integrating the universal truth of Marxism-Leninism with the concrete practice of the Chinese revolution and has enriched and developed Marxism-Leninism by his masterly generalization and summation of the experience gained during the Chinese people's protracted revolutionary struggle.

Comrade Mao Tse-tung's theory of people's war has been proved by the long practice of the Chinese revolution to be in accord with the objective laws of such wars and to be invincible. It has not only been valid for China, it is a great contribution to the revolutionary struggles of the oppressed nations and peoples throughout the world.

The people's war led by the Chinese Communist Party, comprising the War of Resistance and the Revolutionary Civil wars, lasted for twenty-two years. It constitutes the most drawn-out and most complex people's war led by the proletariat in modern history, and it has been the richest in experience.

In the last analysis, the Marxist-Leninist theory of proletarian revolution is the theory of the seizure of state power by revolutionary violence, the theory of countering war against the people by people's war. As Marx so aptly put it, "Force is the midwife of every old society pregnant with a new one."[16]

It was on the basis of the lessons derived from the people's wars in China that Comrade Mao Tse-tung, using the simplest and the most vivid language, advanced the famous thesis that "political power grows out of the barrel of a gun."[17]

He clearly pointed out:

> The seizure of power by armed force, the settlement of the issue by war, is the central task and the highest form of revolution. This Marxist-Leninist principle of revolution holds good universally, for China and for all other countries.[18]

War is the product of imperialism and the system of exploitation of man by man. Lenin said that "war is always and everywhere begun by the exploiters themselves, by the ruling and oppressing classes."[19] So long as imperialism and the system of exploitation of man by man exist, the imperialists and reactionaries will invariably rely on armed force to maintain their reactionary rule and impose war on the oppressed nations and peoples. This is an objective law independent of man's will.

In the world today, all the imperialists headed by the United States and their lackeys, without exception, are strengthening their state machinery and especially their armed forces. U.S. imperialism, in particular, is carrying out armed aggression and suppression everywhere.

What should the oppressed nations and the oppressed people do in the face of wars of aggression and armed suppression by the imperialists and their lackeys? Should they submit and remain slaves in perpetuity? Or should they rise in resistance and fight for their liberation?

Comrade Mao Tse-tung answered this question in vivid terms. He said that after long investigation and study the Chinese people discovered that all the imperialists and their lackeys "have swords in their hands and are out to kill. The people have come to understand this and so act after the same fashion."[20] This is called doing unto them what they do unto us.

In the last analysis, whether one dares to wage a tit-for-tat struggle against armed aggression and suppression by the imperialists and their lackeys, whether one dares to fight a people's war against them, means whether one dares to embark on revolution. This is the most effective touchstone for distinguishing genuine from fake revolutionaries and Marxist-Leninists.

In view of the fact that some people were afflicted with the fear of the imperialists and reactionaries, Comrade Mao Tse-tung put forward his famous thesis that "the imperialists and all reactionaries are paper tigers." He said,

> All reactionaries are paper tigers. In appearance, the reactionaries are terrifying, but in reality they are not so powerful. From a long-term point of view, it is not the reactionaries but the people who are really powerful.[21]

The history of people's war in China and other countries provides conclusive evidence that the growth of the people's revolutionary forces from weak and small beginnings into strong and large forces is a universal law of development of class struggle, a universal law of development of people's war. A people's war inevitably meets with many difficulties, with ups and downs and setbacks in the course of its development, but no force can alter its general trend towards inevitable triumph.

Comrade Mao Tse-tung points out that we must despise the enemy strategically and take full account of him tactically.

To despise the enemy strategically is an elementary requirement for a revolutionary. Without the courage to despise the enemy and without daring to win, it will be simply impossible to make revolution and wage a people's war, let alone to achieve victory.

It is also very important for revolutionaries to take full account of the enemy tactically. It is likewise impossible to win victory in a people's war without taking full account of the enemy tactically and without examining the concrete conditions, without being prudent and giving great attention to the study of the art of struggle and without adopting appropriate forms of struggle in the concrete practice of the revolution in each country and with regard to each concrete problem of struggle.

Dialectical and historical materialism teaches us that what is important primarily is not that which at the given moment seems to be durable and yet is already beginning to die away, but that which is arising and developing, even though at the given moment it may not appear to be durable, for only that which is arising and developing is invincible.

Why can the apparently weak new-born forces always triumph over the decadent forces which appear so powerful? The reason is that truth is on their side and that the masses are on their side, while the reactionary classes are always divorced from the masses and set themselves against the masses.

This has been borne out by the victory of the Chinese revolution, by the history of all revolutions, the whole history of class struggle and the entire history of mankind.

The imperialists are extremely afraid of Comrade Mao Tse-tung's thesis that "imperialism and all reactionaries are paper tigers," and the revisionists are extremely hostile to it. They all oppose and attack this thesis and the philistines follow suit by ridiculing it. But all this cannot in the least diminish its importance. The light of truth cannot be dimmed by anybody.

Comrade Mao Tse-tung's theory of people's war solves not only the problem of daring to fight a people's war, but also that of how to wage it.

Comrade Mao Tse-tung is a great statesman and military scientist, proficient at directing war in accordance with its laws. By the line and policies, the strategy and tactics he formulated for the people's war, he led the Chinese people in steering the ship of the people's war past all hidden reefs to the shores of victory in most complicated and difficult conditions.

It must be emphasized that Comrade Mao Tse-tung's theory of the establishment of rural revolutionary base areas and the encirclement of the cities from the countryside is of outstanding and universal practical importance for the present revolutionary struggles of all the oppressed nations and peoples, and particularly for the revolutionary struggles of the oppressed nations and peoples in Asia, Africa, and Latin America against imperialism and its lackeys.

Many countries and peoples in Asia, Africa, and Latin America are now being subjected to aggression and enslavement on a serious scale by the imperialists headed by the United States and their lackeys. The basic political and economic conditions in many of these countries have many similarities to those that prevailed in old China. As in China, the peasant question is extremely important in these regions. The peasants constitute the main force of the national-democratic revolution against the imperialists and their lackeys. In committing aggression against these countries, the imperialists usually begin by seizing the big cities and the main lines of communication, but they are unable to bring the vast countryside completely under their control. The countryside, and the countryside alone, can provide the broad areas in which the revolutionaries can maneuver freely. The countryside, and the countryside alone, can provide the revolutionary bases from which the revolutionaries can go forward to final victory. Precisely for this reason, Comrade Mao Tse-tung's theory of establishing revolutionary base areas in the rural districts and encircling the cities from the countryside is attracting more and more attention among the people in these regions.

Taking the entire globe, if North America and Western Europe can be called "the cities of the world," then Asia, Africa, and Latin America constitute "the rural areas of the world." Since World War II, the proletarian revolutionary movement has for various reasons been temporarily held back in the North American and Western European capitalist countries, while the people's revolutionary movement in Asia, Africa, and Latin America has been growing vigorously. In a sense, the contemporary world revolution also presents a picture of the encirclement of cities by the rural areas. In the final analysis, the whole cause of world revolution hinges on the revolutionary struggles of the Asian, African, and Latin American peoples who make up the overwhelming majority of the world's population. The socialist countries should regard it as their internationalist duty to support the people's revolutionary struggles in Asia, Africa, and Latin America.

The October Revolution opened up a new era in the revolution of the oppressed nations. The victory of the October Revolution built a bridge between the socialist revolution of the proletariat of the West and the national-democratic revolution of the colonial and semicolonial countries of the East. The Chinese revolution has successfully solved the problem of how to link up the national-democratic with the socialist revolution in the colonial and semicolonial countries.

Comrade Mao Tse-tung has pointed out that, in the epoch since the October Revolution, anti-imperialist revolution in any colonial or semicolonial country is no longer part of the old bourgeois, or capitalist world revolution, but is part of the new world revolution, the proletarian-socialist world revolution.

Comrade Mao Tse-tung has formulated a complete theory of the new democratic revolution. He indicated that this revolution, which is different from all others, can only be, nay, must be, a revolution against imperialism, feudalism, and bureaucrat capitalism waged by the broad masses of the people under the leadership of the proletariat.

This means that the revolution can only be, nay, must be, led by the proletariat and the genuinely revolutionary party armed with Marxism-Leninism, and by no other class or party.

This means that the revolution embraces in its ranks not only the workers, peasants, and the urban petty bourgeoisie, but also the national bourgeoisie and other patriotic and anti-imperialist democrats.

This means, finally, that the revolution is directed against imperialism, feudalism, and bureaucrat capitalism.

The new-democratic revolution leads to socialism, and not to capitalism.

Comrade Mao Tse-tung's theory of the new-democratic revolution is the Marxist-Leninist theory of revolution by stages as well as the Marxist-Leninist theory of uninterrupted revolution.

Comrade Mao Tse-tung made a correct distinction between the two revolutionary stages, i.e., the national-democratic and the socialist revolutions; at the same time he correctly and closely linked the two. The national-democratic revolution is the necessary preparation for the socialist revolution, and the socialist revolution is the inevitable sequel to the national-democratic revolution. There is no Great Wall between the two revolutionary stages. But the socialist revolution is only possible after the completion of the national-democratic revolution. The more thorough the national-democratic revolution, the better the conditions for the socialist revolution.

The experience of the Chinese revolution shows that the tasks of the national-democratic revolution can be fulfilled only through long and tortuous struggles. In this stage of revolution, imperialism and its lackeys are the principal enemy. In the struggle against imperialism and its lackeys, it is necessary to rally all anti-imperialist patriotic forces, including the national bourgeoisie and all patriotic personages. All those patriotic personages from among the bourgeoisie and other exploiting classes who join the anti-imperialist struggle play a progressive historical role; they are not tolerated by imperialism but welcomed by the proletariat.

It is very harmful to confuse the two stages, that is, the national-democratic and the socialist revolutions. Comrade Mao Tse-tung criticized the wrong idea of "accomplishing both at one stroke," and pointed out that this utopian idea could only weaken the struggle against imperialism and its lackeys, the most urgent task at that time. The Kuomintang reactionaries and the Trotskyites they hired during the War of Resistance deliberately confused these two stages of the Chinese revolution, proclaiming the "theory of a single revolution" and preaching so-called "socialism" without any Communist party. With this preposterous theory they attempted to swallow up the Communist party, wipe out any revolution and prevent the advance of the national-democratic revolution, and they used it as a pretext for their nonresistance and capitulation to imperialism. This reactionary theory was buried long ago by the history of the Chinese revolution.

The Khrushchev revisionists are now actively preaching that socialism can be built without the proletariat and without a genuinely revolutionary party armed with the advanced proletarian ideology, and they have cast the fundamental tenets of Marxism-Leninism to the four winds. The revisionists' purpose is solely to divert the oppressed nations from their struggle against imperialism and sabotage their national-democratic revolution, all in the service of imperialism.

The Chinese revolution provides a successful lesson for making a thoroughgoing national-democratic revolution under the leadership of the proletariat; it likewise provides a successful lesson for the timely transition from the national-democratic revolution to the socialist revolution under the leadership of the proletariat.

Mao Tse-tung's thought has been the guide to the victory of the Chinese revolution. It has integrated the universal truth of Marxism-Leninism with the concrete practice of the Chinese revolution and creatively developed Marxism-Leninism, thus adding new weapons to the arsenal of Marxism-Leninism.

Ours is the epoch in which world capitalism and imperialism are heading for their doom and socialism and communism are marching to victory. Comrade Mao Tse-tung's theory of people's war is not only a product of the Chinese revolution, but has also the characteristics of our epoch. The new experience gained in the people's revolutionary struggles in various countries since World War II has provided continuous evidence that Mao Tse-tung's thought is a common asset of the revolutionary people of the whole world. This is the great international significance of the thought of Mao Tse-tung.

Defeat U.S. Imperialism and Its Lackeys by People's War

Since World War II, U.S. imperialism has stepped into the shoes of

German, Japanese, and Italian fascism and has been trying to build a great American empire by dominating and enslaving the whole world. It is actively fostering Japanese and West German militarism as its chief accomplices in unleashing a world war. Like a vicious wolf, it is bullying and enslaving various peoples, plundering their wealth, encroaching upon their countries' sovereignty, and interfering in their internal affairs. It is the most rabid aggressor in human history and the most ferocious common enemy of the people of the world. Every people or country in the world that wants revolution, independence, and peace cannot but direct the spearhead of its struggle against U.S. imperialism.

Just as the Japanese imperialists' policy of subjugating China made it possible for the Chinese people to form the broadest possible united front against them, so the U.S. imperialists' policy of seeking world domination makes it possible for the people throughout the world to unite all the forces that can be united and form the broadest possible united front for a converging attack on U.S. imperialism.

At present, the main battlefield of the fierce struggle between the people of the world on the one side and U.S. imperialism and its lackeys on the other is the vast area of Asia, Africa, and Latin America. In the world as a whole, this is the area where the people suffer worst from imperialist oppression and where imperialist rule is most vulnerable. Since World War II, revolutionary storms have been rising in this area, and today they have become the most important force directly pounding U.S. imperialism. The contradiction between the revolutionary peoples of Asia, Africa, and Latin America and the imperialists headed by the United States is the principal contradiction in the contemporary world. The development of this contradiction is promoting the struggle of the people of the whole world against U.S. imperialism and its lackeys.

Since World War II, people's war has increasingly demonstrated its power in Asia, Africa, and Latin America. The peoples of China, Korea, Viet Nam, Laos, Cuba, Indonesia, Algeria and other countries have waged people's wars against the imperialists and their lackeys and won great victories. The classes leading these people's wars may vary, and so may the breadth and depth of mass mobilization and the extent of victory, but the victories in these people's wars have very much weakened and pinned down the forces of imperialism, upset the U.S. imperialist plan to launch a world war, and become mighty factors defending world peace.

Today, the conditions are more favorable than ever before for the waging of people's wars by the revolutionary peoples of Asia, Africa, and Latin America against U.S. imperialism and its lackeys.

Since World War II and the succeeding years of revolutionary upsurge, there has been a great rise in the level of political consciousness and the degree of organization of the people in all countries, and the resources available to them for mutual support and aid have greatly increased. The whole capitalist-imperialist system has become drastically weaker and is in the process of increasing convulsion and disintegration. After World War I, the imperialists lacked the power to destroy the new-born socialist Soviet state, but they were still able to suppress the people's revolutionary movements in some countries in the parts of the world under their own rule and so maintain a short period of comparative stability. Since World War II, however, not only have they been unable to stop a number of countries from taking the socialist road, but they are no longer capable of holding back the surging tide of the people's revolutionary movements in the areas under their own rule.

U.S. imperialism is stronger, but also more vulnerable, than any imperialism of the past. It sets itself against the people of the whole world, including the people of the United States. Its human, military, material, and financial resources are far from sufficient for the realization of its ambition of dominating the whole world. U.S. imperialism has further weakened itself by occupying so many places in the world, over-reaching itself, stretching its fingers out wide and dispersing its strength, with its rear so far away and its supply lines so long. As Comrade Mao Tse-tung has said, "Wherever it commits aggression, it puts a new noose around its neck. It is besieged ring upon ring by the people of the whole world."[22]

When committing aggression in a foreign country, U.S. imperialism can only employ part of its forces, which are sent to fight an unjust war far from their native land and therefore have a low morale, and so U.S. imperialism is beset with great difficulties. The people subjected to its aggression are having a trial of strength with U.S. imperialism neither in Washington nor New York, neither in Honolulu nor Florida, but are fighting for independence and freedom on their own soil. Once they are mobilized on a broad scale, they will have inexhaustible strength. Thus superiority will belong not to the United States but to the people subjected to its aggression. The latter, though apparently weak and small, are really more powerful than U.S. imperialism.

The struggles waged by the different peoples against U.S. imperialism reinforce each other and merge into a torrential world-wide tide of opposition to U.S. imperialism. The more successful the development of people's war in a given region, the larger the number of U.S. imperialist forces that can be pinned down and depleted there. When the U.S. aggressors are hard pressed in one place, they have no alternative but to loosen their grip on others. Therefore, the conditions become more favorable for the people elsewhere to wage struggles against U.S. imperialism and its lackeys.

Everything is divisible. And so is this colossus of U.S. imperialism. It can be split up and defeated. The peoples of Asia, Africa, Latin America, and other regions can destroy it piece by piece, some striking at its head and others at its feet. That is why the greatest fear of U.S. imperialism is that people's wars will be launched in different parts of the world, and particularly in Asia, Africa, and Latin America, and why it regards people's war as a mortal danger.

U.S. imperialism relies solely on its nuclear weapons to intimidate people. But these weapons cannot save U.S. imperialism from its doom. Nuclear weapons cannot be used lightly. U.S. imperialism has been condemned by the people of the whole world for its towering crime of dropping two atom bombs on Japan. If it uses nuclear weapons again, it will become isolated in the extreme. Moreover, the U.S. monopoly of nuclear weapons has long been broken; U.S. imperialism has these weapons, but others have them too. If it threatens other countries with nuclear weapons, U.S. imperialism will expose its own country to the same threat. For this reason, it will meet with strong opposition not only from the people elsewhere but also inevitably from the people in its own country. Even if U.S. imperialism brazenly uses nuclear weapons, it cannot conquer the people, who are indomitable.

However highly developed modern weapons and technical equipment may be and however complicated the methods of modern warfare, in the final analysis the outcome of a war will be decided by the sustained fighting of the ground forces, by the fighting at close quarters on battlefields, by the political consciousness of the men, by their courage and spirit of sacrifice. Here the weak points of U.S. imperialism will be completely laid bare, while the superiority of the revolutionary people will be brought into full play. The reactionary troops of U.S. imperialism cannot possibly be endowed with the courage and the spirit of sacrifice possessed by the revolutionary people. The spiritual atom bomb which the revolutionary people possess is a far more powerful and useful weapon than the physical atom bomb.

Viet Nam is the most convincing current example of a victim of aggression defeating U.S. imperialism by a people's war. The United States has made South Viet Nam a testing ground for the suppression of people's war. It has carried on this experiment for many years, and everybody can now see that the U.S. aggressors are unable to find a way of coping with people's war. On the other hand, the Vietnamese people have brought the power of people's war into full play in their struggle against the U.S.

aggressors. The U.S. aggressors are in danger of being swamped in the people's war in Viet Nam. They are deeply worried that their defeat in Viet Nam will lead to a chain reaction. They are expanding the war in an attempt to save themselves from defeat. But the more they expand the war, the greater will be the chain reaction. The more they escalate the war, the heavier will be their fall and the more disastrous their defeat. The people in other parts of the world will see still more clearly that U.S. imperialism can be defeated, and that what the Vietnamese people can do, they can do too.

History has proved and will go on proving that people's war is the most effective weapon against U.S. imperialism and its lackeys. All revolutionary people will learn to wage people's war against U.S. imperialism and its lackeys. They will take up arms, learn to fight battles and become skilled in waging people's war, though they have not done so before. U.S. imperialism like a mad bull dashing from place to place, will finally be burned to ashes in the blazing fires of the people's wars it has provoked by its own actions.

The Khrushchev Revisionists Are
Betrayers of People's War

The Khrushchev revisionists have come to the rescue of U.S. imperialism just when it is most panic-stricken and helpless in its efforts to cope with people's war. Working hand in glove with the U.S. imperialists, they are doing their utmost to spread all kinds of arguments against people's war and, wherever they can, they are scheming to undermine it by overt or covert means.

The fundamental reason why the Khrushchev revisionists are opposed to people's war is that they have no faith in the masses and are afraid of U.S. imperialism, of war, and of revolution. Like all other opportunists, they are blind to the power of the masses and do not believe that the revolutionary people are capable of defeating imperialism. They submit to the nuclear blackmail of the U.S. imperialists and are afraid that, if the oppressed peoples and nations rise up to fight people's wars or the people of socialist countries repulse U.S. imperialist aggression, U.S. imperialism will become incensed, they themselves will become involved and their fond dream of Soviet-U.S. cooperation to dominate the world will be spoiled.

Ever since Lenin led the great October Revolution to victory, the experience of innumerable revolutionary wars has borne out the truth that a revolutionary people who rise up with only their bare hands at the out-set finally succeed in defeating the ruling classes who are armed to the teeth. The poorly armed have defeated the better armed. People's armed forces, beginning with only primitive swords, spears, rifles, and hand-grenades, have in the end defeated the imperialist forces armed with mod-ern aeroplanes, tanks, heavy artillery, and atom bombs. Guerrilla forces have ultimately defeated regular armies. "Amateurs" who were never trained in any military schools have eventually defeated "professionals" graduated from military academies. And so on and so forth. Things stub-bornly develop in a way that runs counter to the assertions of the revi-sionists, and facts are slapping them in the face.

The Khrushchev revisionists insist that a nation without nuclear weap-ons is incapable of defeating an enemy with nuclear weapons, whatever methods of fighting it may adopt. This is tantamount to saying that any-one without nuclear weapons is destined to come to grief, destined to be bullied and annihilated, and must either capitulate to the enemy when confronted with his nuclear weapons or come under the "protection" of some other nuclear power and submit to its beck and call. Isn't this the jungle law of survival par excellence? Isn't this helping the imperialists in their nuclear blackmail? Isn't this openly forbidding people to make revolution?

The Khrushchev revisionists assert that nuclear weapons and strategic rocket units are decisive while conventional forces are insignificant, and that a militia is just a heap of human flesh. For ridiculous reasons such as these, they oppose the mobilization of and reliance on the masses in the socialist countries to get prepared to use people's war against imperialist aggression. They have staked the whole future of their country on nu-clear weapons and are engaged in a nuclear gamble with U.S. imperialism, with which they are trying to strike a political deal. Their theory of military strategy is the theory that nuclear weapons decide everything. Their line in army building is the bourgeois line which ignores the human factor and sees only the material factor and which regards technique as everything and politics as nothing.

The Khrushchev revisionists maintain that a single spark in any part of the globe may touch off a world nuclear conflagration and bring destruc-tion to mankind. If this were true, our planet would have been destroyed time and time again. There have been wars of national liberation through-out the twenty years since World War II. But has any single one of them developed into a world war? Isn't it true that the U.S. imperialists' plans for a world war have been upset precisely thanks to the wars of national liberation in Asia, Africa, and Latin America? By contrast, those who have done their utmost to stamp out the "sparks" of people's war have in fact encouraged U.S. imperialism in its aggressions and wars.

The Khrushchev revisionists claim that if their general line of "peaceful coexistence, peaceful transition, and peaceful competition" is followed, the oppressed will be liberated and "a world without weapons, without armed forces, and without wars" will come into being. But the inexorable fact is that imperialism and reaction headed by the United States are zealously priming their war machine and are daily engaged in sanguinary suppression of the revolutionary peoples and in the threat and use of armed force against independent countries. The kind of rubbish peddled by the Khrushchev revisionists has already taken a great toll of lives in a number of countries. Are these painful lessons, paid for in blood, still insufficient? The essence of the general line of the Khrushchev revisionists is nothing other than the demand that all the oppressed peoples and nations and all the countries which have won independence should lay down their arms and place themselves at the mercy of the U.S. imperialists and their lackeys who are armed to the teeth.

"While magistrates are allowed to burn down houses, the common people are forbidden even to light lamps." Such is the way of the imperialists and reactionaries. Subscribing to this imperialist philosophy, the Khrushchev revisionists shout at the Chinese people standing in the forefront of the fight for world peace: "You are bellicose!" Gentlemen, your abuse adds to our credit. It is this very "bellicosity" of ours that helps to prevent imperialism from unleashing a world war. The people are "bellicose" because they have to defend themselves and because the imperialists and reactionaries force them to be so. It is also the imperialists and reactionaries who have taught the people the arts of war. We are simply using revolutionary "bellicosity" to cope with counterrevolutionary bellicosity. How can it be argued that the imperialists and their lackeys may kill people everywhere, while the people must not strike back in self-defence or help one another? What kind of logic is this? The Khrushchev revisionists regard imperialists like Kennedy and Johnson as "sensible" and describe us together with all those who dare to carry out armed defence against imperialist aggression as "bellicose." This has revealed the Khrushchev revisionists in their true colors as the accomplices of imperialist gangsters.

We know that war brings destruction, sacrifice, and suffering on the people. But the destruction, sacrifice, and suffering will be much greater if no resistance is offered to imperialist armed aggression and the people become willing slaves. The sacrifice of a small number of people in revolutionary wars is repaid by security for whole nations, whole countries, and even the whole of mankind; temporary suffering is repaid by lasting or even perpetual peace and happiness. War can temper the people and push history forward. In this sense, war is a great school.

When discussing World War I, Lenin said, "The war has brought hunger to the most civilized countries, to those most culturally developed. On the other hand, the war, as a tremendous historical process, has accelerated social development to an unheard-of degree."[23] Then he added, "War has shaken up the masses, its untold horrors and suffering have awakened them. War has given history momentum and it is now flying with locomotive speed."[24] If the arguments of the Khrushchev revisionists are to be believed, would not that make Lenin the worst of all "bellicose elements"?

In diametrical opposition to the Khrushchev revisionists, the Marxist-Leninists and revolutionary people never take a gloomy view of war. Our attitude towards imperialist wars of aggression has always been clear-cut. First, we are against them, and secondly, we are not afraid of them. We will destroy whoever attacks us. As for revolutionary wars waged by the oppressed nations and peoples, so far from opposing them, we invariably give them firm support and active aid. It has been so in the past, it remains so in the present and, when we grow in strength as time goes on, we will give them still more support and aid in the future. It is sheer day-dreaming for anyone to think that, since our revolution has been victorious, our national construction is forging ahead, our national wealth is increasing, and our living conditions are improving, we too will lose our revolutionary fighting will, abandon the cause of world revolution, and discard Marxism-Leninism and proletarian internationalism. Of course, every revolution in a country stems from the demands of its own people. Only when the people in a country are awakened, mobilized, organized, and armed can they overthrow the reactionary rule of imperialism and its lackeys through struggle; their role cannot be replaced or taken over by any people from outside. In this sense, revolution cannot be imported. But this does not exclude mutual sympathy and support on the part of revolutionary peoples in their struggles against the imperialists and their lackeys. Our support and aid to other revolutionary peoples serves precisely to help their self-reliant struggle.

The propaganda of the Khrushchev revisionists against people's war and the publicity they give to defeatism and capitulationism tend to demoralize and spiritually disarm revolutionary people everywhere. These revisionists are doing what the U.S. imperialists are unable to do themselves and are rendering them great service. They have greatly encouraged U.S. imperialism in its war adventures. They have completely betrayed the Marxist-Leninist revolutionary theory of war and have become betrayers of people's war.

To win the struggle against U.S. imperialism and carry people's wars to victory, the Marxist-Leninists and revolutionary people throughout the world must resolutely oppose Khrushchev revisionism.

Today, Khrushchev revisionism has a dwindling audience among the revolutionary people of the world. Wherever there is armed aggression and suppression by imperialism and its lackeys, there are bound to be people's wars against aggression and oppression. It is certain that such wars will develop vigorously. This is an objective law independent of the will of either the U.S. imperialists or the Khrushchev revisionists. The revolutionary people of the world will sweep away everything that stands in the way of their advance. Khrushchev is finished. And the successors to Khrushchev revisionism will fare no better. The imperialists, the reactionaries, and the Khrushchev revisionists, who have all set themselves against people's war, will be swept like dust from the stage of history by the mighty broom of the revolutionary people.

Great changes have taken place in China and the world in the twenty years since the victory of the War of Resistance Against Japan, changes that have made the situation more favorable than ever for the revolutionary people of the world and more unfavorable than ever for imperialism and its lackeys.

When Japanese imperialism launched its war of aggression against China, the Chinese people had only a very small people's army and a very small revolutionary base area, and they were up against the biggest military despot of the East. Yet even then, Comrade Mao Tse-tung said that the Chinese people's war could be won and that Japanese imperialism could be defeated. Today, the revolutionary base areas of the peoples of the world have grown to unprecedented proportions, their revolutionary movement is surging as never before, imperialism is weaker than ever, and U.S. imperialism, the chieftain of world imperialism, is suffering one defeat after another. We can say with even greater confidence that the people's wars can be won and U.S. imperialism can be defeated in all countries.

The peoples of the world now have the lessons of the October Revolution, the Anti-Fascist War, the Chinese people's War of Resistance and War of Liberation, the Korean people's War of Resistance to U.S. Aggression, the Vietnamese people's War of Liberation and their War of Resistance to U.S. Aggression, and the people's revolutionary armed struggles in many other countries. Provided each people studies these lessons well and creatively integrates them with the concrete practice of revolution in their own country, there is no doubt that the revolutionary peoples of the world will stage still more powerful and splendid dramas in the theatre of people's war in their countries and that they will wipe off the earth once and for all the common enemy of all the peoples, U.S. imperialism, and its lackeys.

The struggle of the Vietnamese people against U.S. aggression and for national salvation is now the focus of the struggle of the people of the world against U.S. aggression. The determination of the Chinese people to support and aid the Vietnamese people in their struggle against U.S. aggression and for national salvation is unshakable. No matter what U.S. imperialism may do to expand its war adventure, the Chinese people will do everything in their power to support the Vietnamese people until every single one of the U.S. aggressors is driven out of Viet Nam.

The U.S. imperialists are now clamoring for another trial of strength with the Chinese people, for another large-scale ground war on the Asian mainland. If they insist on following in the footsteps of the Japanese Fascists, well then, they may do so, if they please. The Chinese people definitely have ways of their own for coping with a U.S. imperialist war of aggression. Our methods are no secret. The most important one is still mobilization of the people, reliance on the people, making every one a soldier and waging a people's war.

We want to tell the U.S. imperialists once again that the vast ocean of several hundred million Chinese people in arms will be more than enough to submerge your few million aggressor troops. If you dare to impose war on us, we shall gain freedom of action. It will then not be up to you to decide how the war will be fought. We shall fight in the ways most advantageous to us to destroy the enemy and wherever the enemy can be most easily destroyed. Since the Chinese people were able to destroy the Japanese aggressors twenty years ago, they are certainly still more capable of finishing off the U.S. aggressors today. The naval and air superiority you boast about cannot intimidate the Chinese people, and neither can the atom bomb you brandish at us. If you want to send troops, go ahead, the more the better. We will annihilate as many as you can send, and can even give you receipts. The Chinese people are a great, valiant people. We have the courage to shoulder the heavy burden of combating U.S. imperialism and to contribute our share in the struggle for final victory over this most ferocious enemy of the people of the world.

It must be pointed out in all seriousness that after the victory of the War of Resistance, Taiwan was returned to China. The occupation of Taiwan by U.S. imperialism is absolutely unjustified. Taiwan Province is an inalienable part of Chinese territory. The U.S. imperialists must get out of Taiwan. The Chinese people are determined to liberate Taiwan.

In commemorating the twentieth anniversary of victory in the War of Resistance Against Japan, we must also point out in all solemnity that the Japanese militarists fostered by U.S. imperialism will certainly receive still severer punishment if they ignore the firm opposition of the Japanese people and the people of Asia, again indulge in their pipe-dreams and resume their old road of aggression in Asia.

U.S. imperialism is preparing a world war. But can this save it from its doom? World War I was followed by the birth of the socialist Soviet Union. World War II was followed by the emergence of a series of socialist countries and many nationally independent countries. If the U.S. imperialists should insist on launching a third world war, it can be stated categorically that many more hundreds of millions of people will turn to socialism; the imperialists will then have little room left on the globe; and it is possible that the whole structure of imperialism will collapse.

We are optimistic about the future of the world. We are confident that the people will bring to an end the epoch of wars in human history. Comrade Mao Tse-tung pointed out long ago that war, this monster, "will be finally eliminated by the progress of human society, and in the not too distant future too. But there is only one way to eliminate it, and that is to oppose war with war, to oppose counterrevolutionary war with revolutionary war."[25]

All peoples suffering from U.S. imperialist aggression, oppression, and plunder, unite! Hold aloft the just banner of people's war and fight for the cause of world peace, national liberation, people's democracy, and socialism! Victory will certainly go to the people of the world!

Long live the victory of people's war!

THE BIG VICTORY
THE GREAT TASK 3

by Vo Nguyen Giap

Vo Nguyen Giap, deputy premier, defense minister, and army chief of Communist North Viet Nam, has built a notable military record. He was the first modern Asian commander to drive a European power out of Asia. He is the only commander in a comparatively small nation who has warred successively on two major powers, first France and then the United States.

Giap was born in 1912 of a poor family in what is now central Viet Nam. Giap's father was an anti-French scholar, and young Giap soon followed in his father's footsteps. Giap pursued his education and at the same time became active in the anti-French underground. At the age of eighteen he was arrested for leading student demonstrations and sentenced to three years in prison. The French police commissioner took a liking to the bright young man, however, and got him released from prison after a few months, thus enabling him to continue his education.

Giap won his baccalaureate degree, studied law, and became a history teacher. His particular interest was Napoleon, and he knew every battle move made by the French emperor. Continuing his studies, Giap earned a university degree and finally a doctorate of laws.

In 1926 Giap had joined the *Tan Viet Cach Menh Dang* (Revolutionary Party of New An Nam), a secret organization that advocated political and social reforms. In 1933 he became a member of the Indochinese Communist Party (ICP). By the time he completed his studies, his party work had brought him into prominence. In 1936 he became one of the leading figures in the "Democratic Front," the legal branch of the ICP

that was set up in Tonkin (now North Viet Nam) to participate in political life while the party itself remained a clandestine organization. After
the ICP fomented an insurrection in 1939, Giap, with other leaders, took
refuge in Kwangsi, Southern China. Giap's wife and her sister, however,
were captured by the French and tried by a military tribunal. The sister
was sentenced to death and guillotined. Giap's wife died in prison.

Giap may have spent some time with the Chinese Communists in
Yenan. At any rate, in 1941 he attended a conference in China that led to
the creation of the *Viet Nam Doc Lap Dong Minh Hoi* (League for the
Independence of Viet Nam), or *Viet Minh*. Giap was given the task of
building up the military apparatus of the Viet Minh, an enterprise in
which he displayed organizational skill. Returning secretly to the mountainous region of Upper Tonkin, he spent the next four years raising and
training a guerrilla army backed by an intelligence network. On 22 December 1944 Giap led a unit of thirty-four men in successful attacks on
two French posts on the Chinese border.

From then on, Giap's forces grew steadily. By the time the Japanese
surrendered at the end of World War II—they had taken away control
of Indochina from the French—Giap's men dominated large segments of
the countryside. Giap seized the city of Hanoi, and the "Democratic Republic of Viet Nam" was born.

In the period that followed, Giap devoted himself to the consolidation
of the Viet Minh regime. His first appointment was as minister of the interior in Ho Chi Minh's provisional government of August 1945. In that
capacity he superintended the liquidation of nationalist parties and the
taking over of key posts in the government by Communists or their supporters. Soon afterwards he extended his sphere of activity by taking on
the post of undersecretary of state for defense.

In the spring of 1946 Giap was promoted to general and commander-
in-chief. He remodeled the army on the Communist pattern, introducing
political commissars and indoctrination methods. In November 1946 he
was made minister of defense, a position he had held for some time in all
but name. In July 1947 he was relieved of the Defense Ministry for a
year, but again was made commander in chief of the army.

Politically he distinguished himself as a firm supporter of a tough policy towards France. During the many talks and negotiations to compose
outstanding differences that took place in the first half of 1946, Giap used
his influence to prevent concessions to the French. Thereafter he actively
prepared for the coming conflict and was instrumental in mounting the
Viet Minh attack on Hanoi on 19 December 1946, at the start of the Indochina War.

The French held the cities; Giap held the countryside. Giap utilized guerrilla warfare to wear away French power, and despite some setbacks when he overconfidently attempted frontal attacks, he eventually did exhaust the enemy and particularly the will of the French back home to continue a war which was heavily draining manpower and resources. When in 1954 the Communists captured the French force deeply entrenched in the town of Dien Bien Phu, the war came to an end. As a result of an international conference in Geneva, the French pulled out of Indochina and four independent nations were established: Laos, Cambodia, South Viet Nam, and (Communist) North Viet Nam.

After the establishment of North Viet Nam as an independent state in July 1954, Giap became deputy premier, while retaining the post of defense minister and commander in chief. He is also a member of the politburo of the ruling *Lao Dong* (Workers') party, a vice-chairman of the National Defense Council, and chairman of the National Scientific Research Commission.

The Communists were not content with the Geneva Agreement division of Viet Nam into independent countries, and within a few years, a guerrilla and terror campaign was under way in South Viet Nam. The campaign grew in intensity, and the United States, committed to defend the independence of South Viet Nam, stepped up its advisory, economic, and military assistance to that country.

Whereas the effort to conquer South Viet Nam was at first carried out primarily by the Viet Cong—the Communists of South Viet Nam—Giap later began sending entire units of the North Vietnamese army to fight in the south. To counter this, the United States dispatched increasing numbers of its own troops to the conflict, and by the mid-sixties the war had developed into major proportions.

After two decades of war, Giap was still fighting.

THE BIG VICTORY; THE GREAT TASK

OUR PEOPLE are living the most glorious years and months in the history of our people's thousands-year-old struggle against foreign aggression and in the history of the decades-old revolutionary struggle under the leadership of our party. In the heroic South, with 170,000 square meters of land, our people are defeating more than a million troops of the U.S. imperialist aggressors and their lackeys and winning increasingly big victories. In the north, our army and people are defeating the U.S. imperialists' war of destruction and thwarting their basic plots while pursuing socialist construction and economic development, consolidating national defense, and fulfilling the duties of the great rear toward the great frontline.

These glorious victories reflect the mountain-moving and river-filling power of our nation and our people. This power is invincible! The anti-U.S. national salvation line of our party, which is very correct, makes our people and our people's armed forces invincible. The sympathy and support of the brotherly socialist countries and the progressive people the world over for our people's anti-U.S. national salvation cause have grown daily and become increasingly effective.

In the enthusiastic atmosphere of carrying out production and fighting to commemorate the August Revolution and 2 September national day anniversaries, looking back at the anti-U.S. national salvation resistance during the past two years, and fully realizing the significance of our big victories and the heavy defeats of the enemy, our army and people are increasingly proud of and confident in our nation, our people, and beloved President Ho. Our nation and people are resolved to heighten their determination to fight, step up their great national salvation resistance, crush all the aggressive plots of the U.S. imperialists, and advance toward final victory.

PART I

The situation of the anti-U.S. national salvation resistance during the past two years.

The Binh Gia victory in January 1965 by the southern army and people marked the fundamental defeat of the special war strategy of the U.S. imperialists in the south of our country. Faced with this situation, the U.S. imperialists, panic-stricken and on the defensive, resorted to all measures to save the puppet authorities and army, who were facing the danger of grave collapse. From the beginning to mid-1965, they carried out a makeshift strategy by hastily introducing a number of U.S. fighting units into the south and, at the same time, expanded the war to the north by using their air force and navy to continually wage a war of destruction, thus hoping to prevent the collapse of the Saigon puppet authorities and army, consolidate and strengthen the reactionary puppet forces in the South, and save their special war strategy from defeat. However, the situation continued to develop in a direction unfavorable to the U.S. imperialists and their lackeys.

Fired with enthusiasm by victories, our people throughout the country unanimously rose up to resist the Americans for national salvation. They continued to develop the initiative on the battlefields and attack the enemy everywhere.

After the Binh Gia victory, between February and June 1965, on the basis of combining armed struggle with political struggle, the southern army and people stepped up the guerrilla war and, at the same time, developed large-scale attacks, completely annihilating puppet companies and battalions in each battle on all battlefields. They drove the puppet troops into a state of collapse, unable to resist the strong attacks of the Liberation Armed Forces.

At that time, the freshly introduced U.S. troops received heavy blows at An Tan, Nui Thanh, Pleiku, Da Nang, and especially Van Tuong. They were tightly encircled in their bases by the guerrilla belts. Neither he United States nor the puppet forces were able to stop the massive, continuous, and victorious attacks of the southern army and people. The U.S. imperialists and their lackeys became increasingly confused.

In the north, as of 7 February 1965, when the U.S. imperialists began using their air force to carry out attacks, our army and people dealt resounding blows to the U.S. Air Force, causing the U.S. imperialists to suffer heavy losses and become more defensive. Faced with this state of defeat and danger, and especially faced with the fact that the puppet troops were being repeatedly attacked and annihilated toward the end of June 1965, U.S. President Johnson, after forcing General Taylor to resign, decided to introduce massive U.S. expeditionary troops into South Viet Nam to participate directly in combat, thus shifting the aggressive war to a new strategic phase: the local war strategy.

In October 1965 after introducing 180,000 U.S. expeditionary troops into South Viet Nam, thus increasing the total of U.S. and puppet troops to 700,000 men, the U.S. imperialists launched their first strategic counteroffensive with the extravagant hope of quickly annihilating the regular units of the southern liberation forces and ending the war in 1966. This strategic counteroffensive developed under the form of two successive major operations during the 1965–1966 dry season.

The first operation was launched during the winter of 1965 with a large force, composed of many of the most seasoned units of the U.S. armed forces such as the First Mobile Division, the First Armored Infantry Division, paratroop units, and so forth. The U.S. imperialists launched their attacks in two main directions: north of Saigon, and the high plateaus, where they believed the liberation troops were concentrating their main forces. Contrary to the desires of the U.S. imperialists, both these attacks failed.

After their heavy defeat in Van Tuong, the Americans and puppets lost many battalions in Bau Bang, Dau Tieng, north of Saigon, Plei Me, the high plateaus, and other areas. Thus, the U.S. troops were defeated right at the beginning. McNamara was very surprised, and Washington was flabbergasted. They hastily increased the number of U.S. fighting men and then launched their second tide of attacks in the spring of 1966.

At that time the total of U.S. troops reached 250,000 men. They poured their entire mobile force into their five-pronged attack, which was aimed in three main directions: eastern Nam Bo, the Trung Bo delta, and the high plateaus, with the aim of annihilating the Liberation Armed Forces and, at the same time, carrying out the pacification task. But again, they failed ignominiously! During this tide of large-scale attacks, in some battles the enemy even used as many as twenty-seven battalions, such as in Bong Son and Binh Dinh.

The enemy was unable to annihilate any liberation detachment. On the contrary, U.S. and puppet troops suffered heavy losses in Cu Chi, Nha Do, Bong Trang, eastern Nam Bo, Phu Yen, Quang Ngai, Binh Dinh, the Trung Bo delta, the high plateaus, and so forth. The first dry-season strategic counteroffensive of the U.S. imperialists ended tragically, with more than thirty battalions annihilated, of which fourteen were U.S. and satellite infantry battalions, and more than 110,000 troops killed or wounded, of whom more than 40,000 were U.S. and satellite troops.

During the 1965–1966 winter-spring period, while U.S. troops sustained heavy defeats during the initial fighting and the puppet troops were continuously on the defensive, the southern army and people, on the contrary, maintained and developed their initiative on the battlefields and stepped up guerrilla and large-size attacks. They took the initiative in counterattacking and annihilating the enemy in his various operations and, at the same time, in attacking and annihilating the enemy deep in his rear—such as the attacks against his lair in Saigon, his barracks and logistic bases in various areas, and so forth.

The southern army and people defeated the U.S., puppet, and satellite troops right in the first round of the local war of the U.S. imperialists. On the basis of the 1965–1966 winter-spring victories, the southern army and people stepped up the combination of military struggle with political struggle and actively attacked the enemy, causing an unstable situation in which the puppet authorities and army encountered crises in all fields and driving the U.S. imperialists into an embarrassed and defensive position. Thirty cities and municipalities throughout the South seethed with the struggle of city people rising up to fight against the introduction of U.S. aggressive troops and against the Thieu-Ky clique. In Da Nang and Hue, the political struggle movement developed most widely and vigorously during this period.

It was obvious that contradictions between the U.S. imperialists and the traitors and the southern people were becoming very fierce. The fierce attacks of the southern army and people caused the Americans and puppets to sustain heavy military defeats and encounter grave political crises. This situation brought about quarrels, conflicts, and discord among the puppet authorities and army in the First Corps area. This crisis lasted over two months and led to a change in commanders five times. Six enemy battalions were dispersed as a result of their shooting at each other.

Faced with this situation and especially with U.S. troop defeats, the decline of the puppet troops was accelerated. In some months, there were 20,000 deserters. At the same time, many military revolts broke out, such as at the first regiment in Thu Dau Mot and other puppet units.

During the summer of 1966, after the defeat of their first dry-season strategic counteroffensive, the U.S. imperialists planned to return to the defensive, avoid the major attacks of the liberation troops, and actively reinforce and increase the U.S. expeditionary troops in order to prepare for their new strategic counteroffensive during the 1966–1967 dry season. But during the summer of 1966, U.S. and puppet troops continued to suffer repeated attacks from the southern army and people on all important strategic battlefields from Tri Thien, the high plateaus, and central Trung Bo to eastern, central, and western Nam Bo.

During the 1966–1967 dry season, after having reinforced and increased the U.S. expeditionary troops to 400,000 men, thus boosting the total of U.S. and puppet troops to over one million men, the U.S. imperialists launched their second strategic counteroffensive. The projected prominent characteristics of this major counteroffensive were: (a) carrying out their two-pronged strategic plan: search-and-destroy and pacification raids; (b) drawing experiences from the defeat of their first counteroffensive, so that this time they concentrated on carrying out the main tasks of the new counteroffensive; (c) achieving a new distribution of labor between the two strategic forces, with the U.S. forces being in charge of the search-and-destroy mission while the puppet regulars were responsible for pacification.

With a very large military force, the U.S. imperialists launched their counteroffensive this time with the aim of destroying the areas in which, they believed, resistance organs were concentrated, trying to annihilate the liberation regulars, and stepped up the pacification task in order to change the situation, win a victory of strategic significance in a short period, and solve the Vietnamese problem quickly. But the U.S. imperialists again sustained heavy defeats during this second dry season strategic counteroffensive and faced a more serious defensive state.

In early winter of 1966, carrying out the NFLSV Central Committee's 17 October 1966 appeal to resolutely fight and defeat the U.S. aggressors during the 1966–1967 winter-spring period, the southern army and people prepared to counterattack the enemy and, at the same time, took the initiative in launching new attacks on all battlefields. After summer ended in 1966, the southern army and people opened a new battlefield in Tri-Thien, attacking the U.S. and puppet troops strongly and repeatedly and forcing them to bring U.S. troops from other battlefields and disperse them to cope with various attacks on this battlefield.

This was a big surprise for the U.S. imperialists which caused them to become passive and embarrassed before pouring their forces into their second dry-season strategic counteroffensive. In the high plateau area, the Liberation Armed Forces lured the U.S. troops into coming to Plei Djereng and annihilated them in bloody battles along the banks of the Sa Thay River. On the Nam Bo battlefield, especially in the Trung Bo Delta, the southern army and people developed a new offensive situation.

The southern Liberation Armed Forces inaugurated the 1966–1967 winter-spring victories by attacking the Long Binh bomb depot on October 28 and shelling the military parade of the U.S.-puppet clique in the heart of Saigon on November 1. These were heavy blows to the enemy.

In eastern Nam Bo, the main target of U.S. troop attacks throughout the 1966–1967 winter-spring period, the enemy launched many military operations. The most important were Attleboro, Cedar Falls, and Junction City. These were defensive operations, aimed at coping with the fierce attacks of the Nam Bo troops and people. For the Attleboro campaign, the enemy mobilized over 30,000 troops. But the campaign ended with heavy losses for the 196th Brigade, units of the 25th Tropical Lightning Division, the Big Red One Division, the 173rd Brigade, and so forth.

The Junction City campaign, begun in February 1967, was one into which the Americans poured the largest number of troops to take a single objective during this dry season. They poured a large force—composed of 45,000 troops and a large number of planes, pieces of artillery, and armored vehicles—into a battlefield of less than 400 square kilometers with the hope of achieving a decisive victory. But this largest campaign was dealt the greatest defeat which ignominiously ended the second dry-season strategic counteroffensive of the Americans. The search-and-destroy operations of the Americans and puppets had failed. Naturally, their pacification task achieved no results.

While fighting fiercely, the southern army and people continued to step up the coordination between the military along with political struggles. The political struggle movement of the southern city people continued to develop strongly. Its anti-U.S. character increased. The southern people's liberated areas continued to be firmly maintained, and some liberated areas were even enlarged. The bitter failure of the U.S. pacification plan was marked by the dismissal of Cabot Lodge and Lansdale. In the second strategic counteroffensive, the U.S. imperialists were defeated more heavily than in the first. Some 175,000 troops were annihilated, including more than 70,000 U.S. troops. A total of ninety-nine battalions and battalion-size units, including twenty-eight U.S. battalions, were put out of action. Some 3,000 aircraft, hundreds of artillery pieces, and other equipment were destroyed.

The U.S. imperialists and their lackeys have been increasingly bogged down and constantly passive. They could not destroy even one small-size unit of the liberation troops' main force, and were annihilated in great numbers. They could not gain the initiative, but had to resist passively our forces on all battlefields.

They have suffered the heaviest defeats wherever the greatest bulk of their forces was concentrated. They planned to send troops to the Mekong River delta, but had to postpone this because the situation on all battlefields was very difficult for them and their lackeys. They intended to save the puppet troops, but the regular puppet troops continued to decline and lose their fighting ability, even in the pacification task.

This summer, following the failure of the second dry-season strategic counteroffensive, a pessimistic atmosphere has enveloped the U.S. ruling clique and the Vietnamese traitors in Saigon. The U.S. aggressors and their lackeys got a headache in the face of increasingly serious and insurmountable political and military difficulties and deadlock. They are embarrassed by the increasingly stronger offensive of the southern army and people and the determination of all the Vietnamese people to oppose the Americans for national salvation. They are encountering the increasingly firm opposition of progressive people in the world and even in the United States.

The ruling clique in the White House and the Pentagon have fiercely quarreled with one another about the seriously deadlocked U.S. situation in Vietnam. Westmoreland was called back to the United States to deliver a speech in which he deceitfully said that there was no deadlock, but he himself had to ask Johnson to send many more reinforcements to the south. U.S. Defense Secretary McNamara, who hurriedly went to Saigon for the ninth time in order to study all aspects of the war, openly criticized Westmoreland for wasting human strength and told him to increase the efficiency of U.S. troops now on hand in Vietnam.

Following this, Taylor, a U.S. strategist, and Clifford, a U.S. intelligence ringleader, toured the satellite countries of the United States in Southeast Asia in order to recruit more mercenary troops, but failed to attain the results desired by the U.S. imperialists.

It is clear that the U.S. imperialists have been increasingly stalemated, following the second strategic counteroffensive. Their local war has been disastrously defeated. As for the southern army and people, following the 1966–1967 winter-spring feats of arms, a stimulating, confident, and seething atmosphere has been reigning over all battlefields and has urged the southern army and people to move forward to score greater and more resounding achievements.

The Liberation Armed Forces have matured swiftly and gained many more fighting experiences and have showed that they are in very good shape. This summer, with the impetus of big victories, the southern army and people continue to develop their initiative, step up both military and political offensives everywhere, and deal the U.S., puppet, and satellite troops painful blows in Con Tien, Gioc Mieu, Gio An, Nong Son, Mo Duc, Tan Uyen, Can Le, My Tho, and Quoi Son, and at many airbases such as Da Nang, Chu Lai, and elsewhere. The above is the war situation in the south during the past two years.

In the same period, in the northern part of our country, the U.S. imperialists used an important part of the U.S. Air Force based in the Seventh Fleet, in the south, and in Thailand to attack the north in an attempt to extricate themselves from their predicament in the south, shake the morale of our people in both zones, and check the northern people's support of the southern compatriots' liberation struggle. This is an important measure of the local war strategy and, at the same time, a passive act of the U.S. imperialists.

At the outset, they attacked the southern areas of the Fourth Military Zone. Following this, they have gradually escalated the war against the northern part of North Viet Nam. On several occasions, they temporarily stopped attacking the north for some time in order to deceive people with their peace tricks and to reorganize their forces, and then continued to widely escalate the war beyond the 21st, 22nd, and 23rd parallels.

On 29 June 1966 they began rashly attacking the capital of Hanoi, thus increasing their war of destruction against the north to the most serious degree. They have also used the naval forces of the Seventh Fleet and the artillery units stationed south of the temporary military demarcation line to supplement the activities of their air force against the coastal areas of the military zone and the southern part of Vinh Linh. Their targets have been axes of communications, industrial sites, dams and dikes, cities, popular areas, schools, hospitals, markets, and so forth.

However, for more than two years the U.S. imperialists' war of destruction in the north has been defeated. The U.S. imperialists have been confronted with an anti-U.S. national salvation high tide of the northern army and people. To date, nearly 2,300 fighter aircraft of the U.S. imperialists have been shot down, and thousands of U.S. pilots have been annihilated or captured in the north. The prestige of the U.S. Air Force has collapsed disastrously. These figures were computed as of September 14, 1967.

In the war, the north has developed the strength of the socialist regime and has fought well, along with achieving good production. The North has constantly insured good communications and transportation and has incessantly developed its economy and culture. Despite many difficulties created by the enemy, the people's living conditions continue to be stabilized. The determination of our people to oppose the Americans for national salvation has been increasingly strengthened.

Meanwhile, in the South, with the spirit, "The North calls, the South answers," the southern army and people have continuously attacked the U.S., puppet, and satellite troops everywhere and have striven to attack their airbases and logistical depots, thus causing them to suffer heavy losses and to be increasingly passive.

Generally speaking, the war developments during the past two years can be summarized as follows:

On the Enemy Side

A. Because of the failure of their special war strategy, the U.S. imperialists have passively shifted to the local war strategy. They have waged an unprecedentedly large local war of aggression. With regard to military strength, they have mobilized more than a million troops, including half a million U.S. troops. As for military means, they have used about one-third of the U.S. Strategic Air Force, as many as 4,000 aircraft of all types, including some 1,300 modern fighter aircraft, and thirteen of the seventeen attack aircraft carriers of the U.S. naval force. They have used very great quantities of the most modern weapons and equipment, except for atomic weapons, in the war.

With regard to their war budget, according to their official sources, in 1966 alone the U.S. imperialists spent as much as 13 billion dollars; they plan to increase this to 30 billion in 1967 and 1968.

The U.S. imperialists mobilized the U.S., rebel, and satellite forces to launch two strategic offensives in South Viet Nam, and have continuously used their air and naval forces to attack the north. Yet they have not been able to extricate themselves from their predicament in South Viet Nam, which is getting worse and worse.

B. The U.S. imperialists have been utterly defeated in all fields—military, political, and tactical—throughout the very important period of the local war. All of their strategic objectives have failed. The U.S. and rebel forces have suffered heavy setbacks, while their pacification plan has gone bankrupt. The puppet administration and armed forces have weakened with every passing day. They are faced with a very bad and seriously stalemated war situation.

C. As a result of their waging of the war of aggression in Viet Nam, the U.S. imperialists are increasingly isolated in the world. The progressive people throughout the world, including the American people, have vehemently condemned the U.S. imperialists for their aggression against Viet Nam and have risen up to struggle against them by all means. Many of the U.S. imperialists' satellite countries have shown themselves indifferent to the war of aggression in Viet Nam. Some of them have even officially protested against it. Even the U.S. ruling authorities themselves have fallen into discord and dissension in the face of their heavy setbacks in Viet Nam.

On Our Side

A. A glance at all aspects of the anti-U.S. national salvation resistance war of our people shows that the war situation has never been so favorable as it is now. The armed forces and people in the entire country have stood up to fight the enemy and are achieving one great victory after another. In South Viet Nam, faced with the U.S. imperialists' change of strategy, the southern armed forces and people have continued developing their initiative, have continuously attacked the enemy on all battlefields, and have defeated two large-scale strategic counteroffensives of the U.S., rebel, and satellite forces. The military struggle has been stepped up in close coordination with the political struggle, which is developing increasingly deeply and widely. The resistance forces of the southern combatants and people have matured rapidly and are strong.

In North Viet Nam, our armed forces and people have defeated and are defeating the U.S. imperialists' war of destruction, have continued building socialism, and at the same time have striven to fulfill the duty of a large rear toward a large frontline. North Viet Nam has become increasingly strong and steady in all fields.

B. The victories achieved by the armed forces and people in the entire country have been of great political and military strategic significance. Our people throughout the country are standing shoulder to shoulder in steadily advancing and pushing the anti-U.S. national salvation resistance war to final victory.

C. Our people's anti-U.S. national salvation resistance war is just and is aimed at safeguarding their independence and freedom. It is of great international significance because it is strongly approved and supported by brother socialist countries and progressive people all over the world. Never has our people's resistance war against foreign aggression been so strongly encouraged and supported by the world's peoples as it is now. The world's revolutionary people consider the anti-U.S. national salvation resistance war of our people as an anti-U.S. front line of the world's peoples and a center of the present national liberation struggle movement.

PART II

The U.S. imperialists were heavily defeated during the very important period of the local war of aggression in South Viet Nam.

Ever since World War II, and especially after their defeats in China, Korea, Indochina, and Cuba, the U.S. imperialists have sensed the inferiority of the imperialist camp and their own inferiority in the balance of power in the world. The imperialist camp, led by the U.S. imperialists, has been forced to take a passive and defensive position in the face of the growth of the socialist camp, of the seething and mounting national liberation movement, and of the continuous offensive posture of the revolutionary movement in the world.

The U.S. imperialists have had to give up their massive retaliation strategy and adopt the flexible response strategy. They maintain that the flexible response strategy, which includes three forms of war—special war, local war, and total war—is the most suitable strategy that may help them find a way out of their passiveness when they are not in a position to prosecute a nuclear war. They add that it is the most positive strategy for implementing their aggressive policy and performing their function as an international gendarme so as to cope with the national liberation movement, which is rising like a storm throughout the world, and to prepare for aggression against socialist countries. They call the special war and the local war a sharp sword that cuts into the national liberation movement, creating favorable conditions for them to prepare for a world war.

In the south of our country, the U.S. imperialists resorted to the special war and failed. They had to shift hastily and defensively to the local war strategy to cope with their dangerous situation. This act not only reflected their failure, but also laid bare their obdurate, aggressive, and warlike nature.

What is the U.S. imperialists' local war strategy? According to their views, local war is one of the three forms of their aggressive war. It is an actual war for the Americans, but with limitations as far as size and scope are concerned. Differing from special war mainly waged by local lackey troops, the local war of the U.S. imperialists is directly waged by U.S. troops.

But the general aggressive policy of the U.S. imperialists is aimed at achieving neocolonialism. Thus, when they wage local war in order to repress the national liberation movement, they must brazenly use local lackey troops and the puppet authorities to wage war along with U.S. troops. They regard the puppet troops and authorities as an important political buttress.

In the U.S. imperialists' local wars aimed at achieving their aggressive neocolonialist policy, the final goal that the war must achieve is: consolidating the puppet army and government and turning them into effective tools for the achievement of neocolonialism. The main military goal of the local war strategy is: annihilating the enemy's military forces. The philosophy of this strategy is: attacking, and attacking quickly in order to solve the war quickly.

The prominent characteristic of the local war strategy is: using U.S. troops in direct aggression, but limiting the war scope; winning military victory in the shortest possible time; and creating conditions for achieving the enslaving domination of neocolonialism.

Limiting the number of U.S. troops means using only a certain part of military forces of the U.S. infantry, air force, and navy in the local war. The U.S. imperialists must restrict the U.S. forces participating in a local war, because without this restriction, their global strategy will encounter difficulties and their influence over the world will be affected. They must achieve this restriction to avoid upsetting political, economic, and social life in the United States. This means that although they wage the war, they do not have to mobilize their forces and they continue to carry out their economic and social programs in the United States.

They impose this restriction because they are convinced that they can achieve victory even if they use only a restricted number of U.S. troops to directly participate in a local war aimed at repressing the national liberation movement in any given country in Asia, Africa, or Latin America.

Having to restrict the number of U.S. troops, the U.S. imperialists pay special attention to consolidating and using the forces of the local lackeys. They believe that if they use a restricted number of U.S. troops as a core for local lackey troops, equipped with modern weapons, to wage a local aggressive war in the countries where the economy is relatively backward or newly developed, they will be able to repress their adversaries, thanks to their superiority in military force and firepower, and will be victorious in a short time. Restricting the strategic goals means restricting the political goals of the war and, in the military field, concentrating forces to quickly annihilate the adversaries' military forces—especially their regulars. They must do this so that they can avoid having to disperse their troops to different targets and so that they can fight and solve the war quickly.

They believe that the adversaries' backbone is their armed forces, and that if they can defeat these armed forces, they can end the war, but that if they cannot do so, the war will last a long time and they will be defeated. They must win, because they want to create favorable conditions for the lackey forces to fulfill the tasks following victory, thus allowing the imperialists to bring their troops home quickly but still maintain political conditions to achieve neocolonialism.

Restricting the scope of the war means waging war only in a certain country or area, thus preventing it from ravaging other countries or areas. They believe that if they cannot restrict the scope of the war, they will become more defensive and face greater defeats, because bigger countries will be forced to join the war. As of now they have not finished making preparations for a new world war.

The U.S. imperialists can restrict the local war to a certain country or area, depending upon concrete conditions. But no matter what the scope is, their objective continues to be quickly annihilate the revolutionary forces and pursue the achievement of neocolonialism.

Having in mind the above-mentioned views about the local war strategy of the U.S. imperialists, we note that the local war which the U.S. imperialists are waging in South Viet Nam has exceeded the original restrictions as far as scope is concerned. The U.S. forces have far exceeded the limitation that each local war may mobilize only between three and six divisions. The U.S. and satellite forces now in South Viet Nam equal eleven divisions, of which nine are American and South Korean.

The U.S. troops' strategic objectives on the southern battlefield are not restricted to annihilating the Liberation Armed Forces, but have included the pacification task. As far as the scope of the war is concerned, the U.S. imperialists have initially exceeded the restriction of limiting the war to South Viet Nam. They have been using their air force and navy to wage a war of destruction against North Viet Nam; they are continuing to intervene with increasing strength in the Laotian kingdom and brazenly provoke the Cambodian kingdom, and they are planning to expand the war to the entire Indochinese peninsula in order to extricate themselves from their dangerous situation in South Viet Nam.

In the south of our country, when the U.S. imperialists shifted to the local-war strategy, they obviously pursued the achievement of neocolonialism. Therefore, although they have sent hundreds of thousands of U.S. troops to the South, they still have had to strive to consolidate the puppet army and administration as a necessary political and military support for their neocolonialist war of aggression. They still capitalize on the name of the puppet administration and strive to consolidate the puppet army.

Along with the military tricks of the war of aggression, they have feverishly carried out the political tricks of neocolonialism. Therefore the nature of the U.S. imperialists' present limited war still is an aggressive war aimed at achieving the political objectives of neocolonialism; it is a neocolonialist war of aggression. The limited-war strategy in particular and the flexible reaction strategy in general are products of the U.S. imperialists' bourgeois military thinking which have come into existence in circumstances under which imperialism has become increasingly depressed, defeated, and passive in the face of a situation in which the balance of power in the world is not favorable for them.

Like their neocolonialist policy of aggression, the U.S. imperialists' limited-war strategy is full of contradictions and insurmountable basic weaknesses. In essence, the contradictions and basic weaknesses of the limited-war strategy are the inherent contradictions and weaknesses of an unjust war of aggression. In the southern part of our country, these contradictions and weaknesses have increasingly worsened and have revealed themselves clearly in the process of development of the U.S. imperialists' war of aggression and of our people's anti-U.S. national salvation resistance.

Since they started the limited war and began to send U.S. troops to wage direct aggression against the South and to use their air force and navy to stage raids against the North, the U.S. imperialists have brazenly revealed their cruel aggressive face and have made the contradictions between themselves and their lackeys and all the Vietnamese people increasingly acute on a national scale. The contradictions between the Vietnamese people and the U.S. imperialists and their lackeys are the main contradictions which will determine the failure of the U.S. imperialists' war of aggression.

The U.S. imperialists have encountered the resistance of an entire people who are courageous, undaunted, full of fighting experiences, and united as one. The south and the north have unanimously taken up arms and have fought shoulder to shoulder for the just cause and for the complete independence and freedom of the fatherland.

In sending U.S. troops to South Viet Nam, the U.S. imperialists have encountered a people's war that has developed to a high degree and is in an offensive position. This people's war has successfully developed the people's strength, has succeeded in mobilizing all the people to fight the aggressors militarily and politically under all forms and with all kinds of weapons—from primitive to modern weapons—and has created a very great combined strength.

This great people's war has gloriously defeated the U.S. imperialists' special war and is on an irreversible trend of vigorous development. Events have proved that from the time they began to send U.S. troops to wage direct aggression in the South, the U.S. imperialists have been defeated. They are being compelled to scatter their forces and are in a passive position on all battlefields. In waging the war of aggression against the north, the U.S. imperialists have knocked their heads against a firm steel bastion.

To protect the North, liberate the South, and proceed toward reunifying the country, the northern armed forces and people have stepped up and are stepping up the violent people's war against the U.S. aggressors' war of destruction. The northern armed forces and people have developed their revolutionary heroism to a high degree, have defeated the U.S. imperialists' war of destruction, and have fulfilled wholeheartedly and to the best of their ability the obligation of the large rear base toward the large frontline.

By sending U.S. troops to wage direct aggression in South Viet Nam, and by using their air force to stage raids against the North, which is an independent and sovereign country and a component of the socialist camp, the U.S. imperialists have made more acute their contradictions with the socialist camp, the national liberation movement, and the progressive people in the world. The more the U.S. imperialists step up their war of aggression in Viet Nam, the more resolutely they make the socialist countries oppose them and more positively help the Vietnamese people in order to protect a member country of the socialist camp and an outpost of socialism, and to fulfill the socialist countries' glorious obligation toward the national liberation movement.

The progressive people of the world have supported more and more vigorously the Vietnamese people's struggle against the U.S. aggressors and are attacking them everywhere in the world. The U.S. imperialists are meeting with vigorous protests from the progressive people in the world, including the American people.

The U.S. imperialists have pursued a policy of neocolonialist aggression. Yet they have had to send U.S. troops to wage direct aggression in South Viet Nam. This has worsened the contradictions between their aim of imposing neocolonialism and their trick of using U.S. troops to prosecute the war. By sending U.S. troops to wage direct aggression in the South. The U.S. imperialists have clearly revealed their brazen aggressive face, which they cannot cover. These contradictions have deepened the many basic political problems of neocolonialism and led the U.S. imperialists toward many difficulties and defeats.

The U.S. imperialists' introduction of troops into the South has been aimed at preventing the collapse of the puppet army and administration and creating new conditions for consolidating and strengthening the puppet forces.

Yet the more the war of aggression is Americanized, the more disintegrated the puppet Saigon army and administration becomes. The traitorous and country-selling nature of the leaders of the puppet army and administration has been exposed. They have been cursed by all our people.

Furthermore, the internal contradictions of the puppet army and administration and the contradictions between the U.S. imperialists and the puppet army and administration have increasingly developed. Those in the puppet army and administration who still have some national spirit have become gradually enlightened. More and more of them have returned to the people. Faced with the towering crimes of the U.S. aggressors and the country-selling traitors, the southern people have become more full of hatred, have tightened their solidarity, and have fought valiantly and resolutely for final victory under the NFLSV's anti-U.S. national salvation banner.

The more they increase the number of their troops in the South and the more they extend the fighting, the more the U.S. imperialists deepen the contradictions between their limited war strategy and their global strategy. The more the limited war in the south is stepped up, the more adversely it will affect the other positions of the U.S. imperialists around the world—especially when they have had to mobilize forces for a limited war which has far exceeded their estimates. As a result, the contradictions between their limited-war strategy and their global strategy have become more acute.

The world revolutionary people can take advantage of this situation to step up their attacks against the U.S. imperialists, with a view to repulsing them step by step and eliminating them part by part. The U.S. imperialists' allies can also take advantage of this situation to wrangle for their own interests, thus creating difficulties for the U.S. imperialists.

In the southern part of our country, during the past two years the U.S. imperialists' limited-war strategy has revealed many basic weaknesses. First of all, the U.S. imperialists' limited-war strategy was adopted on the basis of the defeat of the special-war strategy—the U.S. imperialists have sent U.S. troops to the South in a passive and defeated position and in a situation in which the puppet army and administration have been on the decline. As a result, from the outset their limited-war strategy has become a passive strategy and they have had to accept an unfavorable strategic position.

By waging a limited war, the U.S. imperialists have hoped to ward off the decline of the puppet army and administration, so that they could use them to support politically and militarily their neocolonialist war of aggression. Yet, in the southern part of our country, the puppet army and administration have become impotent and increasingly weakened.

The introduction of U.S. expeditionary troops into the South has been aimed at providing military support for the puppet army. Yet the U.S. troops have sustained continuous defeats and serious losses. The U.S. and puppet troops have not been able to rely upon each other, support each other, or coordinate with each other. As a result, their strategic effect has been reduced. The U.S. imperialists have developed their limited-war strategy in an extremely passive situation. The puppet army and administration have become impotent.

Moreover, the U.S. imperialists have encountered the Vietnamese people who have a determination to fight and win a great people's war, and who have developed to a high degree creative strategy and tactics, and an invincible strength. Therefore, the serious defeats sustained by the U.S. troops have been inevitable.

In the unjust war of aggression in the south, the U.S. expeditionary troops have been fighting without an ideal and, as a result, their morale has been very low. The more they are defeated, the worse this basic weakness becomes. Furthermore, although they are numerous and equipped with modern armaments, they have encountered very great difficulties: topography, climate, and training not suitable to the Vietnamese battlefield. Unaccustomed to the topography and climate, U.S. troops have encountered very great difficulties.

How has the U.S. imperialists' strategic defeat developed during the past two years, during which they have waged a limited war in South Viet Nam? As we all know, when they introduced U.S. troops into the south, the U.S. imperialists wanted to use their great military supremacy, concentrate their military forces, and launch an offensive in an attempt to annihilate the Liberation Armed Forces and regain the initiative. Yet, although they have more than one million troops at their disposal, the U.S. imperialists so far have not been able to realize this strategic design. Although they wanted to concentrate their forces, they have had to scatter them in many theaters and assign them many tasks. From the time they were introduced into the South until the end of 1966, the U.S. expeditionary troops were compelled to scatter in three major theaters—eastern Nam Bo, the highlands, and central Trung Bo—to cope with the vigorously developing people's war.

Recently, U.S. troops have been scattered in another theater: the Quang Tri-Thua Thien theater. Generally speaking, on the southern battlefield U.S. forces have been scattered almost equally in these four theaters.

This scattered deployment of strategic forces runs counter to the U.S. military leaders' plans. It is bitter for the U.S. imperialists to realize that in each of these four theaters, U.S. troops have been thinly scattered.

In the First Army Corps area, U.S. Marines have been scattered over an area of approximately 500 to 600 kilometers. In the highlands, U.S.

forces, which are not large, have been scattered over a 200-kilometer area. In eastern Nam Bo, U.S. troops have had to spread out on many fronts and have found it necessary to defend all areas. As a result, large U.S. forces have become small and have failed to yield adequate strength.

The U.S. and puppet troops have not only been scattered in many theaters, but have been also assigned many tasks. It has been the U.S. imperialists' intention to concentrate U.S. and puppet forces on annihilating the Liberation Armed Forces and, thereby, rapidly settling the war. Yet, faced with the southern people's mounting military and political struggle from the rural areas to the cities, the U.S. imperialists have had to assign U.S. and puppet troops to pacification. The assignment of the bulk of the regular units of the puppet army to pacification is a strategic setback. The assignment of U.S. and satellite troops to pacification will certainly lead the U.S. imperialists to greater political and military setbacks.

Although the U.S. imperialists wanted to launch an offensive, they have fallen into a defensive position. It is an extremely dangerous thing for any aggressive army to have forces scattered, and to remain on the defensive is even more dangerous.

At present, about seventy percent of the U.S. troops perform defensive tasks in South Viet Nam. According to the Pentagon's calculations, at least 200,000 troops are needed to defend U.S. bases of various sizes in South Viet Nam. To defend the Da Nang airbase alone, the U.S. imperialists have mobilized one division of U.S. troops and deployed them over a 25-kilometer perimeter. Recently, the U.S. imperialists estimated that only one out of eight U.S. servicemen in South Viet Nam is engaged in mobile combat. McNamara admitted that the combat efficiency of U.S. troops is very low. He found that of the nearly 500,000 U.S. troops in South Viet Nam, only 70,000 are directly engaged in combat.

The U.S. imperialists have had to commit their combat forces to the defense of their bases, cities, military lines of communications, and even the puppet army, which is being shaken, depressed, and disintegrated. As a result, although U.S. troops are very numerous, they are thinly scattered and lack offensive strength.

The U.S. imperialists wanted to annihilate the Liberation Armed Forces, but they have been seriously annihilated. During the past two years on the southern battlefield, the U.S. imperialists have feverishly concentrated efforts on trying to extricate themselves from their scattered and defensive position. They have continuously increased the number of their troops, and their troops and have conducted offensive operations. Yet they have failed. They sustained very serious defeats in the two "dry-season strategic counteroffensives."

Why do the U.S. and puppet troops not have strategic effect and combat efficiency, although they have conducted many battalion-size, division-size, and even multidivision-size search-and-destroy operations?

To annihilate the enemy it is necessary, first of all, to concentrate forces. The U.S. troops have been scattered to cope with the comprehensive and powerful people's war. They have not only failed to concentrate their offensive forces, but have also been compelled to fight according to the will of the southern Liberation Armed Forces. In actual combat, in most of the battles, U.S. troops have failed to find their targets, not because the U.S. imperialists lack modern reconnaissance instruments, but because in the people's war in South Viet Nam, which has developed to a high degree, targets and battlefronts exist everywhere, yet do not exist anywhere.

The prevalent phenomenon emerging from the war in South Viet Nam is that U.S. troops have always been surprised, caught in the Liberation Armed Forces' traps, and annihilated. U.S. troops have not been able to annihilate the Liberation Armed Forces; on the contrary, they have been seriously annihilated, although they are very numerous and have continuously conducted search-and-destroy operations. This is a strategic and tactical defeat sustained by U.S. troops on the southern battlefield.

The U.S. imperialists wanted to regain the initiative. Yet they have fallen deeper and deeper into a passive position. As everyone knows, initiative on the battlefield is manifested by the facts that one can act freely and at will, that one is fully free to choose the place and time for launching attacks, and that one can maneuver the enemy and compel him to adopt the fighting methods one selects. The most important factor is that one must succeed in annihilating the enemy.

On the southern battlefield during the past two years, U.S. troops have not had freedom of action, have been compelled to fight on the terms of the southern armed forces and people, and have not been able to annihilate any section of the Liberation Armed Forces. How can they regain the initiative on the battlefields?

During the past two years, U.S. troops have been very eager to annihilate the Liberation Armed Forces in eastern Nam Bo, in the highlands, in the delta of the Fifth Zone, and in the Tri-Thien region. Yet it is in these areas that the U.S. expeditionary troops have sustained serious annihilating blows. The Americans have not yet been able to carry out their plan to introduce U.S. troops into the Mekong Delta.

During the past two years, U.S. troops have exerted extensive efforts and conducted thousands of operations of various sizes. Yet they have failed to regain the initiative.

It may seem that U.S. troops have taken the initiative in conducting these operations, which appeared to have an offensive character. Yet, in essence they have had neither combat efficiency nor strategic effect. Therefore, U.S. troops have fallen deeper and deeper into a passive position.

Wanting to engage in a blitzkrieg, the U.S. imperialists have been forced to fight a protracted war. The leading strategic idea of the imperialists' aggressive war is to fight quickly in order to solve the war quickly. Waging the local aggressive war in South Viet Nam under the present situation in the world and the United States, the U.S. imperialists want to fight quickly. But they have been forced to fight a protracted war, although they have boosted the aggressive war to a large scale. They have encountered an adversary—the southern army and people—who is both resolute and clever and who has successively thwarted their blitzkrieg plots since the day they started implementing their special war strategy. They could not fight quickly because they did not know their adversary and because they overestimated their own strongpoints in the fields of numerical strength and modern weapons.

The fact that the U.S. imperialists have been forced to fight a protracted war is a big defeat for them. The more protracted the war is, the more fierce will be the basic contradictions and weaknesses of the aggressive war of the U.S. imperialists in South Viet Nam—contradictions and weakness which will lead them to increasingly big defeats.

The U.S. imperialists have been unable to pacify the countryside and stabilize the situation in the cities. They have used the majority of the puppet troops and a part of the U.S. forces to fulfill the pacification task, but they have failed ignominiously. The pacification plan has not made any progress, and the situation in the cities has become increasingly more troubled. They have bitterly admitted that "the history of South Viet Nam pacification is a list of plans that have collapsed and of talented advisers' boundless efforts that have been reduced to ashes." (AP, January 6, 1967.)[1]

The ultimate goal of the local aggressive war of the U.S. imperialists in South Viet Nam is to consolidate the puppet army and government and to bring about neocolonialism. However, faced with the fierce contradictions between the U.S. imperialists and lackeys and all our people, and faced with the increasingly strong resistance of the southern people, the internal contradictions of the puppet army and government have developed day by day.

The puppet army and government have declined day by day, and will surely arrive at complete disintegration and collapse. This actually has happened and is happening in the south of our country. This proves that the U.S. imperialists have sustained heavy defeats on the path leading to the ultimate goal of their neocolonialist aggressive war.

Thus, the U.S. imperialists have been defeated strategically. What about their tactics? It can be said that after waging the local war for two years, the U.S. imperialists have encountered more and more crises and increasingly greater deadlock in the tactical field. All their offensive and defensive tactics, as well as all private tactics of each branch of the U.S. Armed Forces, have not achieved the expected results.

All forms of tactics—from the search-and-destroy tactic, mop-up operations, pacification measures, and rescue operations to police and security operations, attacks with firepower, chemical poison spraying, and so forth—have proved to be inefficient. The Van Tuoung, Cu Chi, and Plei Me battles as well as the search-and-destroy and mop-up operations during the major campaigns—Five Arrows, Attleboro, Cedar Falls, Junction City, Highway 9, and so forth—have demonstrated the deadlock and failure of these forms of tactics. Modern military bases such as Da Nang and Chu Lai, and logistic bases such as Long Binh, Bien Hoa, and others, have been threatened permanently and attacked repeatedly, and have suffered heavy losses.

The private tactics of each military branch of the U.S. Armed Forces have also been defeated.

Based on the support of armored vehicles, artillery, and aviation, the motorized infantry tactics of the First Division has proved inefficient. Faced with the clever tactics of the liberation troops, this tactic of the First Division has shown many major weaknesses: one is not free to achieve one's own intention, but must comply with the conditions and tactics of the enemy. The Bau Bang, Cam Xe, Nha Do, Bong Trang, and other battles were bitter defeats for this division.

The Air Cavalry Division's massive heliborne tactics have been aimed at staging surprise raids and swiftly annihilating the enemy. Yet, it has never been able to achieve the surprise factor or to annihilate any section of the Liberation Armed Forces. Troops of the Air Cavalry Division are even weaker than ordinary U.S. infantry troops, because they lack the mechanized support and artillery units. Units of the Air Cavalry Division have been battered by the Liberation Armed Forces in Plei Me, Binh Dinh, and other localities.

The U.S. Marines' tactics of blocking defense combined with conducting mop-up operations aimed at pacifying the areas surrounding the military bases has revealed many weaknesses. The U.S. Marine bases at Da Nang and Chu Lai are like isolated islands in the open sea of people's war.

The marines, who belong to one of the armed branches regarded by the U.S. imperialists as the most seasoned, have been most frequently and most seriously defeated, and are being stretched as taunt as a bowstring over hundreds of kilometers in the Tri-Thien region and along Highway 9.

The bombing and strafing tactics, which have been aimed at annihilating the Liberation Armed Forces units, destroying the resistance bases, and massacring the people, have also become ineffective because of inaccurate intelligence information and the failure to identify targets accurately. To date, U.S. Air Force bombings and strafings, including that of B-52 strategic bombers, have not been able to annihilate any Liberation Armed Forces unit, but have only, as the U.S. imperialists have often admitted, shattered trees or destroyed empty tunnels.

Why have the various tactics adopted by U.S. troops been ineffective? As everyone knows, tactics are inseparable from strategy. If strategy becomes passive and stalemated, it will vigorously and adversely affect tactics. The reason for the failure and stalemate of the various tactics adopted by U.S. troops also lies in their erroneous tactical thinking. The U.S. troops' tactics have been based solely upon the power of weapons and upon the assumption that firepower is their soul. Therefore, when these bases—weapons and firepower—are restricted or fail to develop their effectiveness, the U.S. troops' tactics become ineffective and are defeated.

The tactics adopted by the U.S. troops in South Viet Nam are undergoing a crisis and are stalemated not because they are the outmoded tactics of a bourgeois military science but mainly because they cannot match the creative and flexible tactics of the people's war of the heroic, intelligent, valiant, and skillful southern armed forces and people. If U.S. troops were free to fight according to their tactics against an enemy who does not possess fighting experiences, their tactics might develop and have a certain effectiveness. Yet, faced with the strength of the people's war and the skillful strategy and tactics of the southern armed forces and people, U.S. troops have had no freedom of action and, as a result, all their tactics have been ineffective.

The *New York Times* on 28 February 1967 correctly admitted: "How can they—that is, the U.S. troops—win decisive victories over the South Vietnamese people's armed forces, who cannot be defeated? These armed forces have come from the people and are fighting in areas which are very familiar to them. They know how to apply expertly the art and experiences of the war which they have waged for one quarter of this century."[2]

The defeat of the U.S. imperialists' tactics and strategies during the past two years on the southern battlefield was very heavy. Although they have poured in more and more troops to step up their local aggressive war, the U.S. imperialists not only have not achieved their strategic schemes, but also have failed to achieve all their strategic goals.

During the past two years, the U.S. imperialists have expanded the war with the aim of discovering a turning point toward victory; but this turning point has eluded them more and more. Moreover, the turning point toward defeat is drawing increasingly nearer for them. Their aggressive war in the South has exceeded the limitations of a local war. Yet the U.S. imperialists are still unable to find a way out. Johnson continues to find that this war is bloody and stalemated. McNamara and Westmoreland are becoming confused and are quarreling with each other about the problems of increasing U.S. strength or of increasing the U.S. troops' fighting efficiency. All the big shots at the White House and Pentagon have admitted that they cannot defeat the adversary. The *Wall Street Journal* on 20 May 1967 said: "In Viet Nam, the Americans have thrust themselves into a horrible, issueless, eight-diagram battle scheme. It is time to admit that Viet Nam has become an incurable disease for the Americans."[3]

The experiences drawn from the Viet Nam war during the past two years have exposed the fallacy of a series of military views of the U.S. imperialists, as well as of bourgeois military science in general.

The U.S. imperialists maintain that they will surely win if they wage local war with a large army equipped with modern weapons and supported by the air force and navy. The realities on the Vietnamese battlefield have caused this view to go bankrupt, along with the local war theory of the U.S. imperialist aggressors.

First of all, the U.S. imperialists' view that the number of troops decides victory on the battlefield has lost all meaning during the special war as well as the local war. The Americans and their lackeys have continually had more troops than the southern Liberation Armed Forces, but they have never won victory. Facts prove that the U.S. imperialists have been losing on the southern battlefield not because they have lacked troops, and not because their troops have been less numerous than the Liberation troops, but because they have encountered an entire nation which has risen up to resist them resolutely, which has had a strongly developed people's war, and which has had a powerful and inexhaustible political force and Liberation Armed Forces having a high fighting power and clever tactics.

From the purely numerical viewpoint, it is obvious that over a million U.S., puppet, and satellite troops constitute a large force—especially as this force is carrying out aggression on a battleground of only 170,000 square kilometers. But to have numerous troops does not necessarily mean to have powerful and efficient fighting power, since their aggressive war is unjust and since they have no fighting spirit and no appropriate tactics and are in a defensive strategic state. The over one million U.S., puppet, and satellite troops do not have the hoped-for fighting power.

Along with the argument on troop strength, the argument that equipment and weapons can decide victory has also been smashed.

It can be said that on the southern battlefields, those who have a great amount of up-to-date equipment and weapons are the U.S. imperialists. Except for nuclear weapons, all the most up-to-date U.S. weapons and war means have been lavishly expended. Nevertheless, all this equipment and these weapons have been unable to help the U.S. troops protect themselves and develop their effectiveness in annihilating the southern Liberation Armed Forces.

Conversely, although they have no aircraft, armored vehicles, or warships, the Liberation Armed Forces continue to succeed in destroying U.S., puppet, and satellite troops units equipped with up-to-date equipment.

Everyone knows that armed forces must have equipment and weapons and that equipment and weapons are an important factor which creates the fighting strength of armed forces. However, it is obvious that equipment and weapons are not a factor which can decide victory. What decides victory on the battlefields is whether the armed forces have high fighting spirit and good fighting methods. Only with high fighting spirit and proper fighting methods can we develop to the fullest the use of equipment and weapons in order to defeat the enemy.

The arguments on the strength of the air force and on the use of the air force to decide victory on the battlefields has also gone bankrupt. In the south, the U.S. imperialists have a very great superiority in air power. They have used aircraft, including B-52 strategic bombers, to drop bombs of various types in an attempt to destroy the Liberation Armed Forces and massacre the people. However, they continue to be unable to save the U.S. infantry units from defeat and to check the ubiquitous and strong offensive thrust of the southern Liberation Armed Forces.

While it is true that the U.S. troops in the South have a considerable air force, it is obvious that the U.S. Air Force's effect has been limited, because it must cope with the widespread people's war of the heroic southern army and people. From Tri Thien to Ca Mau, there are thousands of targets which the Americans want to attack. Therefore, the U.S. Air Force has been forced to scatter, and, as a result, its fighting effect has not developed as desired. The failure of the U.S. Air Force, from heliborne tactics to large-scale airborne landing tactics, has demonstrated the bankruptcy of the U.S. imperialists' argument concerning air power on the southern battlefields.

In the north, the U.S. Air Force has been dealt fierce blows. Nearly 2,300 up-to-date fighter aircraft of various types of the U.S. Air Force have been destroyed in the northern skies. The U.S. air superiority has disastrously collapsed.

U.S. aircraft, bombs, and bullets cannot intimidate our people. McNamara himself acknowledged that bombs and bullets cannot weaken North Viet Nam. This is an acknowledgement of the inefficiency of the U.S. Air Force in the U.S. imperialists' war of aggression in Viet Nam.

The local-war strategy is collapsing along with the unimaginable strength of the U.S. Armed Forces. The war is not yet ended. However, it can be concluded that the U.S. local-war strategy in the South has proved inefficient and will certainly meet with complete failure. In the unjust war of aggression in Viet Nam, the U.S. expeditionary troops, with nearly half a million men with up-to-date equipment, have not won any victory and are nothing but a defeated armed force.

In war, the ground forces play a decisive role on the battlefields. Nevertheless, the fighting strength of the U.S. ground forces is very poor, their morale is lower than grass, and their fighting methods are bad. The U.S. generals are subjective and haughty and have always been caught by surprise and defeated.

The U.S. imperialists have spent much effort to publicize the so-called unimaginable strength of the U.S. Armed Forces, with the aim of intimidating the world's people—especially the people of small and weak nations. The trick has gone bankrupt. The truth is that the U.S. expeditionary troops are being defeated in the people's war of the Vietnamese, who, although not possessing a vast territory and not having a great population, rely mainly on their own strength and are determined to fight in order to wrest back independence and freedom.

PART III

The people throughout the country have achieved very great victories.

The foregoing is a review of the heavy setbacks, especially strategic and tactical setbacks, of the U.S. imperialists in implementing the strategy of local war of aggression in South Viet Nam during the past two years. For our people, the past two anti-U.S. national salvation years were violent fighting and testing years, during which they achieved very great and glorious victories.

Confronted with the fact that the U.S. imperialists have massively sent expeditionary troops to South Viet Nam and frenziedly stepped up the war of destruction, mainly by means of their air and naval forces, against the North, the people in the entire country find themselves in a very serious situation, that is, the struggle for the country's survival. This situation sets forth for our people throughout the country a common duty: unite the entire people and make both North and South stand shoulder to shoulder in stepping up the great patriotic war and determined to fight to vanquish the U.S. aggressors in order to protect the North, liberate the South, and advance toward the unification of the fatherland.

President Ho said: "At present, struggling against U.S. aggression and for national salvation is the most sacred duty of every patriotic Vietnamese. All our soldiers and people are united and of the same minds, fear no sacrifices and hardships, and are determined to fight until complete victory."

On the South Viet Nam battlefield, with their special war strategy going bankrupt, the U.S. imperialists have been forced to shift to the local war strategy. However, the character of their war still is a war of aggression aimed at achieving the political objectives of neocolonialism. Thus, their war is a neocolonialist aggressive war.

The anti-U.S. national salvation resistance war of the Vietnamese people in South Viet Nam is a revolutionary war, a people's war developed to an unprecedentedly high degree. It is a revolutionary war, a people's war of an entire people against U.S. imperialism's neocolonialist aggressive war.

The great resistance war is developing favorably, because it is directed by an accurate and creative line and because it has synthetically applied and creatively developed all of the valuable experiences and forms of struggle of the Vietnamese revolution, ranging from the political struggle to uprisings and war. Thus our people's anti-U.S. national salvation resistance war is progressing according to all the laws of a revolutionary war against the neocolonialist aggressive war, laws whose main contents are the spirit of indomitable struggle of an heroic people, the spirit of thorough revolution of the working class and the basic masses of workers and peasants, and the skillful and unique combination of all forms of struggle, especially of the political struggle with the armed struggle, in all regions of the country, from jungles, rural areas, and plains to cities.

Naturally, under the direction of all these laws, each form of struggle, such as the armed struggle as well as the political struggle, has its own law. Since our people are already equipped with an indomitable spirit—better to die than agree to serve as slaves—have at their disposal very valuable revolutionary struggle experiences, hold fast to the laws of the revolutionary war against the neocolonialist aggressive war, have very correct strategies and tactics, understand the enemy and friendly situations, and are resolved and know how to fight to defeat the enemy, their anti-U.S. national salvation resistance war has achieved great victories and will certainly achieve final victory.

Holding firm to the character and goal of the U.S. imperialists' local war, our people in South Viet Nam continue developing the achievements scored, strive to step up the people's war, and are resolved to fight and vanquish the U.S. aggressors. The strategies and tactics of the people's war have undergone new developments so that they are consistent with the new situation of the war.

The southern armed forces and people have asserted that their combat targets are the U.S. and puppet forces. These are the enemy's strategic forces to prosecute the war of aggression. They rely on each other and fight in close cooperation. The U.S. troops are the core force which is a military buttress for the puppet armed forces and administration and at the same time the main mobile force. The fact that the U.S. troops are heavily defeated will have a very great adverse effect on the puppet armed forces and administration, causing the puppet troops to disintegrate and the puppet administration to collapse quickly. Since the U.S. armed forces are the most modern armed forces in the capitalist world, they need abundant war means and important logistic bases. Therefore, we seek to destroy not only U.S. military strength but also the enemy's war means and logistic bases.

The puppet armed forces rely on the U.S. forces to survive and to consolidate and develop their ranks. But they play a very important role toward the Americans in the neocolonialist aggressive war. They are the political buttress for the U.S. forces. They are used as both occupation forces and mobile forces on battlefields. They are primarily in charge of controlling and oppressing the people and at the same time carrying out the pacification task. The fact that they are destroyed and disintegrated will deprive the U.S. forces of a buttress for continuing their neocolonialist aggressive war.

The puppet administration is the political buttress and an instrument for the U.S. imperialists to achieve neocolonialism. In view of this, our people in South Viet Nam have combined their armed struggle with their political struggle in order to overthrow the puppet administration, not only at the basic level, as they have done so far, but also at other levels.

On the basis of clearly acknowledging their combat targets, our people in South Viet Nam have correctly and successfully settled the strategic and tactical problems of the people's war. Our people have waged an all-people, comprehensive, and protracted resistance war in which they have always taken the offensive, have relied on their own force which they consider as the principal force, and have highly appreciated the support of brother socialist countries and progressive people all over the world. The resistance war of our people will certainly be victorious, even though it has to undergo sacrifices and hardships.

The participation of all our people in the anti-U.S. national salvation resistance war is one of the basic points in our country's people's war strategy. The objective of the southern compatriots' resistance war is to liberate the south, defend the north, and advance toward the reunification of the fatherland. This objective is entirely consistent with the profound aspirations of all people. This has been instrumental in mobilizing and organizing all people to take part in the anti-U.S. national salvation resistance war, thus forming a large and strong resistance force in which the fourteen million South Vietnamese people are combatants, fighting the enemy by all means and everywhere.

Since the victory of the general uprising, the South Viet Nam National Liberation Front has developed and broadened the great national unity bloc, has succeeded in mobilizing all people to stand up to save the country and themselves, and has insured the practical interests of the people from all walks of life, including the peasants' right to own land. Therefore, the front has been able to consolidate the worker-peasant alliance as a firm and steady foundation for the great national unity front against U.S. aggression and for national salvation.

Ever since the sending of U.S. troops to invade South Viet Nam, the contradictions between the U.S. imperialists and the country-selling Vietnamese traitors and the Vietnamese people have become increasingly acute and deep. Our people in South Viet Nam, millions as one, have closed their ranks in the all-people unity bloc under the NFLSV's invincible banner in order to fight U.S. aggression to save the country. Since our people in South Viet Nam have carried out the slogan of "All people are armed and take part in fighting the enemy," the people's war has been developed deeply and broadly and has produced a great effect.

On the basis of the participation of all people in the anti-U.S. national salvation resistance war, our people in South Viet Nam have built and developed swiftly the liberation armed forces which are composed of three kinds of troops: the guerrillas, the regional units, and the main force units. These three kinds of troops of the Liberation Armed Forces are a core force of the southern people in their anti-U.S. national salvation resistance war. With a large political force and with the increasingly large and strong liberation armed forces, the South Vietnamese people will certainly and completely defeat more than a million U.S., puppet, and satellite troops.

In our country at present, fighting against U.S. aggression and for national salvation is the great, sacred, historic task of the Vietnamese people as a whole. Our people in the South and the North resolutely stand shoulder to shoulder in fighting until final victory in order to achieve independence and freedom for the entire country. Waging a comprehensive resistance war is a very important strategic problem for developing our strength in all fields in order to vanquish the aggressors, an enemy with numerous troops and strong equipment but with many contradictions and weaknesses in the neocolonialist war of aggression.

A striking characteristic of the people's war in our country at present is that even within the local war, the fight against the enemy on all fronts —military, political, cultural, diplomatic, and so forth—is waged at the same time, in which the military struggle and the political struggle are the most basic forms of struggle. The military struggle and political struggle are closely coordinated, assist each other, and encourage each other to develop. The coordination between the military struggle and the political struggle is a law of the revolutionary struggle in our country. It is also an initiative of our people in the process of the protracted revolutionary struggle.

The political struggle plays a very important role throughout the anti-U.S. national salvation resistance. In our country, the political struggle of the masses has always served as a basis for the development of the military struggle. At present in South Viet Nam, our people's struggle has become a direct confrontation with the enemy, and together with the military struggle, has scored repeated and great successes.

In the present local warfare, the political struggle continues to play a very important role. The U.S. imperialists have used expeditionary forces to launch direct aggression against South Viet Nam. But they are forced to carry out a neocolonialist policy, and to resort to all kinds of political maneuvers to fool the people. This constitutes an opportunity for the South Vietnamese people to further step up their political struggle. Moreover, the sending of American troops to directly launch aggression against South Viet Nam has further developed the contradictions between our people and the U.S. imperialists. Therefore, the South Vietnamese people of all walks of life including those who did not realize the true nature of the U.S. aggressors or who were fooled into following them have now stood up to fight the enemy. This constitutes a favorable condition for the South Vietnamese people's struggle to develop and to score great victories.

The main objectives of the political struggle are: to mobilize and organize the people, to guide the people in the struggle against the enemy in all forms, and at the same time to coordinate closely with the military struggle and help it score the greatest victories for the resistance.

The more violent the war becomes, the more strengthened and effective the political struggle will be, especially in the urban centers of South Viet Nam, where there are so many contradictions between the U.S. imperialists and their henchmen on the one hand and our people on the other, contradictions even between the U.S. imperialists, and so forth. In the process of the anti-U.S. national salvation resistance, the political struggle of the urban compatriots of South Viet Nam will play an ever more important role and directly hit the enemy in their deepest dens.

The military struggle is becoming ever more important and is playing a decisive role in directly defeating the enemy on the battlefield. At present the U.S. imperialists are concentrating their forces and resorting to a policy of arms and force to invade South Viet Nam and enslave our people. Therefore our people in South Viet Nam have to resort to revolutionary violence to oppose the counterrevolutionary violence and to use military struggle to oppose the armed aggression of the enemy. The U.S. imperialists are using a huge military force to carry out aggression in South Viet Nam. As a result, the military struggle of our people in South Viet Nam has become ever more important.

The main objectives of the military struggle are: to destroy the enemy military force, to defend the people, to attract the people's sympathy, to coordinate with the political struggle, and to serve and help the political struggle score the greatest victories for the resistance.

Along with the political struggle, the military struggle of our people in South Viet Nam has defeated over half a million rebel troops in the special war, and is now defeating over one million U.S., rebel, and satellite troops in the local war. In parallel with the new progress of the political struggle, the military struggle of the South Vietnamese people has developed and is developing strongly, quickly, and steadfastly in both forms, guerrilla and large-scale combat.

Guerrilla activities and large-scale combat coordinate with each other, help each other, and encourage each other to develop. At the same time, they closely coordinate with the political struggle to score great victories in both military and political fields, thus leading the resistance toward final victory. Protracted resistance is an essential strategy of a people of a country which is not large and crowded and which has restricted economic and military potentials, but who are determined to defeat an enemy and aggressor having large and well-armed forces.

The anti-U.S. national salvation resistance of our people in South Viet Nam must be a protracted resistance, because our people have to fight the imperialists' ringleader, that is, the U.S. imperialists, who have large military and economic potentials. Despite their bitter defeats, the enemy is still very obdurate. In the process of their protracted resistance, the longer they fight, the stronger the South Vietnamese people become. On the contrary, the longer the enemy fights the greater difficulties he encounters. The comparison of forces on the battlefields turns in our people's favor and creates favorable conditions for our people to rush ahead and to completely defeat the enemy. In carrying out their protracted resistance, the South Vietnamese people have frustrated the blitzkrieg strategic scheme of the U.S. aggressor, and forced him to fight in accordance with our strategy, thus causing him to be extremely confused and incapable of escaping complete defeat.

In the present era, with the common offensive thrust of the world revolution, national liberation wars have favorable conditions for developing. National liberation wars can and will certainly score victories without necessarily being connected with a world war or with the revolution right in the country of the imperialist aggressors. Therefore, national liberation wars must allow some time, and a long time, to be able to crush the aggressive desire of the colonialist imperialists and to win final victory.

Our people highly appreciate the struggle of the American people against the aggressive Viet Nam war of the Johnson administration, considering it a valuable mark of sympathy and support of our people's just resistance. Moreover, our people are thoroughly aware that the decisive factor for the success of the anti-U.S. national salvation resistance is our people's objective efforts to turn the comparison for forces more and more in our favor on the Viet Nam battlefield, where there is a firm struggle between the aggressors and the victims of aggression, and where the war situation is developing more and more in favor of the heroic South Vietnamese people.

Our people hold that after the forthcoming presidential elections in the United States, and despite a possible change of presidents, the U.S. imperialists' aggressive policy cannot be changed in nature. The U.S. presidential elections are but a distribution of hierarchies among the personalities of the parties of the ruling capitalist class in the United States. Of course, through the forthcoming elections, the American people will better realize the errors and setbacks of the Johnson administration in the aggressive war in Viet Nam. And so, the struggle of the American people against the aggressive war will be stronger.

The southern people's protracted fighting strategy reflects the determination to fight and the ability of our people to defeat the U.S. imperialists under all war circumstances. The southern people, as well as the people in our entire country, are ready to carry on the resistance for five, ten, twenty, or more years, and are firmly confident of victory. In the protracted resistance against the U.S. imperialist aggressors, our people in the South are able and determined to gain time and to score increasingly greater achievements. The southern people are able to do this because in the past they have scored great achievements and because the resistance forces have swiftly matured.

On this basis, the southern army and people will make greater efforts and will certainly score increasingly greater achievements. The southern people are able to do this, because the U.S. imperialists, following their successive, heavy setbacks, are driven into a strategically deadlocked situation, the U.S. troops' fighting efficiency has increasingly decreased, the U.S. troops are considerably scattered and passive, and the puppet troops and administration are on the verge of collapse. The U.S. ruling circle has been increasingly opposed by the U.S. people and is being isolated politically to a high degree in the international arena.

Although it is great, the U.S. economic and military potential is not boundless. Moreover, the realities of the war in Viet Nam have proved that although they have a great number of troops, good rifles, and much money, the Americans are unable to extricate themselves from defeat and deadlock and will certainly be completely defeated.

Relying mainly on our own force but at the same time seeking assistance from the socialist bloc and the people in the world is a very important strategic matter. This is a manifestation of the masses' steadfast viewpoint, which places absolute confidence in our people and nation, who are imbued with an indomitable tradition and have sufficient conditions and ability to defeat the aggressive enemy, even if it is the U.S. imperialists.

Revolution is the work of the masses. No one can replace our people in carrying out the resistance to wrest back independence and freedom for the Vietnamese fatherland. Only our people can decide their destiny. Relying mainly on our own force and the all-people unity strength and firmly grasping the strategy and tactics of the invincible people's war, our people are determined to defeat the aggressive enemy, the U.S. imperialists.

Relying mainly on their own force, our people have defeated hundreds of thousands of professional troops of the French aggressor colonialists.

Relying mainly on their own force, our people in the South have successfully conducted a general uprising and have defeated the special war of the Americans and the puppets. Relying mainly on their own force, our people have defeated the first phase of the U.S. imperialists' local war strategy and will certainly and completely defeat more than one million U.S., puppet, and satellite troops.

The present era is the era of revolutionary storms. The strong socialist bloc is becoming a factor that decides the development of human society, and the people's liberation movement is boiling throughout Asia, Africa, and Latin America. Imperialism, headed by the U.S. imperialists, is being repeatedly attacked everywhere; our people can and must fully develop the advantages of the present area and positively seek assistance from the socialist countries and the people in the world in order to strengthen our force and ability to defeat the U.S. imperialist aggressors.

Our people do not detach our anti-U.S. national salvation resistance from the present era and highly value the assistance of the socialist countries and our friends in the world. Nevertheless, relying mainly on our own force must be set forth as a matter of primary and decisive importance. In the southern part of our country, the offensive strategy is the strategy of the people's war in the anti-U.S. national salvation resistance.

In the south, the offensive strategy has been carried out by our people since the general uprising period, and the coordinated military and political offensive strategy has scored great achievements in defeating the enemy's special war. Nevertheless, when the U.S. imperialists sent in masses of U.S. troops to directly invade the South, the problem was whether our people would continue to carry out the offensive strategy. The southern people have continued to carry out the offensive strategy, because their resistance has a winning position and because the southern people also possess mature military and political forces, which have conditions for further swift development, while the U.S. imperialists and their lackeys are being heavily defeated and are seriously declining. At the outset, the U.S. expeditionary troops introduced into the South were forced to remain in a strategically passive and scattered position in order to cope with the people's war, which has developed vigorously everywhere.

The striking characteristics of the offensive strategy of our southern people is to comprehensively and continuously attack and to gain the initiative in attacking the enemy everywhere with all forces and weapons and with all appropriate methods. The comprehensive offensive is a coordinated military and political offensive and includes the attacks on U.S. troops and the puppet troops and administration in the mountain and jungle areas, the deltas, and the cities. This requires a very great determination and very flexible, creative attacking methods. Our people have succeeded in doing this, because our people have an extremely valiant fighting spirit, mature political and armed forces, and unique, versatile, and extremely damaging fighting methods.

The southern people have used all methods of the military and political struggles to attack the enemy. It is due to coordinated military and political attacks on the enemy that the southern people's offensive strategy has acquired strong and great effect. It is due to the fact that the offensive strategy has been carried out in a flexible and creative manner, depending upon the place, time, and objective, that the southern people have developed a very steadfast offensive strategy posture and have driven the enemy deep into a passive and defensive position everywhere. Not only have the armed forces, including the three categories of troops composed of guerrillas, regional forces, and regular troops, carried out the offensive strategy, but the women's troops and all the people in the political forces have also repeatedly attacked the enemy.

It is on the basis of this offensive strategy that the revolutionary war in the South, with its various forms, has successfully developed and has acquired increasingly greater strength. It is on the basis of this offensive strategy that the people's army and political struggles have developed successfully from the rural areas to the cities and from the mountain and jungle areas to the deltas, and especially on the battlefields and in various strategic directions. These creative forms of struggle, including the political struggle with its extremely rich contents from low level to high level and the armed struggle from guerrilla warfare to attacks with concentrated forces and with skilled, flexible, and unique fighting methods, have allowed the people's armed forces and political forces to develop their offensive strength to a high degree and attack the areas regarded by the enemy as indestructible, thus opening extremely great new prospects and capabilities for the offensive strategy and giving the offensive strategy— a comprehensive and continuous offensive—an immeasurable strength, an invincible strength.

The foregoing is a summary of the main contents of the people's war strategy, which our southern people have applied in the present anti-U.S. national salvation resistance. This strategy has achieved very great victories and has defeated the local war strategy of the U.S. imperialists during the recent very important phase.

The "all people resist the Americans for national salvation" strategy has caused the large and strong U.S., puppet, and satellite forces of more than a million men to become small and weak. The comprehensive resistance strategy has made the already passive enemy become more passive in all fields. The protracted resistance strategy has defeated the blitzkrieg strategy of the U.S. imperialists and their lackeys. The offensive strategy has developed to a high level the great political and military power of the entire nation and driven more than a million enemy troops deeper into a defensive and passive state.

It is obvious that our people's war strategy is superior to all strategies of the U.S. imperialist aggressors. Every day this strategy has proved that it is invincible. To defeat the U.S. imperialists, our people have not only correct, creative, and very effective strategies but also clever tactics.

We all know that with good tactics a certain number of troops can defeat the enemy, but if the tactics are bad, these troops can hardly be victorious and sometimes sustain losses. In war, to defeat the enemy's strategies and open the way for greater victories, it is sometimes better to fight a few battles with good tactics than to fight many battles with bad tactics. In fighting an enemy having millions of troops, we will encounter many difficulties if we do not have flexible and creative tactics. If we have good tactics, not only can we achieve great results in fighting but also develop the effects of military operations and strategies and deal heavy blows to the enemy aggressors.

In the south of our country, by strongly developing the effects of the people's war strategy, the Liberation Armed Forces have heightened their wonderful courage, resourcefulness, creativeness, and spirit of mastery; developed to a high degree the efficiency of all weapons at hand; limited the efficiency of the enemy's modern weapons; and invented clever, varied, and effective tactics.

All tactics of the Liberation Armed Forces have been invented and developed on the basis of intense patriotism, deep hatred for the enemy, and the spirit of voluntarily, actively, and resolutely finding resourceful and creative means to attack and annihilate the enemy.

On the southern battlefield, the tactics of the guerrilla force have developed in varied ways, thus greatly frightening the enemy. The guerrillas have fought with primitive weapons such as spikes, mines, and traps as well as with semimodern and modern weapons. They have fought with means aimed at decimating as well as annihilating the enemy. The guerrillas have recognized the enemy's weak points and fully developed their own strong points.

They have discovered clever tactics and devoted their courage, spirit of sacrifice, and intelligence to successfully enforcing these tactics. Now the southern guerrillas' tactics are very powerful.

There have been battles in which guerrillas have defeated raids by enemy battalions, in which a guerrilla squad annihilated an entire U.S. company, in which guerrillas have destroyed an enemy command headquarters. Cases of shooting at and burning the enemy's armored vehicles, planes, warships, and so forth have become common among southern guerrillas. Southern guerrillas have stretched out the enemy to decimate and annihilate him, thus sowing great fear among his ranks.

On the southern battlefield, the LAF's method of fighting with concentrated forces to completely annihilate enemy troops has increasingly developed and has been very effective. On the basis of the people's war, which has developed to a high degree, and in coordination with the guerrilla and regional forces, the LAF's main force units have dealt powerful blows to the enemy on all battlefields.

With gallantry and skill and by restricting to a minimum the effect of the enemy's aircraft and artillery, fully developing all kinds of weapons, and deepening the difficulties encountered by U.S. troops—low morale, unfamiliarity with the terrain and climate, poor command, and so forth— the southern LAF have dealt serious, annihilating blows to the enemy, whether he remains in his well-fortified and adequately protected bases, or moves out to launch attacks or conduct mop-up operations, and even if he belongs to seasoned U.S. divisions, such as the First Infantry Division, the Air Cavalry Division, U.S. Marine divisions, etc.

Attacking U.S. military bases and logistical installations is also a powerful fighting method of the LAF on the southern battlefield. Although the enemy stays deep in his extremely well-protected bases, the LAF has been able to penetrate deep into his lairs, inflicted very heavy losses on him, and, as the enemy has admitted, has carried the fear of the war to his bed.

LAF attacks against the U.S. bases at Da Nang and Chu Lai, the large airfields, and the logistical installations at Lien Chieu, Long Binh, and many other areas have brought about very great results which were like the feats of arms scored by a marvelous strategic air force unit of the people's war and which, as the enemy has had to admit, could not be prevented or warded off.

On the southern battlefield the LAF's method of attacking cities is being developed. With the support of the people's political forces, small units of the LAF have succeeded in winning resounding victories and annihilating a substantial part of the enemy's vitality. In particular, the attacks launched by the LAF in the heart of Saigon, Hue, and other cities have supported the struggle movement of the urban compatriots, frightened the enemy, and filled the hearts of our compatriots throughout the country with elation. The attacks on the cities have demonstrated the marvelous courage, skill, and flexibility of the LAF.

On the southern battlefields the methods for attacking military communications, especially important strategic axes of communications, are very effective LAF methods. With them, the LAF have disrupted and paralyzed the enemy's ground logistical supply movement and weakened his mobile ability on the battlefields. The U.S. and puppet troops were forced to shift an important part of their forces to protect and clear their communications, but to date the enemy's military communications still face many difficulties, and his important strategic routes are still constantly and violently attacked and threatened.

The LAF's methods for attacking military communications are developing, thus making the U.S. expeditionary troops unable to develop the effect of their up-to-date equipment and highly mobile ability.

At present in the South, all three categories of troops—guerrillas, regional forces, and regular troops—are very familiar with the methods for attacking military communications and are placing the U.S. and puppet troops in a truly perilous situation on the military communications front.

On the southern battlefields, the LAF forces also have other skilled fighting methods such as those designed to destroy enemy positions, to combine fighting with troop proselytizing in order to disintegrate the enemy ranks, to combine fighting with military revolt in order to destroy one important unit of the enemy after another, to combine political struggle with military struggle in order to destroy strategic hamlets, to foment revolts in the rural areas, etc.

In the process of fighting and defeating the U.S., puppet, and satellite troops, our southern people have constantly sought fighting methods that can help develop the fighting strength of all their military and political forces to a high degree with a view to continuously and comprehensively attacking the enemy at all times and in all places, to thwart all his strategies and tactics, and score increasingly greater achievements.

At present these fighting methods of the LAF have been creatively and effectively applied by the three categories of troops: guerrillas, regional forces, and regular troops. Herewith, I present only the fighting methods adopted by the LAF's main force units and which have undergone development.

The fighting methods are based upon coordination among various armed branches and the independent fighting method of each armed branch. The coordinated fighting method of various armed branches of the LAF is one in which infantry troops constitute the main elements operating in coordination with one or many other armed branches and creating a superior strength and a powerful fighting capacity in order to annihilate major units or command posts of the enemy.

Because of the characteristics of the situation of friendly and enemy units on the battlefield, the organization of coordinated fighting does not depend on the availability of units of all armed branches. The LAF have proceeded from coordinating combat among a few armed branches toward coordinating combat among many on the basis of using infantry troops as the main elements, with a view to developing the decisive role of infantry troops on the battlefield.

Thus, to improve the effectiveness of the coordinated fighting method, the LAF have attached great importance to building and developing many infantry units which fight effectively under all circumstances by coordinating their actions with the armed branches and combining many fighting methods and tactical forms and tricks of the people's war.

In addition to the fighting method based upon coordination among various armed branches with infantry units constituting the main elements, the LAF have also adopted fighting methods based upon coordination among the various armed branches themselves. For instance, coordination between artillery units and crack special units, between engineer and antiaircraft units, and so forth. The existing conditions and the nature of the need to annihilate the enemy serve as a basis for determining the coordination of combat between this armed branch and the other, with a view to adopting a fighting method capable of insuring victory and rapid and complete annihilation of enemy troops.

To insure that the fighting method based upon coordination among various armed branches achieves increasing effectiveness, the Southern Liberation Armed Forces have laid special emphasis on developing the highest efficiency of all kinds of weapons and equipment, developing to a high degree the liberation troops' fighting ability, and using each unit and each armed branch at the right time and place, with a view to raising its level of mastery over the battlefield and completely annihilating large enemy units.

The Liberation Armed Forces' fighting methods based upon coordination among various armed branches is being vigorously developed along with the steady development of the armed branches, especially the development of the infantry units, and in accordance with the growing requirement for concentrated fighting. The fighting method based upon coordination among various armed branches will certainly make a decisive contribution toward annihilating many large units and many important bases of the enemy, changing the situation on the battlefield in favor of the southern people, and providing the southern people with opportunities to move forward to completely defeat more than a million troops of the U.S. imperialist aggressors.

The independent fighting method of each armed branch is a very unique creation of the people's war in the southern part of our country. Not to mention the infantry force, the other armed branches of the Liberation Armed Forces, such as the artillery units, the crack special units, the engineer units, the antiaircraft units, and so forth, have their own independent fighting methods. The common characteristics of the independent fighting methods adopted by various armed branches is the thorough comprehension of the spirit of positively attacking and annihilating the enemy, developing to the highest degree the fighting ability of each armed branch, and contributing toward developing the initiative of the southern armed forces and people at any time, anywhere, and in the face of any enemy. With the independent fighting methods of various armed branches, the Southern Liberation Armed Forces have succeeded in creating many opportunities to attack the enemy and in enabling the armed branches to acquire a tremendous new fighting ability.

The independent fighting method of the artillery units of the liberation armed forces:

On the southern battlefield today, the Liberation Armed Forces' artillery units, in fighting in coordination with infantry units as well as in fighting independently, have increasingly developed their tremendous power. In many independently fought battles, the Liberation Armed Forces' artillery units have rapidly annihilated a substantial part of the enemy troops just as they began to maneuver or assemble. The Liberation Armed Forces' artillery barrages against the enemy's command posts, military bases, and logistical installations, as well as against his bivouacs have inflicted heavy losses on the enemy and rendered him panic-stricken. It goes without saying that for the artillery units, independent fighting is but one method. The primary mission of artillery units is to fight in coordination with infantry units and to support infantry units in major battles in order to annihilate large enemy units.

The independent fighting method of the crack special units, whose numbers are small but whose quality is high, has achieved extremely great results. No matter where the enemy troops are located and no matter how adequately protected they may be, regardless of whether they are U.S. or puppet troops or whether they are in airbases, logistical facilities, U.S. officers' quarters, and so forth, with their independent fighting method the Liberation Armed Forces' crack special units have been able to seriously annihilate them.

With boundless courage, marvelous intelligence, and a thoroughly tested fighting capacity, the crack special units, with their own fighting methods, have dealt vigorous surprise blows at the enemy and rendered him incapable of reacting in time. With small numbers but high quality, the crack special units have defeated the enemy and inflicted heavy losses on him even in areas where large infantry or artillery units have encountered difficulties in organizing combat. The independent fighting method of the crack special units is developing vigorously among the three categories of troops. This has created new fighting abilities and strength for the liberation armed forces to annihilate increasingly larger numbers of the enemy's military forces everywhere.

With their independent fighting methods, the Southern Liberation Armed Forces' engineering units have paralyzed the enemy's communications, cut the important strategic routes, destroyed military bridges, attacked the enemy's mechanized vehicles, and so forth. They have inflicted very serious losses on the enemy. Of course, the engineering units also have the primary task of supporting the infantry and artillery units in combat. Yet, with their independent fighting methods, engineering units have contributed toward effectively annihilating the enemy in a situation in which the Liberation Armed Forces are fighting against U.S. troops, who possess plenty of modern weapons and instruments.

With their independent fighting methods, the Liberation Armed Forces' antiaircraft units have inflicted considerable losses on the enemy's air force and have restricted to a minimum the activities of the enemy's aircraft, especially his helicopters. Although they are newly developed units, the Liberation Armed Forces' antiaircraft units have demonstrated a courageous fighting spirit and resourcefulness and have created fighting methods which are appropriate for the southern battlefields. As a result, they have inflicted considerable losses on the enemy and have caused many difficulties for him in developing the effect of his air force on the southern battlefield. The Southern Liberation Armed Forces' antiaircraft units have increasingly matured in combat and will certainly deal more serious blows at the U.S. Air Force.

The fighting method based upon coordination among various armed branches and the independent fighting methods of each armed branch of the Liberation Armed Forces have indicated that the Liberation Armed Forces know how to apply the universal principle of concentrating forces to annihilate the enemy and, at the same time, know how to apply the principle of using a small number of troops to defeat a large number of enemy troops who possess modern equipment.

This fact indicates another invention of the people's war and the Vietnamese military art: not only in the strategic field do we use a small force against a larger force, but in the tactical field, along with using a large force to strike at a smaller force, we use a small force against a larger force.

Events on the South Viet Nam battlefield have proved that this fighting method is completely and definitely feasible and has been fruitfully implemented. Naturally, when the tactics of using a small force to fight a large force is applied, we must have the following conditions: the quality of units must be high; the targets must be chosen carefully; opportunities must be created and the situation maintained, especially when there are flaws developed by the enemy; actions must be unexpected and swift; and so forth.

With such varied and creative fighting methods, the South Viet Nam Liberation Armed Forces have been able to strike at all targets of the enemy in and outside fortifications, to destroy both the enemy's strength and war means, and to attack even the enemy's military headquarters and bases, logistic bases, communication lines, cities, and so forth, thus inflicting heavy damage on the enemy forces in all domains and everywhere.

With these fighting methods, especially the method of coordinated fighting among various armed branches, not only have the South Viet Nam LAF taken the initiative in counterattacking and smashing the enemy's counteroffensive strategy, but they have also continuously attacked the enemy, achieved glorious victories, and strongly developed their enemy-attacking posture on all battlefronts in the jungle and mountain areas, and in the cities.

With these fighting methods, the LAF have developed to a high degree their militant strength, enabling their three categories of troops to develop their strong offensive force. Not only have the main force units adopted the method of coordinated fighting among various armed branches, but the regional forces and the guerrilla forces are also advancing toward the adoption of this fighting method. As a result of their being closely combined with the methods of the political struggle, these varied and creative fighting methods of the military struggle have become increasingly strong and effective and have brought about resounding victories on battlefields.

A very important factor deciding the victories of the liberation forces in all battles is their skillful and creative fighting methods. Although the U.S. forces have fought many battles, they have not achieved victories because their fighting methods have been clumsy. The fighting methods of the South Vietnamese armed forces and people prevail over those of the U.S., puppet, and satellite forces. They are the methods of a creative people's war and a brave, heroic, unyielding, intelligent, and resourceful people who, though living in a small and less populous country, possess a steadfast determination to fight to protect their fatherland and are resolved and know how to defeat the U.S. imperialist aggressors' armed forces consisting of more than a million men.

We have just dealt with how the strategies and tactics of the South Vietnamese people's war have defeated the strategies and tactics of the limited war of the U.S. imperialists and their lackeys. But besides the problem of strategies and tactics, there is another very basic problem: How many troops do our people need to defeat the U.S. imperialists' aggressive armed forces of more than a million men? Our people in South Viet Nam have settled this problem very satisfactorily and successfully.

On the basis of the development of the people's war, our people in the South have attached importance to the building of military and political forces, considering it a decisive problem in order to implement the strategies and tactics of the people's war.

Our people in South Viet Nam, under the glorious banner of the NFLSV, have developed the experiences of the former resistance war against the French and have been able to develop a policy on the building of armed and political forces, a policy which is consistent with the present conditions of the anti-U.S. national salvation resistance war.

Although South Viet Nam is not large and is less populous, the southern compatriots have been able to build strong military and political forces which have the great militant strength and are fully capable of vanquishing more than a million U.S., puppet, and satellite troops who have modern equipment. This armed forces-building policy consists of mobilizing and arming all people and urging them to participate in the war, in which the armed forces are a nucleus force. It is a policy of building the armed forces, composed of three categories of troops, along with building increasingly large and broad political forces of the people.

Concerning the building of the armed forces, our people in the South maintain that to develop the people's war to a high degree and to step up the armed struggle, it is necessary to pay attention to the building of three categories of troops. It is necessary to build steady, strong, widespread self-defense forces and main-force units.

The building and development of the regional forces and main force units must conform to the practical conditions of each region and of the battlefield. These concentrated armed forces must in fact constitute the core forces in annihilating the enemy's military forces, protecting the people, and achieving increasingly greater successes. The main force units must not necessarily possess a strength equalling that of the enemy. Yet their quality must be high and their fighting methods must be highly effective so that they can deal steel-like blows to the enemy. They must be fully capable of fighting big annihilating battles, dealing serious blows to the enemy, and changing the situation on the battlefield in our favor. Today the southern people's three categories of troops—guerrilla forces, regional forces, and main force units—have developed harmoniously. They have been rationally deployed on various battlefields, have increasingly developed their great fighting strength, and have been able to enhance their position and improve the strategic effect of the LAF in the anti-U.S. national salvation struggle.

The LAF have been fighting while building up their strength and have unceasingly improved their fighting quality. Along with intensifying political education and military training, adequate attention has been paid to improving equipment, weapons, and combat instruments. As a result, all three categories of troops have acquired a greater fighting strength and will certainly deal more vigorous blows to the enemy.

With regard to building political forces, the southern people have satisfactorily settled the relations between developing their political forces numerically and constantly improving the quality of their political forces on the basis of broadening the all-people's great unity bloc and firmly consolidating the key role of the worker-peasant alliance. Today, the southern people's political forces are very numerous and powerful. It is fitting to say that the fourteen million southern people are closing their ranks and moving forward to attack the enemy through military and political struggles.

The political corps, which constitutes the core elements of the people's political struggle movement, has been strengthened both quantitatively and qualitatively and has vigorously developed in the cities as well as in the rural and mountainous areas.

The political forces of the people in southern cities and towns have developed more and more comprehensively and will certainly step up further their political struggle and continuous attacks against the enemy's lairs. The southern people's armed and political forces have been built along a correct and creative line. As result, they have acquired a tremendous strength, which serves as a basis for stepping up the people's war, have closely coordinated armed struggle with political struggle, have achieved extremely great successes, and will certainly defeat completely the U.S. imperialists' war of aggression and overthrow the puppet administration.

If in South Viet Nam our armed forces and people under the NFLSV's leadership have achieved great victories during the past two years, in North Viet Nam our armed forces and people, under the leadership of the party, government, and respected and beloved President Ho, have defeated the U.S. imperialists' war of destruction and frustrated their basic schemes while at the same time continuing to build socialism and wholeheartedly supporting the liberation struggle of the kith-and-kin southern compatriots. We have mobilized and organized all people to participate in resisting the war of destruction by positively fighting the enemy and positively engaging in people's air defense.

In the field of positively fighting the U.S. air and naval forces, we have mobilized all people to fight, using the armed forces as a nucleus. We have simultaneously mobilized and organized all people to emulate in shooting down U.S. aircraft and strengthened the antiaircraft defense forces, the coast guard forces, and the frontier and demarcation line defense forces.

While developing the capacity of all armed branches and the regional forces and the self-defense and militia forces to fight U.S. aircraft, we have developed our antiaircraft defense, air forces, and artillery forces and improved their technical and tactical standards.

We have strongly developed the effect of antiaircraft guns and other ordinary types of infantry weapons, while striving to develop the effect of jet fighter planes and antiaircraft missiles in order to create thick and highly effective fire nets. While fighting, we have carried out training and drawn experiences from the fighting in order to improve the antiaircraft defense quality of our armed forces. We have positively resisted the enemy's planes and warships, while positively improving our combat activity, and we stand ready to fight and defeat the enemy when he ventures to expand the limited war to the North.

The principle of combat adopted by our armed forces in opposing the U.S. imperialists' war of destruction through air and naval power is: positively annihilate the enemy, protect the targets the enemy wants to hit, and preserve and improve our forces. Only by succeeding in annihilating the enemy can we protect our targets from the enemy and preserve and improve our forces. Conversely, only by succeeding in protecting these targets and preserving and improving our forces can we create favorable conditions to annihilate the enemy. On the basis of the concrete situation, sometimes we regard annihilating the enemy as the main task and sometimes we regard protecting targets from the enemy as the main task. Yet normally the principle of positively annihilating the enemy is the most basic and most decisive content of our task.

As a result of their thorough understanding of the principle of fighting against the enemy's aircraft and warships, the northern armed forces, especially the antiaircraft and the air force units, have created many highly effective fighting methods. On the basis of developing the fighting ability of each armed branch and on the basis of the coordination among many armed branches, it is necessary to pay special attention to adopting fighting methods which are most appropriate to each concrete object of combat.

Generally speaking, the objects of combat are the U.S. air and naval forces. However, on the battlefield in general and in each region, each direction, and each battle in particular, it is necessary to determine the concrete objects of combat to be struck, because only by doing so can we fully develop the strength of each armed branch as well as the strength of many armed branches. The basic requirement is to understand firmly the enemy's actions and our own strength and capabilities in order to determine which object must be struck, and how.

In the field of active defense, we have stepped up the people's antiaircraft defense with the aim of restricting the losses in human lives and properties caused by the U.S. Air Force and Navy. We have improved the people's antiaircraft defense organization and the alert-reporting organization and strengthened the construction and consolidation of shelters and communication trenches everywhere. We have evacuated people from the densely populated areas and adjusted the work, study, and life habits to war conditions. We have taken defense measures against the bombings and shellings of the U.S. Air Force and Navy and, at the same time, intensified the protection of security and order and taken precautionary and defense measures against the psychological warfare of the enemy, as well as against the evil plot of the reactionaries and spies.

Events during the two years of struggling against the war of destruction of the U.S. imperialists prove that our defense measures have achieved great results. Although the U.S. imperialists have caused certain damages in human lives and properties of our people, basically the life of our troops and people continues to be stable, the local economy continues to develop, agricultural production continues to increase, communication and transport is not interrupted, and general education, as well as other cultural and artistic activities, continue to develop. Naturally these results have their origin in the fact that our people have satisfactorily fulfilled the task of fighting and producing at the same time. But it is obvious that the defense measures have made an important contribution to this task.

Events during the two years of struggling against the war of destruction and tactics of our army's and people's struggle against enemy planes and warships are completely correct and have achieved great results. We have downed almost 2,300 fighter planes of the U.S. imperialists, sunk and burnt many commando boats and warships of the enemy's navy, annihilated and captured enemy pilots. We have forced the U.S. imperialists to pay a high price for their violations of our airspace and territorial waters.

In addition to actively counterattacking the enemy's planes and warships and actively taking defense measures, we have made timely changes in the direction of our economic building and development and actively maintained and developed communications and transport on all communication lines, especially on roads leading to the front line. This is a very important success which our people have achieved under the leadership of the party, the government, and President Ho.

Thanks to the fact that we have changed the direction of our economic building and development in good time, we have been able to pursue our socialist construction under fierce war conditions. The economy of the socialist north in war time has satisfied people's war and provided our people with sufficient strength to fight victoriously for a long time.

On the production front, our people have strengthened revolutionary heroism, overcome all difficulties, and valiantly produced even though the war of destruction has become increasingly fierce. Even in the areas where the enemy has attacked continuously, such as Vinh Linh, Quang Binh, and other localities, our people have stuck fast to their positions on land and sea and in factories, fighting and producing well at the same time.

Thanks to actively protecting and developing communications and transport, we have satisfactorily insured the demands of the front line, as well as the demands of economic building, cultural development, and the people's life. Our people have smoothed out all our difficulties and hardships and disregarded sacrifices while insuring the continuity of communications and transport with the aim of bringing a large amount of goods to the front line and serving the front line in good time and efficaciously. This is a very great exploit of important strategic significance. This exploit has defeated the wicked and evil design of the U.S. imperialists of creating obstacles to our communications, thus hoping to stop the support of the great rear to the great front line.

It is obvious that our people's war has defeated the war of destruction of the U.S. imperialists. In the fire of war, the socialist North has become increasingly more powerful. The all-people solidarity bloc has become increasingly firm and stable. The people's determination to oppose the Americans for national salvation has become increasingly high. Some seventeen million northern compatriots are siding with thirty-four million southern kith-and-kin compatriots to struggle until final victory.

The U.S. imperialists have sustained heavy defeats in their war of destruction against the north of our country. All their strategic designs have gone bankrupt. It is obvious that the independent activities of an air force —even if it is the modern air force of the U.S. imperialists—cannot have the effect of deciding victory on the battlefield. The U.S. Air Force can cause certain damages to our people, but it surely cannot shake our people's rocklike determination to oppose the Americans for national salvation. It surely cannot save the U.S. imperialists from complete defeat in their aggressive war against the South. The North's big victories demonstrate the great power of the people's war and of the socialist system. This power has dealt and will deal heavy blows at the U.S. Air Force, smashing the so-called superiority of the U.S. Air Force.

Our people throughout the country have won big victories. Our people are taking advantage of these victories to rush forward and defeat the U.S. imperialist aggressors in both the north and south, win increasingly bigger victories, and win final victory.

PART IV

Four conclusions drawn from the two-year old anti-U.S. national salvation resistance.

Basing ourselves on the war situation during the past two years, on the heavy defeats of the U.S. imperialists, and on the big victories of our people, we can draw the following four conclusions:

A. Our people won big victories during a very important phase of the local war strategy of the U.S. imperialists. The possibility of inflicting complete military defeat upon more than a million of U.S., puppet, and satellite troops is becoming a reality.

It can be said that the last two years are a very important phase of the local war strategy of the U.S. imperialists. They have exerted very great war efforts. During the last two years, they have massively increased their troops, boosting quickly the total of U.S. expeditionary troops in South Viet Nam from 50,000 to about 500,000 men and the total of U.S., puppet, and satellite troops to over a million men. They have concentrated their troops to launch two strategic counteroffensives in South Viet Nam and, at the same time, undertaken very serious escalation steps in their war of destruction against North Viet Nam. They have poured an enormous quantity of modern war means into the battlefield and resorted to very cruel war measures, hoping to achieve a decisive victory and bring the war to a turning point.

But they have sustained heavy defeats. They have not only been unable to achieve a turning point toward victory, but have been forced to take a step backward toward defeat. All their strategic objectives—from searching and destroying the enemy's regulars, pacifying the countryside, consolidating the puppet army, and stabilizing the Saigon puppet government to encircling and isolating the southern revolution—have gone bankrupt ignominiously. The strategic efficiency of U.S. troops has been reduced obviously. As for the puppet troops, they seem to be losing in combativity.

During the past two years, our people have passed through many fierce challenges and achieved many big victories, victories having a strategic meaning in both military and political fields. On the southern battlefield—a decisive battlefield—the army and people of the heroic South, under the glorious NFLSV banner, have developed the great people's war to an unprecedentedly high level by stepping up both the military and political struggles and by continually attacking the enemy. The compatriots and liberation armed forces in the south have annihilated an important part of the U.S., puppet, and satellite military forces, developed their own military and political forces very quickly, made the balance of forces tilt in our favor day by day, further developed their initiative on the battlefield, consolidated the liberated areas, further enlarged the front for uniting all the people for the anti-U.S. national salvation struggle, isolated the U.S. aggressors and the country-selling traitors, and continuously heightened the determination of all the people to fight and win.

On the northern battlefield, our army and people under the leadership of the party, headed by respected and beloved President Ho, have successively defeated all the war escalation steps of the U.S. imperialists and inflicted heavy losses upon them, thus causing them to become more embarrassed and stalemated in their aggressive war in Viet Nam. The increasingly strong and powerful socialist north has been strongly developing its role of the great rear toward the great front line.

The victories that our people throughout the country have won during the past two years are comprehensive victories in the military and political fields. In the recent past, the U.S. imperialists have concentrated their troops on carrying out their war policy in order to invade our country. That is why our people have been forced to concentrate our troops and activities on the task of defeating the U.S. bandits on the battlefield. Our people are defeating an army of over a million U.S., puppet, and satellite troops.

This is a military victory of great significance, a heavy blow at the aggressive will of the U.S. war maniacs who are using the policy of force to subdue our people and conquer the south of our country. This great victory of our army and people is eloquent proof demonstrating the great power of the people's war of our country, is a firm argument upon which we can base ourselves to conclude that we are fully able to completely defeat over a million U.S., puppet, and satellite troops in the military field. This ability is becoming a reality.

B. Our people's victory is first of all the victory of the people's warfare strategy and tactics and the victory of the anti-U.S. national salvation victory.

The victory of an armed struggle depends on many factors, the nature of the war, the comparison of forces between the two camps, the strength and quality of the armed forces, the fighting spirit of the armed forces and people, the economic and military potentials, the strategic and tactical leadership, the international assistance, and so forth.

With respect to our country, which is a small and not very populous country and which has to oppose an imperialist ringleader who has carried out a great military buildup with powerful weapons, not only must we have great determination to fight and win, but we must also know how to fight and to win, that is, we must have a good fighting method to be able to defeat the enemy.

The people's warfare strategy and tactics, an important part of our anti-U.S. national salvation struggle, not only have developed the determination to fight and win and the latent potential of our people, but have also developed to the utmost the intelligence and strategem of our people to defeat the enemy. Our people's warfare strategy and tactics have succeeded in concentrating our people's creativeness under the leadership of a correct political and military policy. Moreover, with the experiences of our ancestors in the struggle against foreign invaders in the old days and the experiences of the revolutionary wars in other countries, they brought about glorious victories in our people's resistance against the French colonialists.

Today, our people's war strategy and tactics have further developed in an inspiring and creative manner, have defeated the Americans and puppets in their special war strategy, and are defeating them in their limited war strategy. During the past years, our people's war strategy and tactics have directly tested their strength with that of the strategy and tactics of the U.S. imperialists, the archimperialists, in whom the essence of the bourgeois military doctrine is concentrated. Through challenges, our people's war strategy and tactics have demonstrated their superiority and invincible strength, whereas the enemy's strategy and tactics have proved to be ineffective, old, weak, and decadent along with the decadence and decline of imperialism.

Our people's war strategy and tactics have radically upset the bourgeois military doctrine's viewpoint on the balance of power between two sides and have driven the imperialists' viewpoint on relying upon weapons into complete bankruptcy. Our people's war strategy and tactics have driven the enemy into a situation in which his forces remain insufficient even though they are numerous. He is slow, even though he possesses high mobility. He fails to acquire strength, on the offensive as well as on the defensive, even though he has large numbers of aircraft, artillery pieces, and mechanized vehicles.

Besides, he has exhibited many weaknesses and pitfalls. Although the war has not yet come to an end, it is fitting to say that our people's war strategy and tactics have defeated the Americans' limited war strategy and tactics. The successes and invincible strength of our people's war strategy and tactics are paving the way for greater successes in the days ahead. In a war, once one has fallen into a strategic and tactical stalemate, he can by no means ward off his final defeat even if he possesses plenty of troops, weapons, and money. This is the stalemated situation in which the U.S. imperialists find themselves.

The great successes achieved by our people have proved that our anti-U.S. salvation line is completely correct. Our anti-U.S. national salvation line reflects not only the ironlike determination of our armed forces and people but also the fact that in adopting this line we have ourselves firmly grasped the military science of Marxism-Leninism and the art of war leadership, made a scientific analysis of our own strongpoints and weaknesses and those of the enemy and an analysis of the balance of power between both sides, correctly evaluated the enemy's scheme, thereby setting forth a correct direction with a view to achieving success for our people's resistance.

This line has mobilized and organized all our people and has developed the strength of our entire country to defeat the U.S. aggressors. This line has been deeply imbued with the spirit of independence and the spirit of relying mainly on our own strength, while attaching great importance to the assistance of the fraternal socialist countries and the progressive people all over the world, including the progressive American people. This line has not only held aloft the patriotic banner of our people's struggle for independence and freedom, but has also highly demonstrated our people's proletarian internationalist spirit, because our people's anti-U.S. national salvation struggle is an important contribution to the common struggle for peace, national independence, democracy, and socialism waged by progressive people throughout the world.

It is for this reason that the prestige of our resistance has been increasingly enhanced and the support of the world's peoples for our people has become more and more vigorous. No national liberation struggle in history has ever obtained as much vigorous and comprehensive sympathy and support from the world's peoples as does our people's anti-U.S. national salvation resistance today. The U.S. imperialists have sought by every means to weaken our resistance forces. Yet, they have failed. They have been disastrously isolated in the world. The success of the anti-U.S., national salvation line is also the glorious success of our party's true Marxist-Leninist line and spirit of independence, self-reliance, and international solidarity.

C. The longer the fight, the more mature our forces, and the weaker the enemy forces. Through our anti-U.S. national resistance, all forces of our people have gone through ordeals and become increasingly mature. On the vast front line, through two years of direct confrontation with the U.S. expeditionary troops, not only have the southern army and people scored great achievements, but they have also gained many rich fighting experiences. The liberation armed forces have become increasingly mature, their fighting effect and their strategic efficiency have been more and more increased, and their offensive impetus has become increasingly stronger.

The NFLSV has been increasingly consolidated and enlarged and has increasingly strengthened the people's political forces. The liberated areas have been enlarged and firmly consolidated. The political struggle movement has been widely developed. The people in the southern cities are rising up to struggle more and more fiercely against the U.S. aggressors and the country-selling Vietnamese traitors.

In the North, as the people's armed forces have been developed in quantity, as their quality has been increased, and as they have also learned from the southern liberation armed forces' fighting experiences, their fighting strength has been comprehensively increased.

The U.S. imperialists have attacked the north in a very fierce manner, but our people have never been shaken, and their fighting determination has constantly been heightened. Our army and people have ever more valiantly engaged in production and combat, are determined to insure good communications and transportation, and have devoted themselves to supporting the frontline. Never before was the kith-and-kin Northern-Southern love expressed so ardently and deeply as it is now by the seventeen million Northern compatriots in their production and combat efforts and in support of the frontline. The Northern army and people fear no sacrifice and hardships and are devoting efforts day and night to fulfilling their task toward the vast front line with the spirit of "all for the front line and all for victory."

As for the enemy, although his economic and military potential is great, it is, however, obvious that the more he intensifies the war of aggression in Viet Nam, the more weakened he becomes, and the more difficulties he encounters. Although great, the U.S. military forces have been scattered in many parts of the world. The U.S. imperialists must cope with the national liberation movement, with the socialist bloc, with the U.S. people, and with other imperialist countries.

The U.S. imperialists cannot mobilize all their forces for the war of aggression in Viet Nam. The present force-mobilizing level has far exceeded initial U.S. forecasts and is at sharp variance with U.S. global strategy. At present, the United States does not have enough troops to meet Westmoreland's requirements. In the days ahead, even if the U.S. imperialists send more forces to the south, they will remain unable to stop the decline of the U.S. expeditionary and the puppet troops.

The U.S. troops' fighting spirit has declined, and the U.S. officers' leadership is very poor. Westmoreland remains unable to find any method which can help the U.S. imperialists extricate themselves from their deadlocked situation and to discover any way to help increase the U.S. troops' efficiency and to recover the puppet troops' strength, which has become more and more exhausted.

The enemy's weakness stems from his contradictions and his basic weak points, but is also attributable to a decisive factor: The invincible strength and the great achievements of our people.

Our maturity stems from the radiant just cause of the anti-U.S. national salvation resistance, the all-people great unity bloc with the determination to fight and win, the correct anti-U.S. national salvation lines, and the strategies and tactics of the invincible people's war; the tenacious, indomitable tradition, the potential strength, and the fighting experiences of our people in countering foreign aggression; the absolute superiority of the vast rear—the socialist North—and the strong and wide sympathy and support of the brotherly socialist countries and progressive people in the world. Facts in the past years have proved that the more we fight the stronger we become, and the more the enemy fights the weaker he becomes. This is the law of the protracted, hard, but certainly victorious resistance of our people.

D. The past great achievements are a firm base for our people to move forward to win final victory. The enemy's heavy setbacks will certainly lead him to complete defeat. At the outset, everything is difficult to do. In the past two years, the anti-U.S. national salvation resistance of our people has gone through fierce ordeals and has initially defeated the U.S. imperialists' local war strategy. As we have succeeded in overcoming all difficulties at the beginning, we will certainly succeed in overcoming all the forthcoming difficulties and hardships in a more advantageous manner. The recent great achievements are a firm base for our people to move forward to win final victory.

We do not evaluate our successes subjectively. President Ho has said:

"The nearer victory is, the more hardships there will be." The U.S. imperialists are still very stubborn and cunning. Yet, no matter how frantically they may writhe, they will certainly not be able to change the situation to avoid final defeat. They can by no means turn the cause of defeat into the cause of victory, but will merely deepen the causes leading them toward defeat. Taylor himself, who initiated the flexible reaction strategy and who once directly led the U.S. war of aggression in Viet Nam, had to admit in his latest work, entitled *Responsibility and Response*, that the Americans committed an error in choosing the time, place, and objective in this war. Taylor complained that the Americans have sent troops to South Viet Nam in an instinctive rather than a calculated manner and that the Americans committed themselves too late, yet too deeply, to a war which is very costly in terms of human and material resources. He said that the puppet Saigon army and administration are too weak, are on the decline, and so forth.[4]

The U.S. imperialists will certainly meet with complete defeat in their war of aggression in Viet Nam, because they have encountered a people who not only have a determination to fight and win, but who also know how to fight and defeat all aggressive enemies. The territory of Viet Nam is not vast and its population is not large. Yet, the Vietnamese people possess traditions of indomitability and a very high spirit of self-reliance and have defeated all aggressive enemies. In the past few decades, our Vietnamese people, relying mainly on their own strength, defeated the Japanese Fascists and the French colonialist aggressors and the U.S. interventionists. Today, our people have defeated the Americans' special war strategy and are defeating more than one million U.S., puppet, and satellite troops in their limited war strategy.

This eloquent fact proves that in the present age, even if a people is small, they can have a determination to unite and fight for independence and freedom in accordance with correct and creative political and military lines, know how to rely mainly on their own strength, how to develop the favorable conditions of their time, and how to launch a people's war in conformity with the characteristics and situation of their own country. Having effective fighting methods, they are fully capable of defeating and will certainly defeat all aggressive enemies, including the U.S. imperialists.

Can a small country, which relies mainly upon its own strength, defeat the limited war of aggression of the U.S. imperialists, the archimperialists who possess great military and economic potentials? This is the burning question of our time. The Vietnamese people are replying to this question with their glorious victories. These victories are the Vietnamese people's great contribution to the world's peoples. History has entrusted this glorious mission to our people. Our people are resolved to devote all their minds and abilities to completely defeating the U.S. aggressors and thereby fulfilling this historic task.

PART V

The U.S. imperialists' forthcoming plots and our task.

The U.S. imperialists are confronted with a tragic war situation. On the military front, their strategy has showed that it is ineffective and failing.

Following the failure of the two large-scale strategic counteroffensives, the U.S. imperialists are now at a crossroad: Must the war be limited or expanded? If the war is to be expanded, to what degree must it be expanded? Must efforts be mainly concentrated on stepping up the war of aggression in the South or seeking a turning point by attacking the North? Since the quick victory strategy met with failure and since it is necessary to fight a protracted war, how long will it drag on? What is to be done to increase the U.S. troops' fighting efficiency, which is very poor, to strengthen the puppet troops, who have increasingly declined, and to escape a passive, scattered, and defensive position, and to carry out an offensive strategy?

All these strategic problems are puzzling and very urgent for the U.S. imperialists. From Johnson and McNamara to Westmoreland, they all have clearly realized their bogged down and deadlocked situation in Viet Nam but have not yet found any new solution. They have, at last, resorted to the troop-reinforcement measure. However, they are encountering big difficulties with this problem. If small reinforcements are sent in, it will be impossible to remedy the situation of the U.S. troops who are endangered on the battlefields. If large reinforcements are sent in, this will greatly influence the U.S. people's political and economic life and the U.S. strategy in the world and will not succeed in saving the U.S. imperialists from complete failure.

On the political front, the pacification mission has met with increasingly greater failure and has made no progress. The puppet troops have been increasingly weakened and have lost more and more of their strategic efficiency. Following the deceitful election, the puppet administration remains unable to escape its conflicting, confused, and lost situation. The contradictions among the lackeys of the Americans, among the puppet generals, and between the military faction and the civilian cliques have become ever more acute.

The U.S. imperialists resorted to the deceitful election farce with the aim of applying a new layer of paint on the Thieu-Ky clique. However, through this farce, the Thieu-Ky clique's face of country-selling Vietnamese traitors and lackeys of the Americans has been exposed ever more clearly. U.S. public opinion also acknowledged that Thieu and Ky are shameless and inefficient. The puppet Saigon administration has become increasingly isolated and imperiled in the face of the widespread and vigorous development of the struggle of the heroic Southern army and people.

In the international arena, the U.S. imperialists are also confronted with new difficulties. Since they have been tied firmly to the war of aggression in Viet Nam and have suffered one failure after another, the U.S. imperialists have increasingly revealed their weaknesses and flaws. Revolutionary people the world over have more clearly realized that the U.S. imperialists are wealthy but not strong and that their economic and military potential, although great, are nonetheless limited. The U.S. imperialists are being defeated by a small but heroic people. The more they prolong the war of aggression in Viet Nam, the more the U.S. imperialists are isolated politically in the world.

In the present conflict in the Middle East and Near East, the U.S. imperialists have to cope with a new front. The temporary military victories of the Israeli mercenaries, the lackeys of the Americans, did not put an end to the boiling national liberation movement of the Arab countries in this area but were an event that marked a new step of this movement. The people in the Arab countries are firmly pursuing their struggle and will certainly pursue it to liberate themselves.

The temporary victories of the U.S. imperialists and the Israeli mercenaries have become their mistakes and are causing them increasingly greater difficulties in all fields.

In Latin America, which the U.S. imperialists have always considered an extension of their territory, the revolutionary movement has been developed vigorously, and the Latin American people have stood up to struggle against the U.S. imperialists' interventionist and aggressive policy and the reactionary governments, the lackeys of the Americans, in this part of the world.

In the United States itself, the Johnson government is confronted with the contradictions among the U.S. ruling clique and the U.S. people's increasingly stronger protest. The U.S. Negroes' boiling and widespread struggle is a fierce offensive blow dealt both at the Johnson clique's domestic and foreign policies. Never before has U.S. President Johnson been so deadlocked as he is now. On 14 August 1967 *U.S. News & World*

Report admitted that war, racial conflict, the growing budget deficit, and troubles with the Congress, with the allies, and with the dollar are bad news which are pressing the government from all directions. Suddenly, the situation at the White House has become like that of a building whose roof is about to cave in.[5]

Although they are encountering difficulties and stalemate in Viet Nam, in the world, and even in the United States, because of their stubborn, warlike, and aggressive nature and because they possess economic and military potentials the U.S. imperialists still continue to adopt a policy of military strength in prosecuting their war of aggression in our country. What are the U.S. imperialists' plans?

A. They will continue to step up the limited war on a large scale by increasing the number of U.S. troops in the south and staging fierce raids against the North. After making extensive calculations and weighing the pros and cons, Johnson has decided to increase the number of U.S. troops in the South by another 50,000 men, thus bringing the total number of U.S. forces in South Viet Nam to over half a million by July, 1968.

Yet, the U.S. imperialists are in a difficult and stalemated situation in Viet Nam not because they lack troops, but because their war of aggression is unjust, because they have committed many errors in exerting leadership over the war, and because they have been in a strategic stalemate and tactical crisis. For this reason, even if they increase their troops by another 50,000, 100,000, or more, they cannot extricate themselves from their comprehensive stalemate in the southern part of our country. They cannot overcome their scattered, passive, and defensive battle position, cannot achieve any turning point favorable to them, and can by no means cope with the increasingly vigorous and resolute offensive thrust of the heroic Southern armed forces and people.

It can be asserted that even if they increase the number of U.S. troops in the south by another 100,000, 200,000, or more, the U.S. imperialists will certainly sustain more serious defeats in the southern part of our country.

Recently, on his ninth trip to Saigon, McNamara urged Westmoreland to improve the efficiency of the present number of U.S. troops in the south, in order to raise the present combat ratio of one out of eight U.S. servicemen. Yet, how can Westmoreland do so at a time when U.S. and puppet troops are scattered in many areas and performing many tasks? This situation is irremediable. The organization of the U.S. troops depends heavily upon war equipment and technology and, as a result, it is very cumbersome and requires enormous logistical support. If technical weaponry and logistical support were reduced, the U.S. troops would not be able to perform their combat mission, because they would be deprived of what they regard as their strength. After all is said and done, the ratio of U.S. expeditionary troops actually engaged in combat will continue to be low. This is a bitter fact, a weakness, and a major difficulty for the U.S. imperialist aggressors.

The U.S. imperialists are planning to build a barrier along the temporary military demarcation line. Yet, no well-fortified barrier can avoid collapsing in the face of our people's strength. As a result of the construction of this barrier, U.S. troops would become more scattered and would be trapped in a passive and defensive situation.

The U.S. imperialists hold that to rapidly settle the war, it is necessary for their air and naval forces to intensify their raids against the North. They are stepping up their strikes at our lines of communications on land and on waterways, industrial establishments, cities and towns, populated areas, and so forth. Yet, McNamara himself recently admitted that with the bombing of new targets in the North, no matter what results it may bring, the United States cannot win or shorten the war and that the problem is that the war must be settled on the ground in South Viet Nam.

At present, in their stalemated situation, the U.S. imperialists will writhe even more frantically. They may stage fierce strikes against our cities, villages, and populated areas, further intensify their strikes against our lines of communications, step up their bombing and strafing of our dams and dikes, and strengthen their blockade of our coastal areas. Nevertheless, they definitely cannot shake our people's determination to completely defeat the U.S. aggressors in order to protect the North, liberate the South, and proceed toward reunifying the fatherland.

Our people are not afraid of undertaking sacrifices and hardships and are not afraid of any threat of the Americans. With their intense patriotism, their intelligence and creativeness, and their tremendous organizational ability, our people are resolved to make the North more and more powerful economically and in the field of national defense to insure that production achieves further progress amid the flames of war, to insure uninterrupted communications and transport under all circumstances, and to insure that all our people's needs, especially the requirements of the front line, are met.

Using a large expeditionary corps to wage aggression in the southern part of our country is one of the most serious strategic errors in the history of U.S. imperialism. In this strategic error, the use of air and naval forces to extend the war to the northern part of our country is also one of the most serious errors and one of the most stupid measures adopted by the U.S. imperialists. Regardless of this fact, the U.S. general and field grade officers at the Pentagon have claimed that only by escalating the war against the North can the initiative be regained and the situation reversed.

It is obvious that, faced with continuous defeats, the stupid U.S. imperialists have become more stupid. The more they increase the number of their troops and the further they escalate the war of destruction against the North, the more isolated they become politically, and the more ignominious defeats they will sustain not only in the North, but also in the South, and mainly in the South.

B. The U.S. imperialists may adventurously expand their limited war all over our country. We have adequately prepared ourselves to cope with this possibility. If the U.S. imperialists expand the limited war to the North, it is certain that they will rapidly meet with complete defeat. Although they have more than one million troops at their disposal, the U.S. imperialists have been defeated in the South. If they expand the war to the North with infantry troops, how many more troops would be sufficient? Attacking the North means opening another large battlefield. The U.S. imperialists' forces would become more scattered and would be annihilated more easily.

We have adequately prepared ourselves and are ready to deal annihilating blows at the U.S. imperialists if they adventurously send infantry troops to the North. If they expand the war to the North, the war would become more complex, because by attacking the North they would be attacking the mainland of a member country of the socialist camp. In this enlarged war, the U.S. imperialists would meet with incalculably serious consequences.

The war would not develop according to the U.S. imperialists' subjective expectations. It would also depend on the policy and actions of their adversary. Our people are prepared to annihilate the aggressors. The U.S. imperialists may extend the war to the Royal Kingdom of Laos and intensify their provocations against the Royal Kingdom of Cambodia.

The U.S. imperialists have been passive and defeated in their aggression in South Viet Nam. If they expand the war all over the Indochinese peninsula, they will certainly encounter greater difficulties and sustain more serious defeats. The Vietnamese, Laotian, and Cambodian peoples, united in life as well as in death, will fight side by side against the common enemy, the U.S. imperialist aggressors, to gain complete victory for the three brotherly peoples on their beloved Indochina peninsula. All the activities of the U.S. imperialists clearly prove that they are very obdurate. Despite their bitter defeats, they still persist in continuing their aggression against the southern part of our country. They are striving to step up their criminal war of aggression.

Faced with this situation, the anti-U.S. national salvation resistance of our people sets forth new great and urgent tasks and requirements. With the great victories they have scored, our people in both zones will closely unite, overcome all difficulties and hardships, strongly develop their offensive position, resolutely smash all war attempts of the U.S. imperialists, rush ahead and completely defeat over one million U.S., rebel, and satellite troops, fulfill the glorious historical mission, and lead the anti-U.S. national salvation enterprise to final victory.

In South Viet Nam, the great front line of the fatherland, the compatriots and heroic Liberation Armed Forces have not ceased enhancing their indomitable spirit, bravery, and intelligence, overcoming all hard tests, and writing the most glorious pages of history of the heroic Vietnamese people. The South Vietnamese people have raised high their victorious banner and have shown themselves worthy of the indomitable traditions of Nguyen Dinh Chieu, Truong Dinh, Thu Khoa Huan, worthy of the Nam Ky uprising traditions, worthy of the title of the brass fortress of the fatherland, and worthy of the confidence of the whole nation and of beloved President Ho.

The South Vietnamese people are heroic. The whole nation is directing its eyes toward the compatriots and combatants of South Viet Nam and is closely uniting with South Viet Nam in an unshakable belief that the South Vietnamese people will certainly be victorious. Under the National Liberation Front's leadership, the armed forces and people of South Viet Nam are striving to develop their victories, harassing the enemy, developing their initiatives, and stepping up the people's warfare on the various battlefields.

Following the victorious 1966–1967 winter-spring campaign, the armed forces and people of South Viet Nam are rushing forward and attacking the enemy on both fields, military and political, in the mountain and delta regions as well as in urban centers. From Tri Thien, the Fifth Zone, and Tay Nguyen high plateau, to eastern, central, and western Nam Bo, the guerrilla and large-size forces are strongly developing their effectiveness, inflicting heavy losses on the enemy, and further driving the enemy into a stalemate.

On the South Viet Nam battlefield, the Liberation Armed Forces are clearly showing their ability in destroying U.S. battalions and rebel battle groups. In the days ahead, the Liberation Armed Forces will certainly hit hard and score great victories. They will repeatedly harass the enemy and destroy many large U.S. and rebel units and achieve more resounding victories. On the South Viet Nam battlefield, the guerrilla activities have been further developed. In the days ahead, the guerrilla activities will clearly show their ability in annihilating the enemy everywhere, scattering the enemy in order to fight them, and together with large-size battles, scoring many greater victories.

Along with military activities in South Viet Nam, the political struggles are directly affecting the enemy, destroying the fighting will of the U.S. troops, and dismantling the rebel administration and armed forces. In the days ahead, the political struggle of the South Vietnamese people, especially those in the urban centers, will certainly score more glorious victories. In developing the victorious 1966–1967 campaign, along with the repeated and overall attacks against the enemy, the armed forces and people of South Viet Nam are striving to strengthen and develop the liberated areas and to mobilize more manpower and wealth to further step up and lead the resistance to final victory.

In mid-August, in an enthusiastic atmosphere of the resounding victories throughout the South Viet Nam battlefields, the national liberation front held an extraordinary session to approve the front's political program, aimed at further developing the past great victories of the South Viet Nam revolution, meeting the present requirements of the situation and the revolution, and paving the way for greater victories in the anti-U.S. national salvation struggle of the heroic South Vietnamese people.

The political program set forth the national salvation objectives and tasks of our southern people: to unite all the people, to resolutely defeat the U.S. imperialists' war of aggression, to overthrow the puppet administration, to form a broad national and democratic coalition administration, to build an independent, democratic, peaceful, neutral, and prosperous South Viet Nam, and to proceed toward peaceful reunification of the fatherland. The front's political program is the heroic Southern people's great national unity banner, a banner of determination to fight and win, and a banner of determination to completely defeat the U.S. aggressors.

It is a bugle call which urges the fourteen million Southern people to take advantage of their victories to surge forward to defeat more than one million U.S., puppet, and satellite troops and win great and heroic victories.

In the light of the political program recently proclaimed by the front, the heroic Southern people will certainly develop vigorously all the potential capabilities of the people, develop their offensive thrust, step up their armed and political struggle, make the great people's war develop to a new degree, and completely defeat the U.S. aggressors and their lackeys.

In the North, under the leadership of the party Central Committee and government, headed by respected and beloved President Ho, our armed forces and people are simultaneously engaged, wholeheartedly and to the best of their ability, in production and combat and in resolutely fulfilling the large rear base's obligation toward the large front line. For more than two years, our Northern armed forces and people have overcome all difficulties, fought courageously, and scored many great achievements in production and combat and in serving the front line. Our fight will be more violent in the days ahead. Therefore, the tasks of our armed forces and people will be heavier and require us to make outstanding efforts to achieve greater successes in all fields.

The present glorious and heavy tasks of the north, which have been set forth by our party, government, and President Ho, are: To simultaneously perform production and combat, to pool human and material resources, to contribute toward defeating the enemy's war of destruction against the North, to determinedly step up production under all war circumstances, to support the Southern revolution wholeheartedly and to the best of our ability, and, at the same time, to take precautionary measures against the U.S. imperialists' schemes to expand the limited war all over our country. We must thoroughly and deeply grasp these tasks and strive resolutely to carry them out by every means. Concerning combat, we must step up the people's war, resolutely defeat the U.S. imperialists' war of destruction against the northern part of our country, and hold aloft the banner of determination to defeat the U.S. aggressors through valiant and skillful acts.

Our armed forces and people must appropriately punish all new war escalation steps taken by the U.S. imperialists. We must vigorously develop the moral, material, political, and military strength of the socialist North and, at the same time, effectively use the assistance of the socialist countries in order to defeat the U.S. aggressors. We must regularly heighten our vigilance and firmly grasp the continuous, protracted, and resolute character of our task of fighting against the U.S. imperialists' war of destruction. We have never nourished any illusions about the U.S. imperialists' good will for peace. Only by dealing vigorous and continuous blows at their air, naval, and artillery forces, inflicting heavy losses on them, and reducing their forces and aggressive determination can we check their criminal hands. Dealing vigorous and continuous blows to the U.S. imperialists' air, naval, and artillery forces constitutes the most realistic and most effective act aimed at insuring coordination with the heroic Southern armed forces and people and, at the same time, is a great encouragement for the armed forces and people all over our country.

We must strive to develop the fighting capacity of our armed forces and the various branches of the people's army and make our fire nets against U.S. aircraft, warships, and artillery units increasingly highly effective in order to destroy as many U.S. aircraft, warships, and artillery units as possible and to protect the socialist North more satisfactorily.

We must invent more methods of fighting the U.S. Air Force. For more than two years, as of 14 September 1967, the U.S. imperialists had suffered about 2,300 aircraft shot down over the north.[6] This indicates the tragic bankruptcy of the U.S. Air Force's tactics and proves that we have had creative and appropriate tactics developed by each of our forces and branches.

Now faced with the U.S. imperialists' new plots and acts of sabotage, it is all the more necessary for us to devise more brave and resourceful tactics in order to constantly take the enemy by surprise and to cause him to sustain heavy defeats. We must also pay great attention to improving and developing methods of fighting the U.S. naval force and artillery units. With a steadfast militant determination, heroism, courage, and intelligence, we must do our best to develop the superiority of our existing weapons and be determined to invent highly effective tactics in order to punish the U.S. naval force and artillery units appropriately.

Along with positively fighting the enemy, we must better perform our air defense tasks. It is necessary to continue consolidating our people's air defense system, to consolidate and develop our alert network against the enemy's aircraft and warship attacks, and to consolidate and build more shelters and communication trenches, especially in densely populated places like factories, hospitals, schools, and so forth. It is necessary to promptly commend and reward individuals, units, and localities for their achievements in people's air defense. At the same time, appropriate disciplinary measures must be taken against individuals, units, and localities for their negligence of air defense tasks, negligence which may cause avoidable damage and losses.

On the communications and transportation front, our soldiers and people have made great efforts, have fought valiantly and heroically, and have scored outstanding achievements. In the days to come, we must make greater efforts in order to achieve more glorious victories on this front. No matter how fierce and ruthless enemy attacks may be, we must be resolved to insure smooth communication operations, to meet the demands of the front line and the demands for combat and production, and to insure the people's livelihood.

While continuing their resistance against the U.S. imperialists' war of destruction, the Northern armed forces and people have not stopped preparing to fight and defeat the enemy if he ventures to expand the local war to North Viet Nam. We must continue making more careful and urgent ideological and organizational preparations for vanquishing the U.S. ground force, as well as any of the enemy's armed services, on whatever scale. We must closely combine our fighting against the war of destruction with those preparations in order to defeat the enemy under all other war circumstances.

With regard to production, we must positively implement the policies and plans of the party and the state concerning the change of trends for building and developing the economy and continue building the material and technical base for socialism. We must do our utmost and resolutely fulfill the state plan in order to meet the immediate demands of the anti-U.S. national salvation struggle, the demands for building socialism, and the demands of the people's everyday life.

We must step up agricultural and industrial production, attach importance to developing local industries, and endeavor to increase the economic potentials and national defense force of our people. During the past two years, under the correct leadership of the party and the government and under the violent fighting conditions, North Viet Nam's economy has indicated the superiority of socialism.

North Viet Nam's socialist agriculture is settling with good results such problems as food, irrigation, intensive cultivation designed to increase production, increases in yearly crops, land clearing, and so forth. Our newborn industry has made very positive contributions to developing production, insuring the people's livelihood, and serving national defense.

On the basis of these achievements, our people can and will surely achieve socialist construction in North Viet Nam more satisfactorily under the violent fighting conditions. The anti-U.S. national salvation struggle of our people in the entire country has entered a very urgent state. As a large rear of the entire country, North Viet Nam is resolved to mobilize all of her manpower and wealth to carry out the slogan: "Everything for the front line, everything for victory."

The clear-sighted leadership of the party and the government, the unbroken solidarity of the people, the determination to fight to win, the spirit of sacrificing everything for the fatherland's independence and freedom, and the outstanding efforts of our people are the most basic guarantees for our people to have sufficient strength to fight tenaciously and protractedly to score greater achievements and advance toward the final victory.

Our people's armed forces must be fully and deeply aware of the enemy's schemes and their present revolutionary and military tasks, uphold the spirit of resolutely fighting to achieve victory, and increase their fighting capacity in order to become the truly invincible armed forces of the heroic Vietnamese people. In the past, under the leadership of the party and President Ho, our people's armed forces have upheld revolutionary heroism, developed their "determination to fight and win" tradition, incessantly heightened their fighting strength, fought in an extremely valiant and heroic manner, and won glorious victories on all battlefields. Never before were our people's armed forces so strong as they are now. Our people's armed forces are a heroic community of a heroic people. On all anti-U.S. battlefields, officers and enlisted men and units of our people's armed forces have performed thousands of heroic acts. On all anti-U.S. battlefields, our people's armed forces have stood side by side with the people in raising high President Ho's banner of resolutely fighting to defeat the U.S. aggressors and have achieved glorious victories.

As the shock force of our people in the present anti-U.S. national salvation resistance war, our people's armed forces are highly enthusiastic over their achievements and feats of arms in building their ranks and fighting the enemy. We must not be subjective and conceited and must endeavor to struggle without respite to improve our fighting quality, to develop our fighting force, and to make our people's armed forces, which have fought well, fight better and resolved to fight to vanquish the U.S. imperialist aggressors under all war circumstances.

The present task of our people's armed forces is to fight and at the same time build themselves into an invincible steel-like force for completely defeating the U.S. aggressors. We know that to defeat the enemy, the armed forces must have a certain number of troops and at the same time be of high quality. Of these two aspects, special emphasis must be laid upon quality. To be of high quality, a company must be as strong as ten ordinary companies.

The military theory of Marxism-Leninism points out that the power of a revolutionary force must not be measured by the number of its troops alone. Quantity is necessary, but on the basis of a certain quantity, quality plays a decisive role. The problem of improving quality is a precious tradition and a great experience of our people's armed forces. From the guerrilla units of the pre-1945 general uprising period to the army units during the resistance against the French colonialist aggressors, our people's armed forces, thanks to their high fighting quality, have used small units to defeat larger enemy units and achieved victories everywhere.

The drives for training troops for achieving victories, for training officers and improving soldiers, and for political and military reeducation have helped our People's Armed Forces fulfill in an outstanding way all fighting tasks during the anti-French resistance. During the past few years, the "three firsts" drive and the campaign for building "determination to win" units have made important contributions to making the People's Armed Forces grow quickly and win glorious victories. The burning lesson of the Southern army and people, who are using a force of high quality to defeat an enemy who is superior numerically and who is equipped with stronger weapons, is encouraging us to struggle continually and improve the quality of our People's Armed Forces.

In the struggle against the U.S. imperialists' war of destruction, we have clearly realized the important influence of the task of improving our fighting quality. The Nguyen Viet Xuan anti-aircraft artillery battalion, the Sixth Missile Regiment, the First and Second Companies of the air force, the Seventh Detachment of the navy, many artillery units, many self-defense militia units, and so forth have fought very well: they are typical examples of units having high fighting quality. The anti-French resistance of our people in the past, in its entire process as well as in the development of various combats and campaigns, has brought forth brilliant examples of the great influence of troop quality.

In the present anti-U.S. national salvation resistance, we do not have as many troops and modern weapons as the U.S. imperialists and their lackeys; yet we have defeated the enemy. This proves the great influence of troop quality. After carefully studying the strategic and fighting efficiency of the armed forces in general as well as of each category of troops, each military service, and each unit in particular, we have clearly realized the great influence of troop quality. Therefore, the problem of improving troop quality and developing their fighting power is now a task of strategic significance having a decisive meaning for the task of achieving our people's great determination to completely defeat the U.S. aggressors. To strive to struggle and improve troop quality and to develop the fighting power of all three categories of troops will surely increase by many times the strategic and fighting efficiency of the People's Armed Forces, achieve great progress and a big leap forward, and bring about great changes in the political and military situation of the resistance.

The problem of improving the armed forces' quality must be raised in a comprehensive way, embracing all fields: political, military, logistic, ideological, organizational, and efficiency. We must implement this policy in all three categories of troops—regulars, local troops, and self-defense militiamen—in all military services and branches, and in all military organs at all echelons with the aim of developing the power of all the components of the People's Armed Forces in order to defeat the U.S. aggressors in all war circumstances.

We must endeavor to further increase the regulars' fighting, making all regular units fight better and actually become the iron fists which will win every battle and continually and quickly and completely annihilate the enemy everywhere in our country. We must pay more attention to increasing the fighting power of local troops in order to make the local units from the mountainous region to the coastal areas become strong units having great fighting capacity in the localities and being able to fight independently as well as in cooperation with militiamen and regulars, fulfill all tasks in an outstanding way, annihilate the enemy forces, launch the guerrilla war, and protect the people.

We must pay great attention to increasing the fighting power and numerical strength of the self-defense militia, thus making the self-defense militia become a strong, stable, and widespread armed force ready to fight the enemy and fight him well with all weapons on hand or to be obtained, play the role of a shock force in production, and supply the local and regular forces with good officers and soldiers.

We must pay greater attention to increasing the quality of the armed forces' military organs and schools so that these organs can be of great help to military leaders and commanders, so that these schools can train and improve many officers of high quality, thus actively contributing to the fulfillment of the building and fighting task of the people's armed forces. We must endeavor to satisfy the following requirements:

A. To heighten the political and ideological levels of officers and men so that they can more deeply understand the sacred anti-U.S. national salvation duty, have a boiling revolutionary spirit, have a strong offensive spirit and a high fighting will, unite closely around the party Central Committee, the government, and President Ho, thoroughly implement the policies and lines of the party and the instructions and orders of higher echelons, fulfill all fighting, building, and other tasks, and have the determination to completely defeat the U.S. aggressors and win the greatest victories on the battlefield under any war circumstances.

B. To heighten their technical and tactical levels, it is necessary to pursue the training of officers and men so that they can maintain and cleverly use their weapons and equipment and flexibly and efficiently apply the tactical principles and fighting methods of the people's war. It is necessary to lay emphasis on the quality of resoluteness, courage, resourcefulness, and creativeness in combat and study. We must also pay special attention to training units so that they can launch military operations, station troops, and fight continually on all battlefields under arduous and fierce conditions.

C. To rearrange and improve organizations and equipment in order to fit them to the combat requirements, to the characteristics and duties of different units, to battlefield conditions, and to our capacity, in order to make the various units become orderly, light, and strong organizationally and have great fighting power. It is necessary to streamline the organization, arrange the forces rationally, and build for various organizations work habits and systems to be applied in military operations and combat.

D. To streamline party organizations and mass organizations; to streamline party committees and branches in order to make them strong and stable in all fields; to regularly develop the party; to improve party members so that they will have a high political level and be able to mobilize the masses; to build leading methods for various party echelons from top to bottom; to continuously heighten the leading role of the party under all circumstances; to continue streamlining the mass organizations so that these organizations can fulfill all their tasks and missions, fully develop the intelligence and capacity of all their members, and become a great force in each unit.

E. To improve the troops' material life, heighten their technical level, and improve their stamina and endurance; to strictly enforce the systems of preserving and repairing weapons and military equipment; to rationally use spare weapons, ammunition and military equipment; to strictly enforce the principle of taking weapons from the enemy to equip ourselves; to satisfactorily organize the feeding of troops, their physical training, the improvement of their endurance and stamina, and the improvement of their health, thus insuring a high percentage of fighting men; to satisfactorily organize the treatment of wounded and sick troops so that they will be restored and returned to their units quickly.

F. To develop and increase the efficiency of cadres at all levels. The cadres have played a very important role in building the armed forces and in improving their fighting ability. Only when the cadres are good can units become good and fulfill their fighting task and other tasks. Therefore, it is necessary to strive to develop and increase the efficiency of cadres at all levels and to pay attention to heightening the troop units' leadership, command, and management level and the organizational level in order to fulfill all concrete tasks under difficult, complicated circumstances, especially under urgent, fierce fighting circumstances.

We must have a very high determination and many effective measures in order to swiftly increase the efficiency of cadres at all levels. Only on this basis can we satisfy the early maturity of the armed forces and the war development. At present, the movement to heighten the quality and to develop the fighting strength of the people's armed forces and to increase their determination to fight and defeat the U.S. aggressors is highly significant with regard to the fighting and building task of our people's armed forces. This movement requires all cadres and combatants to make strenuous efforts and to devote themselves to increasing the fighting strength of all units to a new high degree.

The leading and commanding cadres bear a very great responsibility. Cadres and party members must certainly take the lead in this important movement. All cadres at all levels must have a great determination. This is the determination to fight and completely defeat the U.S. aggressors. It is necessary to see all the enemy's setbacks, difficulties, confusion, and deadlock, and, at the same time, it is necessary to see all the great successes and capabilities of our army and people, to make a detailed study of the enemy and ourselves, and to firmly grasp the laws of the resistance and the skilled military art of the people's war. Let all cadres at all levels enthusiastically move forward, be more determined and valiant, and resolutely fight and defeat and know how to defeat the aggressors in order to make valuable contributions to the glorious task of our people and people's armed forces.

On the vast front line, the Southern Liberation Armed Forces are simultaneously fulfilling the fighting and building tasks and have incessantly increased their fighting strength. The resounding feats of arms, the swift maturity, the outstanding progress, and the abundant achievements of the heroic Southern Liberation Armed Forces are vigorously encouraging all cadres and combatants of our people's armed forces. It is hoped that the heroic Southern Liberation Armed Forces will score great achievements in fulfilling their fighting task as well as in fulfilling the task of increasing their fighting strength and will, together with all our people, move forward to completely defeat the U.S. aggressors.

In carrying out President Ho's sacred anti-U.S. national salvation appeal in order to completely defeat the more than one million U.S., puppet, and satellite troops, our people's armed forces must have in mind and carry out his advice: be loyal to the party and the people, fulfill all tasks, overcome all difficulties, and defeat all aggressors. All our cadres and combatants must clearly understand their tasks, strive to struggle, swiftly increase the fighting strength of the people's armed forces, and resolutely fulfill their glorious task as shock forces of all our people in the anti-U.S. national salvation struggle.

The victories on the battlefields are encouraging us and filling us with enthusiasm. All our people are awaiting from our people's armed forces new steps of progress and more resounding and greater feats of arms in the days ahead. The history of our people is the history of a victorious people. Tran Hung Dao, Le Loi, Nguyen Trai, and Quang Trung fiercely fought an enemy of greater strength and were gloriously victorious.

Since the party and President Ho assumed leadership, our people have brought to success the August Revolution and the resistance and successively defeated the Japanese Fascists, the French imperialists, and the U.S. interventionists. In the past ten years, our people have successively defeated all the aggressive schemes of the U.S. imperialists, their neocolonialist aggressive policy with their traditional tricks, and their special war with more than half a million puppet troops, and have defeated and are defeating their local war strategy with more than one million U.S., puppets, and satellite troops in the South and have, at the same time, defeated and are defeating their war of destruction with air and naval forces in the North.

It is obvious that our Vietnamese people have sufficient determination and capabilities and will certainly and completely defeat the U.S. invaders' war of aggression. In the fierce fight against the U.S. aggressors, the most cruel and barbarous imperialist ringleaders in the present war, our Vietnamese people will certainly achieve complete victory, because our great national salvation resistance has been glowing with a just cause, has enjoyed correct political and military lines and the unity strength of our people who rose up to struggle, has possessed a firm determination and skilled fighting methods, and has enjoyed great assistance from the brotherly socialist countries and strong sympathy and encouragement from progressive people in the world, including the U.S. people.

The anti-U.S. national salvation resistance of our people is the continuation and development of the August revolutionary struggle and the anti-French resistance in the past. This resistance must overcome a great many sacrifices and hardships but will certainly score glorious successes. This is the great struggle, which has never been seen before in the country-building and country-protecting history of our people. This struggle is also of great international significance, because it contributes to protecting the socialist bloc and stepping up the movement to liberate the peoples and to protect peace in the world. This struggle is a great contribution of our Vietnamese people to the common revolutionary struggle of the people in the world to oppose imperialism headed by the U.S. imperialists and to achieve peace, national independence, democracy, and socialism.

Under President Ho's "determination to defeat the U.S. aggressors" flag, let all our army and people take advantage of victories to move forward. The Vietnamese people are determined to completely defeat more than a million U.S., puppet, and satellite troops. The U.S. imperialists' neocolonialist war of aggression will certainly be defeated. The people's war of the heroic Vietnamese people will certainly win complete victory!

SOME ASPECTS OF GUERRILLA WARFARE IN VIET NAM 4

by Hoang Van Thai

Lieut. Gen. Hoang Van Thai has long been one of the senior military chiefs in the "Democratic Republic of Viet Nam" (DRV), but little is known about him abroad. He is believed to be a brilliant strategist and to be popular with the army.

Born about 1906 in Thai Binh Province, North Viet Nam, he was trained as a schoolteacher but did not make education his permanent career. Instead, he joined the Indochinese Communist Party (ICP), and became a close friend and associate of Vo Nguyen Giap. When the ICP organized an insurrection in 1939, and as a result was declared illegal, he fled with Giap and other leaders to Kwangsi, southern China.

Though little is known of Thai's activities during the Second World War, he almost certainly played an important part in building up the military forces of the Viet Minh. After the creation of the DRV in August 1945, he had the task of helping Giap to establish a new national army from the limited resources at their disposal. In March 1946 he was promoted to brigadier general and was made deputy chief of staff of the armed forces. For all his power and influence he remained in the background except for such occasions as in 1950, when he became one of the original founders of the Sino-Viet Nam Friendship Association.

In 1958 Thai was made director general of training in the Ministry of Defense and appointed to the National Scientific Research Board. In 1959 he was named chairman of the Central Physical Culture and Sports Committee and promoted to major general. Subsequently he was promoted to lieutenant general.

In addition to his grasp of military affairs, Thai's other asset is his knowledge of political doctrine. He is not content to exercise control from his office. He lectures officers and men on the need for raising their level of "political consciousness"; on the relationship between the army and higher output; and on the "further advance to socialism." Since 1959 he has risen rapidly and his interest in the political "education" of the army has been evident. He is still vice-chief of the General Staff, and in 1961 he was concurrently appointed a vice-minister of national defense. In 1960 he was elected to the Central Committee of the Lao Dong party.

SOME ASPECTS OF GUERRILLA
WARFARE IN VIET NAM

PART I

On Some Fundamental Questions of
Guerrilla Warfare in Viet Nam

VIET NAM, a relatively small country without a very large population, has a long past marked by struggles against foreign invasion and for national construction.

Bachdang, Chilang, Dongda,[1] Dienbienphu, and many other names have been throughout the ages glorious landmarks in the history of the Vietnamese people's struggle for independence.

Since the birth of the Indochinese Communist Party headed by Comrade Ho Chi Minh, the Vietnamese people have scored achievements of unprecedented importance. They made the 1945 August Revolution, broke the French-Japanese yoke and founded the Democratic Republic of Viet Nam, the first people's democratic state in Southeast Asia. Then they vanquished the French imperialists and U.S. interventionists in the first war of resistance (1945–1954). At present, the South Vietnamese people are waging a second war of resistance against the U.S. aggressors and their stooges, a liberation war which is winning ever more decisive successes.

In the course of the revolutionary struggles and wars of resistance in Viet Nam, guerrilla warfare has always occupied a very important place. This short account will deal with some fundamental problems and mention a certain number of experiences relative to that warfare.

Role and Importance of Guerrilla
Warfare in Viet Nam

Marxism-Leninism has taught the Vietnamese people a lesson which has been confirmed by their own experiences: to free themselves from the yoke of the imperialists and their agents, they have no other way than to use revolutionary violence to smash the rulers' administrative machinery and build up for themselves a people's dictatorship.

The Indochinese Communist Party, the present Viet Nam Workers'

Party, have creatively applied Marxism-Leninism to Viet Nam's practical situation. Under their leadership, the Vietnamese people has made a national-democratic revolution along a correct line to overthrow the imperialist oppressors and the reactionary feudal class, and win back national independence and land for the tillers.

This correct line has encouraged the large masses of the people, especially the toiling peasants, to rise up and wage an evergrowing struggle for the accomplishment of the revolutionary tasks set by the party. Availing itself of the experiences drawn by the world proletariat from their revolutionary struggles, our party has worked out adequate forms of political and armed struggle at the various stages of the revolution. At each stage, each form of struggle has a role to play and exercises a definite action. But in the whole process of the revolution, armed struggle has had a direct and decisive action. It has always been linked to political struggle from which it stemmed, then developed into armed insurrection and reached its highest form which was the people's war, a war fought by the entire people on all planes.

In Viet Nam, guerrilla warfare is a form of armed struggle in particular and of revolutionary struggle in general.

It was a guerrilla warfare conducted in localities where conditions were available, which led to the creation of revolutionary conditions in the period of preparation for the 1945 August Revolution in order successfully to stage local insurrections and general insurrection. In this period, guerrilla warfare was a form of armed insurrection for the seizure of power, and a question of revolutionary strategy.

During the first war of resistance (1945–1954), guerrilla warfare helped us to push the struggle ahead and turn the patriotic war against the French imperialists and U.S. interventionists into a real people's war, a war waged by the entire people on all planes. Guerrilla warfare was a school for the Vietnamese people to train themselves in the fight for national salvation, to form cadres and build up military and paramilitary forces. In the enemy's rear, guerrilla warfare demoralized, wore out, disintegrated, and destroyed his troops, pinned down his mobile forces, and coordinated its action with that of the regular warfare in the main theatre of operations. Better still, it was a form of armed insurrection for the seizure of power and establishment of guerrilla base areas. It effectually frustrated the enemy's "lightning war" plan and his maneuvers to feed war with war and make Vietnamese fight Vietnamese. It transformed the enemy's rear into zones of operations and helped us create a permanent strategic offensive position there. During the war of resistance against the French imperialists, guerrilla warfare constituted an important strategic problem, one of the two basic forms of the people's war, gave birth to regular warfare, and coordinated its action with the latter to defeat the enemy.

At present, the struggle for liberation waged by the South Vietnamese people is a guerrilla warfare at its highest stage. It started with local insurrections by which the toiling peasants seized power in the villages and gradually expanded into a vast and steady movement of political struggle by rural and urban masses in coordination with guerrilla warfare which unceasingly grew in intensity everywhere. During the last ten years, with no arms in hands at the beginning, the South Vietnamese people have achieved a great work, liberated four-fifths of the territory with over ten million people, shattered all the U.S. imperialists' aggressive schemes and won glorious victories: Apbac, Chala, Locninh, Bienhoa, Binhgia, Anlao, Pleiku, Quinhon, Phumy, Saigon. . . . All this series of successes testified to the rapid growth of the guerrilla warfare carried out by our fourteen million Southern compatriots, a war long and hard but certainly victorious. It shows that the U.S. imperialists and their agents are doomed to failure: U.S. special warfare has been and will be defeated by the people's guerrilla warfare. At present, guerrilla warfare in South Viet Nam constitutes not only a military tactic or strategy, but also a form of armed insurrection by the peasantry in the process of a protracted revolution taking place in a set balance of forces between revolution and counter-revolution in a backward agricultural country under neocolonialism. Stemming from the people's political struggle, it has become a tool for the maintenance and development of the revolution staged by the masses.

Dominated for many decades by imperialism, Viet Nam was in the same conditions as many other colonial and dependent countries in Asia, Africa, and Latin America. Thanks to revolution and long years of a revolutionary war, North Viet Nam has been completely liberated and is steadily progressing toward socialism, while South Viet Nam has been winning decisive successes. Reality has shown that revolutionary violence, revolutionary struggle, and protracted revolutionary war in which guerrilla warfare occupies an extremely important place are the path our people must follow to reconquer independence, freedom, and happiness. Reality has also shown that in the present juncture of the world, when a people, however small and weak, is united to rise up and follow a correct line, determined to struggle for its dearest aspirations, and creatively applies adequate forms of struggle, that people is fully able to vanquish a powerful army of any imperialist aggressor and his hirelings, be it the U.S. aggressor, chieftain of world imperialism.

Characters and Forms of Guerrilla
Warfare in Viet Nam

In Viet Nam guerrilla warfare is a form of armed struggle of the large masses of the people, of the local military and paramilitary forces which are weak or relatively weak, against much better equipped enemy troops. It consists in dealing blows to the enemy everywhere, with all means and weapons available, in conducting scattered fights and, at the same time, in mobilizing the people for the struggle with most varied forms. It aims at thinning out and destroying the enemy's live force, defending and preserving our political and economic strength. It compels the enemy to disperse his forces, thus creating conditions for us to develop our regular warfare and operate in coordination with it to achieve victory.

In Viet Nam, guerrilla warfare bears the following fundamental characters:

1. Mass character, people's character. Guerrilla warfare is a common form of armed struggle by various strata of the people, old and young, men and women of all religions, nationalities and political tendencies. In a backward agricultural country like Viet Nam, it is the common form of armed struggle by the toiling peasants. "He who has a gun should use his gun, he who has a sword should use his sword, he who has no sword should use picks, mattocks, and sticks."[2] It is in this spirit that every Vietnamese patriot has risen up against the invaders. It is for this reason that guerrilla warfare has developed throughout the country, in delta and mountain, in town and countryside. It constitutes a kind of magic network which holds the enemy in its meshes, scatters his forces, harasses him day and night, wears him out and drives him to a war of attrition without a way out.

2. All-sided character. By means of guerrilla warfare, the Vietnamese people have fought the enemy not only in the military but also in the economic and political fields. The close connection between armed struggle on the one hand and economic and political struggle on the other, is a characteristic of guerrilla warfare in Viet Nam. Economic struggle consists in blocking the enemy's economy, sabotaging his economic bases, frustrating his design of feeding war with war, turning his rear into ours, and depriving him of his sources of manpower and wealth. Political struggle aims at mobilizing and organizing the masses in the enemy's rear to defend their vital rights, denouncing his maneuvers and attacking his political foundations so as to weaken and dislocate them.

In Viet Nam, guerrilla warfare has been waged in the conditions in which the people have to face an enemy much superior in equipment and technique: French imperialism in the first war of resistance, and U.S. imperialism at present. This experience lies within the scope of a general law governing all wars of liberation made by oppressed peoples against stronger imperialist enemies. With their bare hands at the start, the Vietnamese people have resolutely risen up and resisted to the end, carried out construction while combating, grown with the fighting, and equipped themselves with weapons captured from the enemy. They have opposed their courage and self-sacrificing spirit to enemy aircraft, cannons, tanks, and warships. Therefore in Viet Nam, guerrilla warfare has been bitter and fierce, long and hard.

In guerrilla warfare, the Vietnamese people have created extremely varied forms of struggle: sabotage, scorched land policy, noncooperation with the enemy, stratagems to harass or wear out the enemy, spike traps, mine traps, and traps of many other kinds, attacks on communication lines, ambushes, raids against the enemy post network, airfields, dumps, C.P.s, gun-nests. . . . Guerrilla warfare takes higher forms, when the fighters storm the adversary's posts to attract and destroy his reinforcements, frustrate mopping-up operations, raze concentration camps and strategic hamlets while building combat villages. All these forms are suitable to the people's and all-sided character of guerrilla warfare, they are an expression of the large masses' participation in the patriotic war in which weak forces are opposed to strong ones, and rudimentary weapons to modern ones. They drive the enemy's troops into an impasse in spite of his superiority in arms and equipment (aviation, navy, armored force, and others) and make him unable to counterattack efficaciously. U.S. military theoricians have admitted that the war in Viet Nam is holding in store for them surprises which are to be found in no military textbooks. The more developed the guerrilla warfare with an ever larger participation of the people, the richer its concrete forms.

Lessons Taught by Guerrilla Warfare in Viet Nam

The success of guerrilla warfare in Viet Nam is that of a just war waged by the people over the unjust war by aggressive imperialism. It is also that of our correct political and military lines, and of the creative application of Marxism-Leninism to the concrete situation in Viet Nam.

Following are the main lessons we have learnt:

1. We must mobilize, train, and organize the masses and encourage them to participate in ever greater numbers in guerrilla warfare.

Every achievement is performed by the people. We must see to uniting the entire people, mobilizing and arming them. This springs from our following conception: revolution is the work of the masses of the people who precisely decide the outcome of the war. To be able to mobilize and organize the masses, we must first and foremost work out a correct political line likely to satisfy the fundamental aspirations of the toiling masses, particularly the workers and peasants; we must constantly foster their love for the fatherland and their hatred for the enemy, inspire them with high revolutionary consciousness, courage to fight whatever aggressors, spirit of relying on their own strength, and will for independence and sovereignty; we must train them in enduring privations, overcoming difficulties, and fighting resolutely until final victory is won. We must organize them into a broad united national front on the basis of the worker-peasant alliance, unceasingly consolidate the political forces which form the cornerstone of guerrilla warfare, set up the people's military and paramilitary forces, and temper them in the fight.

2. We must constantly and closely coordinate political struggle with armed struggle, firmly grasp the three fundamental tasks of guerrilla warfare, correctly lay down the guiding principle of action in each of the three zones of the country.

As has been said above, the close link between political and armed struggles was in the past a characteristic of guerrilla warfare in Viet Nam; it still is at the present time in South Viet Nam. In tightly coordinating these two forms of struggle we aim at furthering the political supremacy of the masses in rural and urban areas, striking at the weak points of the enemy and shaking to their foundations his political and military bases. For this purpose, we must satisfactorily carry out the three main tasks of guerrilla warfare—armed attack and political attack on the adversary, and agitation in his ranks—in order to put into practice the watchword: "Workers, peasants, and soldiers, unite!" thereby enlarging the revolutionary ranks and, at the same time, weakening the enemy's. The realization of these tasks must follow leading principles suitable to each of the three zones.

a. In the enemy-occupied zone, priority is given to political struggle. Here revolutionary force must be enlarged constantly and the masses trained for struggle in simple and then complex forms.

b. In the guerrilla zone, contended by the two parties, political struggle must be combined with armed struggle and we must stick to the people and the locality where we operate.

c. In the guerrilla base areas, parallel with construction work in all fields, we must prevent and frustrate all the enemy's encroachment attempts.

The question is gradually to transform the guerrilla zone into a guerrilla base area and the enemy-occupied zone into a guerrilla zone, in order to enlarge our liberated zone and narrow down the enemy occupied zone. In this way, guerrilla warfare does not cease to develop and advance to ever higher forms, creating conditions favorable to the promotion of regular warfare to win final victory.

3. We must unceasingly consolidate and extend the guerrilla base areas and build combat villages.

Guerrilla bases and combat villages constitute the rears as well as the fortresses of the guerrilla forces. In consequence, the launching and maintenance of guerrilla warfare are closely connected with the consolidation and extension of guerrilla bases and with the building of combat villages. The primordial condition to set up a guerrilla base is the political consciousness of the masses of the people. Therefore, to build solid guerrilla bases and combat villages, leading cadres and guerrilla forces must stick to the people and the place where they operate. They must constantly educate, organize, and lead the masses to the struggle, see to it that the masses' living conditions be improved and land distributed to the peasants if local conditions permit to do so. We must know how to take advantage of the facilities of the terrain or modify it to make it suit our purpose, erect simple yet efficient defence works, underground hiding-places, spike and other traps, minefields in order to check the enemy's mopping-up operations, and preserve our bases. We must not only constantly consolidate the latter politically, militarily, and economically but also enlarge them by means of transforming guerrilla zones into guerrilla bases and creating as many of these as is possible to establish a system of bases capable of supporting one another to encircle and scatter enemy troops and thus better strike at them.

4. There must be a close coordination of action between the military forces and people's paramilitary forces, especially between local troops and self-defence militia.

The militia constitutes the paramilitary force of the masses, first of all, the toiling peasants. They do not give up production, they carry it on and while embarking in production they fight to safeguard it, they stick to the people and to their locality, forming the core of the guerrilla forces in the villages. Local troops are the armed forces of provinces and districts, the core of the guerrilla forces there, and, at the same time, the link between the militia and regular troops. While the people's militia conducts the struggle in the villages to pin down the enemy and create conditions for local troops to muster and destroy the enemy, the latter assume the heavy task of helping the militia to develop. On the other hand, when regular troops scatter in small units to start guerrilla warfare in the enemy's rear, they must make it a duty to train the local troops and militia. The close coordination between the military and paramilitary forces is a condition to ensure the growth of guerrilla warfare into regular warfare.

5. The principles of guerrilla warfare must be understood thoroughly and applied correctly.

These principles govern all the guerrilla activities of the military and paramilitary forces, they aim at enabling these forces to secure victory over an enemy stronger in equipment and technique. According to our own experience, the following principles must be firmly grasped: to develop to the highest point the moral factor, courage, initiative, and cleverness so as to defeat a much better equipped enemy; to strive to destroy as many enemy live forces as possible while preserving and developing our own; to strive to annihilate enemy forces in small operations, while exhausting him on a large scale; constantly to ensure the initiative of action and never to allow ourselves to be driven to the defensive; always to act with flexibility, in secrecy, and surprise; strike at the enemy where he is weak and exposed, in whatever difficult situation the cadres and militiamen must stick to the people and to their locality and mobilize the masses for the struggle.

Above-mentioned are some fundamental questions of guerrilla warfare in Viet Nam.

Thanks to a thorough understanding of these questions, the Vietnamese people under the leadership of the party of the proletariat succeeded in overthrowing the French-Japanese yoke, vanquished the U.S.-supported French Expeditionary Corps, and at present are defeating the American aggressors in their war of destruction against North Viet Nam. In South Viet Nam, under the leadership of the South Viet Nam National Front for Liberation, the army and people have developed the traditions and experiences acquired in the first resistance war and thoroughly grasp these basic problems. This explains why the further they fight the stronger they become and are now driving the U.S. imperialists into a blind tunnel. For these last ten years and more, the U.S. government representing the U.S. monopolists, has spent more than four million dollars [sic], which it extorted from the American people, and sent to South Viet Nam an important amount of war material, tens of thousands of officers and men; with the local agents at its service, it has conducted "special warfare" aimed at dominating South Viet Nam. To repress the revolutionary movement of the people in South Viet Nam, it has shrunk from no barbarous acts, including the use of noxious chemicals there and attack with air and naval forces on the Democratic Republic of Viet Nam. But all these efforts have failed in the face of the guerrilla warfare waged by the South Vietnamese people in coordination with the telling rebuffs of the North Vietnamese people. Guerrilla warfare is defeating the U.S. "special warfare" and frustrating all attempts at destruction and sabotage against North Viet Nam. This reality shows that guerrilla warfare conducted by the people according to just political and military lines, has all possibilities to vanquish whatever imperialist aggressor.

U.S. imperialism is the enemy no. 1 of the Vietnamese people, the Indochinese peoples, and the peoples of the world. The Vietnamese people distinguish it from the American people who enjoy traditions of freedom and democracy. They are resolved to struggle shoulder to shoulder with the American people and the peoples of the world to destroy the common enemy. U.S. imperialism, a giant on clay feet, is weakened and isolated more than ever.

Final victory belongs to the Vietnamese people, to the oppressed peoples, and to all the peace-loving people of the world.

Lieutenant-General HOANG VAN THAI
Deputy-head of the General Staff
of the Viet Nam People's Army

PART II

GUERRILLA STRATAGEMS

The following stories will show how an entire people, men, women, the aged, and children stirred by patriotism can effectually participate in guerrilla warfare.

STORIES OF THE FIRST WAR OF RESISTANCE (1946–1954)

COUGHING

Gun nests, watchtowers, barbed wire fences, bamboo spikes, nothing was

wanting around that brand-new post which was to bring security to a district in Haiduong province known to be "infested" with guerrillas. The
men in the garrison might set their mind at rest.

The guerrillas came several nights but dared not approach too near.
They blindly fired some shots with their rifles, just to disturb the puppet
soldiers in their sleep. The enemy sentinels on their part did but send now
and then a volley of Tommy gun into darkness.

But one night a cough was heard from the barbed wire fences. "It's
serious this time!" thought the sentries. The alarm was given. Guns of all
calibres spat fire. Hardly had they stopped when the cough was heard
again, more distinctly and more frequently. Great God! the Vietminh
could certainly have slipped through the fences and would be ready to
attack. The powerful batteries of the Kesat neighboring post began to
pound in support of the defence. At daybreak, firing stopped together
with the cough. A narrow escape, indeed!

What actually had occurred? The people's militia of Haiduong had
devised a stratagem to harass the enemy. They had introduced a small ball
of tobacco into the mouth of a toad whose jaws they bound together. The
animal was then hung at the barbed wire fences, at a late hour. With an
irritated throat, it coughed just like a man.

The experience was afterwards popularized among the guerrillas of
other districts so much so toad raising became a special trade occupation
in several villages.

FOREWARNED, FOREARMED?

Highway 5, a hinge of the Red River delta, links Hanoi to Haiphong
port where men and materials would be landed for the French troops in
North Indochina. The daily ambushes and attacks on convoys along this
100-kilometre-long vital communication line caused the French command
serious headache.

One morning of the year 1950, a convoy found a poster planted right
in the middle of the roadway with this notice: "Attention aux mines!"

"That's surely one of their devilish tricks," grumbled the captain while
alighting from his jeep. "If I could take hold of the Vietminh who . . ."

The whole convoy stopped. The sappers had to detect mines all the
same. It might be a serious warning made by our men. The captain boiled
over.

A good hour was lost while the post which had called for reinforcement was waiting impatiently. At last the column could move on after
having found a false mine.

The same irritating trick was met with again on other sections of the road and the drivers paid no more attention to the posters. Every time they came across one of them, they stopped a few seconds, just enough time to pull it up and throw it aside. Some simply dashed at the obstacle and quietly drove on the false mine traps.

One day, a big truck rushed towards Haiduong, a city situated on Highway 5 between Hanoi and Haiphong. The driver pulled up suddenly: he had just noticed one of those posters fixed at a pole. He violently took away the board. A formidable explosion was heard. The driver and forty soldiers were blown up into the air while the truck smashed in a neighboring ricefield.

DIAMOND CUT DIAMOND

This also happened on the famous Highway 5. Ty, a guerrilla of Haiduong province, under favor of the night, hurriedly buried a mine. He lay in ambush, squatting in a dug-out some distance away. At daybreak, there came a patrol. Ty was eagerly waiting for the right moment to pull at the string attached to the detonator. Unfortunately a soldier detected the badly camouflaged mine and warned his fellows. In great anger, Ty had only the time to twist his way along the ricefields to disappear as rapidly as possible. The patrol followed the string and found out Ty's hiding place. They pulled at the string to make the mine explode and burst out laughing cunningly.

For Ty, it was a heart-rending sight. He railed at his inadvertency because mines were not easy to be obtained.

The next morning, he carelessly buried a false mine made of clay at quite visible a spot. The same patrol came to pass. The same trick was repeated. While their commander was exulting near a hillock, six soldiers stepped into the hiding place and pulled at the string. They were blown into the air.

The survivors ran away out of breath. They had not expected that the other end of the string was attached to a real mine planted in the hiding place.

SHADDOCKS

What tempted most the enemy garrison at Camgiang was juicy and delicious shaddocks, which refresh your throat in the dog-days. In shaddock season, every time the French soldiers mopped up the neighboring villages, they did not fail to lay hands on the fruit put up for sale in the market-place or hanging from the trees in orchards.

One day of July 1949, a patrol came across a young woman carrying two big baskets of shaddocks. Frightened she hurriedly turned towards the nearest village. The mercenaries shouted for her; she ran away still faster, scattering the shaddocks all along her way.

Cut to the quick, the gang began to track her. Arrived at the foot of a banyan, the brave woman fell down out of exhaustion, her fruit mingling with a beautiful shaddock which happened to lie on the roadway. She rose up, redoubled her speed and rapidly disappeared behind the bamboo hedge of the village.

The soldiers rushed to the fruit, the most gluttonous of them took as many as four or five. All of a sudden, a mine exploded, flinging four torn bodies onto a ricefield nearby.

The shaddock at the foot of the banyan was a trap and the woman was sent out to lure the French into it.

A BANANA TRAP

It was in the first days of the occupation, the guerrillas had no arms and guerrilla warfare was at its beginning.

At a place in Saigon suburbs, there stood a sentrybox. The sentinel was the same French soldier for several days. He now and then fished from his pockets a sweet or even a banana to eat.

One morning, while on duty he saw two men carrying savory bananas in large baskets with a flail. Unable to resist the temptation, he called for them. To his beckon, one of the man gave him a big bunch of good ripe bananas. He hurriedly reached out his hands to take it when a formidable stroke of the flail at his head sent him to the ground.

The two guerrillas disappeared rapidly with the sentry's gun.

A BOXING MATCH AT A MARKET PLACE

The Go market was known in the whole region of Binhhoa for the abundance and variety of its goods. The peasants streamed there from places ten miles around.

Unfortunately, the enemy came and planted a post in the neighborhood. On market days, the mercenaries from the garrison would come to Go. They would brutalize the women, buy at dirt-cheap prices, or simply plunder.

On March 5, 1948, two French soldiers with Tommy guns in hands, walked into the crowded market as if they were strolling in a deserted place. They waddled about, kicking right and left to break their way through, then stepped over an old woman and trampled under foot the baskets and carrying-poles scattered on the ground. They went so far as blatantly to embrace women and caress their breasts. Finally they entered a cook-shop, leaned their guns against their chairs, and set about to devour plenty of delicious roasted cakes.

Suddenly they heard many shouts of kids. Before them, two lads fought fiercely, using their feet, hands, heads, and even their teeth. People crowded around the fighters. Someone wanted to part them. But with a threatening gesture, the soldiers prevented him to do so and noisily encouraged the boys to go on boxing for them to see gratis. After a few minutes' contest, the vanquished ran away as fast as his legs could carry him, closely followed by the victor.

The two soldiers also stood up to go away, but their Tommy guns had disappeared. Before they could react, they were assailed and beaten by the crowd with the help of the guerrillas who had staged the boxing match. The local militia who so far had but swords and daggers got two Tommy guns, their first firearms.

IN THE HOABINH MOUNTAINS

Late in 1948, Quyetthang village in mountainous Hoabinh province was subject to frequent raids. The population was massacred and paddy buffaloes and poultry plundered. But at each razzia, at least a dozen assailants were killed and wounded chiefly by mine traps.

At last, the enemy came to realize the weakness of the guerrillas and militiamen: they had very few rifles and would immediately withdraw into the forest once their mines had exploded. French and puppet commandos then made it a rule to dash off in pursuit of the guerrillas. Having had a narrow escape many a time, Bui Van Hoa devised a stratagem. Each time he set a mine trap he planted bamboo spikes on the field that the enemy would have to cross. The results were immediate and remarkable. This means of defence was further improved with the local troops' help. Spike traps were set in the vicinity of each mine, particularly near natural obstacles where the guerrillas were supposed to get under cover. The old men who kept the secret of making poison, soaked spike tips with it, and in a matter of seven days five thousand pieces of this arm were ready for use.

Faced with the increased resistance of the guerrillas, the enemy concentrated a battalion-size element to surround Quyetthang by a pincer movement. The population who had been informed evacuated to the forest while local troops and militia feverishly prepared for the defence.

On October 25, 1948, day was breaking on the mountain shrouded with mist. The aged who had prepared the poisoned bamboo spikes together with many others lay hidden in high and well covered spots to witness the fight. The raiders were long in coming. What a pity if they would not come! Were they breakfasting? More probably they were drawing near the village.

Towards noon, an explosion tore the air, followed by others. The firing began. Three enemy detachments came from Vuban in three directions. Though they could not yet get contact with one another, they had to stop and fell down trees and make occasional stretchers to carry the increasing number of killed or wounded by spikes and mines. Casualties amounted to no less than eighty. Starting from the north two other detachments succeeded in joining up at Quyetthang at sunset. But the village was empty of its inhabitants. The mercenaries ransacked the houses and found two jugs of poisoned alcohol which they drank to the last drop.

Early in the morning, the next day, the raiders had to withdraw.

Thus ended the incursion. But to save his face, the same day the enemy brought cannons on Road 12 and pounded at random the surroundings of the mountain.

RICE TRANSPLANTERS

This winter morning promised to be mild and fine. Large sheets of mist silvered by the rising sun were still floating on the bamboo tops of Vanphu.

From the gate made of branches of this little delta village appeared the slender forms of three girls who were nimbly trotting in the path gossiping and laughing. They slowed down when drawing near the temple built on the side of Road 21 where billeted a unit of puppet soldiers wont to illtreat and plunder the passers-by and even the people of the neighboring hamlets.

The girls timidly proceeded toward a ricefield in front of the temple, teased by four soldiers on duty. While puffing away at the hubble-bubble pipe, one of the men said: "What a good luck! Hot tea, fine tobacco with a gurgling pipe, and above all girls near at hand. Life is pleasant here!"

Bending their bodies forward, the transplanters gracefully stuck the young rice plants in straight lines. One of them tunefully sang an old love-song.

The soldiers were all eyes and all ears. All like one they put their rifles in a corner of the temple and went out to accost the girls. In the long run the ice was broken, and with flattering remarks they kept the ball rolling. With some visible reluctance the girls consented to come and have some tea in the temple. While the gallant hosts were busy preparing the "tea party," one of the girls hurled a hand-grenade killing one soldier, wounding another and throwing the remainder to the ground. Her mates, quick as lightning, snatched the rifles.

The three transplanters rapidly headed for Yenduong village. The surviving puppet soldiers hastened to alert a nearby post. Since then, the picket at the temple became less arrogant to the passers-by and the neighboring population.

Stories of the Guerrilla Warfare in South Viet Nam

UNCOMMON GUERRILLAS

H. village in Mocay district lazily stretches along a canal. Coconut-trees with their fine slender leaves and nice round fruit are mirrored in the limpid waters.

On a summer-morning, this charming landscape was troubled by the coming of an enemy battalion to herd the population into a "strategic hamlet." Two companies broke into the village after a preventive fusillade. The third with the battalion commander and the American "adviser," who stationed outside all mortars and heavy machine guns in fighting position, at last entered the village, which the population had visibly evacuated.

Suddenly a deafening buzz was heard.

"Wasps! wasps!" a soldier shouted.

From everywhere big wasps rushed at the assailants who despairingly fidgeted. Some, whose faces and necks were stung by five or six wasps, jumped into the water; each time they emerged they were attacked again, and the pain was still more burning in contact with water. The guerrillas naturally appeared in the nick of time, and with their rudimentary rifles, routed the battalion. The survivors ran at full speed to the post, their faces and hands swollen. The American adviser had to be carried by helicopter to a town hospital. Militiamen and guerrillas captured a large amount of arms and ammunition.

The secret of the victory was rather simple: at the militiamen's suggestion, the population kept scores of nests of wasps of the fiercest kind. These were closely shut and put on the probable passage of the enemy. At the raiders' arrival, the guerrillas pulled a system of strings to release the insects.

Here it is to mention the "father of the bee tactics" of Mocay and how he won this title. A poor peasant named Tu learnt that wasps had been used in the first resistance war against the French. Being himself a guerrilla he set to experimenting on a wasp nest not far from his house. He got stings which once confined him to his bed with a high temperature. He nevertheless spent days and weeks to study the habits of the insects and succeeded in moving the nest without being attacked. In the first campaign his new allies disappeared after the fight. Tu went on experimenting and taming his companions-in-arms. At last they could pursue the enemy on a few kilometres' distance, distinguish friends from foes, and be gathered after each action. Tu also found new methods to multiply wasp swarms.

In 1964, Tu laid some thirty ambushes, combining wasps with bamboo spike traps, and put fifty puppet soldiers out of action.

FOUR CARTRIDGES

A blood-thirsty sergeant made frantic efforts to round up "Vietcong" in the hope of being promoted. For nights on end, he posted his platoon at the village cemetery to catch N.F.L. cadres who usually contacted the population under cover of darkness. Another platoon was on the watch on the other side of the "strategic hamlet" to capture eventual survivors.

Aware of the ambush, three girls, Mai, Zung, and Hoa, were racking their brains for a means to inform the cadres. After heated discussions they unanimously agreed to an original and costless solution.

That night, when the platoons were lying in wait at their position, the girls glided out of their houses and planted spike traps on the shortcut the soldiers would most probably take to reach the hamlet in case of alarm. At some distance between the two detachments, they hid four cartridges in a heap of paddy husk under which they brooded a slow fire.

After midnight when the tired watchers were dozing, four successive detonations were heard.

"Vietcong! Vietcong! Quick, at the double to encircle them," the sergeant shouted triumphantly. He hurriedly led his men to the hamlet, but a bamboo spike pierced his right leg. Others were hit at their chest, belly, and arms. While the slightly injured were freeing themselves with difficulty and the severely wounded howling with pain, bullets whizzed and a machine gun spat fire in their direction. Screwing up their courage the remainder counterstruck. When the fusillade stopped before dawn, one realized that there had been an awkward mistake: the two platoons took each other for "Vietcong" and did their best to kill as many as they could. The sergeant was killed.

FOR WANT OF MINES

On receiving an order to attack the military trains passing in the region, the guerrilla group leader of Vancanh said to his men, "Our stock of mines is sufficient for some operations only. Can we fulfill our mission without using them?"

After heated discussions Le Van Hoi's proposal for the use of creepers to cause derailments was adopted.

On February 6, 1964, by midnight the group headed for a bushy spot where the railway line had a hairpin bend. They unrivetted a section of it, fastened it with strong creepers, and lay in wait.

At dawn, a military convoy came rumbling. The guerrillas pulled on the creepers as strongly as they could. The train ran off the rails then tumbled down with a deafening crash.

The guerrillas rushed at the enemy, killed and wounded a great many of them and collected a lot of booty.

Some time later, three other military trains underwent the same fate. The third was preceded by a passenger, the enemy knowing that the N.F.L. never attacked nonmilitary trains. Informed just a few minutes beforehand the guerrillas could not relay the bolts and held their breath as the passenger train drew near. Fortunately it went on safe and sound. But the following military convoy could not escape in spite of the enemy's trick.

FEET AND WINGS

Since the liberation of the Badang mountain hamlet, the Taois had repelled many enemy razzias with rifles, crossbows, spike and stone traps. The senior of the hamlet having more than one trick up his sleeve, was the soul of the resistance.

The Americans and puppet troops then used the air route to minimize losses on the unsafe paths. Their planes twice strafed the herd of buffaloes at Badang, and killed three which they carried away by helicopters to improve the soldiers' meals.

One evening, the senior convened the hamlet's population in the big communal house and told them:

"We've already cut off the Americans' feet, but they still have wings. What is to be done? My brain, dark as night, has no idea. Who among you has one?"

The meeting ended late at night with a decision of the kind of "Christopher Columbus' egg": one must shoot at enemy planes.

The next day, the senior and his men concealed themselves in ambush on the border of the Rua valley where a score buffaloes were grazing. They waited three days. No plane came. More than one lost patience. The senior said: "A tree stands firm because its roots go deep into the earth. Ants gather grain by grain to fill their nest. Let my men perseveringly wait."

The fourth day three fighters came and strafed two buffaloes. The guerrillas raised their rifles but were ordered to keep quiet.

The fighters were soon replaced by two helicopters. One circled to protect the other which flew very low and dropped a rope-ladder with a soldier standing on it to hook the buffaloes. On the senior's order, his companions fired at both of them. One hurriedly decamped while the other crashed to the earth. The American pilot was killed, two puppet soldiers wounded, and the remainder surrendered.

In the meeting convened to mark the victory, each inhabitant of the hamlet received a share of the buffaloes. Raising a pair of horns the senior said:

"Buffaloes, you die so that your companions live. Thanks to you we've clipped the Americans' wings."

"THANK YOU VERY MUCH INDEED"

In her village young Bay was matchless at making and setting spike traps. She never missed the mark every time the enemy came.

In this atomic era, the Americans probably could not permit a nail to put one of their soldiers out of action or into death. They have made a kind of spike-proof ankle-boots with steel soles. Diamond cut diamond. Bay devised another stratagem.

The village was victim of a new raid. Among the assailants an American shuffled along with new model ankle-boots. Making a false step he walked into a trap-ditch. He howled with pain and fainted. The new pattern trap had a median hinge and iron-spiked leaves, two of which pierced his thigh through. Impossible to take the wounded away. The trap had to be unearthed, and the man together with it were carried to the field hospital.

Bay's self-control, too, inspired her mates. One day, a patrol caught her posing a spiked board into a ditch. As the enemy pointed a machine gun at her imperturbable face, she burst out: "I am unearthing the spikes sowed by the guerrillas last night to avoid a trouble with the authorities and to save you. Is this the way you reward me for my job?"

She showed the puppet soldiers two other traps. "Are there many?" they asked her.

"Oh! yes, but I've only seen those near my home." "Thank you very much indeed," the commander said and the patrol, frightened, went away.

A PIECE OF LUCK

X. village, Duyxuyen district, Quangnam province, had just been liberated. Its population destroyed the "strategic hamlets" into which they had been impounded, and came back to their ancestral houses, ricefields, and gardens. After overthrowing the puppet power the peasants resumed their peaceful work under the protection of the N.F.L., and heightened their vigilance knowing that the garrison of the neighboring post would not let them live in peace.

One morning, an enemy platoon proceeded in single file to X. The guerrillas rapidly laid an ambush at the village outskirts and waited for the aggressors to come within a score meters to open fire. Some mercenaries were killed while the remainder moved back and hastily jumped into the anti-air raid trenches dug on the roadsides. In their hurry two or three of them plunged into one hole: What a piece of luck! They thought they were safe and even could counterattack from excellent positions against rifle-armed guerrillas.

Pan! Pan! Pan! Hand grenades set at the bottom of the ditches exploded. The fortunate survivors were captured or took to their heels.

THE HEN

Born of poor peasants thirteen-year-old Cuc did her best to relieve her parents' burden. She reared poultry, took great care of them, and never let them lack worms. It was a pleasure to look at her plump hens surrounded by pretty chickens. Their big eggs were selling like hot cakes.

One day, in her parents' absence, two puppet soldiers broke into her house. They stopped short, before a beautiful hen scratching for food in the middle of the courtyard. What a blessing! Noticing little Cuc's presence, they told her, "Hullo! young girl, give us the hen. She's fit for eating."

Cuc was in a blue funk. She would be very grieved to part with her pet hen. But what upset her was the presence of a N.F.L. militant in a house nearby. How to warn him of the danger?

An idea occurred to her. She gently came near the soldiers and said, smiling: "You may take the hen but don't run after her. She could escape from you and trample on the young vegetable plants in the kitchen-garden. Aim straight and shoot at her feet."

The two soldiers hastily fired at the bird. Informed by the reports the N.F.L. cadre hurriedly left the hamlet.

CHILI

The little C.N. post struck terror into the local population as there were many torturers in the commando platoon garrisoned there. With its blockhouses, barbed wire, and mine belt it seemed to defy the guerrillas.

One afternoon, three persons were seen shooting slightly smoking garbages on a hillock where the population sometimes got rid of their rubbish at some distance of the post. The wind was rising and drove to the post the acrid, pungent, and nauseous smoke which soon became very thick and infiltrated into all the rooms and even the pillboxes. Rubbing their eyes filled with tears, coughing and sneezing pitifully, many soldiers hurriedly went out and jumped into the river under the post. Unable to help it those in the blockhouses and on sentry did the same. At this very moment shouts "forward" were heard. The guerrillas broke into the fortified compound, tied the remaining mercenaries up, seized their weapons, and pointed the machine guns on the river.

The storming of the post had not cost a single bullet. The guerrillas had hid a mixture of droppings and red pepper powder in paddy husk burning on slow fire and sprinkled on the hillock. This new "chemical" product was quite a success.

PART III

SOUTH VIETNAMESE GUERRILLAS OF THE PRESENT RESISTANCE

"COUSIN LIBERATION"

At the other end of a hamlet the N.F.L. troops and guerrillas' guns crackled. A pale and worn-faced woman about thirty-five years old was hurriedly hiding her child of two months in an underground in the heart of her garden. Then, seizing a shovel and a rifle, she ran to the spot where the enemy raiding troops were trying to open a breach.

She crawled towards a hillock, took position and fired at the assailants. From the top of a dyke a puppet soldier unloaded his deadly weapon. The woman, nimble as a squirrel, skirted the terrain and, taking the enemy in the rear, killed him with an aimed shot. Gathering her strength she then climbed the slope to take away his rifle, but fell exhausted on the ricefield.

"Ut Tich! Ut Tich!" a voice whispered in her ear. She opened her eyes: it was her husband, in N.F.L. uniform, who had left her and her six children since nearly a year.

*

Ut Tich was a poor peasant of Travinh province. Born of a poorest family, she had, when very young, to hire herself as a maid-of-all-work at a big local landlord's. Toiling from morning to night, the thin and lank girl never ate her fill and was daily pummelled or caned. One day, she was tied up by her masters for a slip. A young man servant untied her. They married soon after and together shared the same fate of slavery for over ten years.

The August 1945 revolution liberated them.

But the French soon came back and with them the landlords and their lackeys.

Ut Tich and her husband joined the guerrilla. As a scout, an ambulance worker, then a combatant, she participated in dozens of engagements. During a river ambush she killed two enemies on a barge, and jumping into it, took away a machine gun. After a miscarried attempt on Hum, a post chief notorious for his cruelty, husband and wife were sent to do propaganda work near another garrison. They succeeded in capturing six rifles and blowing up an important bridge on the Coalanh-Longxuyen road.

*

Ten years after, the French withdrew to be replaced by the Americans. Ut Tich and her husband started a new battle for the right to live.

One day, on the way to the market, she met an enemy company going on a raiding operation. She let them pass, then with a borrowed bicycle, took a shortcut through the field to inform her guerrilla group. Before the ambush was ready, she had time to go home to hide her children without forgetting to suckle the youngest. Then rifle in hand, she went to the agreed spot. The enemy taken by surprise suffered heavy losses. During the fight, relaying the badly injured machine gunner, Ut Tich killed two enemies and wounded many others.

Near her house, the puppets' watchtower was a plague for the population. She proposed to remove it by a stratagem. Some time after making acquaintance with the post chief, who was a gourmand, together with her comrades-in-arms she prepared a banquet in a guerrilla's house and invited almost all the garrison. When the hosts were half-drunken Ut Tich took out a Tommy gun hidden a few paces from the table and levelled it at them. The soldiers were at once taken prisoner by the guerrillas. Fifteen rifles were captured, and the post occupied.

Another time, the couple boldly stormed D.T. village post. Then at the point of her Tommy gun Ut Tich forced three puppet soldiers to carry weapons and ammunition to a guerrilla base.

On the 1965 New Year's Eve, though pregnant, she led an armed propaganda group to C., a crowded town. When the work ended at daybreak, Ut Tich ordered her men to withdraw. A Tommy gun slinging across her back, she stayed alone, hidden near the bus station at the locality entrance to distribute N.F.L.'s leaflets, which her groups could not do the night before because of the rain.

A big bus came to stop. The bulk of the passengers were townsfolk, some of them having their children or brothers enlisted in the puppet army. Ut Tich headed towards them and smiling, handed them the leaflets. An old woman, moved to tears, kissed her and turning to the people around, said: "While we celebrate the New Year's Day this pregnant woman wanders on the road. For whom does she endure all the hardships of the maquis?"

She then whispered to Ut Tich's ear,

"My child, tell the Revolution[3] that the people in the town always think of it."

People gathered in a circle around Ut Tich, and asked her about the military situation, the life in the liberated zone, and her own. She answered all the questions, but about her name, she simply said, "Dear compatriots, just call me 'Cousin Liberation.' "

At the First Congress of Heroes and Emulation Fighters of the N.F.L. armed forces early in 1965 Ut Tich was awarded the title Heroine of the Liberation Army.

GUERRILLA WARFARE: A METHOD 5

by Ernesto "Che" Guevara

*"My roving house will have two legs once again,
and my dreams will know no frontiers, at least
until bullets speak."*

So wrote Ernesto Guevara in a book he gave to a friend before setting out on a long journey. Guevara spent a goodly portion of his life in restless traveling. As a youth in Argentina, he took frequent trips into the countryside, traveling by bicycle or motorcycle, sometimes just hiking. In 1952 Guevara broke off his studies in order to set out with the aforementioned friend on a transcontinental trip: motorcycling to Chile, riding a raft on the Amazon, taking a plane to Miami, Florida. He returned to Argentina to complete his studies and receive a medical degree. Then another trip, this time to Bolivia, and on to Peru, Ecuador, Panama, Costa Rica, and finally to Guatemala where Guevara supported the regime of Jacobo Arbenz. When this was overthrown, Guevara went into the Argentine embassy, remaining there until he could go to Mexico.

In Mexico, Guevara had his date with destiny, for it was here that he met the Castro brothers, Fidel and Raúl. The Castros were planning an expedition to Cuba, and Guevara, the restless, agreed to go along as a doctor.

The expedition set out in November of 1956 and landed in Cuba on December 2. Government forces decimated the invaders, but, as history would have it, among the handful of survivors were Fidel and Raúl Castro and Ernesto "Che" Guevara. ("Che" is an affectionate Argentine equivalent of "pal.") The survivors became the nucleus of a guerrilla force which operated in Cuba's Sierra Maestra Mountains and eventually spread out to other mountain regions of the country. The guerrillas rode and were supported by a swelling wave of popular discontent directed against the government of dictator Fulgencio Batista.

Victory came to the rebels—and the population—on the first day of the new year, 1959. Guevara was one of the first rebel commanders to enter Havana to take control of the capital city. Subsequently, he held a variety of official and unofficial posts within the new government: commander of a Havana military bastion, head of an army indoctrination program, president of the National Bank, minister of industries—and always, above all, one of Castro's most influential advisers. Guevara also masterminded Cuba's vast subversive program in Latin America, attempting to create other Communist states in the hemisphere.

Guevara's official tasks, however, did not cure him of his restlessness. He continued his travels to capitals and conferences, the emissary and spokesman of the Cuban regime. In December of 1964 Guevara flew to New York to address the United Nations General Assembly, and then he set out on a long trip that took him to Europe, Africa, and Asia. He traveled for three months, returned to Havana, and then, surprisingly, he completely disappeared from public view.

Not for several years was it possible to reconstruct—and then only partially—the subsequent wanderings of Ernesto Guevara. He went to Africa to lead a guerrilla movement, which failed. He returned to Cuba and there prepared a team of high-level Cuban army officers who would accompany him to his next fighting area, Bolivia, in the heartland of Latin America. From Cuba, Guevara flew to Spain and then to South America, where he slipped into Bolivia.

For precisely eleven months Guevara led a guerrilla movement that operated in the Bolivian hinterland. The guerrillas enjoyed initial successes—the ambushing of Bolivian troops—but the tide began to turn against them. They failed to gain support in either the cities or the countryside. Peasant assistance, so important to guerrillas, was totally lacking: Guevara complained that "the mass of peasants does not help us at all and they become informers."

Guevara's grand scheme had been to draw the United States into "two, three, or many Viet Nams." He hoped that a guerrilla operation in Bolivia, growing and spreading into adjoining countries, would force the United States to send troops to counter the revolution. Instead, the United States provided the Bolivians with needed weapons and trained the Bolivian Second Ranger Battalion in counterinsurgency techniques.

It was this battalion that tracked down and dealt the coup de grace to Guevara's guerrillas. Guevara was captured and shortly afterwards he was executed. In a farewell letter to Castro two years earlier, Guevara had said, ". . . If my final hour arrives under other skies, my last thoughts will be of this country [Cuba] and especially of you." Death had been a frequent companion of Guevara's on his long journeys and in his several wars, and now finally it had claimed him.

GUERRILLA WARFARE: A METHOD

GUERRILLA WARFARE has been used innumerable times in history under various conditions and for different ends. Lately it has been used in various wars of people's liberation where the people's vanguard has chosen the path of unconventional armed struggle against enemies with greater military potential. Asia, Africa, and America have been the sites of these activities when power was sought in the struggle against feudal, neocolonial, or colonial exploitation. In Europe it was used as a complement to the regular armies themselves or allies.

In America recourse has been made to guerrilla warfare on different occasions. The closest precedent is the experience of César Augusto Sandino, fighting against the Yankee expeditionary forces in the Nicaraguan Segovia. And recently, the revolutionary war of Cuba. Since then, the problems of guerrilla warfare have arisen in America in the theoretical discussions of the progressive parties of the Continent, and the possibility and appropriateness of using it is the subject of heated controversies.

These notes will be an attempt to express our ideas on guerrilla warfare and what would be its correct use.

Above all it must be made clear that this type of struggle is a method; a method to achieve an end. That end, essential and inescapable for any revolutionary, is the gaining of political power. Therefore, in the analyses of the specific situations in the various countries of America, the guerrilla concept, reduced to the simple category of a method of struggle to achieve that end, should be used.

Almost immediately the question arises: Is the guerrilla warfare method the only formula for the seizure of power throughout America? or will it, in any case, be the predominant form? or simply will it be one more formula among all those employed for the struggle? and, in the final analysis, is asked, will the example of Cuba be applicable to other continental realities? By way of argument, it is customary to criticize those who want to use guerrilla warfare, adducing that they forget the struggle of the masses, almost as if they were opposing methods. We reject the concept that embraces that position; guerrilla warfare is a people's war, it is a struggle of the masses. To try to wage this type of warfare without the support of the people is a prelude to inevitable disaster. The guerrilla is the fighting vanguard of the people, located in a specific place in some given area, armed, ready to carry out a series of warlike activities leading to the only possible strategic end: the seizure of power. It is supported by the peasant and working masses of the zone and the entire territory involved. Without these conditions guerrilla warfare cannot be permitted.

"In our American situation, we believe that the Cuban Revolution made three fundamental contributions to the mechanics of the revolutionary movements in America; they are: first, popular forces can win a war against an army; second, it is not always necessary to wait for all the conditions for revolution to exist—the insurrectionary focal point can at times create them; third, in underdeveloped America the field of armed struggle should be principally the countryside" (*La Guerra de Guerrillas*, Guerrilla Warfare).

Such are the contributions for waging the revolutionary struggle in America, and they can be applied to any of the countries of our continent in which a guerrilla war is going to be waged.

The Second Declaration of Havana indicates: "In our countries an underdeveloped industry exists side by side with a feudal agrarian system. It is for that reason that, despite the unbearable living conditions of the urban workers, the rural populace lives under even more horrible conditions of oppression and exploitation; but it is also, with some exceptions, the absolute majority, in proportions sometimes surpassing 70 percent of the Latin American populations.

"Not counting the landowners, who often live in the cities, the rest of that great mass eke their sustenance working as peons on the farms for wretched wages or work the land under conditions of exploitation that give the Middle Ages no room to boast. These circumstances are those that cause the poor country population in Latin America to constitute a tremendous potential revolutionary force.

"The armies, which are the force on which the power of the exploiting classes is sustained, organized and equipped for conventional warfare, are absolutely powerless when they have to face the unconventional warfare of the peasants on their territory. They lose ten men for every revolutionary fighter who falls, and demoralization spreads rapidly in them on having to face an invisible and invincible enemy who gives them no chance to display their academic tactics and sword rattling, of which they make so much ostentation to repress the workers and students in the cities.

"The initial struggle of small fighting nuclei is fed unceasingly by new forces, the movement of the masses begins to be unleashed, the old order cracks little by little into a thousand pieces: that is the moment when the working class and the urban masses decide the battle.

"What is it that from the very beginning of the struggle of those first nuclei makes them invincible regardless of the number, power, and resources of their enemies? The support of the people, and they will count on the support of the masses to an ever increasing degree.

"But the peasant is a type that, because of the uncultured state in which he is kept and the isolation in which he lives, needs the revolutionary and political leadership of the working class and the revolutionary intellectuals, without which he could not by himself plunge into the struggle and gain victory.

"Under the present historical conditions of Latin America, the national bourgeoisie cannot head the antifeudal and anti-imperialist struggle. Experience shows that in our nations that class, even when its interests are opposed to those of Yankee imperialism, has been incapable of confronting it, paralyzed by the fear of social revolution and frightened by the clamor of the exploited masses" (Second Declaration of Havana).

Completing the scope of these assertions, which constitute the heart of the revolutionary declaration of America, the Second Declaration of Havana expresses in other paragraphs the following: "The subjective conditions of each country—that is to say, awareness, organization, leadership—can accelerate or retard the revolution according to its greater or lesser degree of development; but sooner or later in each historical epoch, when the objective conditions mature, awareness is acquired, organization is attained, leadership comes forth, and the revolution is produced.

"Whether the revolution takes place through peaceful passages or whether it will come into the world after a painful birth, does not depend on the revolutionaries, it depends on the reactionary forces of the old society, which refuse to allow the birth of the new society, engendered by the contradictions held by the old society. The revolution plays the same part in history as does the doctor who assists in the birth of a new life. He does not use instruments of force unless they are necessary, but he uses them without hesitation each time that they may be necessary to aid the birth. It is a birth which brings the hope of a better life to the enslaved and exploited masses.

"The revolution is inevitable today in many Latin American countries. That fact is not determined by the will of anyone. It is determined by the frightening conditions of exploitation in which the American man lives, the development of the revolutionary awareness of the masses, the world crisis of imperialism, and the universal movement of struggle of the subjugated people" (Second Declaration of Havana).

We shall start from these bases for an analysis of the entire guerrilla problem in America.

We have established that it is a method of fighting to obtain an end. It is of interest, first, to analyze the end and to see if it is possible to succeed in the conquest of power in a manner other than by armed struggle here in America.

The peaceful struggle can be carried out by means of mass movements, and it can—in special situations of crises—force governments to yield, and eventually the popular forces would hold the power and establish the dictatorship of the proletariat. This is theoretically correct. Upon analyzing previous events in the panorama of America, we have to arrive at the following conclusions: On this continent in general there exist objective conditions which impel the masses to violent actions against the bourgeois and landowner governments; power crises exist in many other countries and some subjective conditions also exist. It is clear that, in the countries in which all the conditions are found, it would even be criminal not to act for the takeover of power. In those other countries in which this is not the case, it is permissible to consider different alternatives, and for a decision applicable to each country to spring from theoretical discussion. The only thing that history does not permit is for the analysts and executors of the policy of the proletariat to err. No one can seek to be part of the vanguard as he would seek an official diploma given by the university. To be a member of the vanguard is to be at the head of the working class in the struggle for the seizure of power, to know how to guide it to the capture, and even to lead it through short cuts. That is the mission of our revolutionary parties and the analysis ought to be profound and exhaustive so that there may be no equivocation.

Day by day, a state of unstable balance between the oligarchic dictatorship and the popular pressure is seen in [Latin] America. We call it oligarchy with the idea of trying to define the reactionary alliance between the bourgeoisie of each country and the landowning classes, with the greater or lesser preponderance of the feudal structures. These dictatorships occur within certain frameworks of legality which they themselves set up for their own convenience during the whole unrestricted period of class domination. But we are passing through a stage in which the popular pressure is very strong; the people are knocking at the doors of bourgeois legality, which must be violated by its own authors in order to hold back the drive of the masses. The shameless violations, contrary to all previously enacted legislation—or legislation enacted a posteriori to justify the event—put more tension on the popular forces. Therefore, the oligarchic dictatorship tries to use the old legal arrangements to change the constitutionality and to oppress the proletariat even more, without the collision being head-on. In spite of that, here is where the contradiction takes place. The people no longer support the old nor, still less, the new coercive measures established by the dictatorship, and try to break them. We should never forget the class, authoritarian, and restrictive character of the bourgeois state. Lenin referred to it in this manner: "The state is the product and the manifestation of the irreconcilable character of class contradictions. The state appears in the place, in the moment, and to the extent in which the contradictions of class cannot be objectively reconciled. And vice versa: the existence of the state demonstrates that the contradictions of class are irreconcilable." (*The State and the Revolution.*)

This means that we should not admit that the word democracy, used in an apologetic form to represent the dictatorship of the exploiting classes, loses its depth of concept and acquires the concept of certain more or less optimal liberties given to the citizen. To struggle only to obtain the restoration of certain bourgeois legality without raising, on the other hand, the problem of revolutionary power, is to struggle to return to a certain dictatorial order previously established by the dominant social classes; it is, in any case, to struggle for the establishment of some chains with a ball at the end somewhat less heavy for the convict.

Under these conditions of conflict, the oligarchy breaks its own contracts, its own appearance of "democracy," and attacks the people, although it always tries to use the methods of the superstructure it has created for oppression. The dilemma is stated again at that moment: What must be done? We answer: Violence is not the patrimony of the exploiters, the exploited can use it and, what is more, they ought to use it at the opportune time. Martí said: "He who promotes a war which can be avoided is a criminal; and he who fails to promote an inevitable war is also a criminal."

Lenin, on the other hand, said: "Social-democracy has never viewed, nor does it view now, war from a sentimental point of view. It condemns, absolutely, war as a savage means of settling differences between men, but it knows that wars are inevitable as long as society is divided into classes, as long as the exploitation of man by his fellow men exists. And to do away with that exploitation we cannot disregard wars always and everywhere begun by the very classes that exploit, dominate, and oppress." He said this in 1905; later, in *The Military Program of the Proletarian Revolution*, profoundly analyzing the character of the class struggle, he affirmed: "He who accepts the class struggle cannot help but accept civil wars, which in any society of classes represent the continuation, the development, and the outbreak—which are natural and, under certain circumstances, inevitable—of the class struggle. All the great revolutions confirm it. To deny civil wars or to forget them would be to fall into an extreme opportunism and to deny the socialist revolution."

This means that we should not fear violence, the midwife of new societies; the only thing is that the violence ought to be unleashed at the exact moment when the leaders of the people have found the most favorable circumstances.

Which will these be? They depend, subjectively, on two conditions that complement each other and that in turn continue to intensify during the struggle: the awareness of the need for change and the certainty of the possibility of this revolutionary change. These objective conditions —which are tremendously favorable in almost all of [Latin] America for carrying out the struggle—together with a firm will to achieve the change and the new balances of power in the world, determine the way of action.

No matter how far away the socialist countries may be, their beneficial influence will always be felt by the struggling peoples, and their enlightening example will give them more strength. Fidel Castro said last 26 of July: "And the duty of the revolutionary, above all at this moment, is to be able to discern, to be able to make use of the changes in the balance of power that have taken place in the world, and to understand that change promotes the struggle of the peoples. The duty of the revolutionaries, of the Latin American revolutionaries, is not to wait for the change in the balance of power to work the miracle of social revolutions in Latin America but to take full advantage of everything that the changed balance of power presents to the revolutionary movement and 'make revolutions!' "

There are those who say, "We accept revolutionary warfare as a suitable measure, in certain specific cases, to achieve the seizure of political power. Where do we get the great leaders, the Fidel Castros to bring us to victory?" Fidel Castro, as every human being, is a product of history. The military and political leaders who may direct the insurrectionary struggles in [Latin] America, united, if it were possible, in a single person, will learn the art of warfare in the practice of war itself. There is no occupation or profession which one can learn from textbooks alone. In this case, the struggle is the great teacher.

It is obvious that the task is not easy nor free of grave dangers throughout its course.

During the waging of the armed struggle two moments of extreme danger for the future of the revolution appear. The first arises during the preparatory stage, and the manner in which it is resolved determines the decision to struggle and the clear understanding that the popular forces have of the ends. When the bourgeois state advances against the positions of the people, obviously a defensive process against the enemy must be created which, once it achieves superiority, attacks. If minimum objective and subjective conditions have already developed, the defense should be armed, but in such a way that the popular forces are not converted into mere recipients of the blows of enemies; nor should the stage for armed defense simply be a last refuge for the persecuted. The guerrilla, the people's defensive movement at a given moment, has in itself, and constantly should develop, its ability to attack the enemy. In time, this ability is what will determine its nature as a catalyst of the popular forces. It merits being said that guerrilla activity is not passive self-defense; it is defense with attack, and from the moment it establishes itself as such, its final goal is the conquest of political power.

This moment is important. In the social processes, the difference between violence and non-violence cannot be measured by the number of shots that are exchanged; it yields to concrete and fluctuating situations. And it is necessary to be able to see the instant in which the popular forces, aware of their relative weakness but, at the same time, of their strategic strength, must force the enemy to take the necessary steps so that the situation does not retrocede. The balance between the oligarchic dictatorship and popular pressure must be upset. The dictatorship constantly tries to operate without the showy use of force. Forcing the dictatorship to appear undisguised—that is, in its true aspect of violent dictatorship of the reactionary classes—will contribute to its unmasking, which will intensify the struggle to such extremes that then there is no turning back. The manner in which the people's forces, dedicated to the task of making the dictatorship define itself—holding back or unleashing the battle—carry out their function depends on the firm beginning of a long-range armed action.

Escape from the other dangerous moment depends on the power of growing development which the popular forces possess. Marx always maintained that once the revolutionary process had begun, the proletariat had to strike and strike unceasingly. Revolution that does not constantly become more profound is a regressive revolution. Tired soldiers begin to lose faith and then some of the maneuvers to which the bourgeoisie has so accustomed us may appear. These can be elections with the transfer of power to another gentleman with a more mellifluous voice and a more angelic countenance than the current dictator, or a coup by reactionaries generally led by the army and, directly or indirectly, supported by progressive forces. There are others, but we do not intend to analyze tactical stratagems.

Principally, we are calling attention to the maneuvers of the military coup that was previously mentioned. What can the military give to the true democracy? What loyalty can one ask of them if they are mere tools

of the domination of the reactionary classes and of the imperialist monopolies, and, as a caste, whose value depends upon the weapons it possesses,
aspire merely to maintain their privileges?

In situations difficult for oppressors, when the military plot and oust
a dictator who de facto has already been beaten, it must be supposed that
they do it because the dictator is not capable of preserving their class
privileges without extreme violence, which, in general, now does not suit
the interest of oligarchies.

This in no way means rejecting the use of the military as individual
fighters, separated from the social milieu in which they have operated
and, in fact, rebelled against. But this use must be made in the framework
of the revolutionary course to which they will belong as fighters and
not as representatives of a caste.

In times past, in the preface to the third edition of *The Civil War in
France*, Engels said, "After each revolution, the workers were armed; for
that reason, the disarmament of the workers was the first order of the
bourgeoisie who headed the State. Hence, after each revolution won by
the workers, a new struggle developed that culminated with their overthrow . . ." (Quoted from Lenin, *The State and the Revolution*).

This game of continual struggles, in which formal changes of any type
are attained only to strategically regress, has been repeated for decades
in the capitalist world. But still, permanent deception of the proletariat
in this aspect has been going on periodically for more than a century.

It is also dangerous that, moved by the desire to maintain for some
time the conditions most favorable for revolutionary action by means
of the use of certain aspects of bourgeois legality, the leaders of the progressive party confuse the terms—which is very common during the
course of the action—and forget the final strategic objective: seizure
of power.

These two difficult moments of the revolution, which we have briefly
analyzed, are obviated when the leading Marxist-Leninist parties are able
to see clearly the implications of the moment and to mobilize the masses,
to the greatest extent, by correctly leading them to resolve fundamental
contradictions.

In discussing the subject, we have assumed that, eventually, the idea
of armed struggle and also the formula of guerrilla warfare as a method of
combat will be accepted. Why do we estimate that guerrilla warfare is the
correct method under the present conditions in America? There are
basic arguments which, to our mind, determine the necessity of guerrilla
action in America as the central axis of the struggle.

First: Accepting as a truth the fact that the enemy will struggle to keep himself in power, it is necessary to consider the destruction of the oppressing army; but to destroy it, it is necessary to oppose it with a popular army. This army is not created spontaneously but must arm itself from its enemy's arsenal, and this causes a hard and very long struggle in which the popular forces and their leaders would be continually exposed to attack from superior forces without suitable conditions for defense and maneuverability.

On the other hand, the guerrilla nucleus, settled in terrain favorable to the struggle, guarantees the security and permanence of the revolutionary command. The urban forces, directed from the general staff of the army of the people, can carry out actions of incalculable importance. The possible destruction of these groups would not kill the soul of the revolution; its leadership, from its rural fortress, would continue to catalyze the revolutionary spirit of the masses and organize new forces for other battles.

Furthermore, the organization of the future state apparatus begins in this zone. It is in charge of efficiently guiding the class dictatorship during the entire transition period. The longer the battle, the greater and more complex will be the administrative problems, and in solving them, cadres will be trained for the difficult task of consolidating power and economic development in a future stage.

Second: We have to look at the general situation of the Latin American peasants and the progressively more explosive nature of their struggle against feudal structures in the framework of a social situation of alliance between local and foreign exploiters.

Returning to the Second Declaration of Havana: "The peoples of America freed themselves from Spanish colonialism at the beginning of the last century, but they did not free themselves from exploitation. The feudal landlords took over the authority of the Spanish governors, the Indians continued in grinding slavery, the Latin American man in one form or another followed in the steps of the slave, and the slightest hopes of the people crumbled under the power of oligarchies and the yoke of foreign capital. This has been the situation in [Latin] America, in one form or another. Today Latin America is under an even more ferocious imperialism, far more powerful and ruthless than Spanish colonial imperialism.

"And faced with the objective and historically inexorable reality of the Latin American revolution, what is the attitude of Yankee imperialism? To prepare to begin a colonial war with the peoples of Latin America; to create an apparatus of force, political pretexts, and pseudo-legal instruments signed with the representatives of reactionary oligarchies to repress by blood and fire the struggle of the Latin American peoples."

This objective situation demonstrates the force that slumbers, unproductive, in our peasants and the need for using it for the liberation of America.

Third: The continental character of the struggle.

Could this new stage of the emancipation of America be conceived as the meeting of two local forces struggling for power in a given territory? Only with difficulty. The struggle will be to the death between all the popular forces and all the forces of repression. The paragraphs quoted above also predict it.

The Yankees will intervene out of solidarity of interests and because the struggle in America is a decisive one. In fact, they are already intervening in the preparation of repressive forces and in the organization of a continental fighting apparatus. But, from now on, they will do it with all their energies; they will punish the popular forces with all the destructive weapons at their disposal; they will not permit the revolutionary power to consolidate, and if anyone should do so, they will again attack, they will not recognize it, they will try to divide the revolutionary forces, they will introduce saboteurs of every kind, they will create border problems, they will turn other reactionary states against them, they will try to smother the economy of the new state, in one word, to annihilate it.

With this American panorama, it is difficult to achieve and consolidate victory in an isolated country. The unity of repressive forces must be answered with the unity of popular forces. In all countries where oppression reaches unbearable levels, the banner of rebellion must be raised, and this banner will have, because of historical need, continental features. The Andes Cordillera is called on to be the Sierra Maestra of America, as Fidel has said, and all the vast territories of the continent are called to be the scene of the struggle to the death against the imperialist power.

We cannot say when it will achieve these continental features, nor how long the struggle will last; but we can predict its coming and its success, because it is the result of inevitable historical, economic, and political circumstances, and the course cannot be turned aside. To begin it when conditions are propitious, regardless of the situation in other countries, is the task set for the revolutionary force in each country. The waging of the struggle will continue to control the general strategy. The prediction on the continental character is the fruit of the analysis of the forces of each contender, but this does not exclude, not by a long shot, an independent outburst. Just as the beginning of the struggle at a point in a country is intended to carry it throughout the country, the beginning of the revolutionary war contributes to the development of new conditions in neighboring countries.

The development of revolutions has come about normally by inversely proportional ebbs and flows. The revolutionary flow corresponds to the counterrevolutionary ebb, and vice versa, at the moment of the revolutionary decline, there is a counterrevolutionary rise. At times like this, the situation of the popular forces becomes difficult and they must resort to the best means of defense to suffer the least damage. The enemy is extremely strong, continentally. For this reason, the relative weaknesses of the local bourgeoisie cannot be analyzed for purposes of making decisions of a limited scope. Even more remote is the possible alliance of these oligarchies with the people under arms. The Cuban Revolution has sounded the alarm. The polarization of forces will be total: exploiters from one side and the exploited from another; the masses of the petty bourgeoisie will lean toward one or the other, depending on their interests and the political skill with which they are handled. Neutrality will be an exception. This is what the revolutionary war will be like.

Let us think about how a guerrilla focus could begin.

Relatively small nuclei of people choose favorable places for guerrilla warfare, either to begin a counterattack, or to weather the storm, and thus they begin to act. The following must be clearly established: at first, the relative weakness of the guerrilla movement is such that it must work only to settle in the terrain, establishing connections with the populace and reinforcing the places that will possibly become its base of support.

There are three conditions for the survival of a guerrilla movement that begins its development under the situation just described: constant mobility, constant vigilance, constant distrust. Without the adequate use of these three elements of military tactics, the guerrilla will survive only with difficulty. It must be remembered that the heroism of the guerrilla warrior at this moment consists in the extent of his established ends and the enormous sacrifices he must make to achieve them.

These sacrifices will not be the daily combat, or face-to-face fighting with the enemy. They will take forms that are more subtle and more difficult to resist for the body and mind of the individual who is in the guerrilla movement.

These guerrillas will perhaps be severely punished by the enemy armies. Sometimes they will be divided into groups; those who have been made prisoners, martyrized; persecuted like hunted animals in those areas where they have chosen to operate, with the constant worry of having the enemy one step behind; with the constant distrust of everyone since the frightened peasants will hand them over, in some cases, to be rid of the repressive troops; with no other alternative but death or victory, at times when death is an ever present thought, and victory is the myth about which only a revolutionary can dream.

That is the heroism of the guerrilla. That is why it is said that walking is a form of fighting, that retreat from combat at a given moment is but another form of combat. Faced with the general superiority of the enemy, the plan is to find the tactical form of achieving a relative superiority at a selected point, whether it be to concentrate more effectives than the enemy, or to assure an advantage in making use of the terrain, thus upsetting the balance of forces. Under these conditions a tactical victory is assured. If the relative superiority is not clear, it is preferable not to act. Combat that will not lead to victory should not be carried out, as long as the "how" and the "when" can be chosen.

In the framework of the large political and military action of which it is a part, the guerrilla movement will grow and consolidate. Bases of support, a basic element for the prosperity of the guerrilla army, will then appear. These bases of support are points which the enemy's army can penetrate only with great losses. They are bastions of the revolution, the refuge and springboard of the guerrilla for excursions which are farther away and more daring.

This moment arrives if the tactical and political difficulties have been simultaneously overcome. The guerrillas can never forget their function as the vanguard of the people, a mandate which they personify, and consequently, they must create the necessary political conditions for the establishment of a revolutionary power based on the total support of the masses. The great claims of the peasants must be satisfied to the extent and in the way circumstances warrant, making the population a compact and decided unit.

If the military situation will be difficult at first, the political will be no less ticklish. And if one single military error can liquidate the guerrilla movement, a political error can stop its development for long periods.

The struggle is political and military. That is the way it must be waged and, consequently, understood.

The guerrilla movement, in its growth period, reaches a point where its capacity for action covers a specified region for which there is a surplus of men and an overconcentration in the zone. The bee swarming begins when one of the leaders, an outstanding guerrilla, moves to another region and repeats the chain of developments of guerrilla warfare, subject, of course, to a central command.

Now, it is necessary to point out that it is not possible to aspire to victory without the formation of a popular army. The guerrilla forces can expand only to a certain size; the popular forces in the cities and other penetrable zones of the enemy can inflict damages on him but the military potential of the reaction could still remain intact. It must always be remembered that the final result must be the annihilation of the enemy. Therefore, every new zone which is created, plus the zones of penetration of the enemy behind his lines, plus the forces that operate in the principal cities, must be subordinate to the [central] command. It cannot be claimed that the tight chain of command that characterizes an army exists, but certainly there must be a strategic chain of command. Within determined conditions of freedom of action, guerrilla units must obey all strategic orders from the central command, set up in one of the most secure and strongest posts, preparing the conditions for the union of the forces at a given moment.

Guerrilla warfare or war of liberation will, in general, have three stages: the first, a strategic defense, in which a small hunted force bites the enemy; it is not protected for a passive defense in a small circle, but its defense consists in limited attacks which it can carry out. After this, a state of equilibrium is reached in which the possibilities of action of the enemy and the guerrilla unit are stabilized; and later the final moment of overrunning the repressive army that will lead to the taking of the great cities, to the great decisive encounters, to the total annihilation of the enemy.

After the point of equilibrium is reached, when both forces respect one another, guerrilla warfare acquires new characteristics along the way of its development. The concept of the maneuver begins to appear. Large columns attack strong points. It is a war of movement with a transfer of forces and means of attack of relative strength. But, due to the capacity for resistance and counterattack that the enemy still has, this war of maneuvers does not definitely replace the guerrilla units. It is merely another way they act. It is a greater magnitude of the guerrilla forces until finally a popular army crystallizes into army corps. Even at this moment, marching at the head of the action of the main forces, the guerrilla units will go in their state of "purity," destroying communications, sabotaging the enemy's entire defensive apparatus.

We had predicted that the war would be continental. This means also that it will be prolonged; there will be many fronts, it will cost much blood, innumerable lives for a long time. But, even more, the phenomena of polarization of forces that are occurring in America, the clear division between exploiters and exploited that will exist in future revolutionary wars, means that when power is taken over by the armed vanguard of the people, the country, or countries, that obtain it will have liquidated simultaneously, in the oppressor, the imperialist and the national exploiters. The first stage of socialist revolution will have crystallized; the peoples will be ready to stanch their wounds and begin the construction of socialism.

Will there be other possibilities less bloody?

Sometime ago the last partition of the world was made in which the United States took for itself the lion's share of our continent; today the imperialists of the old world are expanding and the power of the European Common Market frightens the North Americans themselves. All this would seem to indicate that it would be possible to watch an inter-imperialist fight as a spectator and then to make gains, perhaps in alliance with the strongest national bourgeoisie. Without mentioning that a passive policy never brings good results in the class struggle, and alliances with the bourgeoisie, however revolutionary they may seem at a given moment, have only a transitory character, there are reasons of time that lead to taking another position. The sharpening of the fundamental contradiction appears to be so rapid in America that it is disturbing the "normal" development of the contradictions in the imperialist camp in the their struggle for markets.

Most of the national bourgeoisie have joined North American imperialism and must suffer the same fate as the latter in each country. Even in the cases where there are pacts or identity of contradictions between the nationalist bourgeoisie and other imperialisms with the North American, this happens in the framework of a fundamental struggle that necessarily, in the course of its development, will include *all the exploited and all the exploiters*. The polarization of antagonistic forces of class adversaries is, until now, more rapid than the development of the contradictions among the exploiters over the division of the spoils. There are two camps: the alternative is becoming clearer for each individual and for each special stratum of the population.

The Alliance for Progess is an attempt to check the uncheckable.

But if the advance of the European Common Market, or any other imperialist group, on the American markets were more rapid than the development of the fundamental contradiction, the only thing remaining would be to introduce the popular forces as a wedge into the open breach, the latter leading the entire struggle and using the new intruders with full awareness of their final intentions.

Not one position, not one weapon, not one secret can be surrendered to the class enemy, under pain of losing all.

In fact, the birth of the American struggle has begun. Will its vortex be in Venezuela, Guatemala, Colombia, Peru, or Ecuador . . . ? Will these present skirmishes be only manifestations of an unrest that does not bear fruit? It does not matter what may be the outcome of today's struggle. It does not matter, for the final result, that one movement or another may be momentarily defeated. What counts is the decision to struggle that ripens day by day; the awareness of the need for revolutionary change, the certainty of its possibility.

This is a prediction. We make it with the conviction that history will prove us right. The analysis of objective and subjective factors of America and of the imperialist world indicate to us the certainty of these statements based on the Second Declaration of Havana.

OPERATION ANTIAIRCRAFT 6

by Raul Castro

On 22 June 1958, Major Raúl Castro Ruz, commander of the rebel "Second Front" in the eastern portion of Cuba's Oriente Province, issued "Military Order No. 30." This instructed his troops to carry out "the detention of all U.S. citizens" in the area. As the reason for the roundup, the order claimed that almost one hundred air raids had been carried out against "the defenseless peasant population" by government planes. The order assailed "inhuman North American rulers" and charged that the United States had supplied the bombs used by the Cuban government. This, according to Raúl Castro, was a "shameful crime . . . against the defenseless Cuban people." (Together with Military Order No. 30, Raúl Castro issued a manifesto titled "Call to the Youth of the World." This, like the order, was a bitter attack against the United States and alleged U.S. "domination of Latin America.") Raúl Castro's action was a harbinger of the course Cuba would follow once the Castro brothers were in power.

Rebel troops proceeded to seize forty-eight Americans and two Canadians. Two American consuls traveled into the hills to confer with Raúl Castro and to seek the release of the prisoners. After drawn-out negotiations, Castro began releasing the prisoners in small groups until all were free.

Ostensibly the kidnappings had been aimed at forcing the United States to cease shipping weapons to the government of dictator Fulgencio Batista. But, in fact, the United States had already embargoed weapons shipments to Cuba three months earlier.

More important were two other goals that the rebels achieved. In forcing the United States to negotiate with them, they won *de facto* recognition of sorts. And in seizing fifty foreigners and holding them with impunity, they demonstrated to the world the weakness of the Batista regime and the extent to which the rebel movement had developed.

Like his older brother Fidel, Raúl was born (3 June 1931) on the family sugar plantation at Birán, near Mayarí in Oriente. Raúl was the fourth child (of seven) of planter Angel Castro and his second wife, Lina Ruz. Raúl was baptized a Catholic, and he studied at Catholic schools in Oriente and Havana. Then he entered the University of Havana, where Fidel was an important student activist. Raúl listened to his brother's ideas and met Fidel's politically-minded friends. It was a left-leaning student crowd, bent on reforming the world. There were almost certainly Communists among the students.

Raúl moved to the left, and possibly during this period joined the youth branch of the Partido Socialista Popular, Cuba's Communist party. In 1953 he traveled to Europe to attend the Communist-sponsored "International Conference for the Defense of the Rights of Youth" held in Vienna March 22 through 27. After this, Raúl went to Bucharest to attend another Communist meeting, the "World Festival of Youths and Students."

Raúl returned to Havana aboard a steamship, and upon his arrival on June 6 he was detained by customs officials. His baggage was found to contain Communist literature. The literature was confiscated, but Raúl was released.

Batista had staged a successful coup the year before, and Fidel Castro, a member of the opposition Ortodoxo party, was organizing an uprising to take place in the island's second city, Santiago de Cuba. Raúl plunged into the conspiracy.

On 26 July 1953 the rebels attacked Moncada barracks in Santiago and other strategic points. Raúl led a small group that captured the Provincial Courthouse. The uprising failed and the Castro brothers were captured. They were brought to trial, convicted, given fifteen-year sentences, and sent to prison on the Isle of Pines.

Cuba entered a period of comparative tranquility, and, in May of 1955, Batista granted amnesty to a number of political prisoners. Fidel walked out of prison, followed by Raúl.

The brothers remained in Havana, and then, on June 17, Raúl went into asylum in the Mexican embassy. He flew to Mexico a week later and was joined by Fidel. There followed months of planning a new struggle against Batista, organizing a group of followers, raising of needed funds, guerrilla training by Alberto Bayo.

In November of 1956 the yacht *Granma* sailed for Cuba with eighty-two expeditionaries who landed early in December on the western shore of Oriente. Batista's troops and air force went into action, dispersing and pursuing the rebels, killing or capturing many of them.

During a skirmish at a place called Alegría del Pío, Fidel and Raúl were separated. Later—so the story has been told—sitting in a farmer's shack, Raúl heard a radio report that Fidel had surrendered, whereupon he angrily swore that he would seek out his brother and kill him. But Fidel had not surrendered, and the brothers were later reunited.

During the months that followed, the rebels slowly built their guerrilla strength in the Sierra Maestra mountains. Semi-independent commands—"columns"—were set up under the leadership of *Granma* survivors. One of the columns was led by Raúl. He was a harsh commander, but he held the loyalty of his men. He was efficient, he had a talent for organization, he was indefatigable. Despite jungle sores, he marched with his men for days and nights, with only brief pauses. He fought side by side with his troops, and they fought well, in contrast with the slapdash troops commanded by Fidel.

By the first months of 1958 the rebels were in firm control of the Sierra Maestra and looking for new areas to conquer. In March of that year Raúl set out with about one hundred men. They crossed the Central Highway, hid in cane fields, finally made their way to the Sierra del Cristal in the northern portion of Oriente Province.

The rebel group remained in the Sierra del Cristal a while, then headed eastward to the extensive mountainous area of Oriente's far corner. Encountering only token resistance from government troops, most of whom were concentrated in the Sierra Maestra region, Raúl rapidly established control over an area much larger than that held by Fidel. This was the rebels' "Second Front," where Raúl staged the kidnapping of the Americans and Canadians.

Raúl put his organizational abilities to work, established administrative offices, set bulldozers to leveling new roads. A rural intelligence service and the first rebel indoctrination schools were established.

Raúl executed suspected government informers. At the Soledad sugar mill a list of thirty-nine executed men was openly posted on a wall. During two years of guerrilla operations, Raúl was probably responsible for over one hundred executions, more than were carried out by all the other rebel commanders combined. On one occasion a young lieutenant balked at commanding a firing squad, saying that he couldn't deliver the coup de grace. "It's easy," said Raúl, "you just do this," and he pointed his own gun at the ground to demonstrate. On another occasion three prisoners were blindfolded and lined up, ready for execution. The firing squad, however, fired over their heads. Someone shouted: "You missed one! He's still alive." Each of the prisoners thought he was the one that was still alive and presumably would be killed by a new volley. The terrifying mock execution was only meant as a warning, however, and on this occasion, at least, no one died.

As an independent area commander, Raúl Castro was able to indulge his delight in irritating the United States. He kidnapped Americans. He turned the water supply for the United States base at Guantánamo on and off (the water was pumped from a river within Raúl's territory). He attacked the American-owned Nicaro nickel works, forcing the evacuation by the U.S. Navy of American civilian personnel. He kidnapped a Cuban lawyer employed by the Guantánamo base. In effect, Raúl was leading the rebel movement into an increasingly anti-American position.

On 1 January 1959 Batista fled Cuba, and the revolution was victorious. While Fidel and other guerrilla leaders traveled to Havana, Raúl remained in Santiago as commander of all "land, sea, and air" forces in Oriente. He promptly carried out the execution of some seventy Batista followers, who had been given little or no trial. They were buried in a mass grave, not far from famed San Juan Hill.

On January 21, addressing a mass rally, Fidel declared Raúl to be his heir apparent (a status which still prevails). On January 26 Raúl married Vilma Espín, a fanatical young woman who had played a leading role in Santiago's clandestine movement and later joined Raúl in the mountains. Immediately after the wedding, the couple flew to Havana, where Raúl took up a new post as assistant chief of the armed forces under Fidel. Later, when Fidel became prime minister, Raúl took command of all the country's military and police forces.

While Fidel made speeches and traveled around the country and up and down the hemisphere, Raúl built a new military establishment. Raúl saw to it that the troops received political indoctrination. He declared: "We are a political army. . . . It is not possible to be apolitical since to be apolitical means to have no interest in the march of public affairs. And that is precisely why we fought, to transform the economic and social structure of the nation. . . . The armed forces play an important role in the public life of the nation."

Raúl attended cabinet meetings, and on October 20 he was officially given cabinet rank when he was named minister of the revolutionary armed forces, a position which he continues to hold. Upon becoming minister, Raúl declared, "We will not be satisfied until . . . our nation is . . . respected militarily by the small and the powerful." Cuba began making mass purchases of weapons in Europe. At the same time, under Raúl's benevolent eye, Communists steadily gained in power and influence within the Cuban military establishment.

Raúl's activities were not limited to military affairs. He had an important voice in all policy making, he received visiting foreign dignitaries, he was involved in labor affairs, and he even flew to Chile to a meeting of the Organization of American States (but arrived a few hours too late to attend it).

Raúl's greatest power—and the same was true of Ernesto "Che" Guevara—lay in knowing how to handle egocentric and unstable Fidel Castro. Fidel is susceptible to suggestions, and nobody was more adept at guiding him than Raúl and Guevara. After years together with him, they knew how to play on his vanity, how to lead his thoughts, how to convince him to do things without telling him outright to do them. They utilized the fact that Castro seizes and makes his own the thoughts of other people. A true anecdote illustrates how Raúl could influence his brother. Their younger sister Emma was due to be married in April of 1959, and she had asked Fidel to attend the wedding. He agreed to do so and even told friends that he was going to dress up and give the bride away. But Raúl talked to Fidel and asked him, "Do you want your enemies to take pictures of you kneeling in church?" Fidel showed up at the wedding slovenly and twenty minutes late.

Raúl, who had once volunteered to fight with the Allied forces in Korea, became more strongly anti-American as Cuba veered increasingly leftward. On one occasion, he told friends, "It is my dream to drop three atomic bombs on New York." In July of 1960 he flew to Moscow, and there arrangements were made for Cuba to receive over $100,000,000 worth of Communist weapons, ranging from mortars and antiaircraft guns to heavy tanks and supersonic MIGs. Cuba was to become the most powerful military nation in Latin America. But even this was not enough for the Communists. In 1962 Raúl again flew to Moscow, and now preparations were made for Russia to send troops and missiles to Cuba—a move which precipitated the nuclear crisis of October 1962.

Raúl Castro today commands a military organization that numbers approximately half a million troops and militia. In addition to heading the armed forces, he is also deputy prime minister and a member of the Cuban Communist party's Politburo, Secretariat, and Central Committee. He is also president of the party's Armed Forces and State Security Commission.

Fidel and Raúl neatly complement each other. Fidel is the dreamer, the speechmaker, the demagogue. Raúl, however, is the better fighter, organizer, and administrator. Fidel prefers to move around the countryside, to visit farms, to make speeches, to talk with people, to play baseball. Raúl, meanwhile, maintains tight personal control over the military forces that help maintain the Castros in power. Fidel provides the charisma. Raúl provides the muscle.

OPERATION ANTIAIRCRAFT

MIDDAY, 1 March 1958, after receiving instructions on final preparations for the journey, [Juan] Almeida and I, together with officers of both columns, held a final meeting with Fidel at the camp then occupied by Che's forces, at Pata de la Mesa, in the very heart of the Sierra Maestra.

Two new columns broke away from the initial nucleus of the Sierra Maestra Rebel Army, having been born and forged together under enemy fire and with the vast experience accumulated by Fidel during long months of warfare: No. 3 bore the name of the heroic city of Santiago de Cuba and was led by Almeida; No. 6, known as the Frank País,[1] was under my command.

Both began a journey eastward, long forced marches with the purpose of reaching San Lorenzo—the place where [patriot] Carlos Manuel de Céspedes died[2]—where on March 10 I was to leave Almeida, who was striking west of Santiago de Cuba to open a third front. I would march to the northwest of the province, choosing the advantage offered by the darkness of night to cross the Central Highway and the wide strip of land separating us from our column's initial objective. That night enemy soldiers once more would be celebrating the anniversary of Batista's 10 March 1952 military coup. Everything went off in chronological order. The following day at 4 P.M., after ten hours driving in different vehicles and another ten on foot at forced march, we were bombed while leaving the vehicles on the slopes of the mountains near the Central Miranda sugar mill. At dawn that same day we reached the Piloto al Medio district, north of the town of San Luis, Oriente Province, where we camped for the first time on the Second Front, thus complying with orders Fidel had given us in the Sierra Maestra eleven days before.

We took only the necessary time to set up camp, eat and sleep, and organize the first Committees of Revolutionary Peasants in the places where we found the possibility to do so. Taking advantage of brief stops, we also settled accounts with bands of ruffians who, using the name of the Rebel Army as a cover, were actually pilfering and murdering. Then we set out to travel over some of the areas which in the near future were to be part of our Frank País Second Front.

The route we followed went zigzagging toward the northwest to the Sierra Cristal. Later we turned south, having established that the Sierra Cristal was useless for our work, and passed between the settlements of Mayarí Arriba and Calabazas de Sagua, reaching the vicinity of Bayaté, a small village belonging to the municipality of Guantánamo and about two hours northwest of the same. We traveled by jeep over very rough roads.

On March 20 we met detachments led by Captain Demetrio Montseny (Villa) and the then Lt. Raúl Menéndez Tomassevich. With the Tomassevich detachment we formed Company "A" to operate north of Alto Songo; with men under the command of Efigenio [Ameijeiras] and joined by Villa's detachment under the command of the former, we organized Company "B" to operate north of Guantánamo.

With the remainder of Column 6 we advanced some twenty-five to thirty kilometers to the east. In a triangle formed by the three small towns of La Juba, La Escondida,. and El Aguacate, a short distance from each other—a position very advantageous: due to the topography of the land it was easy to defend and was located near a road leading from Guantánamo to Sagua de Tánamo—we installed Efigenio's Command Post, a good base for guerrilla operations. With the three platoons that remained of the original Column No. 6 we continued en route to Guayabal, Palenque, and Delicias, all belonging to the municipality of Yateras, examining and clearing hundreds of armed men operating around there. We organized Company "D," under the orders of Captain Manuel Fajardo, to operate in the Yateras area, and Company "E," with its zone of operations at Baracoa, east of Guantánamo, under Captain Ciro Frías, with Lt. Carlos Laite second in command.

In the meantime, Efigenio had gone north to Moa. He took the town after a brief engagement with some enemy soldiers posted there and occupied the airfield, then waited all night for a plane loaded with arms which, according to instructions from the National Directorate, was to arrive on March 31. Although the date of arrival had been postponed and Efigenio was unaware of this, the journey had not proved entirely unproductive as it gave him the opportunity, of which he fully availed himself, to equip his entire unit with motor vehicles, the property of the Moa Bay Mining Company. On the way back, passing through the Casanova zone, municipality of Tánamo, he was also able to examine and reorganize numerous groups of armed men freely operating on their own in that district. Senior rebels were put in charge of them, and Company "C" was thus organized to function in said municipality.

Near Guayabal de Yateras we laid out an airfield. We used tractors belonging to a lumber company found nearby and waited there until April 8, the day we were told to expect the plane previously expected at Moa. But then we were informed that the plane had detoured to Fidel, where landing facilities were safer.

While there we received news of the impending [general] strike and, after clearing up the last details of organization in the zone and the manner in which operations should proceed according to the terrain, we quickly returned to Efigenio's Command Post at El Aguacate, north of Guantánamo. We installed our headquarters nearby in the little town of La Juba, which we reached the afternoon of the tenth. The outbreak of the general strike had surprised us on the way with the events it precipitated, and our National Directorate asked us to join Guantánamo militia in carrying out immediate action in support of the strike. I sent for Captain Lora, chief of action at Guantánamo. On April 11, together with the various unit heads present, we worked out a plan. The village of Imías, located between Guantánamo and Baracoa, had been attacked the day before with the loss of Captain Ciro Frías. We would attack the barracks at the town of Jamaica, military headquarters for the municipality of Yateras. The operation would be directed by Efigenio, with Yateras troops under the direction of Captain Manuel Fajardo, plus Company "E" of Baracoa under the orders of Captain Félix Pena, substituting for the late Ciro Frías. Troops under my command would attack the Soledad sugar mill. Caimanera was to be attacked by troops of Company "A," Alto Songo, under the command of Captain Tomassevich, and a detachment of Guantánamo militiamen under the orders of Captain Lora. There would also be harrassing actions by mobile patrols in the vicinity of the city of Guantánamo. Meanwhile, in Santiago de Cuba, a column of militiamen under the command of René Ramos (nom de guerre Daniel) would attack the barracks at Boniato.

Thus, in order to occupy a wider stretch of terrain and control hundreds of armed men, it became necessary to release different groups and officers of Column No. 6. To back the strike we realized that one attack, effective as it might be, would not impress the enemy much or stimulate the strike movement as well as would several simultaneous actions. Seen from a strictly military point of view, our disposition of forces in order to carry out attacks in different directions was not advisable. Guerrillas such as ours, whose supply of ammunition depended basically on what we might be able to seize from the enemy in order to keep on fighting him with his own arms, must in every possible way evade battles in which we had no chance to replenish our stores.

We were conscious of the precarious situation that would arise concerning munitions if the strike did not succeed. Of all the military plans, the only complete success was the attack on Caimanera, where the naval and army posts were taken and reinforcements sent from the Guantánamo garrison were forced back with many losses. Some good weapons were captured and our ammunition supply was replenished.

At the other places fighting was hard, but the fact that our forces were scattered did not permit full successes at all points at the same time. Of this we were well aware, and if the operation did not constitute a total victory from the point of view of providing support to the strike, which was the basic objective at the time, it was entirely successful inasmuch as Guantánamo and its surroundings was the city where the general strike lasted longest, after it had been crushed in the rest of the country.

These were, in summary, the rapid events during the first month of the Frank País Second Front. The negative side of those days was the great lack of ammunition, a chronic ailment which we had with us until the war was almost over. On the other hand, we were not unaware that after the strike failed the enemy was not going to lose the opportunity to launch an immediate counteroffensive. At the very first opportunity, Fidel sent us very precise instructions about the need to prepare with all means available and to resist successfully what he rightly described as "Batista's last offensive," in which all reserve forces would be used in a last hope to annihilate the Rebel Army. And that is just what happened.

On our part we did everything possible. We received the reinforcements for the column organized in Santiago de Cuba under Daniel's command during the time of the strike, and as he had to remain in Santiago, directing the movement, we were sent the column under the command of Major Aníbal. These men, having failed in their attempt to take the Boniato barracks, on their way to join the Second Front successfully attacked the Ramón de las Yaguas barracks, where they found weapons and ammunition and took several prisoners. Fidel himself sent us a supply of ammunition. Our clandestine comrades in Santiago de Cuba and Guantánamo did everything possible to help us with all kinds of equipment and projectiles, including cartridges for rifles of all calibers, which in our arsenal we had filled with molded bullets. Our ammunition factory was working around the clock, on twelve-hour shifts, making antitank mines, hand grenades, M-26 grenades—the latter to be shot from rifles by means of blank shells.

We had the advantage that the offensive launched against the Second Front lacked the most elementary coordination on the part of the enemy. In the south and part of the west we fought against troops belonging to the No. 1 Santiago de Cuba Regiment, and in the north and the other part of the west against troops belonging to the No. 7 Holguín Regiment. Between these regiments there was not, apparently, the slightest coordination of action.

If the enemy's infantry troops devoted some days to preparing their offensive, their aviation took advantage of this and from the very moment the general strike ended began a process of methodical and indiscriminate bombing of our camps—whose positions were in some cases known—and defenseless peasant villages. The aviation slowly increased the destructive power of its bombing with the use of bombs of napalm, as well as conventional bombs, and, especially, with accurate rockets. All this material was amply supplied to them by the U.S. Naval Base at Guantánamo Bay, as can be seen in attached documents.[3]

Indicated by their names only, the main combats throughout the front during the month of May and part of June were the following: our attack on the Yateritas Aqueduct; the battle at Abra Mariana, which dominates the entrance to the Caujerí Valley; in the north, battles at Zanja and Gorea, in the municipality of Mayarí; the battle at Jagüeyes, east of Guantánamo; new battles at Abra Mariana; and the battle at La Yuita, south of Casanova, municipality of Sagua de Tánamo.

The same night of this last battle, a patrol of ours broke into the enemy camp and left a known enemy spy hanged in the middle of the camp, while the patrol was being shot at. It was during this action, while firing an M–26 that exploded too soon and too close to his face, that Lt. Ricardo Cisneros, known as "Jotor," lost an eye. Knowing himself injured and unable to see through the bleeding eye, he shouted: "Better a one-eyed Jotor than a dead one!" and went right on shooting at the enemy. This same fellow soldier had distinguished himself during operation Rescate [rescue], which consisted in going down to the towns near the mountains and liquidating isolated enemy pockets, and then returning with their weapons in a type of commando operation that he repeatedly carried out.

Then we had the battle at Bazaar, some thirty to forty kilometers from Sagua de Tánamo, and the battle of El Sitio.

On May 28, anniversary of the battle of El Uvero,[4] in the Sierra Maestra, the enemy launched his strongest offensive on the southern side, using the city of Guantánamo as the starting place. Fighting took place at Marcos Sánchez, some twenty-five kilometers from Guantánamo, and the enemy was driven back and retreated to Cuneira, six and a half kilometers from Marcos Sánchez. The next day they attacked again, managing to break through the first ambush. Fighting was renewed one kilometer from La Lima, where a long struggle for this position began with massive participation by their aviation, their bombing attacks reaching La Juba, El Aguacate, and La Escondida. On May 30 the La Lima battle continued, this being the day when the heaviest air attack was felt. From 5:30 A.M. to 3:30 P.M. there were ten hours of continued bombing, with a brief recess at noon. The battle was being fought now for the heights dominating the village of La Lima, itself already totally destroyed.

On May 31 the La Lima battle entered its fourth consecutive day, and the enemy's army had only managed to advance four and a half kilometers. Troops arriving at Soledad sugar mill tried to get through Cupeyal, where fighting continued all day. On the La Lima right flank, they sought to envelop from the rear our troops who were defending that town. During that day, three enemy attempts to take the Cabeza del Negro height, which dominated the entire scene of the battle, were rebuffed. It became necessary, however, to withdraw to Guanábana, a village located between La Lima and Bayate. As the latter had been heavily struck from the air, all the villagers were ordered to evacuate.

Meanwhile, Major Efigenio Ameijeiras received orders to hold the enemy back as much as possible, preventing any further advance. Fighting continued intensely through June 1 and 2. Outflanked by the enemy, our troops had to retreat, losing Bayate on June 3.

At another defense line established between Bayate and Bambí, in terrain much more favorable to us, the enemy was stopped. They turned to the right and reached Limonar de Monte Ruz, but were unable to proceed. Throughout this long battle for La Lima, the first struggle for positions in which we engaged, Major Ameijeiras[5] distinguished himself, as did the troops under his command. At this time, mobile patrols operating from the coffe plantations harassed the enemy using the roads in that area.

While the battle of La Lima and its surroundings was taking place, our troops were not inactive in other parts of the front. On May 29 Captains Lusson and Oriente Fernández, from Major Aníbal's column, attacked and took the Ocujal Mine, a source of supplies for the Nicaro plant. In occupying the barracks, our forces seized arms, ammunition, and a good quantity of dynamite, as well as a rich booty of trucks, jeeps, fuel, acetylene-welding equipment, etc. During those days our troops attacked also the plant at Guaso, which supplied Guantánamo with water, and harassed the 150-man garrison at Isabel sugar mill, in that same area.

In the following days, the heaviest fighting occurred at Sierra de la Hembrita, northwest of Guantánamo. The enemy was brought to a full halt and his plan to attack Efigenio's base of operations on the right flank was frustrated. Simultaneously, at different places on the front as well as in the enemy's rear, many skirmishes were fought. By the middle of June we had no more reserves of ammunition, not even cartridges for our rifles. All the dynamite we managed to get hold of was quickly used up in the manufacture of land mines and hand grenades, which were immediately sent out to cover the needs at places where there was fighting.

After each bombing it was routine to explore the sites attacked, and often we would find bombs that had failed to explode due to defects in the fuses. We would use the TNT in them for making our own hand grenades and antitank mines.

Many actions were not carried out due to a lack of ammunition. The situation was chaotic. If the enemy had known this, perhaps he would have made an attempt to continue his advance. Our need to fight basically defensive battles slowly used up what scant supplies we had left at the end of the strike. In many places where battles were fought, whatever little ammunition we could take from the enemy had to be used against that same enemy within a few hours. The need to protect rural villages some-times resulted in too much fighting. From the military point of view, in some places it would have been wiser to withdraw, leaving the ground to the enemy when conditions were not favorable for us, then draw him toward terrain where the topography was to our advantage. But it was painful to lose ground and to leave the defenseless towns to an enemy who usually turned them mercilessly into a burning pile after having criminally sacked them. Despite all these difficulties, what were hardest to endure of the enemy's actions were his indiscriminate air attacks, which caused more harm to the civil population than to the forces of the Rebel Army.

Fully conscious of what he was doing, the enemy unleashed all his cowardly fury on the population, terrorizing the people and making them pay a heavy price for the support they were giving the Rebel Army. Be-sides the deaths caused among the civil population, including women and children, and the destruction of all their worldly goods, what was most regrettable was the psychological effect of the bombings on children. The saddest spectacle we saw, worse even than the evacuation of whole peasant villages in the midst of the screams and lamentations of women, was that of children running all over the place at each air attack, and their being gathered up, extremely excited and screaming with all their strength long after the planes had withdrawn. There were whole families who spent weeks and even months huddled in whatever caves and holes were avail-able. The time came when, even though no planes were flying, those people dared only to sit at their cave entrance waiting for a new bom-bardment to start. They would come out for a few hours at night to search in nearby farms and streams for some food and water, and then do their cooking in the dark inside those same caverns.

The moral effects of such conscious and cynical actions by the enemy were soon evident. Many peasants, who did not understand the reasons for the struggle and who lived in great misery and suffered brutal exploita-tion, upon seeing the Rebel Army in their vicinity, felt that this added to their troubles, the worst suffering of all undoubtedly being the bombings. The more backward and less understanding people reasoned thus: "Before we lived badly; but now that the Rebels have come, we live worse!"

At the end of May, our Department of Rebel Intelligence handed me a photograph and a document of exceptional importance. It was a photograph taken inside the United States Naval Base at Guantánamo, where two of Batista's planes could be seen alongside a parked American truck loaded with ammunition. The insignia on the planes, alongside the U.S. emblem on a hut close to the airstrip, left no doubt as to those planes being Batista's and receiving help from the U.S. Naval Base at Guantánamo Bay. The other document, even more important, had been torn from a record book of war material dispatched from the Guantánamo Naval Base. Taken from the files of the base, it was dated 8 May 1958 and bore the signature of an authority in charge of such procedures. This was a detailed account of the shipment of North American war material by the U.S. Naval Base at Guantánamo to the Batista government.[6]

With these two papers in my possession, I remarked: "This is an atomic bomb that we should keep to use at the right moment."

After having received these papers, whenever I thought of the air attacks and of the bodies of civilian victims, women and children killed by bombs, villages destroyed, and I considered how to halt the barbarous methods employed by the enemy against a defenseless population, no matter how I analyzed the question, I always come around to the conclusion that the only way to achieve the objective was to make use of that photo and that document which constituted our "reserve atomic bomb."

In one of the reports that we sent to Déborah (Vilma Espín) and Daniel (René Ramos) in Santiago de Cuba (June 2), telling them of the battles during the last few days, we pointed out the following concerning the enemy: "They are nearly all drunk—or perhaps it is marijuana—and together they make up a swarm of thieves, ruffians, and delinquents of the worst kind. They violate, murder, and steal. Their planes throw incendiary bombs delivered by the Yankees at their naval base at Guantánamo, as happened quite recently, and they order the Trujillos and Somozas to supply Batista with weapons. They cannot do it as brazenly as they had been doing it because of continental pressure. Here our finest men are dying with only a miserable shotgun in their hands. These monstrous crimes must be denounced before the world. . . ."

Around June 17 I was at Major Ameijeiras' Command Post having a meeting with him and several of his officers. Gathered at an old abandoned ranch house, we were analyzing the military operations taking place in his zone when we were surprised by an air attack. To shelter ourselves, we ran towards a nearby coffee grove, seeking a cave that we knew was there.

As we approached, we found it full of peasant families, fright written all over their faces, and some could not help showing how much they disliked us. An old farmer, sorrowful and even with indifference, looked steadily at me and said: "And when is all this going to end?" Not finding much to say, I merely answered, trying to create some feeling of optimism, "Don't worry. It will soon be over!" "Yes," replied the old man as he sat on the floor, "when we all are finished."

I knew an argument would have no validity with those peasants at a time when they could feel the blast of bombs being dropped, shaking the roof of the cave, and they could hear the long volleys of machine-gun fire from enemy aircraft. They also knew that the enemy infantry was quite close, at two different points in the area. In this uncomfortable situation, I decided to leave the cave, so we sat outside in the shadow of some coffee plants, waiting for the bombing to cease. I hung my hammock between two trees some forty to fifty meters from the entrance to the cave, and it was right there, thinking things over, that I decided to detain American citizens within our reach, with whom we could start an international furor, using the evidence already mentioned and much additional we had in our possession.

At the moment, the Central Command of the Second Front was mobile, riding in three jeeps, establishing headquarters wherever we set up camp each day. Together with Captains Augusto Martínez and Jorge Serguera, I headed toward Naranjo Agrio, south of Sagua de Tánamo, where the column commanded by Comrade Belarmino Castilla (Aníbal) was based. We found Castilla ill in bed. On 22 June 1958, after a meeting with different officers of the General Staff, as well as some unit commanders who were present, we reported on the documents in our possession, on the difficult general situation we were facing, and the decision I had taken. Immediately we began to analyze the repercussions as well as the consequences. The gravity of the step we were planning did not escape us.

We analyzed the factors we considered most important: first of all, the responsibility that I would incur taking such an independent decision without consulting the General Command in the Sierra Maestra. To do so would take us no less than twenty days, judging from the delays involved in sending messages through Santiago de Cuba—for we had no direct communication as yet with Fidel and it was only at this time that we were organizing our Communications Department. Judging by what we could see of the situation at the moment—as it usually appeared much graver than it actually was—we believed that the full force of the enemy aviation and army was going to be thrown against us, to annihilate us first and then march on Fidel in the Sierra Maestra. From the scant news we had, we did not know that just the opposite was happening, i.e., that the principal enemy attack was against the Sierra Maestra (although I must say that some days before we had received news of a great concentration in the Bayamo area). The enemy had flung himself against the Sierra Maestra; but we did not know either of the great victories that, under the leadership of Fidel, our men were beginning to achieve in that area. Radio Rebelde in the Sierra could be heard only very poorly.

The other no less grave aspect we had to analyze was the reaction of the American government. Would they go so far as to carry out a military intervention in Cuba? We were not a legally constituted state against which they could take action. Legally, the state was represented by the puppet Batista, and interventions unleashed under any excuse, as in 1898, were no longer possible midway through the twentieth century, nor would world public opinion, particularly in this hemisphere, allow it. The United States would have no other recourse save to come and negotiate with us for the freedom of the North American citizens whose abduction we were considering. In short, we foresaw with great exactitude the events that would follow, as witness the fifth paragraph of the Secret Instructions complementing Military Order No. 30, which said textually: "In view of the certainty that after the detentions are carried out contacts by the U.S. consulates and embassy, as well as by accredited journalists, will be made with the different military commands, be it known that all these people must be treated equally with the greatest courtesies; but they will be kept at a distance from all that concerns our revolutionary army, and kept under vigilance. They must be asked to give complete personal data and explain the reasons for their visits. These data shall be sent urgently to this Command, and instructions awaited concerning the same."

These instructions were drawn up on 22 June 1958, five days before the captures began. We were thus anticipating events that would take place a week later: instead of intervening, Yankee delegates had to come and parley with us.

So we came to the conclusion that we could and should carry out the operation.

We finished our meeting after having studied the immediate effects of the measure. As we had figured, it was going to mean suspension of the machine-gunning and bombing by Batista's aviation in order to give the American government's representatives a chance to confer with us. Having the fullest confidence in the success of what we were doing, the code name with which we designated our plan from then on was "OPERACIÓN ANTIAÉREA."

June 22 I devoted to writing Military Order No. 30 as well as the Secret Instructions[7] that complemented it (documents 1 and 2 of this report), and other instructions concerning said order which different units had to follow. Near our territory, the place where there was the greatest concentration of North Americans was the naval base. We chose the morning of Friday, June 27, to start carrying out the order, taking into consideration that on that day, each week, many U.S. Marines and officers left for the city of Guantánamo on leave. Also marked as basic objectives were the industrial mining center of Moa, the Nicaro Nickel Company, the United Fruit Sugar Company and its plantations at Guaro, and a number of nearby sugar mills owned by North American monopolies. On June 24, in a report sent to comrade Déborah at Santiago de Cuba, after detailing the latest happenings, I made the following remarks:

> ". . . and finally, Déborah, the most important matter I have to discuss with you is the following: next Saturday you must send Anita and Mercedes to pick up Comrade Serguera, who will go to see you to discuss matters of great importance, so delicate I dare not put them on paper. I do not think it necessary to warn you again of the importance of the matter, so you should not fail to send for him on the day indicated. Have them bring him a change of clothes. Although I still have paper and would like to go on writing, I lack time, with which I am in a competitive race.

> Juan Carlos [Raúl]

June 26 all units knew of the mission they had to fulfill. That same night I began to draw up a call to youth[8] (which appears in this report as No. 3). I finished it on the 28 as I had to interrupt it the day before to attend the funeral of Pedro Soto Alba, killed while attacking one of the two garrisons at Moa during the early morning of the 27, and of five others caught in an ambush while retiring from Moa. The names of the latter were Antonio Boizán, Alcibiades Deroncelot, Manolo Ternero, Renato Galbán, and another whose name at this time of writing unfortunately I have not yet been able to obtain.

The report on the Moa action was the first received regarding Operación Antiaérea. It was the only action where fighting was necessary. There had been 120 soldiers, twenty of them in the barracks and one hundred around the Los Mangos district, near the airport. It was not necessary to take either of those groups, just surround them, hemming them in so that nobody could get out, and then on with the basic task, which was to capture the North Americans and to requisition the material and transportation equipment we needed.

Despite the few weapons with which he had been provided for this operation, Captain Soto advanced valiantly until near enough to enemy trenches to jump in. There a grenade killed him. The death of the other five who fell in an ambush while retreating was the result of the irresponsibility and cowardice of two officers, who were later demoted, expelled from the Rebel Army, and sentenced to prison until the end of the war for their lack of responsibility in these events as well as for other faults. The dead were all magnificent fighters who had stood out in the course of the struggle.

I reached the town of Andrés on the banks of the Sagua de Tánamo River, south of the town with the same name, the location of Captain Pedro Soto's Command Post. There, at his own headquarters, from which he had frequently gone out in pursuit of his heroic duties, he and his five soldiers fallen in the Moa action were laid out. Twelve North Americans captured at Moa were there too, but I ordered them taken out of the place so they would not hear our funeral oration for our fallen comrades. I wanted to prevent their being unconsciously linked to the general indignation we were experiencing. I transcribe some notes taken by Captain Cuza of words spoken that afternoon:

"Raúl spoke to us of the importance of the operation that had been carried out. The whole world would know that the people of Cuba were willing to pay any price for their victory, and that the yearning for freedom of our Mambises[9] lived on in our own generation. With the words 'Libertad o Muerte' we were going to win. World public opinion would know that our people were being murdered by the Batista dictatorship with weapons provided by the government of the United States and that in our possession were pictures of the dictator's planes loading bombs at the Guantánamo Naval Base. Raúl spoke of Pedro Soto, of his honesty, of his bravery; of how, having been given up as lost after the *Granma* landing and the battle that followed, he turned up one day in the Sierra Maestra with his own rifle and another one ha had found abandoned by a comrade.

"He recalled how Lt. Pedro Soto Alba, a humble working man, a mechanic from the town of Manzanillo, recently, on May 23, took part in an act of heroism in which he faced 300 soldiers sent from Sagua de Tánamo who were trying to penetrate our free territory; he faced them with only a patrol of riflemen and, as the men used up their ammunition, he ordered them individually to withdraw. When there were only two men with him and he saw that it was impossible to maintain their position, as at any moment they would be surrounded, Soto decided that they should go. But he found he had been crouching so long with his heavy gun that he could not stand up. Once more Pedro Soto's greatness revealed itself, for he unhesitatingly handed his Garand rifle to one of the two comrades who were still with him and ordered them to get out, saving his weapon, while he stayed on fighting with his revolver. He was surrounded and in danger of death when, fortunately, Major Aníbal and one of his units who were in the neighborhood approached, attacking the enemy on a flank, obliging them to withdraw, and pursuing them up to a kilometer from the town of Sagua de Tánamo. Thus Comrade[10] Pedro Soto was spared from certain death. He was decorated with the Frank País Legion of Honor for his unquestionable bravery.

"Raúl explained how when Comrade Pedro Soto fell wounded and near death at the approach to the Moa barracks his last order was 'Save our weapons!' Such was the action of a young revolutionary trained in the stern discipline of the Sierra Maestra. At a time when our lack of weapons and ammunition was severe, his sense of responsibility and care for them was one of his outstanding characteristics during combat duty. Captain Pedro [Soto] Alba was promoted by Raúl to major as a posthumous act of homage. Some day, said Raúl, when together with their freedoms the people will recover their wealth, without which the revolution would not be complete, the Industrial Center of Moa will be named for Comrade Soto, who fell there." (As it is today.) "He also spoke of other fallen comrades, humble workers and peasants, men of the people, tired of wearing around their necks the heavy yokes of exploitation. As Martí taught us, they have taken the star and, with it in front of them, have risen to their feet.[11] 'Eternal Glory to the Immortal Heroes of the People,' concluded Raúl."

That same night, saddened by what I had witnessed, I returned to Naranjo Agrio to continue preparing a call to youth, which I finished the next morning. Copied and mimeographed by Comrade Augusto Martínez, the first copies of these documents I sent to Santiago de Cuba with Comrade Jorge Serguera. From there, once the National Directorate was informed, they would go to the Sierra Maestra. As Serguera was a good lawyer, he would report to Fidel on everything that had happened and would defend our different measures.

With the same papers I sent Comrade Pepe Ramírez, present manager of ANAP[12] in Havana, to get in touch with the comrades of the Political Bureau of the Popular Socialist party (PSP) and request their publication of our documents and dispatch of the same to other progressive organizations. He was also to have them circulate clandestinely throughout the country.

With my staff I immediately left for Calabazas as reports were beginning to arrive of the results of Military Order No. 30 being carried out in different places. The largest detention of North Americans had been realized by men under the command of Captain José Durán (Zapata), from Company "E," Baracoa, who captured a full omnibus traveling between the naval base and the city of Guantánamo with twenty-nine marines aboard.[13] These, with the twelve from Moa, two from Central Ermita, two from Nicaro, and four from the United Fruit Company, totaled forty-nine, including two Canadians who were the first to be released. The names of those detained were:[14]

Moa Bay Company
Anthony A. Chamberlain
Albert M. Ross
Ramón Cecilia
Edwin M. Cordes
James D. Best
John M. Schissler
Eugene P. Pfleider
H. G. Krisjanson
William H. Roster
Howard A. Roach
Edward Cannon Sput

Nicaro Nickel Company
Jaya Poll
Sherman A. White

United Fruit Sugar Company (Guaro)
James Page Stephens
Jesse Gorham Ford
A. F. Smith
Harley F. Sparks

Guantánamo Bay Base Marines

Gerronger, R. C.	Jamson, J. E.
Holt Hous, G. G.	Mpasocos, A. M.
Toxk, B. R.	Keyes, Jr., Til
Asfom, R. A.	Wonall, H. C.
Dubuson, G. L.	Capewell, George H.
Mattewes, A. H.	Marqueg Hobrem, A. E.
Hernández, A. R.	De Faus
Bonde, J. L.	Limbery, C. M.
Anderson, J. J.	Gibson, R. C.
Krown, N. S.	Christre, W. H.
Coly, T. A.	MacArdle, M. P.
Stamb, N.	Worst, R. P.
Sepley, H. D.	Geond, V. W.
Palmer, R. J.	Narváez G.

The names are missing of the two Americans from Ermita and one from Moa.

Military Order No. 30 had, then, been fully carried out. At the end of June comrade Déborah[15] arrived, traveling via Alto Songo, and her arrival coincided with that of the U.S. consul at Santiago de Cuba, Park Wollam, who contacted our advance forces in the neighborhood of Moa. He was taken to Naranjo Agrio and from there to Calabazas, the place chosen for our diplomatic discussions.

The last aircraft of the Batista tyranny that operated during those days over the Second Front territory was a light plane that machine-gunned the jeep in which the U.S. consul was traveling. The government troops fighting our men in different sectors received immediate orders to withdraw. Planes disappeared entirely from the Second Front skies. The war had come to a halt, a necessary breather of which we would take advantage, a fact that had entered into our early calculations.

Women and children came out of their caves and returned to their homes. Happiness appeared on the children's faces. The peasants knew even the name of the operation and, seeing its immediate results, they jokingly remarked to some of our men: "Listen, send a couple of Yankees to our neighborhood. They are antiaircraft batteries, so don't you dare let them go!"

Military Order No. 30 and the Call to Youth were being read to all units and at small gatherings of peasants, to as many as possible.

With comrade Déborah representing the directorate of the movement and also acting as interpreter, Major Aníbal, Augusto Martínez, and I began the diplomatic discussions in an isolated shack belonging to a peasant friend on one of the hilltops overlooking the small Calabazas valley. I deliberately sent for several of the detained Americans who best understood the question and made them take part in our first discussion with Consul Park Wollam.

First we informed them that our measure had been taken, among other reasons, in answer to the continued military help given by the government of the United States to Batista's forces, and that the North Americans had been taken to the Second Front so that with their own eyes they might see what Batista's government had done with the weapons delivered by the American authorities. The consul denied that Batista was being given arms and reminded me of a statement made in March 1958 by Secretary of State John Foster Dulles in which he pointed out that military aid would no longer be given to Batista. We demonstrated the falsity of such arguments by showing him the photographs of Cuban planes loading war material at Guantánamo Naval Base, as well as the photostatic copies of the documents in which it was indicated that during the month of May of the same year, months after the public statement by Foster Dulles, the Batista government had received a load of arms consisting of rockets (rocket bombs for planes), as well as a large number of bomb fuses. About an hour after starting this discussion, the detained Americans, who were also taking part in it, were as talkative as the Cubans and, with a very honest point of view, criticized the consul and the policy of the United States government of using taxpayers' money to give aid to the blood-thirsty Batista government. They concluded severely: "We do not pay income taxes for that!"

Consul Park Wollam, seeing that it was not necessary for any of the Cubans there to say anything in defense of our cause, as the detained Americans were doing it for us, and as his position was rather unfavorable, asked that the meeting be suspended for the day. Consul Wollam, a timid man who in a diplomatic capacity used only the heavy-handed methods characteristic of the system of government in his own country, approached me after the meeting, somewhat enraged, asking me when I was going to release the Americans. I answered that we had agreed to nothing, and he said that he had no authority to agree to anything with me in the name of his government. I answered that there was no hurry, that we were only beginning, and if he was not empowered to agree to anything with me he should retire from the Second Front. So, abruptly ending the brief discussion, I put him in his place. The dull diplomat's face changed color and gave me an idea as to how disconcerted he was. Food and lodging were ordered prepared for him so that we might continue the talk the next day at a wooden house on the edge of a small airfield at Calabazas. Journalists were arriving from different publications, U.S. television, radio, and newsreels, as well as a Brazilian correspondent from the weekly *Manchete*. Some came in their own planes, landing at our airfield, others arrived at Guantánamo and were sent on by the clandestine movement. Some were real journalists, others just CIA agents disguised as reporters. Consul Wollam received a reinforcement, Vice Consul Robert Wiecha, who had been detained by our fighting forces in the region of Caujerí Valley when he entered the free territory following the same route in which the marines from the naval base had been taken. Having seen the good results of our tactics of the day before, it occurred to me that the talks should be witnessed by the detained North Americans as well as by the numerous newsmen who through Vilma's efforts had joined the company. So I said that since we had nothing to hide we favored all further talks being heard by all, detained men and newsmen alike. All were, of course, delighted. When my words were translated for

Consul Wollam, he no doubt remembered his adverse experience of the day before with his fellow countrymen. He found himself on the spot when he opposed our proposal. That was the first blow he received that morning, even before sitting down to talk. I remember that the night before, at supper, someone asked Consul Wollam if he would sign documents in the name of his country as the result of any negotiations with the revolutionary army. Mister Wollam, holding a chicken leg between his teeth—as reported by the Brazilian newsman from *Manchete* magazine —thought for a moment and then replied: "I have no authority with which to sign any document in the name of my country. I have come only to discuss the freedom of all the American citizens." And I thought to myself as I sat at the same table, "If you don't sign, you won't get anyone out of here!"

The conversation that day started cordially. Mr. Wollam kept his temper and mechanically turned down our proposals without the slightest reason. During one of the recesses, while I was standing in the hall reading a document with Vilma, the "cordial" consul of a few moments ago approached me and in a loud and arrogant voice demanded:

"And when do you propose to release the prisoners?"

"When we come to an agreement," I replied.

"I've told you that I am not empowered to do that!"

"And I have also told you that if you have no authority for any such arrangement with us, you can leave," I answered.

"That is not going to please my government; that is absurd," he said.

Up to that moment I had observed all the rules of diplomatic courtesy, in which actually I had no experience. But, as Cubans say, I "exploded," and with a voice as loud as I could make it, I answered: "And what do I care whether your government likes it or not? What concerns me is my people. What we have done is absurd according to you. What you do, giving Batista weapons with which to murder the people, what do you call that?"

Vilma, who besides acting as interpreter now and then put in her own opinions, suddenly struck out at him: "And what you all did at Hiroshima and Nagasaki with the atom bomb, what was that?"

Without allowing him time to answer, I went on: "You expect to intimidate us by force with the power of your country. Do you realize that reason is on our side and that we will fight on and never give up? And this will be a war without end because you will never be able to defeat the Cuban people. Each time I present evidence you come out with agreements and international documents of Mutual Aid for Continental Defense, good for nothing more than spattering the people of Latin America with blood. You say you have not helped Batista for some time. And I say that lately you have even been giving him napalm bombs of gasoline jelly."

"That is a lie!" answered the consul angrily.

"You are the liar," I shouted louder yet.

I immediately had a box brought in containing the remains of a napalm bomb. Luckily these included a large fragment with an inscription in English reading as follows: "Napalm bomb —— pounds. Property of the United States Air Force," followed by the date "May, 195—," with the last digit obviously having been scratched out, but no doubt it was 1958, thus dated after the announcement by the United States government that it was no longer giving Batista weapons. In the face of the argument and the irrefutable evidence, Wollam lowered his head for a moment and then said to me, "That is important evidence. I want to take it to show to my government!" I answered that the evidence was ours and that his government did not need evidence to convince itself of the help which, consciously and while deceiving public opinion throughout the world, it was giving the Batista government.

During the heated words of the discussion I have just related we were approached by Anthony A. Chamberlain, a high official of the Frederick Snare Corporation who directed the building of the industrial center at Moa and who had apparently been listening to the violent altercation while sitting in the living room. Standing before the consul, he reprimanded him, criticizing his attitude and declaring he was not in agreement with his manner of expressing himself and engaging in the discussions. He told him he had to ask our pardon for what he had said. The consul, like an obedient child, sitting on the veranda's bannister, exclaimed in a low voice, head down:

"Kindly accept my apologies."

"They are accepted," I answered. Then I left for a walk down the runway of the landing field.

While I was there, Mr. Chamberlain caught up with me and throwing his arm around my shoulder kept pace with me, and in a paternal tone of voice, in perfect Spanish learned during the long years he had lived in Cuba, tried to give me some advice:

"I'm going to talk to you as if you were my son and ask you a question: Are you crazy? Why are you quarreling like that with the American government? Don't you understand that anyone opposing the Americans here in Cuba won't get anywhere? You may some day even get to be a senator of the Republic when this is over. Don't you realize how strong America really is?"

Despite the basic dishonesty of this proposition of my "improvised papa," I did not feel offended, noticing his conviction in what he was saying. His words reflected the capitalist concept of life and the behavior of men. It would have been absurd of me to try and convince him otherwise, so I confined myself to saying:

"Look, Mr. Chamberlain, we had better not go on talking, as we will never understand each other. You are mistaken. We are not men such as you are accustomed to deal with. We speak different languages, have different ideas about life. We are revolutionaries, not ambitious politicians, against whom we also battle."

Nonetheless, I expressed my appreciation for his opportune interruption in the recent incident with Consul Wollam, and we finished the walk and discussions for the day.

During the days we were holding the diplomatic talks, a commission of officers of our Rebel Army organized different excursions for the detained North Americans to show them the towns destroyed, introducing them to families of dead peasants, and, particularly, to the mothers of children killed in recent bombardments. At this they were so greatly impressed that on the initiative of four of the Moa men under detention the following letter was addressed to the American ambassador in Havana:

28 June 1958

The Honorable Earl E. T. Smith
United States Ambassador to Cuba,
American Embassy
Havana, Cuba

Dear Mr. Ambassador:

You have probably heard from the Moa Bay Mining Company and the Frederick Snare Corporation that a group of twelve men are being held here in the deepest part of rebel territory, where it is virtually impossible to find us, more so as we and the other two groups of four are being periodically moved around. Up to now we have been shown every consideration and courtesy.

During the long and difficult journey to the interior of this territory, we have been shown evidence of the bombing and devastation of certain inhabited areas. The authorities here affirm that the bombs have been obtained from the United States government by means of the Treaty of Western Hemispheric Defense, Mutual Assistance Section. We have been shown a box of ammunition that came from the United States and bore the label of Foreign Aid.

In addition, we have been shown snapshots of Cuban military planes ostensibly loading ammunition at the Guantánamo Naval Base, as well as photostatic copies of requisitions to the U.S. Navy for rocket bomb fuses, presumably for use by the Cuban navy, but it has been reported that they are actually being used to bomb this isolated zone.

Our purpose in writing is to advise concerning the present situation and the fact that, in our opinion, it would be impossible and inadvisable for the Cuban army to try and locate us. We are definitely being held as captives until certain measures are taken. These are: (1) That the U.S. government publicly announce it will cease supplying the Cuban government with arms under the Mutual Assistance Agreement. These people are aware of the fact that the pact has been violated by the use of weapons against civilians. (2) That no Cuban plane be allowed to load arms at the Guantánamo Naval Base.

Naturally, we condemn the use of weapons supplied by our country and our taxes ostensibly for western hemispheric defense but now used for devastation and bombing against the unprotected civil population in a civil revolt. We have been told emphatically that the detention of the twelve guests hinges upon this situation being corrected.

It is hoped that you will quickly take the necessary action to settle this critical problem. Those in command here have warned that the foregoing are the conditions for our release.

Yours sincerely,
FREDERICK SNARE CORP.,
A. A. Chamberlain

MOA BAY MINING CO.,
J. H. Schissler

Román Cecilia
E. P. Pfleider

On June 29 another group of Americans addressed a letter to an American firm with which they apparently had some connection:

Sunday, 29 June 1959

The Stebbin Eng. & Mfg. Co.
Watertown, N.Y.

Dear Mr. Tucker:

Ed Cannon, Henry Salmanson, Bill Koster, and I are guests of the people of Cuba. As soon as you receive this, you should telephone Washington and see what action can be taken concerning the following:

We have been with the 26 of July Movement since the night of June 26. At no time have we been ill-treated or harmed. All conveniences available have been placed at our disposal. The 26 of July Movement has been fighting during the last seven years for the liberation of its fellow citizens. During that time they have sacrificed their families, their homes, and their possessions seeking to liberate the nation from theft and corruption. The movement is made up of many good and intelligent men, many of them very well educated. Above everything, they are not just talking. They have a fervent wish to serve their fellow countrymen. They do not want to control the government but to hold free elections and have a new government free of corruption.

These men have been forced to take a drastic action because AMERICAN (home of the free and land of the brave) bombs and ammunition are killing many innocent persons, including women and children. Certainly a situation so repugnant to any American constitutes a serious insult to the American way of life.

During the three days we have been here we have seen not a trace of communism. In some cases, the weapons these men have are fifty years old. We have seen hand grenades and revolvers that are made here. Such ingenuity would hardly be necessary if Russian weapons were obtainable.

Please tell our wives not to worry as these men do not harm innocent persons. How they can keep from putting their hands on us is a mystery to us.

Our bombs and ammunition have killed so many of them.

This letter has not been written under coercion.

Howard A. Roach
Edward Cannon
Henry Salmanson

William H. Koster
c/o Maurice A. Knight

In the same way, by means of a press communication and letters directed to the families of the Americans detained, we gave our apologies in the following communication:

Free Territory of Cuba

2 July 1958

To the families of American citizens who have been held in the Free Territory of Cuba as international witnesses, and to the people of the United States:

The 26 of July Movement wishes to offer its excuses for the inconveniences caused by the detention of your husbands, sweethearts, fathers, and sons.

Our reason for doing this is to attract the attention of the people of the United States and the world to the fact that American bombs and ammunition are being used in Oriente Province, Cuba, to murder innocent people, including women and children. Homes and farms have been bombed and devastated without there being any military justification for this. We believe such deeds are contrary to the principles of the people of the United States.

Under no circumstances will any North American suffer any harm while in the Free Territory of Cuba.

(The original was written in English.)

The following day Consul Wollam left in the helicopter that had been used as a link with the naval base. With him went four Americans who were ill and had been released, together with one Canadian.

When the helicopter's motor was warming up, ready to take off, Consul Wollam was handed a receipt to sign in which it was made clear that the prisoners entrusted to his care were safe and sound. He refused to sign because at the end of the paper there was the statement that the prisoners were being released to go to the naval base at Guantánamo, and it specified that that was "Cuban national territory." Told that he would have to choose between signing or having the five prisoners taken off the helicopter and nobody going, he decided to do as indicated but not without grumbling something in English. At the same time, he was handed the following letter, expressing our opinion of the talks with him:

Mr. Park F. Wollam
United States Consul at
Santiago de Cuba
By hand.

Sir:
1. In summing up the conversations with this Command, we beg you to be so kind as to inform the State Department at Washington, through the embassy at Havana, of the contents of Military Order No. 30/58, issued by the military commands of this front, of which a copy is attached, specifying these demands:

A. The cessation of the supply of war material to the government of Gen. F. Batista, under the protection of the Hemispheric Defense Pact, whereof an essential clause has been violated by the use of weapons paid for by North American taxpayers in order to maintain in power a government which has been repudiated by a whole nation.

B. The cessation of supplying war material and gasoline, as well as other technical assistance, to the Cuban air force inside the Guantánamo Naval Base, a part of Cuban national territory.

2. We request the U.S. Department of State to appoint a delegate to discuss with the Directorate of the 26 of July Movement, in the Territory of Free Cuba, the measures adopted in said military order and those which in the future it may be pertinent to adopt.

3. We hereby inform you that as of this date and for a period of two days, throughout the territory of the Second Front, said military order is provisionally left without effect and the following U.S. citizens are placed at the disposal of the consul: Messrs. Anthony A. Chamberlain, William A. Koster, Howard A. Roach, and Henry L. Salmanson, as well as Canadian citizen Edward Cannon, all this as evidence of the good faith that guides us in our actions.

4. It is expressly stated that the 26 of July Movement and its revolutionary army are opposed to and will oppose with energy and firmness any attempt by foreign nations to intervene in the internal affairs of our country, and that the measures discussed in these conversations have been aimed precisely at strengthening that strict neutrality which must of necessity govern the relationship between nations that are neighbors and friends.

5. It is equally made clear that Mr. Wollam has declared he has no authorization from his government to receive and transmit this statement.

I remain, with the highest esteem,

> Raúl Castro Ruz, Major
> Commander
> Frank País Second Front

There was speculation in the Yankee press that our objective in the kidnappings was to force the intervention of the United States in our country. Nothing, of course, could be farther from the truth. One of the main objectives sought was precisely to prevent the constant intervention by the U.S. government in a civil war being fought in Cuba by providing Batista with such enormous quantities of arms.

The fourth paragraph of the letter delivered to Consul Wollam made our point of view on this question quite clear.

On July 4, the United States' Independence Day, a banquet was organized for all the Americans we had detained. The place was adorned with American and Cuban flags, made by peasant girls. Our national anthem was sung, and the 26 of July Hymn, as well as other Cuban and American songs.

Two or three days after his departure Consul Wollam reappeared. On landing from the helicopter, with an expression of satisfaction he handed me a copy of the *New York Times* that he had been carrying under his arm. Pointing to the main headline, he said Fidel had ordered the prisoners' release. With a very serious face, I answered that I had no news of any such order, and he replied that the order had been broadcast over Radio Rebelde from the Sierra Maestra. "Then I'll listen and I'll see if I hear it," I answered.

The following nights we were able to hear it, and proceeded immediately to comply. Because the Americans were distributed in different places in small groups, it took several days to get them all together. In our free time during those days, with the war at a standstill as a result of the "antiaircraft Americans," as described by our peasants, we granted some interviews to the foreign correspondents who were there.

Among the questions they asked, there was great interest in knowing our reply as to what the situation was in which the North American citizens found themselves. Were they guests, prisoners, kidnapped, detained, etc.? At this Vilma answered with agility: "The Rebel Army sees them in the position of international witnesses of the events which were taking place in Cuba." Some of the newsmen laughed maliciously and continued asking questions. And with the phrase *testigos internacionales* (international witnesses) the Americans were baptized, involuntarily turning into protagonists of Operación Antiaérea, although, as happens in courts of justice, not always are the witnesses volunteers.

During those days we received our first supply of weapons and ammunition sent by comrades abroad. It consisted of 13,000 bullets, caliber 30.06, and one automatic M-2 carbine. This quantity, today undoubtedly ridiculous, had great importance in those moments and, therefore, constituted a great reinforcement.

From the time we captured the Americans in the territory of the Second Front to the gathering up of the marines who were in the Puriales de Caujerí area, about three weeks had elapsed. During that time we had considerably recovered from our previous situation. Our front had expanded, new fortifications were built on the terrain recovered, and an increase in combatants permitted us to reorganize the units and make five columns of three companies each, considerably increasing our military strength.

In the course of those days we received several letters, which arrived by different routes, from soldiers of the dictatorship who just a few days before had been fighting against us. Upon the detention of the Americans, they had received orders to withdraw from their positions. The soldiers told us in different ways that under no circumstances should we let the Americans go because, if we did, the soldiers would receive orders to return to scale the mountains to fight against us. These letters gave us an idea of the demoralization already undermining Batista's army.

Those most disgusted at the departure of the Americans were the peasants of the zone, who understood that when the last of the detained had left, they would have to take refuge again in the caves, abandoning their homes once more.

Operacion Antiaérea had fully achieved its political, military, and moral objectives. The combatants of the Rebel Army, as well as the worker-peasant masses who supported us throughout the liberated territory, fully understood the measure adopted. It had enabled them to see with greater clarity the true background of the Cuban reality as well as who was basically responsible for the situation, and thus the unquestionable fact that our struggle could not end with Batista's fall but should go further, to the elimination of the real causes of the evils in our fatherland.

When some days later our messenger and lawyer, Comrade Captain Jorge Serguera, returned from the Sierra Maestra, he brought criticism Fidel directed against us. And Fidel was quite right. Before Batista's offensive had begun, he said, Batista was already lost. The offensive constituted his last hope, and once it was repulsed by the Rebel Army, as had occurred, Batista and his regime had no salvation. Therefore, using the pretext of the detention of the Americans, the United States government could have intervened militarily in Cuba and tried to save Batista. Then the situation would have become dangerously worse. Events that occurred months later showed that Fidel was right. The American government realized apparently the mortal gravity of Batista's regime, and accordingly withdrew the garrison of Cuban soldiers who were protecting the Yateritas Aqueduct, which supplied water to the Guantánamo Naval Base. A garrison of U.S. Marines was substituted, in an attitude of military intervention and provocation, and this raised a great protest from all the peoples of Latin America, including some governments. It was no more than a test, an initial step by the imperialists, which, had it been permitted, would have ended in total military intervention in our country in order to save the dying regime of their puppet Batista. These events once more confirmed the arguments provided by Fidel months before.

Today we have not the least doubt that the North American government, when it took the decision to send a detachment of marines to the Yateritas Aqueduct, did it solely with the marked purpose of provoking an attack of ours against that garrison. They had no doubt we would carry out such an attack, taking into account the detention of the American citizens months before.

But this time we had the guidance given by Fidel in the previous case, so we abstained from acting; instead of fighting, the rebel soldiers operating around there received orders to keep away from that zone.

The adverse reaction in all parts of the world against this imperialist measure, frankly interventionist, obliged the Yankees to withdraw their marines, thus frustrating the aforementioned maneuver.

In the midst of the positive results undoubtedly produced by Operación Antiaérea from all points of view, the negative side—my fault, and I will always have to consider it as such—lay in the fact that this had been an action taken on my own in which there was no question I was exceeding the powers entrusted to me as head of a guerrilla front subordinate to the General Command of the Rebel Army in the Sierra Maestra.

The day following the departure of the last detained American for the Guantánamo Naval Base, the aviation of Batista's army carried out ferocious bombings of twenty-four peasant villages throughout the Second Front area, beginning at Calabazas, where the diplomatic discussions had taken place. Again we suffered losses, including more old men, women, and children killed. That was the impotent reply to a guerrilla front already decisively consolidated and a heroic civil population whom they would never govern, much less subjugate.

Days later we took the initiative from the enemy army, and nothing nor anybody could stop us during the uninterrupted series of victories by our people, from 1 January 1959 to the fifth anniversary of Operación Antiaérea, which we recall again when we already are building for the first time in America, triumphant and invincible socialism in our country.

How very far removed are those days of Consul Mr. Wollam!

Patria o Muerte
¡Vencimos!
Major Raúl Castro Ruz

[EDITOR'S NOTE: A number of names were mispelled in the original version of this article. Wherever it has been possible to obtain correct spellings, these corrections have been substituted for the erroneous names. Also see note 14.]

MILITARY ORDER NO. 30

The 26 of July Revolutionary Army
Frank País Second Front

INASMUCH AS: It is a fact that during the first three months of campaigning on this Second Front, towards the end of May, the dictator's aviation effected nearly one hundred raids, and officers of our Department of Rebel Intelligence informed us that our enemies of the Cuban air force were being supplied with bombs of all types by the U.S. Naval Base at Caimanera. From the beginning of the present month, tyrant Batista's aviation has been carrying out three to five raids daily over our territory and alarmingly increasing their power of destruction. During ten consecutive days the villages of La Lima, La Escondida, El Aguacate, and La Juya, all in the Monte Ruz area of Guantánamo, have been experiencing increasing air raids. In the eight days the battle of La Lima lasted they carried out more than twenty raids, including those of May 30, when on the battlefront nine attacks lasted over ten hours. All through the month of May the area of Caujerí Valley was subjected to systematic bombardments which preceded the enemy infantry's attempt to advance. Even jet bombers were used, but the advance failed.

As a consequence of this action, we have seen our brave combatants gather up terrified children who as a result of each air attack scattered in different directions. One hundred families went to live in caves, holes in the ground, and other places of refuge. During endless days of anguish, hunger, and fear it is usual to see whole families evacuating the area on different roads and at all hours of the day and night. Hundreds of humble homes built at great sacrifices and with many years of hard work have now all been razed to the ground.

INASMUCH AS: Engaging in repeated and criminal machine-gunning and bombing, with live phosphorus bombs, napalm (gelatinous gasoline), and rocket bombs, using American planes, American bombs, and pilots trained at American airfields, every day and in an increasing number, dictator Batista's aviation is in action not only against our rebel forces but also against the defenseless peasant population that normally lives in the vast area now controlled by the troops of this Second Front. Besides the merciless hardships during these last three months, there is the scarcity of food due to the hunger blockade imposed on thousands of families living in a rural area of six municipalities in the north and east of Oriente Province.

This Military Command, solely inspired by the desire for peace and tranquility to be restored to so many children, women, and whole families suffering and dying as the result of vandalism and cruelty, knowing that such deeds are perpetrated with the aid, consent, and approval of the government of the United States, is obliged to take pertinent measures tending to eradicate the said evils.

INASMUCH AS: We have patiently awaited the results of efforts directed through different channels to the government of the United States for a cessation of the warlike help offered the tyranny now oppressing the Cuban people. Inside our zone of belligerence are the major interests of the North American government in Cuba, interests such as the Nicaro Nickel Mines, the Cobalt Mines at Moa, the Guantánamo Naval Base, and 100,000 hectares of land, as well as such sugar mills as those belonging to the world-hated United Fruit Company and others, all of which up to the present we have respected. We have been disappointed, however, during the last months. To our great regret, we have been able to verify that the U.S. government, instead of reducing, has increased its aid to dictator Batista, whose military power has been concentrating operations on this Second Front. Furthermore, so-called "Mutual Aid" and "Continental Defense" are criminal covers with which the United States justifies the immoral assistance it now extends to Latin American dictators in order to suit its own financial interests. We now also understand why Colonel [Carlos] Tabernilla Palmero, head of Batista's air force and responsible for the bombing of the cities of Cienfuegos and Sagua la Grande, was decorated by Major General Truman H. Landon, head of the U.S. Caribbean Air Command, under express orders and as the representative of President Eisenhower. Several newspapers in our country highlighted photographs of this.

INASMUCH AS: The inhuman North American rulers, acting in contradiction of the noble sentiments of their fellow citizens, who have repeatedly shown sympathy and support for our honest and just cause, have armed the Batista dictatorship to the teeth to murder our people. We will, in an act of lawful defense, take all such measures as we deem convenient. We will increase their extent in the degree that the United States maintains or increases its aid to the Batista government, and until such time as an end is made to the scandalous traffic in human lives of honest and humble Cubans in exchange for the protection of foreign interests.

THEREFORE: In the use of the powers with which I have been invested and for the reasons previously mentioned,

I Resolve

FIRST: All military commands under the Frank País Second Front Command, immediately and under all circumstances, as of Friday, June 26, of the present year, will proceed to the detention of all United States citizens residing at the points indicated in secret instructions complementing this military order, so that they may be taken and presented for disposition by the Second Front Central Command.

SECOND: Be it known by the authorities in charge of implementing this military order that, as is our custom, persons arrested should be treated with due consideration; it is made clear that this order does not refer to women or children of the indicated nationality.

THIRD: In view of the fact that the civil population has given repeated evidence of its aversion to North Americans, knowing that the government of the same supplies the dictatorship's planes with bombs and ammunition, it is resolved that those detained will be kept in secret places to prevent their being exposed to public anger.

FOURTH: This military disposition is due to the fact that American citizens themselves, living as they do in our midst—and we have nothing against them—may thus personally comprehend the shameful crimes committed by their government against the defenseless Cuban people. The only danger threatening those detained citizens will be the same as we endure with each air raid.

FIFTH: Let the present military order be made known to all unit chiefs under this command. They, in turn, will inform their forces of exactly what is hereby determined.

Given at the Second Front, on the twenty-second day of the month of June, of the year nineteen hundred and fifty-eight.

LIBERTAD O MUERTE

RAÚL CASTRO RUZ
Commander Chief
FRANK PAIS SECOND FRONT

ONE HUNDRED FIFTY QUESTIONS TO A GUERRILLA

7

by Alberto Bayo

One of the more colorful figures on the periphery of the Cuban revolution in its early years was Alberto Bayo Giraud, a professional soldier who had utilized his talents on three continents. In a sense, Bayo enabled the revolution to survive at a critical moment: it was the training Bayo had given Castro and his men that helped them to keep going during the first perilous weeks in the Sierra Maestra.

Bayo was born in 1892 in Camagüey Province in Cuba, then still a Spanish colony. After the conclusion of the Spanish-American War, the Bayo family moved to Spain, and Bayo joined the army as a private. In 1912 Bayo enrolled in the Infantry Academy in Madrid, and three years later he graduated as a second lieutenant.

Bayo then entered the Military Aviation School, receiving his pilot's license in 1916. He served with the Spanish air force for six years in North Africa, where he participated in the campaign against the rebellious Moors. Later he was transferred to the Spanish foreign legion, and it was with the legion that he gained his first knowledge of guerrilla warfare. As a captain and company commander, he fought the wily Riffs, who were applying age-old guerrilla tactics against the Spanish forces. Bayo was wounded in combat.

The Riffs were finally subdued around 1926 by French and Spanish forces, and Bayo returned to Spain to do administrative work in the army. The political situation in Spain was deteriorating, however, and finally it erupted into the bloody civil war. At the time, Bayo was serving as an aide-de-camp to the military commander of Barcelona.

Bayo's main claim to fame during the civil war was his command of an amphibious expedition in the Balearic Islands. Several of these islands, including the largest, Majorca, had been taken over by the rebels, and because of their strategic location astride the sea lanes in the western Mediterranean, Bayo's expedition was sent in August of 1936 to recapture them. Bayo commanded some 3,000 men, plus a flotilla that included a battleship, two destroyers, a submarine, and four transports.

Italian forces were actively engaged in the Spanish conflict, and they had established air bases on Majorca. Bayo tried for a month to capture the big rebel island, but his forces floundered under the pounding they received from Italian warplanes. Finally, the expedition was ordered to give up the effort and return to Spain. The *New York Times* noted on 8 September 1936 that "the ill-fated Majorca venture . . . was abandoned as a useless waste of energy now that more important military problems are pressing."

After returning to Spain, Bayo began advocating the use of guerrilla tactics against the insurgent armies, much as Spain had employed these tactics against the French invaders over one hundred years earlier. Bayo penned a pamphlet, *La Guerra Será de los Guerrilleros.*

Bayo served as an air commander in southern Spain; then he was authorized to establish a guerrilla training school in Barcelona. This came too late, however, for the Loyalist cause was already lost. Bayo was caught in a bombing raid on Barcelona and as a result he lost his left eye.

Bayo now began the long journey that would eventually carry him to his fateful meeting with Fidel Castro. He was evacuated to France; then he traveled back to his homeland, Cuba. At a Havana school Bayo taught mathematics and languages.

Bayo moved on to Mexico, where he became an instructor at the Military Air Academy at Guadalajara. He also went into business as the owner of a furniture factory. Central America during this period bore a strong resemblance to the Balkans: conspiracies, expeditions, and revolutions were commonplace. Bayo found a demand for his services. He trained a group of Nicaraguan revolutionaries, and later he trained Dominican revolutionaries. Then, in 1955, he was approached by a Cuban revolutionary. Fidel Castro asked Bayo to prepare a group of his followers, who would then launch an expedition to Cuba.

Castro, however, at this time had neither sufficient men, funds, nor equipment with which to set up a training base. After listening to a lengthy Castro harangue, Bayo agreed to prepare Castro's men if he could raise funds and recruit enough followers. In the months that followed, Castro succeeded in obtaining funds and in putting together the elements of a small force. A training site was selected about twenty-five miles from Mexico City: the large Santa Rosa ranch, nestled amidst mountains and harsh terrain—an ideal place for guerrilla training.

The preparation for revolution was intense and rugged. The Cubans were taught how to handle weapons, how to make Molotov cocktails, how to organize their forces, how to counter the use of aviation by the enemy, how to fight at night, and all the other things that Bayo had learned in his long military career. The men climbed sheer cliffs, participated in long endurance marches, crawled around cactuses while live ammunition was fired over their heads. Almost every moment of the men's lives was regulated, and the amount of time they could spend off the ranch was strictly limited.

A system was followed under which the trainees were graded by Bayo, as well as by each other. The man who was usually at the top of the lists: Ernesto Guevara, the Argentinean whom Castro had recruited in Mexico City.

On 25 November 1956 Castro, his brother Raúl, and eighty other revolutionaries, including Guevara, sailed from Tuxpan on the Gulf of Mexico aboard the 62-foot yacht *Granma*. The rest is history.

Bayo remained behind. He trained additional Cuban revolutionaries, and, once Castro was firmly established, he maintained a correspondence via courier with his pupil. He provided Castro with advice, such as: "Start activating a program of agitation on a large scale to encompass the most important cities. . . . Have the women in your group wear black dresses to impress the people . . ."

Bayo spent several months in the United States, during which time he trained a group of expeditionaries in Florida for ex-Cuban President Carlos Prío. The expedition was launched in May of 1957, but it was quickly destroyed by government forces after it landed in Cuba. Castro was Bayo's only successful pupil.

Once Castro had won, Bayo returned to Cuba. Dressed in his Spanish Republican uniform, he was duly honored by the Castro regime. Other Spanish exiles gathered around him. And once again Bayo's talents were put to work. He had a hand in the training of the new Castro military forces, and, more ominously, he was involved in the training of other Latin Americans who were to be sent back to their homelands to spread the Castro revolution. Bayo headed a subversive training school that was established at Tarará, a few miles outside of Havana.

Another contribution to subversion that Bayo made was the preparation of *One Hundred Fifty Questions to a Guerrilla*. Printed in booklet form, as well as published in the official Cuban daily *Revolución*, the work has been widely distributed among subversive and guerrilla groups in Latin America.

Bayo died in August of 1967. He was a "comandante," highest rank in Castro's army.

ONE HUNDRED FIFTY QUESTIONS TO A GUERRILLA

1. In order for a guerrilla war to succeed, exactly what preconditions should exist?

To be right in your struggle against the injustices which a people suffer, whether from foreign invasion, the imposition of a dictatorship, the existence of a government which is an enemy to the people, an oligarchic regime, etc. If these conditions do not exist, the guerrilla war will always be defeated. Whoever revolts unrighteously reaps nothing but a crushing defeat.

2. Who should take part in a guerrilla unit?
— Primarily only young men and women who are firm in their convictions, cautious in their dealings, have proven their spirit of self-sacrifice, personal courage, patriotism, and great dedication to the cause of the people should take part in a guerrilla war.

3. In addition to these moral qualifications what else must one who intends to join our guerrilla organization do?
— He must truthfully and in detail answer questions on a questionnaire which includes such information as the applicant's full name; place and date of birth; marital status; names of parents; names of spouse, children, etc.; places of work since the age of eighteen; names of friends in the Revolutionary Movement; whether he has ever been arrested; and many other questions which our Movement has worked out. The applicant must give a history of his political position. After completion of the questionnaire and our obtaining a favorable impression from the investigation of the data supplied, he will be admitted to the appropriate guerrilla unit.

4. If the results of the investigation of his questionnaire reveal the applicant to be an informer or spy who intends to enter our ranks to betray us, what shall we do with him?
— He will be judged by the Summary Court Martial as a traitor to the revolution.

5. If in spite of all steps we take, a despicable spy infiltrates the organization, what shall we do with him?
— Once his status has been verified as such, he will be judged by Court Martial and without pity sentenced to death. We can pardon a political enemy who fights for an ideal which in our estimation is wrong, but never

a spy. Such a man deserves no consideration even though to the enemy he may be a hero or martyr. The accused should be given every right which his situation warrants, especially since he may really be an agent working for us who was ordered by his supervisors to engage in counterespionage.

6. *How many guerrillas work in a guerrilla unit?*
— The ideal number is between cen and twenty. The fewer the men, the greater the mobility.

7. *How fast does a guerrilla unit make an amphibious landing and how is it achieved?*
— The unit is only as fast as the slowest of its members. To effect a landing everything must be planned and rehearsed in advance so that as soon as the unit hits the beach every member moves quickly, silently, well disciplined and well briefed in his particular task. Those who are assigned to take the hills commanding the beach move off to the left flank; those who are to take and hold the center run forward and assume their positions, then rapidly unload the material from the boat as quickly as possible, maintaining discipline and absolute silence as though they were a group of deaf mutes, not even being able to signal to one another.

8. *What is done with guerrillas who cannot withstand long marches?*
— They are brought together to form slower units within which, however, everyone has to keep up.

9. *Who should captain a guerrilla unit?*
— The captain should be the one who because of his special qualifications of command ability, character, intelligence, caution, zest for combat, etc. is nominated for the position.

10. *Should a guerrilla be informed of the higher command organization?*
— Yes, he should know it and abide by it so that when there are casualties there will be no disagreement as to who is to command a unit. Vacated positions are taken over by the person with the next highest authority and who will be respected and obeyed by all subordinates.

11. *What weapons should a guerrilla unit carry?*
— The unit should be equipped with the same type of rifles to facilitate the supply of ammunition, and in addition, it is good to have a light machine gun which is always useful in our operations. Each guerrilla should

always carry his own first-aid kit, canteen, a watch synchronized with the unit leader's, and many need field glasses. A guerrilla should also wear as a belt a rope some six feet long which can be used at night by a companion who holds on to one end thus not losing contact with his unit. This "tail" is worn wound around the waist. The part left over is what his companion, following behind, holds on to. No one is ever lost this way, no matter how dark the night is. It can be used in scaling peaks, crossing rivers, and for tying up bundles of firewood.

12. *How should the guerrilla unit be equipped?*
— Its men should have good heavy shoes with thick soles and count on one good compass per unit. These are indispensable. Maps of the sector should always be available in order not to have to ask directions of any peasant. But if necessary he should only be used to confirm data already on the map.

13. *How should a guerrilla unit be organized?*
— Exactly like an army corps, with its staff, its different positions and responsibilities filled by guerrillas so all the work does not fall on one man. Therefore the guerrilla unit is composed of the following sections: intelligence, operations, sabotage, recruiting, training, armament, munitions, quartermaster, sanitation, and propaganda.

14. *What are the duties of each of these sections?*
— Intelligence should compile all the information it can on all members of the guerrilla unit, all enemies, those indifferent to the movement; on the location of water, springs and rivers; on roads, highways, trails, bridges; on the conduct of the guerrilla members; on sympathizers who wish to join the unit; on soldiers, informers, spies, etc. At the same time it will obtain or make maps of the terrain and the principal targets in the sector assigned to the unit. It will conduct espionage and counterespionage activities, keep records on unit personnel regarding all combat performance whether outstanding or unimpressive; and carry on cryptographic work (coding and deciphering messages, documents of courts martial, etc.).

The Intelligence Section should be under the direction of the second in command of the guerrilla unit, who should himself possess a high degree of intelligence, wisdom, and caution.

The Operations Section will supervise all attacks and other missions the unit undertakes and will evaluate the results of these endeavors. It consults with the comrades responsible for carrying out the missions, keeps the commander posted on the development of projects so he can make the final decision as to whether the operation will be put into effect. When the captain is unable to command a unit because of wounds, severe illness, or necessary absence, the head of Operations takes over his command, filing all data required for operations, both proposed and ready for accomplishment, along with different scale maps of the sector.

Leadership of the Sabotage Section, the main one of the ten composing our staff, falls to an active officer, extraordinarily dynamic, extremely intelligent and clever, having a creative imagination, adaptability, and a real vocation for his assignment. He must conduct his missions so that all types of sabotage are exploited to the fullest; if possible hitting new objectives daily.

The Recruiting Section obtains personnel to fill out our ranks or replace our losses. It will list names of young volunteers separating them into three groups. In the first group will be those who are to replace our casualties; in the second, those who can serve as machete men or demolition agents; and the third group, used only for the construction of fortifications and other such tasks.

The officer in charge of training will supervise the training in handling firearms and close order drill, literacy courses for peasants, and all educational and cultural programs of the guerrilla unit.

The Armament Section is concerned with the maintenance of the unit's weapons; with the shotguns of the shotgunners serving with our forces as well as with our hand guns.

It will keep lists of instructors and armorers and their assistants, providing for the acquisition of replacement parts needed to maintain our arms in good repair.

The Munitions Section is in charge of everything pertaining to the guerrilla unit's ammunition. It trains civilians who are to pass cartridges on to the guerrillas, and furthermore maintains small caches of cartridges and spare parts so that in no encounter will the guerrilla be without munitions.

The Quartermaster Section, because of its vital importance, will be the province of one of the most responsible men in the unit. This section sees to it that food is never lacking for the troop, rationing intelligently whatever it has, and assuring by its negotiations, orders, and purchases the feeding of the unit.

The Sanitation chief doesn't have to be a doctor or nurse, although it would be helpful if he were. This section has the responsibility for keeping a complete stock of medicine, and whatever else is needed to bring our comrades back to health. This includes the addresses of doctors and nurses in our sector who will either voluntarily treat our men or who will be forced to do so when called upon.

The man in charge of Propaganda will make known all our successful exploits in newspapers and magazines throughout the country; and if that is not possible, then by means of letters, mimeographed bulletins, etc. This publicizing of our military accomplishments will raise the morale of our people and wear down the morale of our enemies.

In Combat

15. *What physical training should a guerrilla have before going on missions?*
— He will engage in even longer marches until reaching a total of fifteen hours duration with only a short rest of ten minutes every four hours; besides, he will practice night marches of seven hours, at least.

16. *How should one move about in the field at night?*
— One should walk as though riding a bicycle, lifting the feet high each step in order not to trip over stones, tree trunks, or other objects in your way. Use your compass at least every hour to check your directions. If you have no compass you can orient yourself by the polar star whose location you will learn in our manuals. On starless nights you can get your bearings from the trees. In our countries, the north side of live trees has either no bark or the bark is thin and worn.

17. *How should guerrillas treat one another?*
— Everyone should be friendly or at least cooperative. Practical jokes and tricks are considered bad taste. They cause enmity among the men, weaken the unit's strength, and therefore are forbidden in our organization.

18. *How can one orient himself during the day?*
— By means of the sun. Stand pointing your right arm and side toward the place the sun has risen. This arm points toward the east; the opposite side is the west; in front of you, north; and at your back, south.

19. *When in the field we come upon a house or peasant's hut, how should we proceed before entering for the first time?*
— Only two of our number will go in; the others will let the occupants of

the building know they are surrounded in case they are enemies or intend to betray us. When a careful search of the house has been made and the possibilities of betrayal or the hiding of enemies in the house have been ruled out, the rest of the guerrilla unit can enter after lookouts have been placed on the hills overlooking the road along which enemies might come. While we are inside, we will not let anyone leave, for he might warn an enemy. The recruiting officer will be in charge of interrogating the owner and discerning his true feeling toward us. Afterwards he will be asked to help as an informal agent, or as a farm guerrilla. If he refuses, showing open sympathy for the enemy cause, he will be made to leave the area; for it is impossible in an area where the guerrilla unit is operating to allow freedom of movement to individuals who might be working against us. Once he has been told to leave his house or farm we will attach all of his property without any compensation. All his belongings will become the property of the armed forces of popular liberation.

20. *What shall we do with the young men who wish to join our unit?* — The recruiting section will process them one by one, investigating their merits and deciding whether we can accept them as fellow-soldiers in our revolutionary struggle. In case we can, they are trained to be farm guerrillas; if we have the weapons and the need for more people, they can be taken in as regular guerrillas after receiving the proper training. I personally trained Calixto Sánchez's guerrilla leaders who later landed in Oriente, and in Cabonico, and whose initial operation was a complete success. Not a cartridge was lost; only one boat, which got stuck on the beach. Many times in my classes I emphasized that those who did not voluntarily offer to join up might be accepted one at a time, searched, and given a rigorous interrogation by the recruiting officer to decide who should be assigned to our elite, to the regulars (the less inspired), or to the third section—the unreliables. But we never accept people merely because they claim to be on our side. Calixto Sánchez's leaders did not follow this warning, one which I learned well in a hundred encounters with the enemy. When a group of soldiers dressed as peasants came up shouting, "Viva Fidel Castro!", our people received them with open arms. The soldiers then drew their pistols from hiding and arrested our men saying they were surrounded by many others in the mountains. Our guerrillas, new at the tricks of war, were stricken by fear, the disease that all unseasoned troops are subject to. The rest is well known. They were taken prisoners and that butcher Colonel Cowley assassinated all that were with Calixto Sánchez. Cowley, in turn, was later brought down by a heroic

shotgunner of the 26th of July Movement. Only the seven men in Calixto
Sánchez' advanced guard, commanded by Héctor Cornillot, survived this
encounter and later most of them joined the Sierra Maestra units.

21. *What should the guerrilla unit do after an amphibious landing?*
— Once on the beach, we march toward the highest ridge offering con-
cealment. Of course this is after hiding in the most appropriate places all
the heavy materiel we have unloaded. If we succeed in moving inland in
secrecy, we carry along our materiel to hide in even safer places in the
highlands.

22. *Can you tell me some of the assignments in which volunteers of
both sexes can assist?*
— Here are some of the missions they can undertake:
    1. To form a small platoon of attendants for each guerrilla unit.
    2. To provide pairs of people to serve as scouts in front and on the
flanks.
    3. To provide liaison pairs to give proper personnel status reports to
the command post.
    4. To act as runners to maintain contact with the flanks.
    5. To provide large platoons to comb (clean) the enemies from our
zone of control. This job must be done frequently.
    6. Other platoons can ask the loan of hammers, nails, saws, picks, shov-
els, hoes, barbed wire, food, canteens, empty bottles and tin cans, and
typewriters that the commander requires.
    7. Others may compile a list of volunteers, both men and women, of
the proper age to give service.
    8. To form political groups to inquire of the political leanings of the
people in our zone.
    9. To select individuals who are ready and able to make our status re-
ports, plans, selected scale maps, detailed operational information, to keep
guerrilla service records, speeches to the people, etc.
    10. Printers, typists, mimeographists, and others may work in the
propaganda section.
    11. To form brigades of propagandists of our revolutionary ideas to
carry out meetings in plazas and other places.
    12. To form police platoons, in which women should participate, to
impose order and to prevent robbery, pillage, violations, and abuses.
    13. To provide and guard storage for our material.
    14. Women will also be used to bring complete information from

cities not yet dominated by us. By sending many of them to the same place without their knowing that they have the same mission, more complete and cross-checked information will be gained.

15. To form water carriers and quartermaster personnel and distributers of provisions from the women.

16. Women can be used to form a corps of nurses and helpers.

17. To form the sections of carrier pigeons.

18. To establish a report-carrying section using trained dogs.

19. Cooks.

20. Cook's helpers.

21. Wood carriers for the kitchen.

22. Kitchen dishwashers.

23. Water carriers for the kitchen.

24. Seamstresses.

25. Clothes ironers.

26. Laundresses.

27. Registerers of home residents (preferably women).

28. Bathkeepers.

29. Typists, for consignment to sections that ask for them.

30. Separation, storage, and control of captured enemy clothing.

31. Hospital personnel.

32. To form units of saboteurs of trains, highways, bridges, wire communications, etc.

33. To make groups of slingers and throwers of incendiary bombs.

34. Teams of sling instructors.

35. To provide picked groups designated to prepare incendiary bottles, filling them with gasoline and capping them, so that they will be ready at the proper time.

36. From the most intelligent and brave women, to form sowers of fear.

37. Statisticians.

38. To form a group of carpenters to make sawhorses, barbs, fence stakes, trench floors when the ground is wet, grenade boxes, frames to mount rails in trenches, etc.

39. As groups to collect rails for fortification works.

40. To carry the rails to the place of their use.

41. To form recruiting parties to bring people from villages not yet controlled.

42. To form espionage and counterespionage sections.

43. To make up flag and signal communication sections.

44. For fortification works, using whatever workshops that are available.

45. To provide day and night relief teams.

46. To form cavalry with whatever animals are available among the people.

47. Enemy aircraft spotters.

48. Basket carriers to carry dirt from the trenches.

49. Arms cleaners.

50. Cold steel weapons (cutting weapons) storage.

51. Providers of horse rations.

52. Investigation of traitors.

53. Food storage.

54. Throwers of incendiaries against vehicles on the roads.

55. Personnel to set up and improve airfields.

56. Tree cutters.

57. Keeper of the "operations diary."

58. Correspondents.

59. Letter carriers.

60. Tool keepers.

23. What is the first offensive action that a recently formed guerrilla unit should take?

— Our first action, as soon as we reach our sector, is to cut in as many places we can, all roads and railroads so that our enemies will only be able to travel on foot. We must force them into infantry roles. Because of their inferior training, lack of morale, because they are armed forces at the service of the oligarchic enemies of the people, and because of their lack of fighting spirit they should be very inferior to our forces who, with greater nobility and efficiency of personnel, are in better condition than the enemy. We should not become panic-stricken under any circumstances, even though the enemy might throw thousands of men at us. We will have a better chance to inflict casualties on him. It would be more dangerous to our guerrilla team of fifteen men if they assigned twenty-five soldiers to hunt us down. This is worse than having a thousand after us. Always remember that Sandino fought against the Americans for seven years without once being cornered in spite of his pursuers' many thousands of perfectly trained men with motorized units and dozens of radios beaming concentric rings around the Sierra de Segovia where our hero was fighting. After seven years of fruitless pursuit they had to grant him a truce on his own terms. Augusto César Sandino, the Nicaraguan

patriot, was assassinated a short time after leaving the Segovia highlands.

24. What should we do with the peasants who wish to join us?

— The recruiting officer will organize them into two different divisions.
Into the first one will be put fighting men whom we trust completely, and
into the second will go those who can be utilized on secondary combat
tasks such as water carriers, wood cutters for the mess units, and porters
for long marches. To those individuals who display an avid desire for
combat and have unquestionable backgrounds will be issued machetes
and incendiary bombs. They will march along with our unit as members
of machete and bomb squads.

25. When should we do battle with the enemy?

— This is the prime question for a guerrilla unit. The answer should be
learned by heart and always put into practice. The perfect guerrilla, that
is the one who best serves the daily interests of the peoples revolutionary
cause, is one who never invites the enemy to do battle. Nor does he accept challenge to fight the enemy who hopes to meet us where he would
hold the advantage. Every good guerrilla should attack by surprise, in
skirmishes and ambushes, and when the enemy least suspects any action.
When the soldiers load and prepare to repel our attack, we should all fade
out of sight and redeploy in safer places. Obviously, in all actions we try
to inflict the heaviest possible casualties. We will never lose visual contact with our enemies; that is, we will accompany them from afar keeping
within field glass range so that we are constantly aware of their position.
If we do not fire into their quarters every night we are not performing
our duty as guerrillas. A good guerrilla is one who looks after his men not
exposing them to enemy fire; he makes sure they cannot see his troops
with camouflage and skillful tactics. He hounds the enemy day and night,
carrying on "minuet" tactics. That is, he advances when the enemy falls
back; retreating to our right when the enemy plans to encircle us on that
flank. We always keep the same distance from the enemy forces: some
800 to a thousand yards by day, sending two or three of our sharpshooters
up as close as possible during the night to pester them, and thus bringing
about the highest number of casualties.

26. How should a police headquarters be attacked?

— If the headquarters is built in the center of a lot one hundred yards
wide by fifty in length, there will be fifty yards between the building and
the fence surrounding it.

First, we have to take the adjacent buildings and with our fire force the garrison to take cover, waiting for reinforcements and outside help. Once in possession of a neighboring building and setting our riflemen around the headquarters so that no one can escape, we will begin our plan of attack as follows: In the building we have taken, we will dig a tunnel toward the center of the headquarters. Once we have the first shaft and the tunnel begun, we put two men with pick axes shoulder to shoulder digging a six-foot-high tunnel. Each one digs out a cubic yard of earth. They then withdraw while the dirt is quickly removed by others with shovels and baskets. When one side of the tunnel is clear of loose dirt, the shovel and basket men withdraw and the pick men begin again. All the workers thus have a break and can perform their tasks with greater efficiency. The tunnel bores away underground, just wide enough to allow two to work without interference. All work as fast as possible; the supervisor relieves the men when they seem to be slowing down.

It is next to impossible for reinforcements to reach the garrison by day so it will probably surrender. If it does not do so soon, it should be blown up—first with the object of taking it over; secondly, as a lesson for other police hedaquarters to surrender quickly. To hasten the job, not only one tunnel will be dug, but many leading under the headquarters. We do not know what kind of earth we will encounter in any one tunnel, nor whether the first mining attempt will be successful. A second or third bombing may be needed.

If on igniting the charge we discover that the blast is not underneath the building, our soldiers, ready and waiting, should be sent into the tunnel to reach the garrison from the crater or at least to occupy the crater. It has to be somewhere near the building and as such serve as a good place to attack the building from.

For these operations we need the following teams: strong men for the picks, shovelmen, and basketmen; those to handle the lanterns and other tunnel lights; those who will shore up the tunnel after it is dug; and finally those who will set the charge, as well as soldiers to race down the tunnel after the explosion.

Before setting off one tunnel explosion under the headquarters, all other tunnel activities from other buildings must be halted so as to safeguard our comrades.

We have to be prepared at all times for a counterattack from the garrison itself as well as by the army, keeping a 24-hour guard posted. We also will make beforehand the necessary preparations for accommodating the wounded, prisoners, and the dead resulting from the attack. One man will be assigned to take care of all equipment we might capture. All enemy survivors will be given a thorough interrogation to learn what should be done with them.

If, after the first explosion the garrison still does not surrender, we keep up work intensively on the other tunnels as well as in the first one. After an unsuccessful first attempt we should be able to correct the angle for the next try. Up to the time of the second bomb, the first crater can be used to pin down the occupants of the building from close by.

After the headquarters has been taken, the teams we have utilized in the tunnel operations will be sent on to other targets to do similar work.

When all garrisons in our zone have fallen, these specialists will be given jobs in our corps of engineers. The leaders of tunneling operations will at all times inform the general staff of their progress.

As a closing note to this section keep in mind that from all of the world's famous prisons, men have escaped by digging their way under walls and past sentinels.

27. *What should be done before attacking from a tunnel?*
— If it is not possible to achieve a surprise attack, an intense psychological campaign should be carried out making use of emissaries, wives of the besieged, local bigwigs, and enemy prisoners taken in previous attacks.

28. *How is a guerrilla column on the march made up?*
— The guerrillas cover their flanks (right and left sides), an advance party (those preceding the main body) and rear guard (protecting from behind) utilizing peasants who volunteer (as they all should) to help us, as well as troops from the guerrilla unit itself.

29. *What should appear on service records?*
— The dates and places where each guerrilla has fought in addition to his rating as a soldier in each action, and whether he received any distinction for his performance. It is important to be precise in keeping service records so that promotions can be given to the most valuable men.

30. *How can you make a hand grenade?*
— Take an empty condensed milk can, dry it thoroughly inside; put in a dynamite cap, nails or small pieces of iron; press smoothly so no sparks are produced; be careful not to jar or hit it. Continue inserting other dynamite caps and more shrapnel, tamping gently each time until the can is full. A wooden or metal cover is then placed over the can after the contents have been compressed as much as possible. The cover should be pierced to allow a fuse with a percussion cap at its end to make contact

with the dynamite. On lighting the fuse, the percussion cap is exploded, which in turn ignites the dynamite in the grenade.

31. *How can you make a land mine?*
— Take a length of pipe, seal it at one end by welding or screwing on a pipe cap. Fill it with dynamite and cover the open end, leaving a small hole in the cap for the fuse. Insert a tube about ⅛ of an inch thick with a percussion cap in the end contacting the dynamite. In the other end of the fuse, place a wad of cotton impregnated with potassium chlorate and sugar. Another wad of cotton, and next to this a little glass chamber containing sulfuric acid are next inserted into the fuse tube, making certain the glass receptacle is well-sealed to keep the acid inside. Next, stick in a length of metal or wood for a plunger that can slide easily down the tube to break the glass. This releases the acid which forms a chemical reaction with the sugar and potassium chlorate, producing a flame to ignite the fuse and percussion cap. Set the mine in a road with a board attached to the plunger. The first vehicle or pedestrian to pass over ignites the charge.

32. *How do you make a time bomb?*
— Use the same system as for the land mine, adapting to the fuse a connection to drive the plunger with an alarm clock, whose alarm bell of course will be removed.

33. *How do you make a delayed action fire bomb?*
— Take a small bottle and fill it with sulfuric acid; then cap it with a wad of cloth or newspaper (one page). The paper is attached to the bottle with a rubber band. Cut off the end of the cover that sticks out. This is done so that the acid is not wasted in this material. Then take another small bottle with a slightly larger mouth so that the top of the first bottle can fit into it. Into the second bottle put twelve tablespoons of potassium chlorate and four of ordinary sugar. Mix up the sugar and potassium chlorate. Now set the first bottle upside down in the mouth of the second. The acid eats through the paper or cloth and on reaching the potassium chlorate and sugar, produces a large multicolored and long-lasting flame. If we have taken the precaution to set the bottles next to inflammable materials, we are assured of a good blaze.

34. *What happens if acid and glycerine are used instead of acid alone?*
— The action of the bomb can be delayed up to five or six days depending upon the amount of glycerine to acid. Experiments with different mixtures should be made to establish formulae for various time durations.

35. *How can you obtain the maximum delay?*

— By putting the sulfuric acid into a covered bottle with a siphon in the top which reaches well below the level of the acid inside. The acid slowly evaporates on contact with the air and consequently fills the siphon with vapor. Later, the vapor condenses and drips onto the chlorate in an adjoining bottle, producing the combustion. A bomb like this can be set to explode weeks or months later.

36. *What is the principle of the military time fuse?*

— Military time fuses which can produce results days, weeks, or even months later are used by all modern armies. The triggering device consists of a plunger on a compressed spring. Acid eats at the wire compressing the spring. When the wire is cut through, the released spring drives the plunger into a priming tube containing the combustible acid, touching off the bomb. This was the type bomb used by the anti-Nazis against Hitler in 1943. The attempt to blow up the German dictator's plane failed due to the discovery of the bomb by vigilant crew members.

37. *How do you make an incendiary bomb?*

— Incendiary bombs should be used by the masses to insure our victory. Every man, woman, and child should know how to handle them. By converting everyone into a combatant and hurling thousands of incendiary bombs against the defenders of tyranny, no enemy can stand before us and victory will certainly be ours.

An incendiary bomb can be made with any kind of a bottle, a rag fuse, and gasoline. These can easily be found in any town. Fill the bottle with gasoline and put in a piece of cloth; any size will do so long as it reaches the bottom and has a bit sticking out to light. The bottle is closed with a cork stopper, paper, cloth, or can even be left open. Light the fuse and throw the bottle at the target. When it breaks open on striking the hard surface, the gas is spilled out and ignites. There is first a huge flame and small explosion which cannot hurt the thrower, even though he is close by. The flame lasts a few minutes depending upon the amount of gasoline in the bottle. The bottle with its lighted fuse, whether uncovered or not, *never explodes*. It makes no difference whether the bottle is open or covered, the gas fills a third, a half, or two-thirds of the container, or whether the bottle is carried around for hours. It will not explode in your hands.

We emphasize this so that the future bomb throwers will know that only those on the receiving end can be injured by this bomb. It is advisable to cover the bottle, however, so that upon being thrown no gasoline spills out on the ground, but all of it hits the objective. Suggested training exercises include using a bottleful of water to begin with, though actually lighting the fuse each time. Using a thick glass bottle, like the Coca-Cola ones, practice throwing as far as possible over soft earth. Plowed earth makes a good "range" to practice on. Thus you can use the same bottle many times over, practicing daily for accuracy and distance. Later, practice with different-size bottles to achieve versatility. In actual combat conditions thin-walled bottles are best as they require less energy to smash on reaching the target.

Incendiary bombs can be used to good effect at night since their flames illuminate the enemy objective and thus help make the bomb thrower's position less visible.

When attacking the military garrison in a town, the revolutionaries should proceed as follows: Everyone at a predetermined time will appear on all the surrounding flat-roofed buildings. Five minutes later everyone lets fly with a rain of incendiary bombs against all the walls of the building, trying to hit doors and windows. Revolutionaries in the streets also hurl the bombs they can against the walls at the same time, trying for the same prime targets. Especially those in the streets will throw rocks and shoot at doors, balconies, and windows.

If the police or soldiers come out they will be riddled with bullets, rocks, and bombs by the whole populaces, and especially by those on rooftops. Outnumbered like this, not one garrison can hold out.

If the garrison is constructed of wood, fire bombs can be used to good effect no matter where they hit; but even in this case doors and windows should be the prime targets. Even uncapped bottles can be used without having to light the fuses first, if a good blaze is already going. Gasoline can even be thrown in cans and earthen pots. It is well to have our revolutionaries also practice with slings, as do shepherds and country folk, so they can hurl gasoline bombs with them. You make a sling with a piece of rope two yards long, into the middle of which you attach a can, piece of heavy cloth, or leather pouch (from a handbag, etc.) where the missile is placed. We then tie one end of the rope to the right wrist. Put the gasoline bottle into the pouch (or even into a partially unwoven and widened section in the middle of the rope). Grabbing both ends of the rope, swing the sling with the bottle around your head (like hill people do all over when they want to hit a hog, bull, or horse) until you build up speed. When ready, take aim and release the free end of the rope, sending your projectile smashing into its target. That is, if you have been practicing!

Time spent in practicing bomb-throwing with a sling is really worthwhile. You can become invaluable to the revolutionary cause as a precision bomb marksman being much more valuable than the hand thrower.

Another way of throwing fire bombs is with large launchers similar to the slingshots used by children in hunting birds. The elastic bands of course must be heavier and more powerful.

Patriots in towns should become skilled in throwing fire bombs by hand, sling and slingshots; then engage in contests with one another. It goes without saying that all this is to be carried out under the utmost secrecy and with the least possible noise so as not to arouse the suspicions of the police.

These marksmen will be in the front line when the revolution comes.

When the day of the revolution comes, these units should attack the town garrison, the houses, and other places the enemy is holding out. If all the enemy strongholds in your town are immediately smashed, the whole bomb squad should report together immediately afterwards at other localities where their services are needed. If all the objectives (town garrisons, barracks, forts, etc.) are successfully taken, the Revolutionary Command will assign them to the highways to attack, from a distance, all vehicles moving through the area. These operations are best carried out in daylight and from ambush. Other bomb throwers should be ready to defend the first attackers should enemy parties pursue them from the highway.

Ideally, every revolutionary, man woman, or child (over twelve), should know how to wield incendiary bombs. To achieve this goal, not one day should go by without our practicing with water-filled bottles.

In order to prepare for the eventual battle of liberation from the forces of oppression, exploitation, and the bourgeois dictatorship, all revolutionaries should continue collecting all the empty bottles they can (even buying them), as well as storing gasoline, old rags, and matches so that when the crucial day arrives nothing will be wanting. Empty cans and cardboard boxes, well lined with paper so that no liquid comes through, should be kept. Wooden boxes can be made if bottles and pots are unavailable.

Teamwork makes for efficient fire bomb attacks. Comrades should aid the bomb thrower; some filling the containers with gasoline; others sticking in fuses; others closing the bottles with corks, paper, or rags; and still others lighting the fuses.

In a fire bomb attack, our people should be well hidden so that the police or soldiers, when driven from their refuges by the heat and flames, can be fired upon with rifles, pistols, and rocks and given the warm reception they deserve.

If, after the bombardment, there still remain inside the garrison enemies who have not surrendered, then platoons of volunteer machete men should rush in, being careful to divide up the rooms to be attacked. Some will only go down the main corridors, others into the rooms on the left, others into the ones on the right. As soon as they have eliminated the enemy occupants of the rooms, they should cut a hole no more than a yard from the floor to let their comrades in the next room know they are in command there and not to use fire bombs against them. When one side of a garrison is in our power, the revolutionaries should come out into the street to help the others attacking the other sides. This draws enemy fire and attention from our forces inside and thus shares the burden of the siege.

38. *How can communication be organized between various guerrilla sectors?*
— Portable walkie talkie radios are used by wireless experts these days for communication among groups in the field.

It is understandable that for guerrillas who have to scale high mountains and engage in long marches heavy communication equipment is out! We cannot count on vehicles to carry the equipment, nor even on hand generators which are also heavy. For our operations we are limited to only the lightest of apparatus, working off dry cells. Even these need to be replaced. The 114 mc. (two-meter) band is the best. On the air, keep your messages clear and to the point to guarantee speed and security in communication.

Groups in the field should communicate with each other directly and privately. Each group should carry a small transmitter-receiver and maintain contact on a previously determined wave length adjusted on their sets by means of a crystal oscillator. Other groups intercommunicate with one another in the same way. If various groups gather in one place they can contact a shelter or supply depot over the same system to acquire more and better equipment and aid.

When making preliminary incursions in unfriendly territory it is not advisable to complicate this basic system of communications. Radio sets can be acquired or even built, and tested before their being put to use. Sets measuring 2½ x 3½ x 10 inches powered by a 3-volt A battery and a 90-volt B battery have a 15-mile range and, in favorable conditions, twice as far.

The sets are delicate, precision-made instruments, and should be handled with care.

39. *How should guerrillas report current developments to their superiors?*
— Each guerrilla leader should report such happenings on three different

sheets. One of them furnishes valuable *personnel* information; another lists the *materiel* on hand at the moment of its signature; and the third concerns *political military* information from the sector. This last report might include the latest rumors, enemy troop movements, new men who have joined us, data on informers and spies, etc. These three parts are sent to the chiefs of the personnel section, the materiel and armament section, and the intelligence section, respectively.

40. *How should guerrillas in neighboring sectors communicate with one another?*
— They should report their strength and the state of their supplies. These reports should be delivered verbally and in person by liaison officers of the utmost confidence. The officers should also have the authority from their superiors to set the day and hour for combined operations, including their own and another or possibly two other units.

41. *Should reports be made in code?*
— It is advisable to code messages which might be captured by the enemy. Usually duplicate messages are sent, cast in special language. Two men, or better yet, two boys start out at different times with the same message. These runners should be natives of the region, clever fellows and fleet of foot.

42. *What is the complement of a guerrilla company?*
— The tactical unit designated as the company contains one hundred men including the commander, a captain. A company has four lieutenants, each commanding a section. Including their lieutenants in command, the first three sections each contain twenty-five men, except for the last. The captain is the twenty-fifth member of the fourth company.

Each section has two sergeants who in turn command a platoon apiece of eleven men. Each platoon has two corporals who command squads of five men each. In the squads a second corporal assists the corporals.

43. *What is the complement of a battalion?*
— A battalion has five companies. In the fifth company are the cooks, helpers, mechanics, barbers, tailors, cobblers, office personnel, and all those who because of the nature of their work are relieved of instruction and daily activities. Of course even this company reports for duty when the guerrilla war has attained the magnitude approaching a civil war. In other respects, the fifth company is like any other.

44. *Is it necessary for all guerrilla companies to keep this same complement?*
— In order to have complete and precise control over all units it is indispensable. If all the units are the same size you can at all times know your total strength. The quartermaster, for example, must know that three companies contain exactly 300 men, etc., without having to make any calculations. All units can then contribute equally in whatever they are called on to perform. An undermanned company could not be expected to obtain the same results as one fully staffed. Also important: no guerrilla wants to be held back in his career for having been associated with an ineffectual outfit.

45. *When your complement is full and you still have extra men, what do you do with them?*
— Report the fact at once to your immediate superior so that he can order the men sent to other units as yet undermanned. If, after all units have been brought up to full strength you still have extras, then new units can be made up with the additional men.

46. *If we have said previously that the ideal guerrilla unit in the interest of mobility is composed of fifteen men, why are we now talking of companies of one hundred?*
— Because this organization has nothing to do with combat operational necessities. A captain can command a hundred men, but does not have to use all of them together. On certain occasions, for example, in the siege of an army or police garrison defended by a small detachment, it is a good idea to use the whole guerrilla company for the assault. The captain who operates in certain sectors assigned to him by the Guerrilla Staff has his platoons of twelve men trained to be perfect guerrillas; he will sometimes utilize groups of twenty-five men commanded by lieutenants.

47. *What is the best procedure for replacing battle casualties?*
— The captain should have in some strategic site, out of the enemy's range, if possible, a training base where new guerrillas spend all their time undergoing intensive training, including the memorization of this manual and other necessary information. After having tested these trainees, a ranking will be made according to each man's knowledge, aptitudes, and intelligence section report. As necessary, to fill vacancies, the new men are then sent to active units. After reporting to the captain in charge they are given their permanent assignments.

48. *What are close order and extended order drill?*
— Close order drill is a type of exercise designed to instill habits of discipline in the troops. The guerrilla must surrender his own will completely to the one in command, no matter who it may be. While close order drill is part of the training of armies all over the world, it is no longer employed in combat. It is merely a preliminary form of exercise and does produce good results. Extended order drill is used in the field to deploy troops in the various positions of combat formations.

49. *If while on the march, in camp, or at any other time you are fired upon by the enemy, what is your first move?*
— The first thing to do is to hit the ground and as best you can lie facing the direction the shots are coming from. Then space yourself as far as possible from your comrades who will be doing the same. Thus if the enemy fire misses the one aimed at, there is no possibility of a lucky hit on another man.

After this choose the best protection within reach and take cover. If you are a captain or in command of a smaller unit, order your men to take cover as well. Do not counterattack, but try to find some way out of the ambush as quickly as possible. If the fire is too heavy and the enemy is not cutting down our men, because of lack of morale, or in fear of our return fire (which will probably be the case), you might sit tight and wait for nightfall. A daylight retreat would probably cost you too many casualties. After dark, slip out of the trap.

50. *What shall we do with our dead and wounded in the field?*
— If we have time, we will bury our dead, first seeing to it that our wounded are removed from the scene of combat; and when possible, taken to where our comrades can administer medical treatment. If there is no time nor possibility for burial of the dead, we must face the necessity of leaving them. When absolutely imperative, we leave a dead companion; but never one who is wounded.

51. *What should we do so as not to lose visual contact with the enemy?*
— When you withdraw, leave one or two men (better one than two) to keep an eye on the enemy. These observers should never open fire on the enemy, but rather do nothing to let him know he is being watched. When the enemy makes camp for the night one of the observers should report the enemy position so that some of our men can be sent to harass them during the night.

52. If the enemy continues marching during the night, what should we do?

— In that case we will follow him, keeping him in sight. The party we send out to follow him should stick as close as possible to him, maintaining harassing tactics as he marches. If the enemy later makes camp or stops to rest or eat, we continue annoying him.

53. How many men should the harassing party contain?

— Very few—perhaps two or three. The rest of our men should get their sleep. Our snipers, taking care not to be surrounded, will spend the night firing into the enemy. We will cover both of our flanks while they are resting, so that the snipers can do their job without unexpected risks. This harassment should be carried out every night without fail. You would not be doing your duty if you overlook it.

54. What is the difference between a spy and a counterspy?

— Espionage and counterespionage are arts which all guerrillas should become proficient in, since wars are not won only by using one's head, but also by using one's foot in tripping up the enemy as often as possible. A spy is a peasant working for us who accompanies the enemy troop pretending to be their friends and selling them anything they need. The type of article sold or his profits or losses are of no consequence. The important thing is that he become friendly with as many of the enemy, of all ranks as possible. He should never ask them for any information whatsoever, but rather report everything, every movement, he sees; about the equipment the enemy has; information on their delays, etc. Women are invaluable in this role. That is after they have had the proper training. Their reports should be brought in by intermediaries, and in code. If the information is of extreme urgency, by oral message. A counterspy is one who works with the enemy forces, or is a volunteer in the ranks of the oppressors. Once in their confidence, he goes to work for us, keeping us up to date with firsthand intelligence information.

In wartime, counterespionage is of greater service than simple espionage.

55. How is a secret society formed?

— A secret society is always formed with a maximum of three members. A fourth member is never admitted, but one can operate with two members. Experience has shown that anything can be done with three agents; any more get in each other's way. Besides if we have the misfortune (and

it is to a certain extent inevitable) to have one of our cells infiltrated by a
spy, the most that are lost to us are two agents. This does not represent
too great a risk nor expense. We must abolish those cells containing eight
to ten where each member is in turn the leader of another cell with ten
or twelve members, and so on.

56. How does the sabotage section operate?

— A secret society will never be given more than one mission. Giving the
cells many of them has always produced poor results. Each society should
choose a special name for identification purposes, such as José Antonio
Galán, Antonio Nariño, or names of other martyrs to our cause. The
sabotage section will assign but one mission to each such cell. This way
they will have ample opportunity to do a good job.

57. Does only the sabotage section have secret societies?

— No. The Intelligence Section can and should have their information-
gathering suborganizations, but these never engage in sabotage.

58. How many types of guerrillas are there?

— Two types: Field troops and farm troops.

59. What are farm troops?

— Farm troops are those who work as farm hands, apparently neutrals
politically, who operate periodically, perhaps two or three times a month.
They get their arms from the cache, carry out a night mission, then return
to the farm and go to work the next day as though nothing had happened. If questioned, they know nothing of the operation, but all say
they have seen a few armed men at a distance whom they thought to be
guerrillas.

60. How can you blow up sizable buildings, barracks, etc?

— The easiest, surest, and least dangerous way to blow up big barracks or
buildings like the Presidential Palace is by digging a tunnel ending just
below the center of the building.

61. How do you dig the tunnel?

— First one must select a house in the neighborhood. It doesn't matter if
the house is not too close to the objective. It might be more dangerous if
the house is not close since the larger the distance to the objective the
bigger the risk, but distance might help in order to ensure the operation
without arousing suspicions. Once the house is obtained the tunnel can be

started from it, but before anything else is done canned food should be acquired and kept in the house. Food should be enough for the four or five men who are to dig the tunnel, however these men should not give the impression of being the tenants of the house.

On the first day a shaft has to be made in one of the rooms of the house reaching farther down if the building to blow is very big, and less if the building is not as heavy. Introduce in the shaft a log shaped like an E without the middle line, the one in between, the log looks then like a C with the top and the bottom straightened. The top arm of the log must be oriented toward the objective and consequently the parallel bottom arm will equally point toward the objective. The tunnel must be started in this direction and only one man will work in the shaft since it has to be narrow in order to avoid earth slides. When this man has dug out enough earth, a second man will remove it with a shovel and a third man will take it out of the tunnel with a basket. This operation will go on until the tunnel has become long enough.

62. *What do you do with the earth removed?*
— When the blasting takes place within a city it is hard to take the earth out of the house without being noticed since in these cases you have to handle a great deal of earth. The best way to handle it is by simulating in the house a business that requires loading and unloading operations. This way sandbags can be taken to an unnoticeable place or preferably cast into the river, the sea, etc.

63. *How long does it take to dig a tunnel?*
— When the earth is of average hardness a man can remove a cubic meter of earth per hour. It is easy to determine how long it will take to cover the distance between the house and the objective.

64. *How do you estimate the distance to the objective?*
— An exact calculation requires a comrade with some knowledge of trigonometry and of how to resolve triangles. Otherwise you will have to use your eyes and discuss repeated measurements with other comrades until the estimate is as accurate as desired.

65. *How much dynamite has to be placed below the building to blow it out?*
It depends on how heavy the building is but it is better not to underestimate the amount. Let's say that it is safe to use 500 to 1000 kilos of dynamite.

66. *How do you go about blasting?*

— A technician should be in charge of the operation, but everybody should know that the dynamite will only blow by means of a fulminant detonator inserted into the load and in contact with a fuse that will carry the fire from afar. To ensure the blasting it is better to use two different detonators and two fuses, and if one fails use the other.

67. *How do you place the detonator in the dynamite?*

— Pick up a sharp stick and make a hole in the dynamite, then place the detonator in the hole. Don't ever use metalic tools to open the hole unless you want to go to heaven instead of fighting in the guerrilla.

68. *How do you attach the fuse to the detonator?*

— The fuse is introduced in the open side of the detonator and is fixed with special pliers (crimpers) pressing evenly around the open side of the detonator, which prevents loosening of the fuse and failure of the blasting. If pliers are not available at blasting time bite the detonator, it is not dangerous, it is the most common method among guerrilla men.

69. *What would happen if dynamite burns or is exposed to fire?*

— It doesn't blast, it is just consumed as a melting sugar lump.

70. *How do you burn the fuse?*

— With a cigarette, and if there are two fuses both must be burned simultaneously.

71. *How can you achieve a sympathetic blasting?*

— The formula for sympathetic blasting is $S = 0.9 \times K$ (Kilos). The number of kilos of the load multiplied by 0.9 will give us the distance in meters (ms) from where to blast the other bomb. If the bomb weighs 23 kilos, multiplying 23 by 0.9 the result will be 20.7. Any bomb exploding within this distance will make the other blow up, but if we increase the distance no matter how well prepared the bomb is it will not explode.

72. *What precautions must the chief of the force have in mind before the blasting is ordered?*

— He must send an officer to every tunnel to make sure that nobody is still there, he will also make sure that each man knows what to do the minute he hears the blast. He will make a speech to encourage speed in the assault and will indicate that shameful acts during the attack will be severely punished.

73. *What else should be kept in mind for after the explosion?*
— Before lighting the fuse the chief will announce to the troop that the blasting time has arrived and, immediately after the explosion, all our fighters will approach the building to be taken from all sides, taking advantage of the confusion that will necessarily follow the explosion. This attack must be carried out fast for better results.

74. *What is to be done with used cartridges?*
— We better keep them, we can always find an officer or a sergeant among the enemy who will exchange them for new ones to make friends with us. He can very well say that they were used by his own troops in order to turn them in and get a resupply; besides, we must not keep the enemy informed about the state of our supply by letting them know how many shots were made.

75. *If our fighters could take advantage of a plain to build an airfield, how would they go about it?*
— The terrain must be cleared of stones, holes straightened, and hills made even. The field selected must be 1000 meters long and some 400 meters wide. Close obstacles like trees, telegraph poles, etc., must be removed.

76. *How can the field be made available for the use of our planes?*
— First it will be convenient to send our side information about the existence of the field, and a chart of it indicating its exact dimensions and location in a chart at a scale of 1/10,000; if possible send also a photograph. When we get news of the day and hour in which our planes will land on the field, right on that day logs and branches of trees will be placed around the perimeter of the field. As the plane appears on the horizon at the fixed hour, signals will be made with a whistle or a flag and the logs set on fire so that the plane may find the field, determine its limits as pointed out by the fires and find out the direction of the wind, since landing must be made always against the wind.

As soon as the plane has landed all the fires will be put out, things transported by the plane unloaded and the plane itself pushed by hand to the extreme end of the field where it will be again facing the wind. Only then, if the pilot requests it, which he shouldn't, a single fire will be set to indicate the direction of the wind in case the pilot cannot determine it himself by using a handkerchief. The pilot will see to it that the plane does not remain longer than necessary in order to prevent identification.

If there were any mountains around the field we will place a machine gun on the top to harass enemy airplanes that might appear on the horizon.

77. What is to be done if the plane must land during the night for security reasons?

— At the day and the hour which the plane will be directly over the field we will light the fires and keep somebody minding the fires so that they are burning constantly to let the pilot know where to land. Night landing is usually very dangerous for the pilot, since even with a good compass precise positioning over the field is always hard to achieve due to the winds which might deviate the plane without allowing the pilot to find the field. To prevent this from happening, landing may be fixed at an hour that will allow the pilot some visibility. Landings will be accordingly fixed for one hour before dawn, unless repeated utilization of the field by the same pilot makes disorientation improbable, in which case landing may be fixed for an earlier time.

After a night landing, whistles or a shot will indicate that it is time to put the fires out. If it is still dark after unloading and the plane must leave, fires will be started again all along the runway for good orientation and put out when the plane has been for fifteen minutes in the air.

78. How does a plane take off and land?
— Always facing the wind.

79. How will our men be busy when there is no immediate task?
— They will relax during the day, wash their feet daily and take care of their toenails since feet and legs are the engines of the guerrilla. They will study the maps of the region, memorizing the names of all nearby villages, and their population and some of the names of the people, they will identify on a blank chart all rivers, tributary rivers, springs, reservoirs, and wells. They will learn the distances between different points within that sector and the location of bridges and sewers that might be used for train sabotage. In other words they must learn by heart whatever piece of information might be helpful to carry on the war or to facilitate the tasks of other sections of the militia.

80. How are they given such training?
— They are first enlisted as bomb and machete men and will go with us on the marches. Beginning as scouts and carriers of water and ammunition for the guerrilla, then they will take over the watching as sentinels while the fighters rest and will be given rifles for the moment in the capacity of fighters for the first time. Then they will be employed in assaults on the police headquarters or refuges of counterrevolutionary forces, etc.

Finally when new rifles captured from the enemy are available, they will be given the rifles and promoted to guerrilla fighters.

81. *What is the standard procedure to administer capital punishment to traitors?*
— They must be given an opportunity to defend themselves, and as in the army, the regular procedures of a court martial will be followed.

82. *What are we supposed to do with sick comrades?*
— When a comrade is sick we will leave him with a family that can be trusted if they make themselves responsible for his cure and protection. They will be better off hiding in some place other than peasant huts even though attended by the peasants.

83. *What is understood by the term resupply storage?*
— Weapon and ammunition officers will keep their supplies hidden in secret places or buried close to peasants' huts.
Since it is better not to keep all the eggs in the same basket lest they be broken, resupply storages will be dispersed in strategic sectors so that we may have recourse to the supplies regardless of our position at any moment.

84. *What is the attitude of the fighters with regard to peasants?*
— All food taken from them must be paid for at a good price, thanks must be repeatedly expressed and peasants made aware that they are helping their own cause. Our men will try to repair things in the house such as beds, closets, tables that might be ruined. They will help the peasant in fencing his lot or in sowing or clearing the fields, and in so doing they will clearly show our sympathy and attract the peasants to our cause so that we may eventually request their help any time.

85. *How is the defense of a town taken from the enemy organized?*
— In order to organize this defense, the town must be rearranged to take the configuration of a complex of fortifications by opening connecting passages between adjacent houses. These passages must be small, letting only one man crouching go through, so that if it is an enemy he can be easily disposed of and if it is a friend he may go through with only the relative discomfort of bending his knees. Once all the houses are connected, those facing the street where the enemy will attack first will have in the front several holes like small vents from which to shoot. These

openings will be made at a level higher than the regular stature of a man so that even bullets that occasionally go through them will not hit our men. Of course, in order to shoot from these openings one must be standing on a chair.

86. *What will be our attitude toward the population of the town?*
— We will try to convince them gently that they must evacuate their houses, that it is an imperative of the war to fortify them. If this can't be achieved peacefully then they will be evacuated by force as an imperative of war.

87. *What will be done with the furniture?*
— All the furniture, good or bad, will be used to connect houses of separate blocks. Blocks must be connected by barricades made of furniture, stones, bricks, etc.

88. *What about military defensive organization?*
— The chief of highest seniority or rank will appoint his deputies for different sectors of the captured town that is to be defended. Every chief responsible for a sector will see to it that houses and blocks are prepared to conform to the specified defense configuration.

89. *What will be the role of the groups operating in the vicinity of the town during the course of the enemy attack?*
— They will be in constant activity, striking at the rear guard of the besiegers and most of all their supply sources.

90. *How can we slow down the capture of entire blocks by the enemy?*
— We will have parapets in the corners of all the roofs and firing from them will deny the enemy access to the houses. We will also have in the houses dry husk and rags impregnated with cheap oil. If a house is taken, the husk set on fire will have the effect of a smoke grenade stopping enemy advance.

91. *How long can we keep defending a town in this manner?*
— It may last for years. This was the type of defense put into practice during the defense of the University district of Madrid; Franco's troops never went through it.

92. *What if the enemy completely cuts the water supply to the town?*
— It was presupposed that the activity of the outside guerrillas would

make it frightful and unacceptable for the enemy to maintain a protracted assault; however, if after all there is no other alternative the best way to escape is to break through the enemy lines in the middle of the dark and flee to the hills.

93. *Which must be the main concern of the fighter while in the hills?*
— His main concern must be the care of his gun, since the weapon is his friend and protector, his means of survival. The rifle must be kept clean and oiled, especially when you are out in the country, marching by dusty paths where guns easily get dirty.

94. *Who can be properly called a hill fighter?*
— He who is in open and declared rebellion against the oligarchy, against bourgeois dictatorship, against the people's enemies; in other words, all regular soldiers in the guerrilla who wage war against oppression and exploitation.

95. *Which is the maximum time for a guerrilla to remain in the same place?*
— Three days is the longest they can stay in one particular place. On the third day they must start toward a position far away from their previous one.

96. *What qualifications make a perfect guerrilla fighter?*
— To correctly handle a gun, a rifle, a machine gun, and a revolver.
To be able to fight with a knife and fence with a stick.
To be able to throw a knife well and hit a distant target.
Horseback riding, bicycle driving, automobile driving.
Making and using bombs.
Know how to take and develop pictures.
Know how to use the phone.
Typing.
Chart designing.
An elementary knowledge of topography.
Know how to read a chart and interpret contour data.
Know how to whistle loudly.
Practice in climbing ramparts and walls using ropes or human towers.
Practice in twelve-hour marches through rugged hills with slight descents.
Swimming, rowing, motor boat driving.
Practice in climbing trees and telegraph poles rapidly.

Familiarization with piston-engine parts.

Know how to start a car with a crank, how to reach the fuel tank, how
    to fill the tires of a car or a bicycle, how to change the tires fast.

Know the Morse Code.

Know how to start the propeller of a light plane.

Extreme tolerance to all religions.

Finally to be courageous, daring, cunning, to anticipate needs and dan-
    gers, to avoid ties with things or persons; to love danger.

97. *Are all those conditions indispensable to become a guerrilla fighter?*
— Those are qualities of the perfect fighter only and are only achieved
at the peak of the fighter's performance. Take Pancho Villa for instance.
He was an outstanding fighter and nevertheless he was an illiterate. However, all those qualifications must be required as an ideal, as they are required by military academies to graduate officers who can defend the
fatherland in case of aggression.

98. *What items should be on hand for the guerrilla?*
— The perfect guerrilla must have:

Combat boots for the men.

Thick socks.

Pants reenforced with inside and back patches.

Thick and resistant belts that eventually can be joined together as the
    links of a chain and be used in crossing rivers, climbing walls and
    obstacles . . . They are called "tails" by the fighters.

Coats according to the weather (jackets).

Compasses.

Good watches.

Knives and folding knives.

Scissors to cut hair.

Scissors to cut nails (especially toenails).

Soap for clothes washing.

Guns, submachine guns.

Grenades.

Combat binoculars.

Medicaments proper for the guerrilla in the first aid kit.

Pliers with oilskin handle (you can also use a thin pipe to cover the
    handle).

Hatchets to cut wood.

Razors and blades.

Flashlights.

Forehead lights (of the kind that can be attached to the head, as the miners do).

Batteries for all these lights.

Three-corner files.

Saws.

Threads and fishhooks for fishing.

Lighters.

Hammocks.

Wirecutters.

99. *Isn't that too much to be carried by the fighters?*

— For sure, but it can be taken by the irregulars who always accompany the guerrilla. The list is just a catalog of things that we should have on hand at one time or another and that eventually will all be needed, but that doesn't necessarily mean that all of them should be taken in every raid.

100. *What precautions must we have before attacking a village?*

— In order to attack a village we must know first all the details about it. Some of the most important details will be:

Whether or not it has telegraph or telephone communications. Whether or not there are troops guarding communication centers.

If there are no troops to guard them, where (how far) is the closest communication center.

How many civilians have rifles.

Whether there is in the village an amateur radio transmitter.

Names of traitors and executioners, domiciles of the best known oppressors of patriotic and revolutionary agents.

Location of the railway or road bridges closest to the village and size of the guard.

Distance to the closest airfield.

Timetable of trains passing through the village and of trucks or buses of lines regularly serving the town.

Analysis of the topography of the local area and all other useful data that could possibly be collected.

Once the information has been gathered, the data should go into the Staff Section (Operations), which will prepare plans for the assault based on the information received. Assaults are possible without all these requirements, but this is the technical approach that will give us the highest probability of success.

101. *Once plans have been prepared how does the operation develop?*

— The precise time must be fixed. Each special task is assigned to a special team. These teams must operate fast and with decision, without being concerned with the development of the operations of the other teams, or with the failure of these operations. A team will cut telegraph and telephone communications at the entrance of the village, another team will cut them at the exit. Since individuals possessing weapons are known, a team guided by friendly villagers will break into the houses of these individuals and take their weapons along. The addresses of these individuals and the order in which these searches will take place will be specified in the lists that the chief of the team will be given. Other teams will pick up squealers, spies, or traitors.

All these things must be done "electrically," that is, in the least possible time, and the faster we do it the greater the success will be, even in terms of convincing the enemy about our great discipline and morals. This way hopeful revolutionaries will see with their own eyes that our organization can do the job. After the operation is finished we will leave the village by car, meeting the vehicles in predetermined places where they will be waiting with their engines running.

102. *What will be the mission of a guerrilla chief in an area under control?*
— He will organize, under the guidance of the recruiting officer, several groups with the following purposes:

A. One unit will "comb" the area, that is, it will inspect all the houses and sectors where there are enemies of the people's cause. This same unit will carry out the requisition of all the combat elements that we may need by searching wherever they may be.

B. Another unit will intensify propaganda for our cause in that area. Both units will be integrated by honest personnel who are notoriously incapable of stealing or of abusing those whom they dislike or their personal enemies.

103. *What will be the punishment for those who commit abuses?*
— Those who would dare to steal in these circumstances, or perpetrate abuses or infractions, must immediately undergo a drum-head court martial and after conviction sent to the firing squad without wasting any time.

104. *How will the execution take place?*
— It will take place at an hour that will permit attendance of a large audience. It will be publicly announced and dramatically set. An officer will address the crowd explaining that the man to be shot is guilty of rape, murder, theft, or of any other shameful and antirevolutionary action that

he may have accomplished. He will use this occasion to emphasize the honesty of the People's Army and praise it in the most laudatory terms insisting upon the fact that shameful acts against the dignity of the people will never be left without their rigorous and well deserved punishment.

105. *What is the most important advice that should never be overlooked in the marches?*

— Combat marches will mainly be accomplished during the night, especially when our purpose is to be seen again far away from our previous position and let the enemy think that there are two different units in operation. During the day we will be sleeping, studying, or occupied in activities proper of the guerrilla, such as care of the weapons, distribution of ammunition, care of the feet, study of the map of the region, attention to the business of the sections of the guerrilla, memorizing names of nearby villages or individuals living within the sector, etc. Don't forget the names of the ranches that we visit, etc. But in marching during the night it is a must that we walk in the most absolute silence and without smoking; otherwise, the entire unit might be destroyed.

106. *How must we proceed in a surprise enemy attack after taking shelter?*

— First we will try not to answer enemy fire, and then, even if they seem to be fewer than we are, wait until the day is over to retreat. If we were superior in number, we engage them for a short time and cause them some casualties. If the situation is not clear it is better to disappear because it might be a decoy or a stratagem to surround us with superior forces.

The course of action must be resolved by the chief of the guerrilla who knows by heart that our tactic is not to engage the enemy but to hit and run.

107. *Is the purpose of such skirmishes to cause casualties or to cause psychological effects?*

— Our aim is to destroy enemy morale, keeping their mercenaries from relaxing. If a troop does not sleep during the night they are worthless during the day and slow in the marches. Therefore, the enemy will not be left in peace for a single night.

108. *Shall we take turns in this mission?*

— Of course. This is a mission that should be shared by all members of the guerrilla for several reasons:

They must all share the honor of harassing the enemy, our fighters must acquire more experience in this type of actions to improve their morale, and finally it is known that when a soldier does not shoot he gets more and more paralyzed, rusty, useless.

109. *Which is the most vulnerable part of a camp?*
— Kitchens, stables, dispensary, etc. These are points that can't be defended and where the combat morale would be lower.

110. *How will we keep weapons in a peasant hut?*
— It would be a big mistake to keep it in boxes in the hut itself. They must be buried in boxes with an inner cover of zinc, in other words the box will be patched up inside with straightened oil or gasoline cans that will be nailed to the box. The weapons should be wrapped in rags if time permits. Then the box must be closed tight and well hidden in the hole. There you have your hideaway.

111. *How deep should the boxes be buried?*
— Always rather deep to prevent any soldiers from digging around the field close to the house and finding the boxes there (although even this is improbable).

112. *How far from the house should the boxes be buried?*
— Rather far, between 30 and 60 meters from the house, and the place will be known only by the man who buried them and two other fighters; one of whom must always be from the weapons section and the other will, in each case, be from a different one.

113. *What should be done from time to time in order to prevent rifles from getting rusty when in use?*
— They should be examined by the weapons expert that always goes along with the guerrilla and in all cases the fighter must take care of his own weapon with love and dedication, for it is an insurance policy for his life and for those who are in his company.

114. *How many times a week do the chiefs of the sections report to the commander of the guerrilla?*
— Twice a week, during the stops in the marches, the commander will call his chiefs of sections away from the rest of the comrades in a spot called the "office," close to a rock or a tree; the commander will talk with each one of his chiefs separately, starting with the Information chief. The commander will ask as many questions as he thinks fit. One after the other

all the chiefs will be examined by the commander about the status of every branch in his section and about the efficiency of their activities.

115. *What basic knowledge should the guerrilla fighter possess?*
— They all should have an idea of plotting, plot reading, contour interpretation and be able to reproduce at a different scale a map of installations or facilities such as schools, court buildings, police stations, barracks, etc.

116. *If we have on hand a map of Colombia, for instance, and we want to change it from a scale of 1:300,000 to a scale of 1:5000, what is the best way to do it?*
— Since the quotient of 300,000 divided by 5,000 is 60 it would be very hard and bothersome to enlarge the map on a paper 60 times larger than the original, and besides, many parts of the map would not be of interest for guerrilla operations. Therefore, it is better to design first a map four times larger covering only the part in which we are interested. The new scale would be 1:75,000 (300,000 divided by 4). After this we place within a square the zone of operations and enlarge it to 1:15,000; finally by a similar operation we enlarge only a concrete part of the zone of operations making it three times larger or to a scale 1:5,000. Instead of a direct 60 times enlargement, we enlarged a part of the original 4 times, a part of that 5 times and then a portion of the latter 3 times. The scale is: $4 \times 5 \times 3 = 60$ times larger.

117. *What shall we do with the maps 1:75,000 and 1:15,000 that were made and will not be used?*
— Give them to the Operations Section which can certainly use them.

118. *What does the fraction 1:100,000 mean in a map scale?*
— It means that every meter on the map will represent 100 kilometers in reality, that is, 100,000 meters on the ground.

119. *What is the best scale for maps used in guerrilla operations?*
— The best scale is 1:10,000 or 1:5,000.

120. *What acts of sabotage can be accomplished by isolated patriots?*
— Those who don't feel that they have the courage to get together and form secret societies and those who don't trust anybody around but still would like to cooperate by means of individual action may carry out the following tasks:

a. If they are working at a post office they could slow down service or send official communiques to the wrong place or in the wrong direction, always avoiding the possibility of being suspected.

b. If they work on a phone board they can boycott the service and slow it down.

c. Mailmen may pick out letters addressed to important personalities in the regime and open them by steam, learning about their contents. If they contain intelligence data they will pass these data to the Intelligence Service.

d. Phone operators will try not to miss a word of interesting conversations and will communicate all useful information to our movement. The operator should do this by telephone without disclosing her name.

e. Those who work in garages will put emery powder in the oil of automobiles used by mercenaries or by officials who are against the people. If emery were not available they may use sand or pulverized rocks, etc.

f. If they work in garages belonging to the armed forces or in official maintenance depots, they will ruin the supplies, hide the tools, misuse gas either in engine tests or by washing their hands often, always trying to throw away some.

g. If they are government chauffeurs they will try to ruin the tires with nails if they can do it in the garage or by driving close to the sidewalk to scratch their sides or by driving over rocks.

h. Schoolteachers will talk to their pupils about the greatness of progress, of beautiful ideals, about love among human beings and solidarity among nations, looking after each other even within the moral slavery in which they find themselves.

i. Everybody will pass on gossip about the exploitation that the people suffer, the increasing prices of essential goods, and complain about the miserable life they are leading.

j. Workers will ask for leave affecting sickness, and request increases in salaries or try to manufacture defective articles especially if the factories are managed by a few enemies of the working class.

k. Wherever there are no water or light meters people will leave faucets open and the lights on.

l. Government employees will not brief or correct their subordinates, instead they will criticize all orders from above and emphasize the defects of their superiors. They will use their time as much as possible in telephone conversations, coffee breaks, reading newspapers, will change the sense of documents, cause disorder, break the furniture, break machines, etc.

m. When opportune, they will change personnel, reprimand those who are friendly with the regime, and at the same time they will appear to be the most fanatic supporters of the government and of the people's enemies. They will ruin the urinaries, bathrooms, water, light, and gas installations, not only in the public offices but in cafes, casinos, theaters, etc. The best way to destroy a urinary is by throwing cotton packages and newspapers mixed with nails and wire into it.

n. In larger offices they will let loose rats and feed them with cheese until they adapt to the place and can operate by themselves. They will also try to blow the light bulbs in the offices and try to cause a short-circuit.

o. While traveling on the train or other public means of transportation they will cut the seats with razors or scissors, etc. In the stadiums or other games they will protest and disturb the peace by yelling against the authorities, the police, etc.

p. In the streets they will try to stop the traffic by going against the traffic regulations.

q. On the anniversaries of traditional commemorations that are not celebrated by the bourgeois government they will be in the streets marching past military, government, and police offices, in a silent protest against the arbitrary government of the oligarchy. They must also go to the plazas where there are statues of freedom heroes and circle around until their presence is noticed, and attract other demonstrators provoking police intervention. Then they will all start booing the police, manifesting indignation. They will convene crowds large enough to break police ranks and to expand and shrink like an accordion, rushing like gigantic waves toward the enemy only to disperse in the collision and to reorganize, forming other waves to clash with police trucks or armored cars or army tanks or "steel helmets." If there is opportunity and impunity they must boo the most prominent figures of the bourgeois landowners and the dictatorship, yelling "down with them," and encouraging revolt so as to form a massive clamor, howling and wild. The idea is to cause methodically the greatest disorder possible. If political debates with mercenaries take place try to keep the opponent surrounded by comrades, especially if he is a police official, and try to out-yell him and out-act him.

121. *What is to be done if the police or the troops open fire on the people?*
— If in a street fight either the police, the armed forces, or the "steel helmets" open fire against the crowd, the next day all our friends and comrades in the work must be induced not to go to work so that a protest may be transformed into a revolutionary general strike. If this end is achieved all efforts will be directed toward generalization of the strike so that bus-

iness will stop and nobody will dare to work in the factories. To this end we must recruit the help of all our friends and use coercion and energetic measures upon shy and cowardly people.

122. *How do we use rumors?*
— We echo all sorts of rumors and fibs to discredit the most prominent figures of the oligarchy, including presidents elected in a referendum, and we "improve" these rumors. They may also discredit chiefs of police, army, or secret police.

123. *How should we react in the event of a vehicle collision?*
— When we are present at the scene of a collision and one of the drivers is a government driver we must direct the indignation of the people against him.

124. *What shall we do if a fire starts?*
— If a fire starts we will attempt to interfere with the work of the firemen. We will make a call from a distant place from which escape is easy and give the firemen a wrong address. (This refers to fires due to sabotage of government facilities or of offices of prominent figures in the regime.)

125. *How can we use vacant apartments?*
— If we can get vacant apartments for rent belonging to persons in favor of the regime we will throw gasoline, or any other inflammable on hand, into them and set them on fire, escaping only after the fire starts.

126. *How do you spoil gasoline?*
— To sabotage gasoline it is sufficient to put some water or sugar in it.

127. *How do we sabotage a machine or a car?*
— To sabotage a car it is enough to take a small part essential to make it run; it is better to pick out parts that cannot be easily found in the store and must be ordered. Summing up, all efforts must be directed to paralyze regular work, whether in government offices or in private factories, especially wherever it may affect influential figures. We must never give a peaceful moment to the representatives of the criminal bourgeois dictatorship. We will never stop until we see the ultrareactionary dictatorship collapse violently and lose the power that it held for so long at the expense of the people, while the peasant and working majorities and the middle classes suffered misery and hunger and strains and worries.

128. *How do we distribute the troops in order to defend a village?*
— The village itself must be divided into four zones, each one under a responsible chief who will operate independently from the other but keeping them posted as to the steps that he takes so that they can all depend on each other although they are all subordinate to the commander of the village.

129. *How will the troop itself be divided by its commander?*
— The troop will be classified in three categories: roof shooters, balcony shooters, and window shooters.

130. *How will the sentries on the roofs react in case of an air attack?*
— They will get out of reach of the planes' machine guns, but if a plane is flying low they will open fire against it trying to be always under the cover of walls or old ramparts and aiming at the bushing of the propeller.

131. *How do we keep the doors of the houses?*
— The front doors will be all locked and if possible blocked so that the only way to get in the house is by destroying them.

132. *Should we remove all doors within the house?*
— All the doors within the house must be removed or pulled away except those of the rooms where food and ammunition are kept.

133. *How do we arrange the houses that make one block?*
— They must all be connected by passages made in the separation walls; these passages should not be higher than one meter or wider than sixty centimeters so that people can go through one by one only and stooping. This prevents the enemy from entering a house ready to attack the defenders.

134. *What shall we do about women and children living in these houses?*
— Women, children, and elderly people will be evacuated. Some women, useful old men, and children over sixteen will be allowed to stay if they want to fight for the revolutionary cause. These women and old men will be used in the many jobs and arrangements that defense requires, such as preparation of the blocks, recruiting, encouraging those who don't dare to fight, and especially distributing the ammunition, because at fighting time all men should be shooting and it should be these women who take care of providing men with ammunition.

135. *What will people evacuated from the houses be allowed to take with them?*
— All their private things, except weapons, ammunition, even if it is only shot cartridges, knives, hatchets, picks, bottles, gasoline, alcohol, or anything that might be helpful in the battle.

136. *What shall we do with requisitioned food and ammunition?*
— They will be kept in a room of the house especially adapted for this purpose, the food in one room and the ammunition in another together with everything useful in battle. Those who guard the food will be made aware that they will be responsible for every crust of bread, and will not take anything for themselves unless they want to be accused of disobedience, irresponsibilty, cheating their comrades, and of faults against the ethics of revolutionary war.

137. *Who will guard the rooms where food and ammunition are kept?*
— Both rooms will preferably be guarded by women who can be trusted with this task, since men will be dedicated to missions requiring more strength or to missions of more responsibility and risk.

138. *What kinds of communications will be maintained?*
— Communications from house to house and between the zones and the headquarters of the defense. Communications may be verbal, but it is better if it is done by writing. Other communications will be conducted by means of flags or other signals previously agreed upon, such as cloth hanging from the balconies, etc. We will also have to manage to establish communications with the guerrillas in the hills.

139. *What kind of discipline will be maintained in the confusion originated by our occupation of private quarters?*
— We will be more severe with our own men than with the population. We will shoot right away those who trespass or steal for their own pocket, and severely punish those who beat, insult, or humiliate civilians who refuse to give up their houses or goods or who don't understand our explanations for breaking into their houses. Our troops will take whatever is necessary without cruelty or insults and will evacuate people from their homes only as a necessary imposition due to the war.

140. *How do we attend to the care of the wounded?*
— The wounded from all houses will be gathered in a house well adapted

to their care that will be as far as possible from enemy fire. Since all the houses will be connected, as we said before, it will be possible to transfer the wounded from house to house and from block to block to the point where they will be attended.

141. *What shall we do if the enemy takes one house in the village?*
— We will defend the next house room by room.

142. *What if they take several blocks?*
— We will defend the village block by block until there is none left. It should be clear that this is only done in the phase of open war with the enemy and not in the phase of guerrilla warfare in which this type of combat is never admissible.

143. *What is our answer to those who argue against this phase of combat saying that we are destroying the fatherland?*
— We will contend that the best way to destroy the country is by allowing the enemies of the people from all the parties of the oligarchy to eat it up and give it up to Yankee imperialism. We will tell them that the shame of living under oppression, under the dictatorship of the bourgeoisie, is worse than to fight for the fatherland and for true freedom, even if we have to start reconstruction from scratch. Finally we will tell them that we prefer to build the new walls at the expense of the blood of our brothers rather than leave the old walls to serve as prisons for the eternal seclusion of the workers, the peasants, the students, the employees, etc.

144. *Is it convenient to have in our cause people working in counterespionage?*
— Undoubtedly. Persons in the villages who do this job will render a better service than anybody who would give us fifty machine guns.

145. *Should the counterspy take part in the battles against our own men?*
— A counterspy should take part in such battles, but his role should be to show off as much as possible without causing great damage to the guerrilla, without really hurting anybody.

146. *What services can be rendered by a counterspy who serves as an officer in the enemy ranks?*
— He may give us details about the strength of each one of the units that

follow us, names of their officers, material at their disposal, maps of the places where they are assigned, information about the morale of these troops, ammunition supply, and movements planned, etc. etc. One of the best services that he may render is to assign pickets to engage a guerrilla in places previously agreed upon among us or to leave a small garrison in a particular place, impeding their defense by leaving them short of ammunition or by leaving in command a cowardly sergeant or corporal who would waste the ammunition, or by moving their soldiers some place so that we may attack them in this way at a determined place and time, etc. An officer of the enemy forces that collaborates with us is more useful than ten of our own officers fighting the enemy. For this reason those who work in counterespionage must always volunteer to participate in actions against us or in outfits set for repression of guerrillas, such as the so-called "peace guerrillas" organized by the dictators Laureano Gómez and Rojas Pinilla, among others, in Colombia, etc.

In the Occupied Zones

147. *What precautionary steps must we take after occupation of enemy territory?*
— Small units will be formed with men that don't move as fast as the other fighters because of injuries, wounds, physical defects, or exhaustion. These units will "comb" the area. In these circumstances all the sections will be able to work efficiently, without rush or fears.

The Information Section will gather information as necessary, Operations will interrogate the peasantry about bridges and sewers and will mark them in their maps, Sabotage will increase its manpower with as many men as they please, instructing and training the men to form new secret societies. Recruitment will take care of the necessary propaganda to add new men to the guerrilla, checking with Information before making the selection. Training will carry out its mission by establishing camps, selecting and stimulating the instructors who will produce good hill fighters and refined technicians in the specialty of demolition, etc. Armament will make an inventory of the material at the disposal of the different sections, requesting and accepting from the General Staff orders to the effect that all units report to our rearguard facilities for armament inspection and repairs. Ammunition will be able to select good places for their secret storages and make a status report on their supply and will also from time to time dig out their stocks and expose them to the sun. Supply can take care of the purchases of food and will catalogue requisitioned items in their storages. All of which will be done more accurately now that the pressure of the fight is overcome. Finally, Health and Propaganda will carry out their own missions.

In Victory

148. *What will be done by the chief when he sees that victory is coming?*
— He will carefully attempt to separate those who will volunteer to fight at the last moment from those who are truly our own men. He will attempt to keep a good record of his own men and of those who in the last minute jumped onto the bandwagon of revolution. These new volunteers will be registered in a card with complete information and two pictures, and will be requested to sign their service record which will be passed to purging committees for verification.

149. *What will be the attitude of the chief toward the indignation of the masses and their intentions of revenge against the agents and spies of the people's enemies and the mercenaries of the dictatorship?*
— He will strongly and effectively oppose those attitudes, because it is prescribed that all persons suspected of being war criminals will have the right of self defense, and especially because there were many among the enemy who were secretly doing counterespionage, and risked their lives for the victory of our cause.

150. *What is the greatest danger that we face after victory over the bourgeois dictatorship and over the oppression and exploitation of the various oligarchical regimes?*
— The greatest danger is dissipation of our victory. The forces of evil and oppression, the historical legions of the reactionary classes never give up. They are like snakes that always fight back even after we step on their poisonous throats; they crawl and crouch, only to get ready to jump over the people. They never give up, they always resist, they are always trying to stifle us.

Some of these snakes are the politicians in the clergy who hardly deserve the name of Christian or Catholic. They are the ones who want to do in Latin America as they did in Spain where they achieved complete domination of the Spanish people after a horrible mass murder. And thus they preach in the Dominican Republic the slogan of God and Trujillo and have the shamelessness of repeating in our countries, exhausted by exploitation, misery, oppression, injustice, and by bourgeois reactionary dictatorships that call themselves democratic, that heaven is for the poor in spirit.

This clergy, by nature reactionary and always meddling in politics, should not call itself Christian or Catholic since their only ambition is to use religion as a cover to justify the oppression of the minorities and to deceive the peasants and workers by forming the so-called "Christian" and "Christian Democratic" or "Social Christian" parties, or others with equal pretensions, and to them they preach that there should not be hatred nor aversions, that God will judge humanity, that the conquerors should be lenient with the defeated. It must be noted well that these individuals, who don't believe in God or in anything of the kind, mean "the God Capitalism," "the God Exploitation" when they mention God.

They never preach these things when it is the enemy who have their feet on our neck, but no sooner is the war over when they will tell you this and more. They will go around shrieking to stop our fight against reaction if it ever makes a show; and so they will carry out their "missions" for the benefit of the enslavers. But you, revolutionary son of the people, beware of "the incense of the sacristy."

Watch over and mind your own victory, never let clerical winds impress or hypnotize you, beware of those who in all nations dominated by capitalism or imperialism adulate and support exploiters and oppressors: beware lest those hypocrites of the "kyrieleison" undermine your heroic and well-deserved victory.

[Translators' Note: Inconsistencies in the original have been translated without comment or correction.]

NOTES

Notes to the Introduction

1. *Time*, 24 September 1965. Since that date, additional conflicts have included Ernesto Guevara's 1966–1967 Bolivian operation, the Nigerian internal struggle that began in 1967, the Israel-Arab War of 1967, later followed by guerrilla warfare, the Soviet-Red China border clashes that began flaring in 1969, and the Salvador-Honduras war of 1969.
2. *Current Digest of the Soviet Press*, vol. XIII, no. 4, 22 February 1961.
3. Actually, this was a designation meaning "Seat of the Border County Prefecture." The real name of the town was Muong Thanh. But then, "Bay of Pigs," of Cuban fame, is a misnomer too. "Cochinos," as used in Bahia de Cochinos, refers to a type of local fish, not to pigs.
4. Bernard B. Fall, *Hell in a Very Small Place—The Siege of Dien Bien Phu* (Philadelphia, 1967).
5. This subversive campaign is detailed in Jay Mallin, *Fortress Cuba* (Chicago: Henry Regnery Company, 1965).
6. Mao Tse-tung, *Basic Tactics* (New York, 1966).
7. Mao Tse-tung, "Problems of Strategy in Guerrilla War Against Japan," *Selected Military Writings of Mao Tse-tung* (Peking: Foreign Languages Press, 1963).
8. Mao, "Concentrate a Superior Force to Destroy the Enemy Forces One by One," *Selected Military Writings*.
9. Vo Nguyen Giap, "The People of the Entire Country Are of One Mind in Stepping Up the Great Patriotic War and Are Determined to Fight and Vanquish the U.S. Aggressors," *Nhan Dan*, Hanoi, 16, 17, and 18 January 1966.
10. Giap, *People's War, People's Army*, Hanoi, 1961 (as reprinted by Frederick A. Praeger, Inc., 1962)
11. Ibid.
12. Giap, *The South Vietnam People Will Win* (Hanoi, 1965).
13. Ibid.
14. Ernesto Guevara, *La guerra de guerrillas* (Havana: Departamento de Instrucción del MINFAR, 1960).
15. In a speech delivered in San Diego, Calif., on 23 June 1969, the comman-

dant of the Marine Corps, General Leonard F. Chapman, Jr., spoke of groups who are against the war in Viet Nam. He differentiated between sincere dissenters and those who are "in accord with the principles of the enemy." Of these latter groups, Chapman said: "Like our enemy in Viet Nam, they fight a guerrilla war. They too have a freedom of movement, and the advantage of doing battle when and where they choose. Their sanctuary is the honesty and integrity of the other . . . groups . . ."

16. The Chinese Communists view even the Negro civil rights movement in the United States as part of the "world revolution." In a statement issued 16 April 1968, Mao declared: "The struggle of the black people in the United States for emancipation is a component part of the general struggle of all the people of the world against U.S. imperialism, a component part of the contemporary world revolution. I call on the workers, peasants, and revolutionary intellectuals of every country and all who are willing to fight against U.S. imperialism to take action and extend strong support to the struggle of the black people in the United States!"

17. The other great powers, Soviet Russia and Red China, have demonstrated through their Czechoslovakian and Korean interventions that they also believe that intervention is justified when what they consider to be their own strategic areas are threatened.

18. The question has been raised, however, whether the peasant whose home has been damaged hates the Americans more, or the Viet Cong whose presence brought about the American raid. Raúl Castro encountered this same problem in Cuba (see "Operación Antiaérea" in this volume).

19. " 'Americans Will Lose,' Says Gen. Giap," by Oriana Fallaci, *The Washington Post*, 6 April 1969. In regard to the Communist unconcern about the loss of lives, it may be recalled that to Mao is attributed the remark that if a war were to kill 300,000,000 Chinese, there would still be 300,000,000 left.

20. Ibid.

21. *Report on the War in Vietnam*, by Admiral U. S. G. Sharp and General W. C. Westmoreland (Washington, 1968).

22. Ibid.

23. Ibid.

24. "Big Guns Not Answer," by Brigadier General S. L. A. Marshall (Ret.), *The Washington Post*, 16 July 1967, as reprinted in *Vietnam: Anatomy of a Conflict*, edited by Wesley R. Fishel (Itasca, Illinois, 1968). In a letter to Mallin, General Marshall stated: ". . . The artillery shell is the costliest item of the war. We spend around $2 billion on it. Most of these rounds are spent on I & H (interdictory and harassing) fires, approximately 80 percent of which are a total waste. They are not only unnecessary, but they do more harm than good, and keep the countryside stirred up. I would not cut off all I & H fires, but would keep them to the bare minimum, registering on known VC base camps and other sensitive points only. . . ." In regard to the use of air power, Marshall said: "In the employment of the B-52s, some strikes are redundant and ill-advised. Nevertheless, I do not believe that strategic air power proved

itself inapplicable to irregular warfare in this case. We simply used it too gingerly. As to tactical air, it is not used to excess. The fault is that too many times it is called in too late. We could profitably use more of it were it better coordinated."

25. William R. Corson, *The Betrayal* (New York: Ace Books, Inc., 1968).
26. "We Could have Won in Vietnam Long Ago," by Admiral U. S. Grant Sharp (Ret.), *The Reader's Digest* (May, 1969).
27. Ibid.
28. General Maxwell D. Taylor (Ret.), "Post-Vietnam Role of the Military in Foreign Policy," *Air University Review* (July–August, 1968).
29. "Rebuttal of Hamburger Hill," *Time*, 6 June 1969.
30. Colin Leinster, " 'One Day They Will Go It Alone,' " *Life*, 25 April 1969.
31. *Pacification of Quang Dien District—An Integrated Campaign*, published by Headquarters, U.S. Military Assistance Command, Viet Nam (1969).
32. Ibid.
33. Ibid.
34. Letter from Lt. Colonel George L. Weiss to the editor.
35. Text provided by the White House.

Notes to *On Protracted War*

[The following notes are reprinted as they appeared in *Selected Military Writings of Mao Tse-tung*, published by Peking. Page references, therefore, are to this volume]

1. This theory of national subjugation was the view held by the Kuomintang. The Kuomintang was unwilling to resist Japan and fought Japan only under compulsion. After the Lukouchiao Incident (July 7, 1937), the Chiang Kai-shek clique reluctantly took part in the War of Resistance, while the Wang Chin-wei clique became representatives of the theory of national subjugation, was ready to capitulate to Japan, and did in fact subsequently do so. However, the idea of national subjugation not only existed in the Kuomintang but also affected certain sections of the middle strata of society and even certain backward elements among the laboring people. As the corrupt and impotent Kuomintang government lost one battle after another and the Japanese troops advanced unchecked to the vicinity of Wuhan in the first year of the War of Resistance, some backward people became profoundly pessimistic.
2. These views were to be found within the Communist party. During the first six months of the War of Resistance, there was a tendency to take the enemy lightly among some members of the party, who held the view that Japan could be defeated at a single blow. It was not that they felt our own forces to be so strong, since they well knew that the troops and the organized people's forces led by the Communist party were still small, but that the Kuomintang had begun to resist Japan. In their opinion, the Kuomintang was quite powerful, and, in co-ordination with the Communist party, could deal Japan telling blows. They saw only one

aspect of the Kuomintang, that it was resisting Japan, but overlooked the other aspect, that it was reactionary and corrupt, and they therefore made this erroneous appraisal.

3. Such was the view of Chiang Kai-shek and company. Though they were compelled to resist Japan, Chiang Kai-shek and the Kuomintang pinned their hopes solely on prompt foreign aid and had no confidence in their own strength, much less in the strength of the people.

4. Taierhchuang is a town in southern Shantung where the Chinese army fought a battle in March 1938 against the Japanese invaders. By pitting 400,000 men against Japan's 70,000 to 80,000, the Chinese army defeated the Japanese.

5. This view was put forward in an editorial in the *Ta Kung Pao*, then the organ of the Political Science Group in the Kuomintang. Indulging in wishful thinking, this clique hoped that a few more victories of the Taierhchuang type would stop Japan's advance and that there would be no need to mobilize the people for a protracted war, which would threaten the security of its own class. This wishful thinking then pervaded the Kuomintang as a whole.

6. The English text is based on Edgar Snow's *Red Star Over China*, with some alterations made in accordance with the Chinese record of the interview.

7. The Reform Movement of 1898, whose leading spirits were Kang Yu-wei, Liang Chi-chao, and Tan Sze-tung, represented the interests of a section of the liberal bourgeoisie and the enlightened landlords. The movement was favored and supported by the Emperor Kuang Hsu, but had no mass basis. Yuan Shih-kai who had an army behind him betrayed the reformers to the Empress Dowager Tzu Hsi, the leader of the die-hards, who seized power again and had the Emperor Kuang Hsu imprisoned and Tan Sze-tung and five others beheaded. Thus the movement ended in tragic defeat.

8. On January 16, 1938, the Japanese cabinet declared in a policy statement that Japan would subjugate China by force. At the same time it tried by threats and blandishments to make the Kuomintang government capitulate, declaring that if the Kuomintang government "continued to plan resistance," the Japanese government would foster a new puppet regime in China and no longer recognize the Kuomintang as "the other party" in the negotiations.

9. Referring chiefly to the capitalists of the United States.

10. Referring to the governments of the imperialist countries—Britain, the United States, and France.

11. Comrade Mao Tse-tung's prediction that there would be an upswing in China during the stage of stalemate in the War of Resistance Against Japan was completely confirmed in the case of the Liberated Areas under the leadership of the Chinese Communist Party. But there was actually a decline instead of an upswing in the Kuomintang areas, because the ruling clique headed by Chiang Kai-shek was passive in resisting Japan and active in opposing the Communist party and the people. This roused opposition among the broad masses of the people and raised their political consciousness.

12. According to the theory that "weapons decide everything," China which

was inferior to Japan in regard to arms was bound to be defeated in the war. This view was current among all the leaders of the Kuomintang reaction, Chiang Kai-shek included.

13. See "Problems of Strategy in Guerrilla War Against Japan," note 9, p. 184 of this volume.

14. Sun Wu-kung is the monkey hero of the Chinese novel, *Pilgrimage to the West*, written in the sixteenth century. He could cover 108,000 *li* by turning a somersault. Yet once in the palm of the Buddha, he could not escape from it, however many somersaults he turned. With a flick of his palm Buddha transformed his fingers into the five-peak Mountain of Five Elements, and buried Sun Wu-kung.

15. *"Fascism is unbridled chauvinism and predatory war,"* said Comrade Georgi Dimitrov in his report to the Seventh World Congress of the Communist International in August 1935, entitled "The Fascist Offensive and the Tasks of the Communist International." In July 1937, Comrade Dimitrov published an article entitled *Fascism Is War*.

16. Lenin, "Socialism and War," Chapter I, and "The Collapse of the Second International," Section 3, *Collected Works*, 4th Russian ed., vol. XXI.

17. *Sun Tzu*, chapter 3, "The Strategy of Attack."

18. Chengpu, situated in the present Fanhsien County in Shantung Province, was the scene of a great battle between the states of Tsin and Chu in 632 B.C. At the beginning of the battle the Chu troops got the upper hand. The Tsin troops, after making a retreat of 90 *li*, chose the right and left flanks of the Chu troops, their weak spots, and inflicted heavy defeats on them.

19. See "Problems of Strategy in China's Revolutionary War," note 24, p. 148 of this volume.

20. In 204 B.C., Han Hsin, a general of the state of Han, led his men in a big battle with Chao Hsieh at Chinghsing. Chao Hsieh's army, said to be 200,000 strong, was several times that of Han. Deploying his troops with their backs to a river, Han Hsin led them in valiant combat, and at the same time dispatched some units to attack and occupy the enemy's weakly garrisoned rear. Caught in a pincer, Chao Hsieh's troops were utterly defeated.

21. See "Problems of Strategy in China's Revolutionary War," note 25, pp. 148–149 of this volume.

22. See ibid., note 26, p. 149 of this volume.

23. See ibid., note 27, p. 149 of this volume.

24. See ibid., note 28, p. 149 of this volume.

25. See ibid., note 29, p. 149 of this volume.

26. In A.D. 383, Fu Chien, the ruler of the state of Chin, belittled the forces of Tsin and attacked them. The Tsin troops defeated the enemy's advance units at Lochien, Shouyang County, Anhwei Province, and pushed forward by land and water. Ascending the city wall of Shouyang, Fu Chien observed the excellent alignment of the Tsin troops and, mistaking the woods and bushes on Mount Pakung for enemy soldiers, was frightened by the enemy's apparent strength. Cf. "Problems of Strategy in China's Revolutionary War," note 29, p. 149 of this volume.

27. Referring to the fact that Chiang Kai-shek and Wang Ching-wei, having betrayed the first national democratic united front of the Kuomintang and the Communist party in 1927, launched a ten-year war against the people and thus made it impossible for the Chinese people to be organized on a large scale. The Kuomintang reactionaries headed by Chiang Kai-shek must be held responsible for these mistakes.

28. Duke Hsiang of Sung ruled in the Spring and Autumn Era. In 638 B.C., the state of Sung fought with the powerful state of Chu. The Sung forces had already deployed in battle positions when the Chu troops were crossing the river. One of the Sung officers suggested that, as the Chu troops were numerically stronger, this was the moment for attack. But the duke said, "No, a gentleman should never attack one who is unprepared." When the Chu troops had crossed the river but had not yet completed their battle alignment, the officer again proposed an immediate attack, and once again the duke said, "No, a gentleman should never attack an army which has not yet completed its battle alignment." The duke gave the order for attack only after the Chu troops were fully prepared. As a result, the Sung troops met with a disastrous defeat and the duke himself was wounded.

29. Han Fu-chu, a Kuomintang warlord, was for several years governor of Shantung. When the Japanese invaders thrust southward to Shantung along the Tientsin-Pukow Railway after occupying Peiping and Tientsin in 1937, Han Fu-chu fled all the way from Shantung to Honan without fighting a single battle.

30. The Kuomintang expanded its army by press-ganging. Its military and police seized people everywhere, roping them up and treating them like convicts. Those who had money would bribe the Kuomintang officials or pay for substitutes.

Notes to *Long Live the Victory of People's War!*

[These notes are part of the original document as printed by Peking]

1. Under the influence of the Chinese Workers' and Peasants' Red Army and the people's anti-Japanese movement, the Kuomintang Northeastern Army under Chang Hsueh-liang and the Kuomintang Seventeenth Route Army under Yang Hu-cheng agreed to the anti-Japanese national united front proposed by the Communist party of China and demanded that Chiang Kai-shek should stop the civil war and unite with the Communist party to resist Japan. Chiang Kai-shek refused. On December 12, 1936, Chang Hsueh-lian and Yang Hu-cheng arrested him in Sian. Proceeding from the interest of the entire nation, the Chinese Communist Party offered mediation and Chiang was compelled to accept the terms of unity with the Communist party and resistance to Japan.

2. Mao Tse-tung, "Win the Masses in Their Millions for the Anti-Japanese National United Front," *Selected Works*, Eng. ed. (Peking: Foreign Languages Press, 1965), I:290.

3. The "three thirds system" refers to the organs of the political power that were established according to the principle of the Anti-Japanese National United Front and in which the members of the Communist party, nonparty progressives, and the middle elements each occupied one-third of the places.
4. Mao Tse-tung, "Current Problems of Tactics in the Anti-Japanese United Front," *Selected Works*, vol. II.
5. Mao Tse-tung, "The Chinese Revolution and the Chinese Communist Party," *Selected Works*, vol. II.
6. Mao Tse-tung, "On Coalition Government," *Selected Works*, vol. III.
7. The Three Main Rules of Discipline and the Eight Points for Attention were drawn up by comrade Mao Tse-tung for the Chinese Workers' and Peasants' Red Army during the Agrarian Revolutionary War and were later adopted as rules of discipline by the Eighth Route Army and the New Fourth Army and the present People's Liberation Army. As these rules varied slightly in content in the army units of different areas, the General Headquarters of the Chinese People's Liberation Army in October 1947 issued a standard version as follows:

   The Three Main Rules of Discipline:
   (1) Obey orders in all your actions.
   (2) Do not take a single needle or piece of thread from the masses.
   (3) Turn in everything captured.
   The Eight Points for Attention:
   (1) Speak politely.
   (2) Pay fairly for what you buy.
   (3) Return everything you borrow.
   (4) Pay for anything you damage.
   (5) Do not hit or swear at people.
   (6) Do not damage crops.
   (7) Do not take liberties with women.
   (8) Do not ill-treat captives.
8. Frederick Engels, "Possibilities and Perspectives of the War of the Holy Alliance Against France in 1852," *Collected Works of Marx and Engels*, Russ. ed. (Moscow, 1956), VII:509.
9. Mao Tse-tung, "On Protracted War," *Selected Works*, vol. II.
10. Mao Tse-tung, "A Single Spark Can Start a Prairie Fire," *Selected Works*, Eng. ed. (Peking: Foreign Languages Press, 1965), I:124.
11. Sparrow warfare is a popular method of fighting created by the Communist-led anti-Japanese guerrilla units and militia behind the enemy lines. It was called sparrow warfare because, first, it was used diffusely, like the flying sparrows in the sky; and because, second, it was used flexibly by guerrillas or militiamen, operating in threes or fives, appearing and disappearing unexpectedly, and wounding, killing, depleting, and wearing out the enemy forces.
12. Mao Tse-tung, "Problems of Strategy in China's Revolutionary War," *Selected Works*, Eng. ed. (Peking: Foreign Languages Press, 1965), I:248.
13. Mao Tse-tung, "The Present Situation and Our Tasks," *Selected Works*, Eng. ed. (Peking: Foreign Languages Press, 1961), IV:161.

14. Mao Tse-tung, "Interview with Three Correspondents from the Central News Agency, the *Sao Tang Pao* and the *Hsin Min Pao*," *Selected Works*, vol. II.

15. Mao Tse-tung, "We Must Learn to Do Economic Work," *Selected Works*, vol. III.

16. Karl Marx, *Capital*, Eng. ed. (Moscow: Foreign Languages Publishing House, 1954), I:751.

17. Mao Tse-tung, "Problems of War and Strategy," *Selected Works*, vol. II.

18. Ibid.

19. V. I. Lenin, "The Revolutionary Army and the Revolutionary Government," *Collected Works*, Eng. ed. (Moscow: Foreign Languages Publishing House, 1962), VIII:565.

20. Mao Tse-tung, "The Situation and Our Policy After the Victory in the War of Resistance Against Japan," *Selected Works*, Eng. ed. (Peking: Foreign Languages Press, 1961), IV:14-15.

21. Mao Tse-tung, "Talk with the American Correspondent Anna Louise Strong," *Selected Works*, Eng. ed. (Peking: Foreign Languages Press, 1961), IV:100.

22. The Statement of Chairman Mao Tse-tung in Support of the People of the Congo (Leopoldville) Against U.S. Aggression, November 28, 1964.

23. V. I. Lenin, "For Bread and Peace," *Collected Works*, Eng. ed. (Moscow: Progress Publishers, 1964), XXVI:336.

24. V. I. Lenin, "The Chief Task of Our Day," *Collected Works*, Eng. ed. (Moscow: Progress Publishers, 1965), XXVII:162.

25. Mao Tse-tung, "Problems of Strategy in China's Revolutionary War," *Selected Works*, Eng. ed. (Peking: Foreign Languages Press, 1965), I:182.

Notes to *The Big Victory; the Great Task*

1. The Associated Press states, "We cannot find in our files any dispatch with phrasing such as that attributed to AP" (letter to the editor from Samuel G. Blackman, general news editor, 21 August 1969). Other transcripts of the Hanoi broadcasts do not indicate Giap was quoting AP.

2. *The New York Times* on 28 February 1967 carried an editorial titled "Escalation by Whatever Means." It contained this statement: "It is clear that the United States has embarked on a substantial escalation of its war effort in Vietnam. . . . The tragedy is that the escalation will almost certainly prevent the world from finding out whether the possibility exists for ending the fighting . . ." Giap's alleged quotes do not appear in the editorial.

3. On 2 May 1967 *The Wall Street Journal* carried an editorial titled "The Least Among Evils." It stated: "It is time to recognize, we think, that Vietnam has become a sickness without a cure. The best hope now is to choose the least among evils where every course inevitably means further anguish. . . . The United States, with the best intentions but possibly not with the best judgment, has got itself into a frightful maze from which there is no good way out. . . . What should occupy us now is

trying to find the path pointing to the least tragic results for this nation."

4. General Taylor comments: "What I said in *Responsibility and Response* with regard to the war in Vietnam is available to the reading public and anyone who cares to check the record can appraise Giap's accuracy. I doubt that any such check would reveal much resemblance between my stated views and the Giap quotation." (Letter to the editor, 11 August 1969.)

5. *U.S. News & World Report* stated on 14 August 1967: "Suddenly, at the White House, it must seem as though the roof is falling in. War, race strife, a soaring deficit, troubles with Congress, allies, and the dollar— bad news is pressing in on the Administration from all sides."

6. The U.S. Air Force reported that as of 20 September 1967, 681 aircraft had been shot down over North Viet Nam.

Notes to *Some Aspects of Guerrilla Warfare in Viet Nam*

[These notes are part of the original document]

1. Victories over foreign invaders won by the Vietnamese armed forces and people:

Bachdang (1288): A river in North Vietnam where General Tran Hung Dao destroyed an army half a million strong under Gengis Khan's grandson.

Chilang (1427): A mountain pass in North Vietnam where Le Loi gained a victory over the Mings, crowning ten years of people's resistance.

Dongda (1789): A place near Hanoi where Nguyen Hue, leader of a peasant insurrection, defeated a 200,000-strong army of the Tsing invaders.

2. Appeal by President Ho Chi Minh for national resistance (December 1946).

3. The people usually call N.F.L. "Liberation" or "Revolution."

Notes to *Operation Antiaircraft*

1. Frank País was an underground leader who was killed in Santiago de Cuba.
2. In 1874, when Cubans were warring against Spanish domination.
3. Not included in the *Verde Olivo* article.
4. One of the earliest victories won by Fidel Castro's guerrillas. They overran a small army post in the hamlet of El Uvero.
5. Ameijeiras served as chief of police during the early years of the Castro regime, but later fell in disgrace.
6. American officials explained that the shipment was of live replacements for practice warheads mistakenly sent to the Cuban government in 1957 under a mutual security agreement.

7. These Instructions were not published with the Raúl Castro article in *Verde Olivo*.

8. Not published in *Verde Olivo*.

9. Cubans who fought in the wars of independence against Spain.

10. Castro uses the word *compañero*, which literally means "companion" but which now in Cuba has become a euphemism for "comrade," in the Communist sense of this word.

11. Reference to a poem, "Yoke and Star," by Cuban independence hero José Martí.

12. National Association of Small Growers.

13. Actually, there were eleven marines and eighteen sailors aboard the bus. Another American sailor was kidnapped separately.

14. The U.S. State Department, basing its information on U.S. Navy reports, has provided the following list of the men kidnapped by the guerrillas:

Name	Affiliation
Edward Cannon	Moa Bay Mining
Henry Salmanson	Moa Bay Mining
William Koster	Moa Bay Mining
Dr. A. A.Chamberlain	Frederick Snare Co.
Howard Roach	Stevens Corporation
Alfred G. Smith	United Fruit
Jessie Ford	United Fruit
Harley F. Sparks	United Fruit
J. H. Schissler	Moa Bay Mining
E. P. Pfleicher	Moa Bay Mining
Román Cecilia	Frederick Snare Co.
Edward Gordes	Moa Bay Mining
H. G. Kristyanson (Canadian)	Moa Bay Mining
Sherman A. White	Nicaro
James A. Poll	Nicaro
James P. Stevens	United Fruit
Damon Elmore	Central Ermita
Jones Best	Moa Bay Mining
Albert Ross	Moa Bay Mining
T. R. Mosness	USN (Navy)
Richard A. Sargent (Canadian)	Central Isabel
Charles B. Young, Jr.	USMC (Marines)
Valentine W. George	USN
Alfredo R. Hernández	USN
William H. Christie	USN
Robert E. Gibson	USN
Noble S. Brown, Jr.	USMC
Billy R. Fox	USN
Jorge Rescalla (Chaieb) (Cuban national, bus ticket collector)	Gtmo Base
Lawrence E. Jamison	USN
Michael P. McCardle	USN
Hal C. Worrall	USMC

Angelo Mpazocos	USN
Hannibal E. Holmes, Jr.	USMC
Robert C. Gerringer	USN
Merrit H. Stuck	USN
Albert H. Matthews	USN
Thomas W. Cody	USMC
Carmelo Dejesus-Narváez	USMC
Waldo Reyes, Jr.	USMC
Jack R. Palmer	USN
Joseph J. Anderson	USMC
Gerald L. Dickenson	USN
John L. Bondi	USN
Robert D. Lepley	USN
Robert A. Asfour	USN
Charles Lindberg	USN
Adelberto G. Márquez	USMC
Robert P. Wurst	USN
George H. Capewell	USMC
Gerald G. Holthaus	USMC

Totals: 21 civilians (2 Canadians, 1 Cuban), 30 military personnel. [It is not clear whether the Cuban bus driver, Alberto Tito Rodríguez, was also kidnapped.]

15. Vilma Espín later wed Raúl Castro.

SOURCES

Mao Tse-tung. "On Protracted War." In *Selected Military Writings of Mao Tse-tung*. Peking: Foreign Languages Press, 1963.

Lin Piao. *Long Live the Victory of People's War!* Peking: Foreign Languages Press, 1965.

Vo Nguyen Giap. "The Big Victory; the Great Task." In *Nhan Dan* and *Quan Doi Nhan Dan*. Hanoi: broadcast on 17–20 September 1967.

Hoang Van Thai. *Some Aspects of Guerrilla Warfare in Vietnam*. Hanoi: Foreign Languages Publishing House, 1965.

Guevara, Ernesto "Che." "Guerrilla Warfare: a Method." In *"Che" Guevara on Revolution*, edited by Jay Mallin. Coral Gables, Florida: University of Miami Press, 1969.

Castro, Raúl. "Operation Antiaircraft." Translated by Beatrice M. Ash. In *Verde Olivo*. Havana, 15 and 22 September 1963.

Bayo, Alberto. *One Hundred Fifty Questions to a Guerrilla*. Translated by Robert I. Madigan and Dr. Angel de Lumus Medina. Published by courtesy of the Air University.

BIBLIOGRAPHY

Innumerable books on guerrilla warfare have been published in the United States and other countries. Any effort to provide a definitive listing would be futile. Accounts of guerrilla combat go all the way back to the Bible (Judah waged guerrilla warfare against the Syrian armies). The following is a list of books that are generally considered useful by authorities in the field. They constitute a basic bookshelf on guerrilla warfare in these times.

General

Bayo, Alberto. *Ciento cincuenta preguntas a un guerrillero*. 28th ed. Havana [probably], 1961.

Campbell, Arthur. *Guerillas*. New York: John Day Company, 1968.

Condit, D. M.; Cooper, Bert.; et al. *Challenge and Response in Internal Conflict*. 3 vols. Washington: Center for Research in Social Systems, 1967 and 1968.

Counterguerrilla Operations. Department of the Army, Headquarters. Washington, 1967.

Cross, James Eliot. *Conflict in the Shadows*. Garden City, N.Y.: Doubleday & Co., Inc., 1963.

Crozier, Brian. *South-East Asia in Turmoil*. Baltimore: Penguin Books, 1965.

Dach Bern, Major H. von. *Total Resistance*. Boulder, Colorado: Panther Publications, 1965.

Debray, Régis. *Revolution in the Revolution?* New York: Grove Press, Inc., 1967.

Galula, David. *Counterinsurgency Warfare*. New York: Frederick A. Praeger, 1964.

Guerrilla Warfare and Special Forces Operations. Department of the Army, Headquarters. Washington, 1961.

Guevara, [Ernesto] Che. *La guerra de guerrillas*. La Habana: Departamento de Instrucción del MINFAR, 1960.

Heilbrun, Otto. *Partisan Warfare*. New York: Frederick A. Praeger, 1962.

Levy, "Yank" Bert. *Guerrilla Warfare.* Boulder, Colorado: Panther Publications, 1964.

Mallin, Jay, ed. *"Che" Guevara on Revolution.* Coral Gables, Florida: University of Miami Press, 1969.

Ney, Virgil. *Notes on Guerrilla War.* Washington: Command Publications, 1962.

Osanka, Franklin Mark, ed. *Modern Guerrilla Warfare.* New York: The Free Press of Glencoe, 1962.

Paget, Julian. *Counter-Insurgency Operations: Techniques of Guerrilla Warfare.* New York: Walker and Company, 1967.

Paret, Peter and Shy, John W. *Guerrillas in the 1960s.* New York: Frederick A. Praeger, 1962.

Pomeroy, William J. *Guerrilla and Counter-Guerrilla Warfare.* New York: International Publishers, 1964.

Pustay, John S. *Counterinsurgency Warfare.* New York: Free Press, 1965.

Special Forces Handbook, 1965.

Special Forces Operations—U.S. Army Doctrine. Department of the Army, Headquarters. Washington, 1969.

Taber, Robert. *The War of the Flea.* New York: Lyle Stuart, 1965.

Thayer, Charles W. *Guerrilla.* New York: The American Library, 1965.

The Guerrilla—and How to Fight Him. Selections from the *Marine Corps Gazette.* New York: Frederick A. Praeger, 1962.

Trinquier, Roger. *Modern Warfare.* New York: Frederick A. Praeger, 1964.

U.S. Army Counterinsurgency Forces. Department of the Army, Headquarters. Washington, 1963.

Viet Nam

Bain, Chester A. *Vietnam—The Roots of Conflict.* Englewood Cliffs, N.J.: Prentice-Hall, Inc., 1967.

Browne, Malcolm W. *The New Face of War.* Indianapolis: The Bobbs-Merrill Company, Inc., 1965.

Corson, William R. *The Betrayal.* New York: Ace Books, Inc., 1968.

Duncan, David Douglas. *I Protest!* New York: The New American Library, 1968.

Fall, Bernard B. *Street Without Joy.* 4th ed. Harrisburg, Pa.: Stackpole Co., 1961.

Fall, Bernard B. *Hell in a Very Small Place.* Philadelphia: Lippincott Company, 1966.

Fishel, Wesley R., ed. *Vietnam: Anatomy of a Conflict.* Itasca, Ill.: F. E. Peacock Publishers, Inc., 1968.

Mallin, Jay. *Terror in Viet Nam.* Princeton, N.J.: D. Van Nostrand Company, Inc., 1966.

Marshall, S. L. A. *Battles in the Monsoon.* New York: William Morrow and Company, Inc., 1967.

Pike, Douglas. *Viet Cong—The Organization and Techniques of the National*

Liberation Front of South Vietnam. Cambridge, Mass.: The M.I.T. Press, 1966.

Tanham, George Kilpatrick, *Communist Revolutionary Warfare.* New York: Frederick A. Praeger, 1967.

Valdés Vivó, Raúl. *Relatos de Viet Nam del Sur.* [and] Rojas, Marta. *Viet Nam del Sur: su arma estratégica es el pueblo.* La Habana: Editora Política, 1966.

Vo Nguyen Giap. *People's War, People's Army.* New York: Frederick A. Praeger, 1962.

Cuba

Batista, Fulgencio. *Cuba Betrayed.* New York: Vantage Press, 1962.

Dubois, Jules. *Fidel Castro.* Indianapolis: The New Bobbs-Merrill Company, Inc., 1959.

Franqui, Carlos. *El libro de los doce.* La Habana: Instituto del Libro, 1968.

Guevara, Ernesto "Che." *Pasajes de la guerra revolucionaria.* La Habana: Ediciones Unión/Narraciones, 1963.

Mallin, Jay. *Fortress Cuba.* Chicago: Henry Regnery Company, 1965.

Matthews, Herbert L. *The Cuban Story.* New York: George Braziller, 1961.

Taber, Robert. *M-26—Biography of a Revolution.* New York: Lyle Stuart, 1961.

China

Mao Tse-tung. *Selected Military Writings of Mao Tse-tung.* Peking: Foreign Languages Press, 1963.

Mao Tse-tung. *Mao Tse-tung on Guerrilla Warfare.* New York: Frederick A. Praeger, 1963.

Snow, Edgar. *Red Star Over China.* New York: Grove Press, Inc., 1968. [First published in 1937]

Malaya

O'Ballance, Edgar. *Malaya: The Communist Insurgent War, 1948–60.* Hamden, Conn.: Archon Books, 1966.

Pye, Lucian W. *Guerrilla Communism in Malaya.* Princeton, N.J.: Princeton University Press, 1956.

The Philippines

Valeriano, Napoleon D., and Bohannan, Charles T. R. *Counter-Guerrilla Operations.* New York: Frederick A. Praeger, 1962.

Indonesia

Nasution, Abdul Haris. *Fundamentals of Guerrilla Warfare.* New York: Frederick A. Praeger, 1965.

Cyprus

Grivas, George. *General Grivas on Guerrilla Warfare*. New York: Frederick A. Praeger, 1965.

Colombia

De la violencia a la paz—Experiencias de la Octava Brigada en la lucha contra las guerrillas. Manizales, Colombia: Imprenta Departamental de Caldas, 1965.

Venezuela

Soto Tamayo, Carlos. *Inteligencia militar y subversión armada*. Caracas: Ministerio de la Defensa, 1968.

Peru

Las guerrillas en el Perú y su represión. Lima: Ministerio de Guerra, 1966.

Bolivia

Guevara, Ernesto "Che." *El diario del Che en Bolivia*. La Habana: Instituto del Libro, 1968.

Algeria

Behr, Edward. *The Algerian Problem*. New York: W. W. Norton and Company, Inc., 1962.

Bocca, Geoffrey. *The Secret Army*. Englewood Cliffs, N.J.: Prentice-Hall, Inc., 1968.

INDEX

"It is the oldest of adages that the prime requirement, if one is to conduct war successfully, is to know the mind of the enemy. In our past trials at arms we have occasionally failed of that aim, though the blighting effects were always temporarily discomfiting, and never finally fatal.

"Today it is a good question whether the American people, and more particularly the men at the top who shape policy and make the pivotal decisions, have even begun to understand the minds of such men as General Giap and Ho Chi Minh. More disturbing, it is no more possible to give a positive answer to the question now than it was a decade ago, though in ten years of ever-broadening contact one should make some advance through hard-won experience."

Brig. Gen. S. L. A. Marshall

Although unconventional or guerrilla warfare is not a Communist invention, it has become their most important lever for revolutionary expansion. Perhaps because guerrilla war inverts so many of the principles of traditional war, the Western world has been agonizingly slow to understand it. Nowhere has our lack of comprehension been more costly than in Viet Nam.

In his timely compilation of the writings of communism's leading guerrilla strategists, Jay Mallin has provided a firsthand account of the purposes and tactics of the Communist brand of unconventional warfare. Including material that has been previously inaccessible or unavailable in English, *Strategy for Conquest* contains selections from the writings of Mao Tse-tung, Vo Nguyen Giap, "Che" Guevara, Lin Piao, Raúl Castro, and others. From General Marshall's scathing indictment of U.S. military conduct in Viet Nam, through the editor's thoughtful survey of how some events have borne out Communist proclamations, to the fundamental writings of the ideologists themselves, this book offers the hard truths of what we face in remote jungles and in our own city streets.

(Continued on back flap)

Jay Mallin, an experienced correspondent for *Time, Life,* and other major media, has been an on-the-scene observer at trouble spots around the world, including Viet Nam, Bolivia, and Cuba. Mr. Mallin is a recognized authority on guerrilla warfare and the author of *Fortress Cuba,* dealing with Castro subversion, *Caribbean Crisis,* about the 1965 Dominican uprising, *Terror in Viet Nam,* and *"Che" Guevara on Revolution.*